Antique Trader®

TOYS

Price Guide

**EDITED BY KYLE HUSFLOEN
CONTRIBUTING EDITOR DANA CAIN**

Published by
Antique Trader Books, A Division of

**krause
publications**

700 E. State Street • Iola, WI 54990-0001
Telephone: 715/445-2214
Web: www.krause.com

Please, call or write us for our free catalog of antiques and collectibles publications.
To place an order or receive our free catalog, call 800-258-0929.
For editorial comment and further information,
use our regular business telephone at (715) 445-2214.

Library of Congress Catalog Number: 00-111281
ISBN: 0-87349-221-8

Printed in the United States of America

TABLE OF CONTENTS

INTRODUCTION

In 1994 Antique Trader Books began to publish an expanded selection of specialty price guides to compliment our long-established annual Antiques & Collectibles Price Guide. Various popular categories of antiques and collectibles have been covered since then in price guides on ceramics, glassware, furniture metals, Art Pottery and Country Americana.

Now we are proud to introduce our newest specialty price reference *Antique Trader Books Toy Price Guide*. Toys have long been a mainstay of the collecting world and this popularity shows no signs of waning as we enter the 21st century. From the earliest surviving mass-produced toys of the 19th and early 20th century right up to current toy lines, this field offers something of interest to every level of collector, no matter what their budget restraints may be.

Since most toy collectors tend to specialize in pieces from a certain time period, manufacturer or related to a specific topic, we have arranged this new guide in a logical format that we hope will make it easy to use as well as comprehensive. Basically the contents are divided into two broad categories— "Antique & Vintage" toys, predating World War II and "Modern" toys, dating after World War II and through to the present. This way readers can more easily zero in on the segment of the toy hobby that has the most direct interest to them and still have a pricing guide which will allow them to study and learn about the many major specialties in toy collecting. Our two main sections are then divided into various chapters that are listed in our Table of Contents.

Each listing in each chapter is arranged alphabetically according to the toy name, manufacturer's name or a specific character name, as in the case of Disney Toys & Collectibles. Since some character toys may fall into any of several chapter categories we will conclude this book with a comprehensive Index with cross-referencing provided so you can check for the pages where the listings for Donald Duck or Star Wars items will be found. Each chapter is also abundantly illustrated with fine photos, a total of nearly 1,000 pictures in all, in addition to a special 16-page full color supplement.

A guide of this nature, needless to say, takes a great deal of time and effort to compile. My staff and I have drawn on our own database of toy listings but were also very fortunate to obtain the help of several toy specialists. Dana Cain, noted writer and collector, served as my chief contributing editor and offered tremendous help in compiling material on Modern toys. Her special feature on this topic follows here and is certain to prove of great interest to all readers. Also offering invaluable assistance was Joe Fex, an associate of Dana Cain, who provided our comprehensive chapter on "Model Kits." Writer and researcher Jim Trautman, added further breadth to our guide with chapters on "Playsets by Marx" and "Toy Soldiers." We also appreciated the assistance of Stuart W. Wells III, author of Krause Publications *Science Fiction Collectibles - Identification & Price Guide*, for further data on that special field of collecting.

We have taken great care in preparing all the thousands of detailed entries included here, and we feel it offers a comprehensive and up-to-date reference which all those who collect, deal in or research toys will find invaluable. We all have memories of a special toy and, if we are lucky, we may have preserved it into adulthood. If not, many of us will happily spend time and money to "recover" that lost treasure. Many toy collectors start out this way and we hope this new guide will help you better understand and appreciate the playthings that have a special appeal to you. Whether you're building a collection around an antique toy passed down through the family or a boomer-era toy less than a quarter century old, you'll find lots to intrigue you in Antique Trader Books Toy Price. Take it along on all your toy hunting forays and good luck on your special toy hunt.

—Kyle Husfloen, Editor

Please note: Though listings have been double-checked and every effort has been made to insure accuracy, neither the compilers, editors nor publisher can assume responsibility for any losses that might be incurred as a result of consulting this guide, or of errors, typographical or otherwise.

PHOTOGRAPHY CREDITS

Photographers who have contributed to this issue include: Susan Eberman, Bedford, Indiana; Scott Green, Manchester, New Hampshire; Charles Hippler, Monticello, Illinois; Robert G. Jason-Ickes, Olympia, Washington; and Joyce Roerig, Waltersboro, South Carolina.

For other photographs, artwork, data or permission to photograph in their shops, we sincerely express appreciation to the following auctioneers, galleries, museums, individuals and shops: American Eagle Auction Company, Circleville, Ohio; American Social History and Social Movements, Pittsburgh, Pennsylvania; Bertoia Sales, Vineland, New Jersey; Christie's, New York, New York; Collector's Auction Services, Oil City, Pennsylvania; Collector's Sales & Services, Middletown, Rhode Island; DeFina Auctions, Austenburg, Ohio; DuMouchelles, Detroit, Michigan; Glen Erardi, N. Andover, Massachusetts; Garth's Auctions, Inc., Delaware, Ohio; Deborah Gillham, Gaithersburg, Maryland; Grunewald Antiques, Hillsborough, North Carolina; the Gene Harris Antique Auction Center, Marshalltown, Iowa; K. Hayes & Associates, Louisville, Kentucky; International Toy Collectors Association, Athens, Illinois; Jackson's Auctions, Cedar Falls, Iowa; James Julia, Fairfield, Maine; Peter Kroll, Sun Prairie, Wisconsin; Russ McCall Auctioneers, Onawa, Iowa; McMasters Doll Auctions, Cambridge, Ohio; Parker-Braden Auctions, Carlsbad, New Mexico; Skinner, Inc., Bolton, Massachusetts; Slawinski Auction Company, Felton, California; Sotheby's, New York, New York; Stanton's Auctioneers, Vermontville, Michigan; The Auction House - Paine Auction Service, Sacramento, California; Theriault's, Annapolis, Maryland; Lee Vines, Hewlett, New York; Todd Wagner, New Middletown, Ohio; and Woody Auctions, Douglass, Kansas.

ON THE COVER

FRONT COVER: Back left - Battery-operated "Mr. Robert" by Cragston, ca. 1950s, $1,155; Back right - Fisher-Price "Mr. Doodle" pull toy, No. 132, 1957, $143. Front - Tin "Atom Jet" racing car, ca. 1950s, $1,320.
BACK COVER: Top - Pressed steel airplane, Tri-motor No. 30, Schieble, ca. 1930, $1,705; Center - G.I. Joe Action Solider box, complete with action figure and Army manual, $88. Bottom - Fiction action "Condor" motorcycle and rider, IYO, Japan, 1950s, 11 3/4" l., $900-$42,700.

All color photos courtesy of International Toy Collectors Association, RR #2, Box 90-V, Athens, Illinois 62613.

SPECIAL CATEGORY CONTRIBUTORS

Modern Toys
Dana Cain
5061 South Stuart Court
Littleton, CO 80123
e-mail: dana.cain@worldnet.att.net

Books:

"Collecting Monsters of Film and TV" (Krause Publications, 1997); "UFO and Alien
Collectibles," (Krause Publications, 1999); "The Encyclopedia of Saturday Morning TV
Collectibles," (Krause Publications, 2000); "Film and TV Animal Star Collectibles,"
(Antique Trader Books, 1998); "Japanese Movie Monster Collectibles," (Antique Trader
Books, 1998); "Dinosaur Collectibles," (with Mike Fredericks, Antique Trader Books,
1999); "501 Collectible Horses," (with Jan Lindenberger, Schiffer Publishing, 1995);
"Fun Collectibles of the 1950s, 60s and 70s," (with Jan Lindenberger, Schiffer
Publishing, 1995).

Model Kits
Joe Fex
5061 South Stuart Court
Littleton, CO 80123
e-mail: joefex@att.net
Model Collector, painter and dealer

Wooden Toys
Richard Friz
P.O. Box 472
Peterborough, NH 03458
(603) 563-8155
e-mail: joshdickmad@monadnet.com

Lionel Trains and Toy Soldiers
Jim Trautman
R.R. 1
Orton Ontario, Canada
L0N 1N0
e-mail: emjaygee@inetarena.com

Jigsaw Puzzles
Chris McCann
Collectors Press, Inc.
P.O. Box 230986
Portland, OR 97281
(503) 684-3030
fax: (503) 684-3777
e-mail: rperry@collectorspress.com

COLLECTING TOYS
1950 - NOW
by Dana Cain

A Brief History of Modern Toys

The 1950s

The chain of events leading to the toy boom of the 1950s and '60s was an almost magical convergence of diverse factors. The three primary ingredients for the toy boom recipe were: 1) more kids, 2) more television, and 3) more plastic. Let us review:

In the late 1940s, soldiers returned home to loving wives after World War II and the baby boom was launched. As the new legions of youngsters began to grow, so did another new addition to the American landscape — television. During the 1950s, television and the all-American family became intertwined. Naturally, with fathers at work and mothers busy around the home, it was the kids who were perhaps most mesmerized by the TV, and advertisers began to take note.

At the same time, the development of plastics was also maturing, as more and more people were finding uses for the inexpensive, highly versatile substances. Consequently, a variety of plastics were beginning to infiltrate the toy manufacturing business, helping make toy production easier and less expensive.

The stage was set. We had lots of kids, lots of television shows and lots of plastic. Put them all together and stir in the idyllic social atmosphere of the 1950s, and the golden age of toys was born. For the first time, kids could bug their parents to buy them the toys they'd seen on television. The old days of Pa whittling out a wooden doll were over. Now, the mass media had taken hold, and toys would never be the same! For the first time, kids all over America could see the new toys on television, advertised on their favorite shows, and for the first time, the kids began clamoring for the same toys — the new toys being mass marketed in plastic and tin by companies like Marx, Mattel and Ideal.

The 1960s

By the time the 1960s rolled around, the advent of toys being mass-marketed to kids through television had escalated beyond the wildest dreams of most toy companies. More and more families were purchasing televisions, and more and more televisions were airing children's programming and ads aimed at children. Consequently, more and more toys were being produced and introduced to the market. Now, the success of a toy meant that it would spawn "sequel" toys. The Barbie doll, introduced by Mattel in the late 1950s, had proved so popular that she now needed friends and family members in the 1960s just to keep up with demand. And the kids of the 1960s knew how to demand! Toy companies scrambled to keep up. They introduced all sorts of new toy lines and gave new spins to many of the classics. Diecast cars, introduced decades before in Europe, became faster, wilder, and with bright orange track when the Hot Wheels phenomenon was born. Dolls, popular with girls for centuries, now were marketed to boys with the advent of the GI Joe line. But, they couldn't call it a "doll," so the Action Figure was born. Battery-operated toys flourished as kids wanted more complex and entertaining toys. And perhaps the fastest-growing area of all in the toy arena was the explosion of character toys, paying homage to the television shows and movies that the kids loved.

The 1970s

By the 1970s, the toy explosion of the past two decades seemed old hat. The mountains of mass-marketed toys had simply become part of our way of life. In terms of toy manufacturing history, it seems much of the 1970s was devoted to the development of the action figure as a major force in the toy world. Mego led the way here, with a barrage of high-quality, very poseable figures keying in on a wide variety of media characters, from monsters to TV stars to superheroes and more. Many other companies, like Mattel, Remco and Hasbro also helped to develop the action figure during the 1970s.

Part of the development included a radical downsizing — not in production, but in the size of the figures. Earlier action figures, in the 1960s, had measured about 12 inches or more. Mego brought the average size down to about 8 inches in the mid-1970s, and by the end of the decade, the 3-3/4 inch action figure, with fewer points of articulation, had become the new standard. Never again, could an action figure be confused with a doll.

Another primary focus of '70s toys was a new emphasis on safety. Sure, fewer babies were choking on small parts, but the days of firing plastic bullets from Johnny Seven One-Man-Army machine guns was gone. No longer could we heat up our Thingmaker ovens and burn our fingers on the metal Creepy Crawler molds. Something had been lost forever.

The 1980s

Just as the danger had been stripped from toys in the 1970s, it seemed all other potential evils were banished in the 1980s. Monster toys, so popular in the 1960s and on into the 1970s, were all but obliterated, as a new tidal wave of "cuteness" swept the land. This was the decade of Care Bears, My Little Pony, Strawberry Shortcake and Rainbow Brite. While the grown-ups were learning to be successful yuppies and visiting their therapists weekly, kids were also being taught to "share their feelings" and be nice and good. This trend carried through most of the decade, but was somewhat cooled by the introduction of He-Man toys, Transformers and Teenage Mutant Ninja Turtles toys later in the '80s.

Which brings us to another '80s earmark. Suddenly there was a major "flip-flop" in toy-making logic. Whereas before, character toys were released to play on the popularity of a TV or film character, suddenly, the tables were being turned. TV shows were being created to embellish the popularity of existing toy lines! In fact, companies like Mattel were now funding and helping create shows like "He-Man and the Masters of the Universe" to advertise their toy lines. Instead of buying an ad on the show, they just created an entire program based on the toy characters. My Little Pony, Strawberry Shortcake and Cabbage Patch Kids all had amazing success with this tactic. And the marriage of toys and TV grew even stronger. A toy without TV exposure began to seem as implausible as, oh, say a TV show without a toy line.

To further cement the bond, there was a strong swing toward games that were played on the television set, as video games became a favorite pastime of many American kids.

The 1990s

With these trends locked in place for the 1990s, another new factor emerged. Suddenly, everyone was a collector. The comic and trading card industries endured massive booms and then busts as America went "collector crazy." Now, words like "mint condition" and "limited edition" became more important than ever, and all of these concerns and factors were being mirrored in the toy industry. Toys were now marketed with limited edition numbering and phrases like "Special Collectors Edition" printed on the packaging. Fewer and fewer toys were being removed from their boxes and played with. More and more toys were being snatched from toy stores and whisked away to collector shops and shows with elevated prices reflecting the exploding demand.

Meanwhile, all of the trends of the past decades were being magnified. Remember how TV influenced kids to want the same mass-marketed toys in the 1950s and '60s? Well, now each Christmas was characterized by one toy that caused riots in shopping malls. Remember how action figures were gaining a stronghold in the 1970s? Well, now the action figure market was completely flooded with high demand figures and collectors were clamoring for the rarest of the rare — the figures in mislabeled packages, the figures that were "short packed" in each case, the figures that were specifically introduced as very limited runs, which immediately sold for hundreds of dollars despite their $8.95 price tags. And, remember how the 1980s saw the fast-growing popularity of

video games? Well, by the 1990s, parents were expected to provide kids with a library of various video games, all of which were to be replaced every two or three years with the advent of a newer, fancier game system.

And, it was amid this intensely active toy collecting environment that the marketing group at Ty, Inc. hit upon a gold mine that would, once again, change toy collecting forever. Ty introduced its line of Beanie Babies in 1994, and within a couple of years, the cute little $5 toys had become a national phenomenon, with rarer examples selling for thousands of dollars each.

At the same time, Todd McFarlane revolutionized action figure collecting with his extremely detailed and well-sculpted Spawn figures. And, the popularity of *Star Trek: The Next Generation* had propelled science fiction action figures to new heights, in terms of sales and production. Meanwhile, companies producing diecast cars, model kits and more began cranking out nostalgic reproductions of 1950s and '60s toy lines.

And everything was geared toward collectors.

The Challenges and Rewards of Becoming a Toy Collector

Settling on a Strategy

Toy collectors these days tread a fine line. We learned in the 1990s that we should have taken care of our old toys and kept them all mint in package. We also learned in the '90s that it was possible to buy lots of NEW toys and keep them all mint in package. So, today's collectors are expected to not only seek out vintage treasures, but also keep tabs on new collectible toys. No longer can we say, "Oh, that's too new."

Anyone can tell you that a two-year-old designer Barbie can easily bring more than a 40 year-old vintage Barbie, these days. It just depends. You have to know what you're doing! (Hey, that's why you buy price guides, right?)

It's hard to predict which new toys will spike in value upon release, only to become passé (i.e. Tickle Me Elmo) two months down the road. How can we tell which toys will endure as collectibles (i.e. Beanie Babies)? In fact, there may be no accurate way to predict these things.

In the end, there may be only one collecting strategy that makes sense. Collect what you love. This way, you never have to worry about being "stuck with" a pile of worthless action figures or a room full of dusty Teddy bears. Whether or not your toys escalate in value, you can enjoy them for years!

For those intent on collecting as an investment, avoid gathering toys marked "collectors edition." If the toy claims to be collectible, chances are good that hundreds or thousands of other people are buying it for the same reason you are. So, a year or two or five down the road, when you're ready to cash in on your investment, you find these toys are plentiful, as everyone else had the same idea. They are all still mint in package and are basically worthless. It happens too often.

Collect from the heart. It's more fun.

The Happiest Hunting Grounds

Where do toy collectors go to find their treasures? Collectors of newer toys have the option to pop into Toys R Us or Kmart, and some opt to rush in when the doors first open for the best selection. For others, it's not so easy. Vintage toys occasionally pop up at yard sales, flea markets and thrift stores. It's always a special treat to find that vintage Charlie's Angels doll for $1 at the bottom of a box in someone's garage! Of course, you have to root through a lot of junk to make these magical discoveries. For those less patient, most large cities have one or more collectible toy shows, a one- or two-day event that draws private sellers and collectors from the regional area. Check your local classified ads for listings. And, for those who want it NOW, there are a growing number of shops, nationwide, specializing in collectible toys. Some of these shops carry vintage toys exclusively, but many cater to collectors of vintage and newer collectible toys. Check your Yellow Pages under "Collectibles." Of course another important source for those looking to buy and sell all types of toys is *Toy Shop*, the bi-weekly tabloid publication produced by Krause Publications of Iola, Wisconsin, the parent company of Antique Trader Books.

And, then of course, there's eBay and the other online auction Web sites. Certainly no other single element has changed toy collecting as much as the advent of the online auction. Log on, type in what you want and place your bid. It's so easy. Toys that have eluded collectors for years are suddenly available in quantity. Prices vary, conditions vary and there's a whole new world of global Internet commerce to contend with. This is certainly the trend to follow into the next decade, and an invaluable asset to the serious — or the frivolous — toy collector.

Learning the Ropes

What do toy collectors look for in a toy? Some of the primary considerations are: 1) rarity; 2) desirability and demand; 3) condition, and 4) cost. These considerations are in no particular order, and the importance of each will certainly change from collector to collector. But, these are the things that are important.

Of all these considerations, the one that is probably the least understood is "condition." Condition is VITAL to a toy's collectiblity. A #1 Barbie doll can easily bring more than $3,000. But if her hair's been cut, you might not get $500. A vintage glossy Breyer horse may be worth $65, but if his ear's chipped and he has a few paint rubs, he's a $5 horse. A vintage Hot Wheels car with red lines on the tires can sell for $85, but if the paint job is shot, figure on $10 or less.

Another common misconception is that "age = value." This is not necessarily true. A wooden toy boat from 1950, for instance, typically isn't worth much. Yes, it's old. But it doesn't have the fan base to make it valuable. No one cares. It isn't sought after. The same is true for certain character toys. How collectible is the character? A Captain Kangaroo coloring book may be old, but it may not be worth $10, while a Howdy Doody coloring book from roughly the same era may sell for more than $100. Even though both pieces are in good shape, and both are old, there are simply more people actively seeking Howdy Doody toys than Captain Kangaroo toys (apologies to Bob Keeshan, Bunny Rabbit and Mr. Moose, all of whom I love dearly).

Toy collecting is definitely a dynamic hobby. There is always more to learn, more to know and more avenues to explore. Every collector develops his or her own strategies and secrets, preferences and passions. That's what makes it fun. Toys were invented to bring fun into our lives. And that's the bottom line.

Top 25 Collectible Post WWII Toys

(Note: This list is based on Dana Cain's opinions. What is your list like?)

1. Barbie
2. Hot Wheels
3. Beanie Babies
4. Marx playsets
5. 1960s monster toys
6. Vintage plastic model kits
7. Lionel trains (and other vintage train sets)
8. Pre-1970 pressed steel trucks
9. Breyer Horses
10. GI Joe
11. Mego action figures
12. Tin space toys and robots
13. Superhero action figures & accessories
14. Vintage tin litho battery-ops and wind-ups
15. Vintage Star Wars/Star trek
16. Character dolls
17. Pinball machines/arcade games
18. Metal lunch boxes
19. Pez candy dispensers
20. Mattel thingmaker toys
21. Vintage Fisher Price
22. Vintage cap guns
23. Transformers/transforming robots
24. View-Master
25. Pedal cars

Section I
ANTIQUE & VINTAGE
(PRE-WORLD WAR II)

Chapter 1

CHARACTER TOYS — COMIC & RADIO

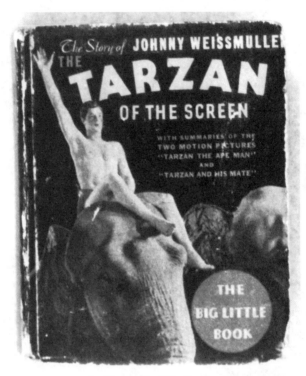

Tarzan Big Little Book

Andy Panda doll, stuffed cloth, 1940s **$600**

Barney Google figure, Syroco, marked on front "Barney G." & "KFS 1944" on back, 4" h. (near mint condition) **135**

Barney Google & Spark Plug

Barney Google & Spark Plug, jointed wood, comic strip characters, cloth outfit & blanket, Albert Schoenhut, the pair (ILLUS.).. **1,500**

Rare Betty Boop Composition Doll

Betty Boop doll, jointed composition, painted features, black dress w/red heart decal, near mint, Cameo Doll Co., 1930s, 13" h. (ILLUS.) **2,255**

Buck Rogers Space Gun

Buck Rogers Space Ranger Kit

Alexander Dionne Quintuplets Dolls

Ella Cinders Doll & Book

Early Felix Jointed Figure

Felix the Cat figure, painted silhouetted cut-out wood w/hinged joints, black & white w/red nose, 1930s, 7" h. (ILLUS.) 550

Felix the Cat figure, bisque, ca. 1930s, 2" h. 90

Felix the Cat Schoenhut Figure

Felix the Cat figure, jointed wood, painted black & white w/leather ears, decal on chest & trademark under foot, Schoenhut, ca. 1924, slight face paint wear, needs restringing, 8 1/8" h. (ILLUS.) 374

Flash Gordon Signal Pistol

Flash Gordon pistol, Signal Pistol, lithographed tin, green w/red fin & tip, decal w/bust of Flash & his name on side, Marx, 1935, 7" l. (ILLUS.) **1,600**

Flash Gordon Rocket Fighter

Flash Gordon toy, windup tin, "Flash Gordon Rocket Fighter," futuristic space ship w/Flash aiming a gun from the cockpit, Marx, ca. 1930s, missing back fin, minor paint loss, 12" l. (ILLUS.) 275

Foxy Grandpa figure, nodder-type, painted cast iron, Kenton Hardware, ca. 1910, 6 1/4" l. 345

Gene Autry cap pistol, cast iron, 1930s, very fine.. 90

Gene Autry photograph & letter, written to a fan, signed by Autry as Technical Sergeant in U.S. Army Air Forces, 1940s, photo 5 x 7", 2 pcs... **45**

Gene Autry songbook, "The Oklahoma Yodeling Cowboy," 28 cowboy songs & mountain ballads, great cover graphics, 1934... **45**

Happy Hooligan figure, china, reclining figure w/full-color underglaze paint, early 20th c., 3" l. **65**

Harold Lloyd bell toy, lithographed tin, Germany, 6 1/4" l., excellent.......................... 275

Hopalong Cassidy cookie jar, ceramic, tall barrel-shape in tan w/brown specks 525

Katzenjammer Kids figure, "Hans," Syroco pressed wood, 1944 King Features Syndicate copyright, 3" h. 55

Laurel & Hardy game, Magnetic Pie Toss....... 100

Little Lulu doll, stuffed cloth, pressed cloth face w/painted features, yarn hair, red dress, Georgine Averill, 1930s, 36" (doll fair condition, dress faded) **201**

Little LuLu perfume bottle, ca. 1940 102

Lone Ranger arcade card, photo of Lee Powell as the Lone Ranger wearing a net mask 45

Lone Ranger badge, Secret Compartment-type, w/instructions & mailer......................... 175

Large Lone Ranger Doll

Lone Ranger doll, composition w/cloth cowboy hat & outfit including shirt, vest, scarf, badge, chaps & cuffs, minor rub on nose, 1930s, 20" h. (ILLUS.) 688

Lone Ranger figure, chalkware, 1930s............. 78

Lone Ranger guitar, child's, pressed wood, by Supertone, ca. 1940s 150

Lone Ranger pencil box, 1930s 88

Lone Ranger pinback button, celluloid, red, white & black round picture of the Lone Ranger & Silver in the center, white border w/black wording "The Lone Ranger - Sunday Herald and Examiner," newspaper premium, ca. 1930s, excellent condition 28

Lone Ranger pressbook, 1938 serial 900

Maggie & Jiggs Dolls

Maggie & Jiggs (Bringing Up Father comic), jointed wood, comic strip figures, cloth outfits, Maggie w/rolling pin, Jiggs w/bucket of corned beef, Albert Schoenhut, the pair (ILLUS.) **1,200**

Maggie & Jiggs (Bringing Up Father comic) salt & pepper shakers, chalkware figures, full original paint, ca. 1920s, pr. **85**

Mutt (Mutt & Jeff comics) pitcher, milktype, figural, porcelain w/full-color underglaze decoration, ca. 1920s, mint, 5 1/4" h. **158**

Nancy doll, stuffed cloth, marked on wrist tag "Georgene," Georgene Novelties, New York, New York, cloth mask face, painted black eyes, pug nose w/accented nostrils, closed smiling mouth, applied ears, cloth body jointed at shoulders & hips, original black fuzzy hair, black & white striped cloth lower legs for socks, beige flannel felt for shoes, wearing original black, orange & white dress, nylon panties, w/original marked box, 13" h. (ILLUS. left w/Sluggo) **850**

Orphan Annie tea set: cov. teapot, cov. sugar bowl, creamer & two cups & saucers; porcelain, lustre trim, Japan, ca. 1930s, the set **295**

Orphan Annie & Sandy dolls, composition head, pale blue painted eyes, closed mouth, molded & painted hair, original red dress, orange composition dog, Freundlich, marked "Harold Gray" on paper hang tag, 12" Annie, pr. **575**

Orphan Annie & Sandy teapot, cov., child's, porcelain, color decoration of Annie & Sandy on a lustre ground, Japan, ca. 1930s **95**

Popeye bank, ceramic, figural, American Bisque **450**

Popeye bank, dime-type, lithographed tin, ca. 1929 .... **99**

Popeye bubble blowing set, ca. 1936 .... **58**

Popeye Christmas tree light set, eight light shades in original display box, Mazda, ca. 1920s, the set **250**

Popeye knockout bank, lithographed tin, very good, Straits Mfg. Co. **900**

Popeye pencil, large metal-type, 1929, in original box, 8" l. **75**

Popeye pencil sharpener, Bakelite, ca. 1930s **125**

Popeye pencil sharpener, lithographed tin **165**

Popey e puzzle, hand-held dexterity-type pinball style, 1929 .... **75**

Porky Pig figure, chalkware, early carnival-type, w/coin slot, ca. 1945, 12" h. **33**

Shirley Temple chalk figure, gold, "Shirley" on base, 4" h. **125**

Shirley Temple doll, marked "Ideal Doll, ST - 35 - 38 - 2," vinyl head, hazel eyes w/real lashes, feathered brows, painted lower lashes, open-closed mouth w/six upper teeth, rooted hair, original yellow nylon dress w/attached slip, 36" h. **1,300**

Shirley Temple doll carriage, wooden, decals on side, all original, 1930s **875**

Georgene Nancy & Sluggo Dolls

Sluggo doll, stuffed cloth, marked on wrist tag "A "Georgene" Doll, Georgene Novelties, Inc., New York 10, N.Y., Made in U.S.A.," doll unmarked, cloth mask face, painted black eyes, pug nose w/accented nostrils, closed smiling mouth, applied ears, jointed body, beige flannel feet for shoes, dressed in original blue pants, striped knit shirt, black jacket & brown cap, in original box w/marked label "A Georgene Product, No. 6102," three small dirty smudges, 13" h. (ILLUS. right) **775**

Superman badge, "Superman of America Club," figural, brass **180**

Superman bubble bath bottle, plastic, figural Superman, Soaky, Colgate-Palmolive, 1965, 10" h. **40-75**

Rare Large Superman Doll

Superman doll, jointed composition, painted blue & red outfit w/original cloth cape, Ideal, 1940, some crazing, 13 1/2" h. (ILLUS.) **1,595**

Superman figure, jointed plastic w/removable clothes, Mego, 1972, 8" h.. **50-115**

Superman toy, plastic, Kryptonite, glow-in-the-dark, boxed, 1970s **10-30**

Tarzan Big Little Book

Tarzan Big Little Book, #778, "Tarzan of the Screen," 1934 (ILLUS.) **35**

Tarzan book, "Tarzan and the Lost Empire," cover by A. W. Sperry, hardcover, 1931-1940, Grosset & Dunlap **50**

Tarzan book, "Tarzan of the Apes," first edition, cover by Fred Arting, hardcover, 1914, McClurg............................. **19,550**

Tarzan book, "Tarzan of the Apes," four volumes in one, cover by J. Allen St. John, hardcover, 1988, Avenal Books **15**

Tarzan book, "Tarzan of the Apes," hardcover, 1927, Grosset & Dunlap **50**

Tarzan book, "Tarzan of the Apes in the Land That Time Forgot," undated, Treasure Hour Books, art by Russ Manning **20**

Tarzan book, "Tarzan The Invincible," cover by Studly Burroughs, hardcover, 1933-1940, Grosset & Dunlap **50**

Tarzan book, "The Beasts of Tarzan," cover by J. Allen St. John, hardcover, 1927-1940, Grosset & Dunlap **50**

Tarzan book, "The Return of Tarzan," hardcover, 1927-1940, Grosset & Dunlap **50**

Tarzan book, "The Son of Tarzan," cover by J. Allen St. John, hardcover, 1927-1940, Grosset & Dunlap **50**

Tarzan figure, ceramic, 1930s, Foulds, 4" h.. **75**

Tarzan movie lobby card, "Tarzan The Mighty," 1928, Universal Pictures **300**

Tarzan movie lobby card, "Tarzan's Secret Treasure," 1941, MGM **185**

Tarzan movie lobby card, "The New Adventures of Tarzan," 1935, Burroughs/Tarzan Productions........................ **75**

Tarzan movie poster, "Tarzan's Revenge," 1938, Twentieth Century Fox **3,000**

Tarzan paperback book, "Tarzan of the Apes," 1943, Armed Forces edition **500**

Tarzan toy, tin whistle, Japan, 1930s **75**

Tom Mix bird call & telescope, w/papers & mailer **175**

Tom Mix "bullet" telescope, Ralston premium **70**

Tom Mix cowboy boots, child's, in original box **375**

Tom Mix good luck spinner, Ralston premium **50**

Tom Mix magnet ring **45**

Tom Mix Premium Set

Tom Mix secret manual & decoder badge, original Ralston premium set also including booklet titled "The Life of Tom Mix," mint & unused in original mailing envelope, the set (ILLUS.) **66**

Uncle Wiggily doll, unmarked, cloth swivel head w/mask face, black glass eyes, multi-stroke brows, painted upper & lower lashes, open-closed mouth w/two teeth, cloth ears attached to black felt hat, cloth body, original white collar, red felt jacket w/black snap buttons, blue pants w/red & white striped cuff, 13" h......... **155**

Uncle Wiggily doll, marked "A Georgene Product" on doll, "Uncle Wiggily (Long Ears), The Famous Story Book Character, Copyright 1943 Howard R. Garis, Trade Mark Reg." on one side paper tag, "Georgene Novelties, Inc. New York, Exclusive Licensed Manufacturers" on the other, cloth body, applied long ears, original white shirt, gold felt vest, blue felt jacket w/red lapels, blue pants w/red polka dot cuffs, blue ribbon tie, holding black felt hat, 20" h. **550**

Yellow Kid (early comics) pincushion, metal figure w/cushion, ca. 1890s, 3 1/2" h. **350**

Yellow Kid toy, Yellow Kid in goat cart, cast iron, Kenton Hardware, early 20th c., 7 1/2" l. (overpainted) **345**

Chapter 2

CHILDREN'S DISHES & MUGS

Nursery Rhyme Pattern Children's Punch Set

DISHES

Berry set: master bowl & six sauce dishes, clear pressed glass, Pattee Cross patt., the set $55

Butter, cov., pressed glass, Drum patt., clear 145

Butter dish, cov., clear pressed glass, Tulip & Honeycomb patt., large size.......................... 66

Butter dish, cov., pressed glass, Tappan patt.,clea 75

Butter dish, cov., pressed glass, Tulip & Honeycomb patt., clear 32

Cake stand, pressed glass, Rexford patt., clear 35

Castor set, four-bottle, clear bottles & shaker in clear pressed glass, American Shield patt., in a silver-plated frame w/flaring openwork foot, ring holder & central handle w/top loop centered by a small figural bird, late 19th c., the set (ILLUS. left) 121

Castor set, four-bottle, two shakers & two bottles in clear pressed glass, Flute patt., in a silver-plated frame w/high stamped-design foot, ring holder & central handle w/a large top loop centered by a sitting girl, late 19th c., the set (ILLUS. right).......... 220

Coffeepot, porcelain, embossed scroll & grape leaf design w/cobalt blue trim, Germany, 5" h. 88

Two Children's Castor Sets

Children's Creamer

Creamer, pressed glass, Drum patt., clear (ILLUS.)... 55

Monopteros Children's Dinner Service

Creamer, pressed glass, Pennsylvania patt., clear 35

Creamer, pressed glass, Tulip & Honeycomb patt., clear 17

Creamer & covered sugar bowl, earthenware, footed boat-shapes w/flaring rims, light blue transfer-printed design of an Oriental landscape on each, ca. 1840, pr. (unseen chip on lid rest of sugar base) 165

Cup & saucer, handleless, earthenware, Casino patt., transfer-printed in light blue, Adams, England, ca. 1830-40 50

Cups & saucers, handleless, earthenware, transfer-printed light blue decoration of a lake w/towers, geometric border w/medallions of the view, England, ca. 1830-50, five sets & one extra saucer, the group 303

Dinner service: 15 dinner plates, four soup plates, four platters, one well-and-tree platter, two gravy boats, two soup tureens w/undertrays & ladles, one cov. soup tureen, undertray & ladle; transfer-printed design w/geometric & Greek key banding, blue on white, Staffordshire, England, 19th c., platter 5 3/4" l., the set (minor chips, cracks, restoration) 230

Dinner service: two 2 3/8" d. plates, one 3" d. plate, three 3" d. soup plates, one 5 1/2" l., 3 1/2" h. cov. soup tureen, two 3 1/4" l., 2 1/2" h. square cov. vegetable dishes, two 1 3/8" h. gravy boats & one 3 1/4" l. oval platter; earthenware, Monopteros patt., medium dark blue design of ancient ruins, Rogers, ca. 1830, the set, some damages (ILLUS. above) 660

Gravy boat, earthenware, transfer-printed light blue floral designs, England, ca. 1830-40 55

Pitcher, lemonade, pressed glass, Oval Star patt., clear 65

Plate, round w/flanged rim, the center w/a relief-molded turkey, lightly embossed rim w/six green enamel dots, turkey lightly colored in black & brown, first half 19th c., 4" d. 94

Plate, round w/flanged rim, center w/a blue transfer-printed sheep, the border embossed w/a monkey, dogs & foxes highlighted in blue, green & bluish green, probably Adams, first half 19th c., 4 3/4" d. 220

Plate, octagonal, center red transfer-printed scene of four men sitting around a table & drinking, titled "Pot Boys," flanged rim embossed w/stars & florets, 5 1/2" w. (two tiny chips) 110

Plate, round, flanged rim, center w/a black transfer-printed scene of a British soldier titled "A Soldier Visiting Home," the rim embossed & crudely painted in red, green, blue & purple, mid-19th c., 5 1/2" d. (two minute nicks on rim) 66

Plate, octagonal, flanged rim, central black transfer-printed scene w/the Farmer's Arms including wheat, farming tools, flowers, hay, etc., banner w/"Our Bread - Untaxed - Our Commerce - Free," trimmed in blue, yellow & red, border band of embossed stars & florets w/pink lustre rim band, first half 19th c., 6" w. 220

Plate, round w/flanged rim, the center w/a dark blue transfer-printed design of three men fishing, border embossed w/flower clusters trimmed in red, green, black & orange, first half 19th c., 6" d. (two unseen chips on the back) 88

Punch bowl, pressed glass, Inverted Strawberry patt., clear 65

Punch bowl, pressed glass, Oval Star patt., clear w/gold rim 55

Punch bowl, pressed glass, Wheat Sheaf patt., clear 30

Punch bowl, pressed glass, Wild Rose patt., clear 45

Punch cup, pressed glass, Wheat Sheaf patt., clear 8

Punch set: punch bowl & six cups, clear pressed glass, Wheat Sheaf patt., Cambridge, the set 121

Punch set: punch bowl & six cups; pressed glass, Nursery Rhyme patt., blue opaque, the set 460

Children's Porcelain Tea Service

Children's Punch Set

Punch set: punch bowl & six cups, pressed glass, Nursery Rhyme patt., milk glass, the set (ILLUS.) **225**

Sauce dish, pressed glass, Wheat Sheaf patt., clear **9**

Children's Spooner

Spooner, pressed glass, Hawaiian Lei patt., Higbee mark, clear (ILLUS.) **35**

Sugar bowl, cov., clear pressed glass, Amazon patt. **33**

Sugar bowl, cov., Menagerie patt., figural sitting bear, clear **149**

Sugar bowl, cov., pressed glass, Drum patt., clear **150**

Sugar bowl, cov., pressed glass, Hawaiian Lei patt., Higbee mark, clear **40**

Sugar bowl, cov., pressed glass, Oval Star patt., clear **30**

Sugar bowl, cov., pressed glass, Tulip with Honeycomb patt., clear.................................... **25**

Table set: cov. butter, cov. sugar bowl, creamer & spooner, clear pressed glass, Button Panel No. 44 patt., the set **198**

Table set: cov. butter, cov. sugar, creamer & spooner, clear pressed glass, Rexford patt., the set... **72**

Table set: cov. sugar, creamer, cov. butter dish & spooner, Nursery Rhyme patt., clear, the set... **220**

Table set: cov. sugar, creamer, spooner & cov. butter dish; Vine & Beads patt., clear, the set **175**

Table set: creamer, cov. sugar, cov. butter & spooner; pressed glass, Wild Rose patt., milk white, 4 pcs. **275**

Table set: creamer, sugar, cov. butter, spooner & matching tray; clear pressed glass, Hobnail w/Thumbprint Base patt., 5 pcs. **275**

Table set: creamer, sugar, cov. butter & spooner; pressed glass, Arrowhead in Ovals patt., clear, the set **100**

Table set, pressed glass, Oval Star patt., clear, 4 pcs. **175**

Tea service: 3 1/2" h. cov. teapot, 2 7/8" h. cov. sugar bowl, 2 1/2" h. creamer, 3 1/2" d., 2 1/2" h. waste bowl & six handled cups & saucers; porcelain, boat-shaped serving pieces, all decorated w/overall h.p. enameled floral sprigs in blue, brick red & orange, ca. 1820, the set, some damage (ILLUS. above) **440**

Tea set: cov. teapot, cov. sugar bowl, creamer & four cups & saucers; pearlware w/a light blue transfer-printed Willow-like patt., boat-shaped serving pieces, marked "Semi China," ca. 1840, teapot 3 1/4" h., the set (teapot spout chip, chips on sugar lid, surface flakes or pinpoints on saucers) **220**

Tea set: cov. teapot, cov. sugar, creamer, waste bowl, six handled cups & saucers & six 5 1/2" d. plates; overall red spatter decoration, serving pieces w/tall cylindrical bodies, marked "Staffordshire, England," ca. 1900, teapot 5 1/4" h., the set (teapot spout chip, small hairline in creamer) 358

Tea set, porcelain, yellow lustre ground w/color scenes of little girls & their Teddy bears, early 20th c., 15 pcs. 375

Tea set: cov. teapot, creamer & sugar bowl, waste bowl & six cups & saucers, iron-stone, Moss Rose patt., 16 pcs. (teapot damaged) 220

Tumbler, pressed glass, Oval Star patt., clear 11

Water set: pitcher & five tumblers; clear pressed glass, Pattee Cross patt., the set 66

Water set: pitcher & seven tumblers; pressed glass, Nursery Rhyme patt., clear, 8 pcs. 198

Mugs

"Count Down, Blast Off" Whistle Mug

Ceramic, "Count Down, Blast Off," space mug, rocket ship on handle is whistle, bottom says "Personal Property of (space for child's name)" (ILLUS.) 25-35

Bear "Drink Milk and Whistle" Whistle Cup

Ceramic, "Drink Milk and Whistle," three small bears play on front while little bear sits on handle, ceramic whistle is separate piece (ILLUS.) 35-45

New Hampshire Souvenir Whistle Cup

Ceramic, "Old Man Of The Mountain, Franconia Notch, NH," souvenir whistle cup, bird tail is the whistle (ILLUS.) 45-55

Pressed glass, Beaded Column & Panel patt., clear 15

Pressed glass, Butterfly patt., clear 38

Pressed glass, Diagonal Flowered Band patt., clear 25

Pressed glass, Grapevine with Ovals patt., clear 21

Pressed glass, Little Bo Peep patt., clear 85

Pressed glass, Little Bo Peep patt., clear, etched 65

Pressed glass, Ribbed Forget-me-not patt., clear 23

Pressed glass, Robin patt., amber 25

Pressed glass, Scampering Lamb patt., clear 59

Staffordshire pottery, cylindrical w/molded base & C-scroll handle, black transfer-printed design representing the month of December w/a young girl w/a cart full of guns, drum, fiddle, doll, a British flag & a rhyme, 2 1/8" h.. 61

Staffordshire pottery, cylindrical w/molded base & C-scroll handle, black transfer-printed design representing the month of August, shows men, women & children hand-harvesting wheat w/a printed rhyme, 2 1/4" h... 77

Staffordshire pottery, cylindrical w/molded base & C-scroll handle, blank transfer-printed design of a young girl grooming a large dog, the ground littered w/bones & a food dish, 2 3/8" h. 33

Rare Washington-Lafayette Mug

Staffordshire pottery, cylindrical, blue transfer-printed sheep in front of a cottage above the words "A PRESENT FROM WASHINGTON," blue line border, ca. 1820-30, 2" h. **605**

Staffordshire pottery, cylindrical, black transfer-printed scene titled "Cornwallis Surrendering His Sword at Yorktown," pink lustre border, probably by Wood, first quarter 19th c., 2 1/16" h. (line across the base, repair to base chip damages part of the title) **413**

Staffordshire pottery, cylindrical w/C-form handle, black transfer-printed decoration, one side w/an oval leafy medallion w/the words "Washington - His Countrys Father" enclosing a bust portrait of Washington, the reverse w/a similar wreath w/the words "Fayette - the Nations Guest" enclosing a bust of the Marquis de Lafayette, on the front the Seal of the United States w/the wording "Republicans Are Not Always Ungrateful," base

rim chip, unseen table ring flake, minute rim nick, 2 3/8" h. (ILLUS. above) **1,540**

Staffordshire pottery, cylindrical w/C-form handle, pearlware, red transfer-printed American eagles on a shell on the sides, the front w/a scroll cartouche enclosing "Prosper Freedom," 2 3/8" h. (overall mellowing) **440**

Staffordshire pottery, cylindrical, brown transfer-printed scene of a cat & her kittens, trimmed in green, red & yellow, 2 1/2" h. (chip on base) **99**

Staffordshire pottery, cylindrical, polychrome decorated "Keep thy Shop & Thy Shop will Keep Thee," 2 1/2" h. (hairline) **50**

Staffordshire pottery, cylindrical w/molded base & C-form handle, black transfer-printed medallion enclosing a bust profile of Benjamin Franklin within a leafy wreath, reverse w/a farm scene of three men talking, highlighted in blue, red & green, 2 3/4" h. (minor rim flakes) **550**

Chapter 3
DISNEY TOYS & COLLECTIBLES

Early Snow White & Dwarfs Dolls

Bambi figure, ceramic, standing w/butterfly on tail, American Pottery, 1947, 8" h............. **190**

Bambi Bank by Leeds

Bambi bank, ceramic, marked "Leeds" (ILLUS.).. **$68**
Bambi charm, metal, 1940s.................................. **55**
Bambi figure, ceramic, prone position, American Pottery, Evan K. Shaw.................. **150**
Bambi figure, ceramic, American Pottery Co., 4 1/2" h....................................... **145**

Bambi & Thumper Movie Cel

Bambi movie cel, gouache on trimmed celluloid applied to a Courvoisier background, a scene of Bambi looking down at Thumper perched on a rock, stamped "W.D.P." on mat w/Courvoisier Galleries label on back, 1942, 7 x 7 1/2" (ILLUS.).. **4,025**
Bambi pencil sharpener, Bakelite **35**

Bambi pin, sterling silver, Art Deco style, Bambi in rectangular frame, "Coro" 90

Bambi planter, ceramic, butterfly on the tail, American Pottery 200

Bambi planter, ceramic, depicts Bambi looking into a pond, 7 x 10" 70

Bambi sheet music, "Love is a Song" 38

Bambi & friends coat hangers, set of 5 45

Bambi & Thumper planter, china, marked"Walt Disney," 7" h. 60

Big Bad Wolf (from "Three Little Pigs") doll, stuffed cloth, colorfully dressed in blue felt trousers and a tall red felt hat, standing w/his mouth open & tongue hanging out, about to devour a sandwich containing one of the pigs, 20 1/2" h. 1,050

Big Bad Wolf (from "Three Little Pigs") figure, bisque, 1930s, 3" h. 105

Big Bad Wolf (from "Three Little Pigs") figure, rubber, standing position, brown w/painted details, Seiberling Products, 1930s, w/original box, 10" h. (some cracking) 900

Big Bad Wolf (from "Three Little Pigs") sheet music, "Who's Afraid of the Big Bad Wolf," 1932 50

Big Bad Wolf (from "Three LIttle Pigs & The Big Bad Wolf"), Ingersoll, 1930s 675

Big Bad Wolf (from "Three Little Pigs") doll, cloth, felt face w/toothy open mouth & button eyes, plush body, wearing red pants w/patches at the knees, foot stamped w/mark of Knickerbocker Toy Company, 1930s, 18" h. 1,000

Blue Fairy (Pinocchio) movie drawing, graphite & colored pencil on paper, a large full-figure drawing of the Blue Fairy grasping her wand, production numbers stamped in lower right corner, 1940, 12 1/2 x 15 1/2" 1,035

Early Clarabelle & Horace Glasses

Clarabelle Cow tumbler, clear slightly tapering glass decorated w/black enamel, Clarabelle seated looking in a mirror (ILLUS. right) 151

Disney characters book, Annual 1937, w/dust jacket, 10 1/2 x 13 1/2" (well worn dust jacket) 360

Disney characters book, "Disney's Silly Symphonies," 1930s 27

Disney characters book, "Peculiar Penguins," published by David McKay, 1934 120

Disney characters book, "School Days in Disneyville," 1939 30

Disney characters book, "Silly Symphony Book To Color, "Whitman No. 660, 1932....... 75

Disney characters book, "The Three Caballeros," Walt Disney Productions, 1944, excellent condition.................................. 60

Disney characters book, "Walt Disney Comics & Stories, No. 11, Vol. 3," August 1943... 1,400

Disney characters book, "Walt Disney's Forest Friends," 1938, hard cover, w/dust jacket 78

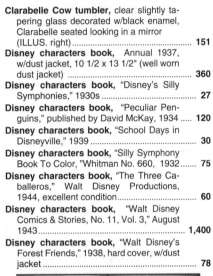

1942 Disney Characters Calendar

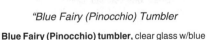

"Blue Fairy (Pinocchio) Tumbler

Blue Fairy (Pinocchio) tumbler, clear glass w/blue figure, ca. 1940 (ILLUS. right) 19

Clarabelle Cow book, "Story of Clarabelle Cow," story & picture book w/adventures of Donald Duck & Mickey Mouse & Clarabelle as a secondary character, Whitman Publishing, child's scrawled name & date on cover, 1938, 94 pp., 5 x 5 1/2" (ILLUS. center w/Goofy book) 48

Disney characters calendar, 1942, color lithographed paper, advertising promotion for Morrell's Ham, each month w/a different color scene of various Disney characters, each page shrinkwrapped individually, minor soiling & edge creasing, each 8 1/4 x 17 3/4" (ILLUS. of part)......... 1,150

Disney characters cartoon drawing, graphite & colored pencil on paper, a storyboard drawing of Katharine Hepburn as Little Bo Peep w/four large sunflowers behind her, from "Mother Goose Goes Hollywood," 1931, 6 3/4 x 8 1/2" 920

Disney characters charm bracelet, 14k gold, w/Dumbo, Bambi, Jiminy Cricket, Thumper, Pluto & Flower, the skunk, together w/an enameled piano, key & heart, 7" l. 550

Disney characters Christmas tree lights, Silly Symphony series by NOMA, ca. 1930s, original box 405

Disney characters coloring book, "Silly Symphony," Whitman, 1934, 34 pp. 45

Disney characters cookie tin, long, low rectangular metal container w/a colorfully printed lid featuring a landscape scene full of Disney characters including the Three Little Pigs, Mickey & Minnie Mouse, Donald Duck, Goofy & Snow White, ca. 1940, 12 x 18" (minor dents & scratches) 125

Disney characters dinner set, china, "Three Little Pigs and Red Riding Hood Set," imported from Bavaria by Schumann Bros., a sub license from George Borgfeldt, 1932, the set...... 180

Disney characters doll, cloth, from "Babes in Toyland," features "Mary, Mary Quite Contrary," w/printed features, dressed in original dress, ca. 1930s, 18" 205

Disney characters drum, lithographed tin, illustrates Mickey & Minnie Mouse, Donald Duck, Pluto, etc., Ohio Art Co., (Bryan, Ohio), 6 1/2"...... 305

Disney characters entertainment program, World War II era, illustrations of Mickey, Donald, Minnie & several other characters dressed as soldiers, red, white & blue, mint condition 125

Disney characters music box, "Melody Player" w/five paper rolls, J. Chein & Co., 6 1/2" x 7" 125

Disney characters sand set, sprinkling can, small bucket, little shovel w/Disney characters plus sand mold & scoop in box, with sand elevator, Ohio Arts, Inc., the set 750

Disney characters Silly Symphonies book, pop-up type, King Neptune/Babes in Woods, Walt Disney Enterprises, 1934, hard cover, w/dust jacket...... 575

Disney characters toy, windup tin "Disneyland Roller Coaster," figure-8 roller coaster w/two passenger cars, J. Chein & Co., 1940s, 10" h. 450

Donald Duck alarm clock, Bayard Co., France, dated 1956 145

Donald Duck ashtray, china, trapezoidal dish w/two cigarette indentations at front edge & two Donald Duck figures perched on back edge, glossy glaze w/painted trim, Japan, ca. 1935, 3 1/2" h...... 725

Donald Duck bank, composition, w/life preserver, Crown Toy Co., ca. 1938, 6" h. 350

Donald Duck bank, dime register, lithographed tin, Louis Marx & Co...... 300

Donald Duck book, "Donald Duck & The Mystery of the Double X," Better Little Book...... 15

Donald Duck cartoon cel, gouache on trimmed celluloid applied to a drawing of a tree branch & nest, Donald, w/outstretched arms & a menacing squawk, approaches the eagle's nest, from "Alpine Climbers," 1936, 9 3/4 x 11"...... 1,035

Donald Duck cartoon drawing, graphite & colored pencil on paper, an angry Donald w/hammer & horseshoe in hand, from "The Village Smithy," production notes throughout, 1942, 10 x 12"...... 517

Donald Duck cartoon drawing, graphite & pencil on paper, from "Orphan's Benefit," Donald attempts to recite "Little Boy Blue Come Blow Your Horn," 1935, 9 1/2 x 12"...... 345

Donald Duck charm, sterling silver...... 145

Donald Duck doll, cloth, long-billed Donald dressed in a blue & green sailor suit, red bow tie & blue cap, w/original Knickerbocker tag, ca. 1930s, 13" h. (some stains)...... 900

Large Donald Kickerbocker Doll

Donald Duck doll, stuffed cloth & felt, Donald dressed in a red bandleader's uniform w/gold trim & brass buttons, w/a "bearskin" tall black hat & wooden baton, Knickerbocker, ca. 1930s, 21" h. (ILLUS.)...... 1,200

Donald Duck figure, bisque, long-billed Donald, 1930s, 1 3/4" h. 105

Donald Duck figure, bisque, w/horn, ca. 1930, 3" h...... 110

Donald Duck figure, rubber, Seiberling, 5 1/2" h 105

Donald Duck Advertising Blotter

Donald Duck ink blotter, advertising-type, "Sunoco," color-printed paper, rectangular w/a color scene of a laughing, waving Donald seated in an open auto racing across a snowy landscape w/a Billy goat butting the back of the car, reads "A Quck Start - Blue Sunoco (in logo) - Peps Up Cold Motors," ca. 1938, edge wear, scratches, soiling, small tear at top (ILLUS.) **149**

Donald Duck nodder, celluloid figure on metal base, Japanese, 6 1/4" h., very good **880**

Donald Duck paint box, Transogram, 1938 .... **65**

Donald Duck pencil sharpener, celluloid, figure w/sharpener inside, ca. 1930s **185**

Donald Duck ring, sterling silver, full-figure raised image of Donald waving, late 1930s **105**

Donald Duck sheet music, "Der Fuehrer's Face," 1942 .... **38**

Donald Duck toothbrush holder, bisque, long-billed Donald in typical sailor suit, Japan, 1930s, 5 1/4" h. **390**

Donald Duck toothbrush holder, bisque, modeled as two long-billed Donalds standing side to side, Japan, ca. 1935, 4" h. **400**

Donald Duck toy, makes quacking noise, very good, Sun Rubber Co. **25**

Early Donald Duck Tumbler

Donald Duck tumbler, clear glass w/blue printed long-billed Donald Duck, ca. 1930s (ILLUS.) **186**

Donald Duck umbrella, figural Donald head handle, yellow silk, Louis Weiss Company, ca. 1930s **125**

Donald Duck valentine card, dated 1939, mint condition **40**

Donald Duck wristwatch, round, Donald's hands indicating the minutes & hours, three Mickey figures on subsidiary seconds dial, leather band w/enameled metal figures of Donald, Ingersoll, 1935-39 .... **400**

Donald Duck & nephew cookie jar, turn-about-type, ca. 1940s **90**

Donald Duck & Joe Carioca cookie jar, ceramic, turnabout-type, Leeds China Co. **500**

Donald Duck & nephews tumbler, colored scene of Donald & his nephews as Boy Scouts, 1942 series **52**

Donald Duck & Pluto toy, composition, metal & wood, h.p. figures riding a railroad flatcar on which Pluto's doghouse is placed, The Lionel Corporation, 1938, w/original box, 10" l. **1,400**

Donald Duck & Pluto toy, Donald & Pluto in car, Sun Rubber Co., 6 1/2" l. **125**

Dumbo bank, china, marked "W. Disney U. S. A.," 1940s **75**

Dumbo book, "Dumbo of the Circus," 1942 .... **60**

Dumbo book, "Dumbo the Flying Elephant," Whitman, 1941 .... **28**

Dumbo cookie jar, ceramic, "Dumbo's Greatest Cookies on Earth," California Originals **625**

Dumbo figure, pottery, American Pottery, w/paper label, 6" h. **145**

Dumbo planter, ceramic, American Pottery, 4" l. **145**

Dwarf Bashful doll, composition head, cloth body, Knickerbocker Toy Co., 1930s **195-225**

Dwarf Bashful figure, bisque, 1930s, 3 1/4" h. **75**

Dwarf Bashful figure, bisque, playing saxaphone, 1930s, 4 1/2" h. **125**

Dwarf Bashful figure, ceramic, Evan Shaw, 6 1/4" h. **125**

Dwarf Bashful movie drawing, graphite & colored pencil on paper, a production drawing of Bashful walking forward, 1937, 10 x 12" **460**

Dwarf Bashful Toothbrush Holder

Dwarf Bashful toothbrush holder, porcelain, figural, Bashful standing next to a textured brown container w/a blue rim, h.p. clothing & face, Japan, 1930s, 3 1/2" w., 4" h. (ILLUS. previous page) 110

Dwarf Doc animation drawing, graphite on paper, outline sketch of Doc smiling & looking to his right, 1937, 10 x 12" 575

Dwarf Doc doll, stuffed cloth, Knickerbocker Toy Co., 11" h. 98

Dwarf Doc figure, bisque, 1930s, 5" h. 105

Dwarf Doc glass, dairy, 1938 28

Dwarf Doc lamp, ceramic, Walt Disney Productions, dated 1938, 7" h. 250

Dwarf Doc toothbrush holder, ceramic, "Doc Says Brush Your Teeth," 1930s 280

Dwarf Dopey bank, composition, 1938 180

Dwarf Dopey carpet sweeper, musical, Fisher-Price 225

Dwarf Dopey doll, composition, movable arms, original paint & cloth costume, marked "Walt Disney, Knickerbocker Toy Co.," 9" h. (some wear)................................... 400

Dwarf Dopey figure, bisque, 1930s, 5" h. 105

Dwarf Dopey pencil sharpener, Bakelite, figural, 1930s... 95

Dwarf Dopey pin, plastic, Dopey on skis, 1940s, on original card 75

Dwarf Grumpy doll, stuffed velvet, Knickerbocker, dated 1938 on original tag, 10" h. 450

Dwarf Grumpy figure, bisque, Walt Disney Enterprises, 1930s, 3" h. 40

Dwarf Grumpy soap, Castile, w/original box 38

Dwarf Happy Birthday card, "Disney Birthday Card," 1938, excellent condition 80

Dwarf Happy figure, bisque, 1930s, 2 1/2" h. 40

Dwarf Happy figure, rubber, Seiberling, 5" h... 85

Dwarfs Happy & Doc toothbrush holder, ceramic, Maw, England, 1938, 4" h. 445

Dwarf Sleepy doll, Ideal, w/original 1937 tag, 12" h.. 550

Dwarf Sleepy figure, bisque, 1930s, 5" h. . **95-105**

Dwarf Sneezy charm, silver, movable head 65

Dwarf Sneezy figure, bisque, 1930s, 4 1/2" h. 85

Dwarf Sneezy toothpick holder, china, 1937.. 180

Dwarf Sneezy valentine card, mechanical, Walt Disney Enterprises, 1938 37

Dwarfs Doc, Dopey, Sleepy, Grumpy, Sneezy, Happy & Bashful movie cel, gouache on one piece of trimmed celluloid, a scene depicting all seven of the Dwarfs dancing jubilantly as Prince Charming's kiss brings Snow White back to life, 1937, 6 1/4 x 13" 5,750

Dwarfs Bashful, Doc, Dopey, Sleepy, Sneezy & Happy figures, hard rubber, Seiberling, 1938, 5 1/2" h., set of 7.. 600

Dwarfs Grumpy & Dopey hairbrush set, large & small brush, pr.................................... 140

Elmer Elephant book, "Elmer Elephant", 1936, McKay 78

Elmer Elephant toothbrush holder, twin Elmer Elephants, both w/movable trunks, Borgefelt.. 1,200

Evil Hag (Snow White & the Seven Dwarfs) production drawing, graphite & colored pencil on paper, showing a half-length portrait of the Evil Hag in profile, stamped w/production numbers in lower left corner, 1937, 10 x 12" 977

Faline (from Bambi) figure, ceramic, American Pottery Co., 4 1/4" h...................... 125

Fantasia book, "Fantasia Paint Book," 1939, #689.. 120

Fantasia book, "The Sorcerer's Apprentice," 1940, w/dust jacket........................... 40

Fantasia figure, ceramic, Ostrich bowing, Vernon Kilns, 6" h.................................... 1,100

Fantasia figure, ceramic, Ostrich, Vernon Kilns, 9" h... 1,400

Fantasia figure, ceramics, Mr. Stork, Vernon Kilns, Incised in the unglazed cavity, plus ink markings, "Disney Copyright 1941 Vernon Kilns U. S. A.".......................... 1,800

Fantasia figure, china, Centaurette, black, Vernon Kilns, No. 24 1,000

Fantasia figure, china, Centaurette, blonde, Vernon Kilns, No. 18...................... 1,000

Fantasia Centaur Movie Cel

Fantasia movie cel, gouache on celluloid, a male centaur spots the approaching centaurettes, from the "Pastoral Symphony" segment, 4 1/2 x 7" (ILLUS.) 920

Fantasia movie cel, gouache on celluloid applied to a Courvoisier background & mat, a centaurette looks down as her attendant grooms her, from the "Pastoral Symphony" segment, w/a skirt airbrushed onto the background & stamped "W.D.P.," 1940, 3 1/4 x 4 1/2" oval 690

Fantasia Mushroom Dancers Cel

Fantasia movie cel, gouache on celluloid applied to an airbrushed Courvoisier background, scene of The Mushroom Dancers lining up in two rows while Hop Low bows to them, "W.D.P." stamped in lower right corner & Courvoisier Galleries label on back, 1940, 6 x 6 3/4" (ILLUS.) **2,300**

Fantasia "Sorcerer's Apprentice" Cel

Fantasia movie cel, gouache on trimmed celluloid, Mickey timidly peers up the steps to see if Yen Sid has left, from "The Sorcerer's Apprentice" segment, 1940, 4 3/4 x 5 1/4" (ILLUS.) **4,887**
Fantasia movie cel, gouache on trimmed celluloid, the ballerina ostriches line up on point in the "Dance of the Hours" sequence, 1940, 7 x 8 1/2"................................ **920**

Fantasia Mickey Production Drawing

Fantasia production drawing, graphite & colored pencil on paper, showing Mickey Mouse directing his new-found magic powers, from "The Sorcerer's Apprentice" segment, 1940, 10 x 12" (ILLUS.)...... **2,875**
Ferdinand the Bull book, 1939, linen-like cover **45**
Ferdinand the Bull bracelet, marked "Walt Disney Enterprises".......................... **80**
Ferdinand the Bull cartoon cel, gouache on trimmed celluloid applied to a Courvoisier airbrushed background, Ferdinand charges down a field while astonished men look on, 1938, 9 1/4 x 9 3/4"..... **1,725**
Ferdinand the Bull coloring book, 1938 .... **25**
Ferdinand the Bull costume, mask includes horns, by Fishbach, New York, ca. 1940, w/original box **85**
Ferdinand the Bull figure, bisque, Japan, 1930s, 3" h.. **75**
Ferdinand the Bull figure, ceramic, large, Brayton Laguna.............................. **500**
Ferdinand the Bull figure, composition, jointed, signed Walt Disney Enterprises & Ideal **280**
Ferdinand the Bull figure, rubber, Seiberling, 1938-40, 5 1/2" l. **125**
Ferdinand the Bull hand puppet, cloth w/composition head, w/flower in hand, Walt Disney Enterprises **120**
Ferdinand the Bull toy, windup tin, Ferdinand & the matador, Louis Marx & Co., 1938, mint in box **950**
Figaro (Pinocchio's cat) cookie jar, ceramic, featuring two kittens, one on the jar, the other on the cover, ca. 1940s, 11" h. **190-225**
Figaro (Pinocchio's cat) doll, mohair w/oilcloth face, ca. 1939 .... **150**
Figaro (Pinocchio's cat) figure, ceramic, Figaro w/bowl, Brayton Laguna.................... **280**
Flower the Skunk (Bambi) figure, ceramic, American Pottery Co., 3" h. **105**
Geppetto (from Pinocchio) figure, pressed wood, Multi Products, 1943, 5" h... **118**

Gideon from Pinocchio Movie Cel

Gideon (from Pinocchio) movie cel, gouache on trimmed celluloid applied to a Courvoisier veneer background, full figure of Gideon sitting, Courvoisier Galleries label on back, 1940, 5 1/4 x 5 3/4" (ILLUS. previous page) **1,150**

Goofy book, "Dippy the Goof," hardbound, Whitman, 1938 .... **65**

Goofy, Clarabelle & Minnie Books

Goofy book, "Dippy the Goof," small hardbound story & picture book, Whitman Publishing, 1938, child's scrawled name & date on front, some wear, 94 pp., 5 x 5 1/2" (ILLUS. top) **48**

Goofy figure, bisque, 1930s, 3" h. **165**

Goofy pencil sharpener, celluloid, Walt Disney Productions **185**

Goofy & Donald Duck cartoon drawing, graphite on paper, outline sketch showing a surprised Goofy & Donald, from "Mickey's Service Station," 1935, 9 1/2 x 12" **690**

Horace Horsecollar tumbler, clear cylindrical glass w/red & blue enamel decoration of Horace playing a flute (ILLUS. left w/Clarabelle Cow) **151**

Jiminy Cricket (from Pinocchio) doll, made by Knickerbocker Toy Company, paper wrist tag, composition character head w/large painted eyes, closed smiling mouth, composition cricket body, painted yellow gloves & black shoes, original black jacket w/long tails, orange felt vest, blue felt hat w/yellow band, ca. 1939, 10" h. **1,100**

Jiminy Cricket (from Pinocchio) doll, velvet body, felt jacket & vest, 13 1/2" h. (hat missing) **105**

Jiminy Cricket (from Pinocchio) movie cel, gouache on celluloid applied to a prepared background, Jiminy, standing in front of a large eight ball threatens to knock Lampwick's block off after having been sunk in the corner pocket, 1940, 7 x 9" **1,955**

Jiminy Cricket (from Pinocchio) wristwatch, Ingersoll, in box **300**

Joe Carioca pencil sharpener, Bakelite, 1940s **50**

Joe (Jose) Carioca toy, balancing-type, lithographed paper on metal Joe Carioca balances on a metal base finished in black, France, 1940s, 12" h. **185-225**

Little Red Riding Hood figure, bisque, marked "Walt E. Disney - Borgefeldt - 1934," 3" h. **400**

Mickey Mouse alarm clock, animated, Ingersoll, 1930s **2,700**

Mickey Mouse animation drawing, graphite on paper, from "Alpine Climbers," 1936, 4 x 4 1/2" **1,500**

Mickey Mouse ashtray, ceramic, a stylized figure of Mickey sits playing a guitar, trimmed in yellow & brown w/black outlines, Holland, 8" h. **1,600**

Mickey Mouse ashtray, ceramic, triangular dish base w/figure of Mickey standing at short end playing the saxaphone, handpainted, Japan, ca. 1930s, 5" w. **300**

Mickey Mouse baby rattle, light blue plastic, early **275**

Mickey Mouse baby rattle, wood, pie-cut eyes, ca. 1930 .... **95**

Mickey Mouse bank, book-shaped, red leather & brass, Zell Products Co., 1930s, (Moore No. 197) **175**

Mickey Mouse bank, composition, Mickey w/movable head standing beside chest, Crown Toy Co., 1940, 6 1/4" h. **600**

Mickey Mouse bank, dime register, lithographed tin, dated 1939, 2 1/2 x 2 1/2" **195**

Mickey Mouse bank, Mickey w/mandolin seated on drum, pot metal, England, 1930s, 5" h. **525**

Mickey Mouse bell toy, Mickey on rollerskates painted on wood, 6" d. metal wheels w/large paper lithograph of Mickey on hubs, marked "WD Ent.," Mickey 7 x 8", overall 7 x 14" **600**

Mickey Mouse book, "Book for Coloring," die-cut, shows Mickey skating, 1936 .... **105**

Mickey Mouse book, "Hello Everybody," Bibo and Lang, 1930 .... **875**

Mickey Mouse book, "King Arthur's Court," pop-up type, 1933 .... **1,050**

Mickey Mouse book, "Mickey Mouse Cru-
soe," 1938 165
Mickey Mouse book, "Mickey Mouse & His
Friends," linen, Whitman No. 904, 1936,
12 pp. 185
Mickey Mouse book, "Mickey Mouse Pic-
tures to Paint," 1931, #210, Saalfield
Publishing Co. of Akron, Ohio 240
Mickey Mouse book, "Mickey Mouse Pre-
sents Walt Disney's Nursery Stories from
Walt Disney's Silly Symphony," Whit-
man, 1937, 212 pp. 125
Mickey Mouse book, "Mickey Mouse's
Summer Vacation," 1948 48
Mickey Mouse book, "Mickey Never Fails,"
hardbound, Heath, 1939 95
Mickey Mouse book, "Mickey & The Gold-
en Touch," 1937, mint w/dust jacket 105
Mickey Mouse book, "Silly Symphony
Babes in the Woods," pop-up type,
1930s 115
Mickey Mouse book, "The Sorcerer's Ap-
prentice," 1940 38
Mickey Mouse book set, "The Mickey
Mouse Box," #2146, includes "Brave Lit-
tle Tailor," "Mother Pluto," "The Practical

Pig," "Timid Elmer," and "The Ugly Duck-
ling," set, Whitman Co., 1939, set 275
Mickey Mouse booklet, "Sun Oil Automo-
tive" premium, 1938 25
Mickey Mouse bowl, Beetleware, w/alpha-
bet & numerals on rim, Walt Disney
Ent., ca. 1930s, large 105
Mickey Mouse bridge score pad, large
illustration of Mickey on cover 95
Mickey Mouse buttons, dress-type, Walt
Disney Enterprises, ca. 1930, on original
card, set of 4 95
Mickey Mouse candy box, lithographed
tin, elliptical shape w/colorful images of
Mickey w/top hat & cane bowing to Minnie on the lid, & ice skating around the
sides, 4 1/2 x 8" 705
Mickey Mouse cartoon cel, gouache on
trimmed celluloid applied to an airbrushed Courvoisier background, from
"Brave Little Tailor," Mickey the Tailor
leans out a window, flyswatter in hand,
1938, 7 1/2 x 8 3/4" 4,025
Mickey Mouse cartoon drawing, graphite
& colored pencil on paper, a production
drawing of Mickey in bed reading "The
Cry in the Night," ca. 1930s, 9 1/2 x 12" 575

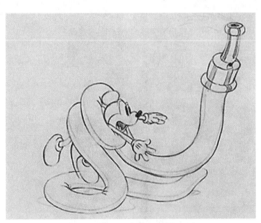

Mickey Mouse Cartoon Drawing

Mickey Mouse cartoon drawing, graphite
& colored pencil on paper, a scene of
Mickey wrestling w/a huge garden hose,
from "Mickey's Garden," 1935,
9 1/2 x 12" (ILLUS.) 805
Mickey Mouse cartoon drawing, graphite
& colored pencil on paper, Mickey recoils
in horror at the sight of his new family,
from "Mickey's Nightmare," 1932,
9 1/2 x 12" 920
Mickey Mouse cartoon drawing, graphite
& colored pencil on paper, showing Mickey dangling from a vine, in full cowboy at-
tire, from "Two Gun Mickey," full production notes throughout, 1934, 9 1/2 x 12" 690
**Mickey Mouse cartoon production draw-
ing,** graphite & colored pencil on paper,
large image of Mickey ready to swing a
golf club, from "Canine Caddy," 1941,
10 x 12" 1,035

Mickey Mouse charm, sterling silver, 3/4" 140
Mickey Mouse Christmas card, die-cut,
Walt Disney Enterprises, 1936 200
Mickey Mouse clothes hanger, wooden,
marked "Walt Disney Enterprises" 65
Mickey Mouse costume, cloth & rubber, in-
cludes mask, skull cap, long-sleeved
shirt w/Mickey Mouse patch, shorts
w/four metal buttons, red scarf & rubber
tail, Wornova Play Clothes, New York,
New York, ca. 1930s, size 6, w/original
box, box 11 1/2 x 12", 7" h. (shorts fad-
ed, box w/edge wear & tears) 431
Mickey Mouse creamer, china, gold & blue
lustre finish, 1930s 125
Mickey Mouse decals, "Mickey Mouse
Transfer-O-S for Easter Eggs," Paas Dye
Co., Newark, N.J., Walt Disney
Enterprises, ca. 1930 78

Very Rare Mickey Mouse Cowboy Doll

Mickey Mouse doll, cowboy, jointed composition, character head w/large "pie" eyes, large orange hands w/three fingers & a thumb, original red bandanna, white leather fur chaps w/red belt, two metal guns, made by Knickerbocker Toy Company, paper wrist tag, w/original box missing top flaps, ca. 1936, 9 1/2" h. (ILLUS.).................**12,100**

Mickey Mouse doll, cowboy, made by Knickerbocker Toy Company, paper wrist tag, swivel cloth character head w/large "pie" eyes, string whiskers, painted open-closed mouth, applied felt ears, large orange hands w/three fingers & a thumb, original red bandanna, white leather fur chaps w/red belt, two metal guns, holding rope lariat & felt cowboy hat, ca. 1936, 11" h. **3,900**

Mickey Mouse doll, plush, stockinette mask face, painted black eyes, painted upper lashes & black nose, open-closed mouth, black felt ears, unjointed black plush body w/white felt hands, yellow felt feet, original red felt short pants, tag on foot w/"Merrythought Ironbridge Shops, Made in England," 12" h. (nose touched up)....................**90**

Mickey Mouse Doll & Toy

Mickey Mouse doll, stuffed cloth, sharp rat nose, pie-cut eyes, broad stitched grin, four-fingered hands w/golden satin gloves, velveteen body, red shorts & orange shoes, tail missing, one finger w/tear, early Charlotte Clark model, ca. 1934, 13" h. (ILLUS. left)............................**2,185**

Mickey Mouse doll, stuffed cloth, velour face w/pie-cut eyes, sharp nose, long whiskers & felt ears, dressed in double-button shorts, gold gloves & orange shoes, distributed by George Borgfeldt, ca. 1936, 15" h..............................**900**

Mickey Mouse doll, stuffed w/oversized hands, Margarete Steiff, 6 3/4" h. (missing tail & button) **770**

Mickey Mouse egg cup, china, 1930s..............**160**

Mickey Mouse feeding dish, heavy white china, center w/pie-eyed Mickey wearing red pants & yellow shoes & playing one-string guitar, border w/alphabet in black, marked "Mickey Mouse China, Authorized by Walter E. Disney, Made in Bavaria," excellent conditon, 7 3/4" d............**190**

Mickey Mouse figure, bisque, Mickey holding baseball glove & ball, ca. 1930, 3 1/4" h. **195**

Mickey Mouse figure, bisque, Mickey playing a mandolin, 1930s, 5" h. **600**

Mickey Mouse figure, bisque, Mickey riding Pluto, 1930s, 3 1/4" h..........................**150**

Mickey Mouse figure, bisque, Mickey wearing green shorts, hinged arms, the base inscribed "Mickey Mouse" & stamped "Japan," 1930s, 7 1/4" h..................**375**

Mickey Mouse figure, bisque, playing French horn, 1930s, 3 1/2" h. **600**

Mickey Mouse figure, celluloid, cowboy w/jointed arms & legs, 4 1/2" h.......................**350**

Mickey Mouse figure, celluloid, Mickey on ball, 1930s, 2 1/2" h. **295**

Mickey Mouse figure, chalkware, 1930s,
10" h. 300

Mickey Mouse Fun-E-Flex Figure

Mickey Mouse figure, jointed wood & com-
positioin, Fun-E-Flex, painted composition head & wood jointed body w/mov-
able limbs, cloth-covered tail w/wooden
knob at end, George Borgfeldt, marked
"Mickey Mouse Des. Pat. 82802 by Walt
Disney," ca. 1930s, 7" h. (ILLUS.) 2,860
Mickey Mouse figure, jointed wood, two
decals on feet, marked "A Fun-e-Flex
Toy," excellent paint, 1930s, 7" h.
(minor flaking on chest decal)........................ 650

Very Early Mickey Mouse Figure

Mickey Mouse figure, painted wood, leatherette & rope, when tail pushed down, his
head bobs up, thought to be the very first
American Mickey, marked "ca. 1928-30
by Walter E. Disney," 6 1/4" h.
(ILLUS.).. 1,750-1,900
Mickey Mouse hairbrush, tin, ca.1930s 45
Mickey Mouse handkerchiefs, printed cot-
ton, Days of the Week series, ca. 1930,
set of 7... 398

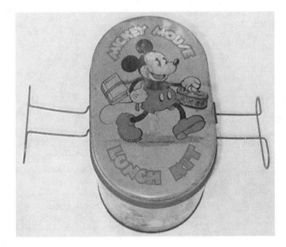

Early Mickey Mouse Lunch Kit

Mickey Mouse lunch kit, lithographed tin,
an oval box & cover w/hinged wire bail
side handles, green ground decorated on
the cover w/a picture of Mickey walking
to school, marked "Walt Disney Enterprises," 1930s, some paint wear,
(ILLUS.) 500

Mickey Mouse marionette, composition,
dressed in a striped shirt, shorts & shoes,
by Madame Alexander, 1938-39,
9 1/2" h. marionette, overall 21" h.............. 1,250
Mickey Mouse napkin rings, wooden,
painted Mickey Mouse head w/ring body
& feet, stand upright, 3" h., pr........................... 69

Mickey Mouse pen knife, bone handle, "Chicago World Fair, 1933" souvenir, 4" l. **89**

Mickey Mouse pencil box, rectangular, yellow & red, pictures Mickey w/Donald Duck, 1930s (very slight wear at corners) **90**

Mickey Mouse pencil sharpener, celluloid, figure of Mickey, 1930s.................................... **125**

Mickey Mouse pillow case, embroidered, 1932.. **180**

Mickey Mouse planter, china, lustre ware, Mickey playing saxophone, 1930s, 4" l. **235**

Mickey Mouse pocket watch, die-stamped picture of a standing MIckey on the back, Ingersoll, 1933, mint in box **1,400**

Mickey Mouse rocker, wooden, each side painted w/an early Mickey lying in a pool of water, the sides connected by a seat & play rack, the Mengel Company, ca. 1935, w/a photo of the toy & its original owner, 35" l. (some flaking on one side)....... **575**

Mickey Mouse sheet music, "The Wedding Party of Mickey Mouse," 1936 .... **80**

Mickey Mouse sled, by Allen CO., Philadelphia, PA, 1935-1940, 2 sizes (Sm + L) depicts Mickey on sled w/Minnie, small size **450**

Mickey Mouse sled, decorated wood, Allen Co., Philadelphia, depicts Mickey on sled w/Minnie, large size, 1935-1940 .... **600**

Mickey Mouse slot machine, life-size figural Mickey Mouse, wood-cased cast aluminum front slot machine as Mickey's chest & waist, 5-cent play, 62" h. **4,888**

Mickey Mouse table set: cov. sugar bowl, salt & pepper shakers & tray; china, each modeled as a long-nosed Mickey on a shaped triangular tray, black & white w/yellow shoes, marked "Made in Germany," mint condition, ca. 1930s, sugar bowl 4" h., the set **3,000**

Mickey Mouse Porcelain Tea Set

Mickey Mouse tea set: cov. teapot, cov. sugar bowl, creamer, six cups & saucers in original cardboard box; porcelain, transfer decorations in color of Mickey in different poses, golden lustre trim, Japan, ca. 1930s, the set (ILLUS.) **578**

Mickey Mouse toy, airplane, "Mickey's Air Mail," rubber, "S-12019" on wings (replaced propeller) **77**

Mickey Mouse toy, lithographed tin, colorful Mickey w/sharp rat nose playing a saxophone, when wire in back is squeezed Mickey stretches his arms to the side as his feet clash the attached cymbals together, some scuffs & discoloration, ca. 1934, 6" h. (ILLUS. right with doll) **1,955**

Mickey Mouse Floor Walker Toy

Mickey Mouse toy, floor walker-type, painted & hinged wood, standing wearing yellow shorts, hands on hips, hinged straight square wooden legs w/green block feet, stick handle at back, ca. 1930s, 13 1/2" h. (ILLUS.)............................. **138**

Mickey Mouse toy, Mickey on tractor, rubber w/metal axles, black & peach Mickey, red tractor w/white tires, both sides marked "Mickey's Tractor," bottom marked "Sun Rubber Co.," 4 1/2 x 4 1/2" **125**

Mickey Mouse toy washing machine, tin, marked Walt Disney Enterprises, Ohio Art Co. **105**

Early Mickey Mouse Tumbler

Mickey Mouse tumbler, clear glass w/black printed Mickey, ca. 1930s (ILLUS.) **110**

Mickey Mouse & Horace Horsecollar porringer, silver plate, engraved illustration of Mickey & Horace in the center of the bowl & engraving of Mickey on the handle, International Silver Co., ca. 1930 .... **360**

Mickey & Minnie Mouse cartoon cel, gouache on trimmed celluloid applied to a Courvoisier background, Mickey & Minnie take a dangerous curve in their new "horsecar," from "The Nifty Nineties," 1941, 5 3/4 x 6 3/4" **4,887**

Early Mickey & Minnie Drawing

Mickey & Minnie Mouse cartoon drawing, graphite & colored pencil on paper, a large drawing of a jubilant Mickey & Minnie being carried atop the winning football goal post after Mickey has made the winning touchdown, from "Touchdown Mickey," 1932, 9 1/2 x 12" (ILLUS.)............ **2,070**

Mickey & Minnie Mouse coin purse, metal mesh w/metal frame decorated w/Mickey

& Minnie Mouse in yellow, red & green, fringed bag painted w/an impressionistic design in pink & yellow, Whiting-Davis Co., ca. 1930s, 4 1/4" l. **300**

Mickey & Minnie Mouse creamer, china, blue luster glaze, Japan, 1930s **235**

Mickey & Minnie Mouse dolls, flannel, each w/flannel bodies, felt ears, swirling tails & stitched smiles, Mickey dressed in red flannel shorts, Minnie wearing a bubble & dot print green dress, Mickey 15" h., Minnie 14" h., pr. **950**

Mickey & Minnie Mouse figure group, bisque, Mickey & Minnie seated on a couch w/Pluto at their feet, hand-painted, pie-cut eyes, decal on Mickey reads "Niagara Falls," Japan, 3 3/4" h. **462**

Mickey & Minnie Mouse figures, bisque, Mickey playing drum, Minnie playing accordion, 1930s, 3" h., each **265**

Mickey & Minnie Mouse figures, glazed china, Mickey wearing long pants & Minnie wearing balloon skirt, ca. 1940, 3" h., pr. **155**

Mickey & Minnie Mouse figures, wooden, w/decals on front, Borgfeldt, 1934, 3 1/2" h., pr. **195**

Mickey & Minnie Mouse marionettes, composition & wood, composition heads & wooden bodies, Mickey w/painted pie-cut eyes, rat teeth grin, gold plush hands & red velvet pants, Minnie w/painted closed eyes & closed mouth smile, wearing a white & red polka dot skirt & green shoes, each 9" h., pr. **2,760**

Mickey & Minnie Mouse pencil case, Dixon No. 2909, depicts Minnie Mouse waving from balcony to Mickey in car, includes newer Disney pencils & some original crayons, pull-out drawer w/original protractor, 6" w., 10 3/4" h. **58**

Mickey & Minnie Mouse Plaques

Mickey & Minnie Mouse plaques, die-cut cardboard, colorfully printed, one w/Mickey & the other w/Minnie, each w/a small sign at the bottom, Mickey's reads "Lo Mickey," Minnie's reads "Hello Folks," ca. 1930s, 10 1/2" h., facing pr. (ILLUS.)............ **165**

Mickey & Minnie Mouse plate, lithographed metal, depicts Mickey & Minnie doing dishes, 4" d. **60**

Mickey Mouse Hand Car

Mickey & Minnie Mouse toy, windup tin, Mickey & Minnie Mouse handcar, composition figures on each end of the center handlebar, red car, w/original box, Lionel, 1930s (ILLUS.) **1,265**

Micke y & Minnie Mouse & Donald Duck toothbrush holder, marked "Walt Disney," original paint, 1930s **325**

Mickey Mouse & Pluto figure, bisque, Mickey riding on Pluto, George Borgfeldt, ca. 1930s, 2 1/4" h. **65**

Minnie Mouse book, "Story of Minnie Mouse," story & picture book, Whitman Publishing, child's scrawled name & date on cover, 1938, 94 pp., some wear, 5 x 5 1/2" (ILLUS. bottom w/Goofy book) **48**

Minnie Mouse doll, black cloth body & tail, black felt ears, white felt face w/stitched smile & eyebrows, pie-cut eyes, dressed in white pantaloons & red velvet skirt, red felt high heel shoes & flesh-colored felt hands, 16" h. **585**

Minnie Mouse doll, cloth, Minnie w/felt ears, wearing polka dot cloth skirt, original Mickey Mouse paper label for the Knickerbocker Toy Company, 1930s, 21" h. (tears around neckline) **1,410**

Minnie Mouse earrings, lacquered wood, 1940s **145**

Minnie Mouse figure, bisque, Minnie carrying purse & umbrella, 1930s, 4 1/2" h. **150**

Minnie Mouse figure, celluloid, jointed arms, wearing a white skirt, red bloomers & blue shoes & hat, Japan, ca. 1930s, 6" h. **675**

Minnie Mouse figure, jointed wood, "Fun-e-Flex," 5" h. **285**

Minnie Mouse figure, jointed wood, w/cloth skirt, marked "Walt E. Disney," 1934, 3 1/2" h. **325**

Minnie Mouse lawn chair, wood & canvas, 1930s, child's size **440**

Minnie Mouse mug, china, pictures Minnie reading a letter, England, 3" d. **125**

Minnie Mouse pillow cover, pictures Minnie powdering her nose, 1930s **105**

Minnie Mouse plate, Bavarian china, Minnie playing coronet & chased by two cars, 1930s, 6" d. **125**

Minnie Mouse toothbrush holder, bisque, movable arms, 1930s **450**

Minnie Mouse tumbler, clear glass w/black figure of early Minnie w/parasol, late 1930s (ILLUS. center w/Blue Fairy tumbler) **41**

Oswald the Lucky Rabbit doll, stuffed cloth figure w/large floppy ears, carpet slippers, short pants w/button nose & eyes, by Deans Rag Book, 1930s, 15 1/2" h. **4,950**

Pinocchio bank, composition bank w/trap door bottom & key, marked "Walt Disney," 5 1/4" (some peeling around coin slot) **83**

Pinocchio bank, composition, Pinocchio leaning on tree, signed "Disney Enterprises" 1940s **233**

Pinocchio book, "Pinocchio," Heath Publishing Co., 1940, illustrations by Walt Disney Studio **25**

Pinocchio book, "Pinocchio," Walt Disney, Coco Malt ad back cover, 1939 .... **55**

"Walt Disney's Pinocchio" Book

Pinocchio book, "Walt Disney's Pinocchio," colorful picture of Pinocchio & friends on the cover, hard cover, full-color, Whitman, 1940, 9 1/4 x 13" (ILLUS.) **33**

Pinocchio doll, composition, Knickerbocker, 16" h. **450**

Pinocchio doll, composition, large features, Steiff, Germany, 1938, 15" h. **700**

Ideal Jointed Pinocchio Doll

Pinocchio doll, composition & wood segmented, original clothing, Ideal, early 1940s, 10 1/2" (ILLUS.) **256**

Pinocchio doll, jointed wood, painted red & yellow w/white gloves & wearing a blue ribbon w/Disney stamp on stomach, Ideal, ca. 1940, 20" h. (paint cracking & crazing overall) **400**

Pinocchio Doll

Pinocchio doll, jointed wood, very good, Walt Disney Enterprises, 6" h. (ILLUS.) **95**

Pinocchio doll, made by Knickerbocker Toy Company, paper wrist tag, composition character head w/large painted blue eyes w/shadow, closed smiling mouth, molded & painted hair, molded & painted yellow gloves & green shoes, original red romper w/blue sleeves & white collar, yellow felt hat w/red trim & blue band, early 1940s, 10" h. **900**

Pinocchio doll, wood-jointed, Ideal, mint in original box, 12" h. **400-600**

Pinocchio Carnival Chalk Figure

Pinocchio figure, carnival-type chalkware, 1940s, 16" h. (ILLUS.) **65**

Pinocchio figure, jointed wood, "Fun-e-Flex," colorfully painted, marked "Pinocchio copyright Walt Disney - Geo. Borgfeldt Corp., New York," 4 3/4" h. **285**

Pinocchio figure, pressed wood, Multi-Wood Products, 1940s, 8" h. **185**

Pinocchio figure, rubber, squeak-type, Seiberling, 6" h. **40**

Pinocchio lunch pail, tin, cylindrical w/swing handle, various characters march around the sides, dated 1940, 6 1/4" h. **375**

Pinocchio mirror, Pinocchio & other characters from the movie embossed around the frame, 20" oval **400**

Pinocchio phonograph record, 78 r.p.m., ca. 1940 .... **55**

Pinocchio record album, original movie sound track, cover decorated w/movie scenes, Walt Disney Enterprises, 1939, 3 records **195**

Pinocchio sand pail, tin, green background w/two pictures of Pinocchio, 1940s, 4 1/2" d. 175

Pinocchio sheet music, "When You Wish Upon A Star". 12

Pinocchio tea set, lithographed tin, Ohio Art, w/box 375

Pinocchio tumbler, clear glass w/a single color picture of Pinocchio, part of a dairy promotions series, 1940 40

Pinocchio Valentine card, 1939, 5" h., excellent condition 20

Pinocchio, Cleo, Figaro & Geppetto masks, paper, pull-out type, dated 1939, Gillette Blue Blades advertising premium, in original brown envelope, set of 4 60

Pinocchio & Figaro planter, ceramic, standing Pinocchio & Figaro beside a square container, unmarked 89

Pinocchio & Geppetto tray, serving-type, lithographed tin, Ohio Art, 1939 105

Pluto book, "Story of Pluto the Pup," 1938, hardbound 48

Pluto figure, ceramic, crouching position, Brayton Laguna, unsigned, 1938-40 200

Pluto figure, ceramic, reclining Pluto w/legs crossed, American Pottery, ca. 1940s 225

Pluto pencil sharpener, Bakelite, figural, 1940s. 45

Pluto "Pop-Up Kritter" Toy

Pluto toy, "Mickey's Pal Pluto Pop-Up Kritter," yellow dog w/black tail, red collar & black oilcloth ears on a guitar-shaped base, Model 210, Fisher-Price, Inc., 1936, mint condition (ILLUS.) 400

Pluto tumbler, clear glass w/black Pluto figure, ca. 1936 (ILLUS. left w/Blue Fairy tumbler) 19

Saludos Amigos cartoon cel, gouache on trimmed celluloid applied to a Courvoisier wood veneer background, Donald Duck smiles & points upward, stamped "W.D.P." on mat, w/Courvoisier Galleries label on back, 1943, 5 1/2" sq. 920

Snow White bank, ceramic, figural, Leeds China Co. 86

Snow White book, "Snow White Sketch Book," coffee table-type, Collins, 1938 950

Snow White book, "Snow White Storybook," Walt Disney Productions, 1938 60

Snow White candy container, glitter covered papier-maché, Walt Disney Productions 68

Snow White Christmas tree lights, NOMA, 1930s, boxed set 195

Snow White cut-out book, all characters & Dwarfs' house in lustrous color graphics, 1937, 13 x 13" 150

Snow White doll, dressed in original clothing, Ideal Toy Corp., mint w/original tags, 1930s, 16" h. 400

Snow White figure, bisque, 1930s, 2 3/4" h. 85

Snow White figure, ceramic, American Pottery, 9" h. 275

Snow White figure, chalkware, early Carnival-type, 14 1/2" h. (some paint loss) 58

Snow White flour sack, pictures Snow White rolling dough (unused) 40

Snow White ironing board, lithographed tin, Ohio Art Co., 1930s 150

Snow White lamp, plaster composition, figural, made by La Mode Studios for Walt Disney Enterprises, dated 1938 525

Snow White movie cel, gouache on celluloid applied to an airbrushed background, Snow White improvises while cleaning the Dwarfs' cottage by using a young deer to hang laundry on, 1937, 5 1/2 x 6" 1,265

Snow White Movie Cel

Snow White movie cel, gouache on trimmed celluloid applied to a Courvoisier airbrushed background, Snow White sitting under a quilt w/two rabbits in her lap, 1937, 6 1/4 x 7" (ILLUS.) 6,325

Snow White movie cel, gouache on trimmed celluloid applied to an airbrush-on-patterned paper Courvoisier background, scene of Snow White preparing a pie w/the help of squirrels & four birds, 1937, 7 x 7 1/2" 4,600

Snow White pencil sharpener, Bakelite, late 1930s 80

Snow White pencil sharpener, celluloid, Snow White playing mandolin 135

Snow White refrigerator, lithographed tin, Wolverine 25

Early Snow White & Dwarfs Dolls

Snow White & the Seven Dwarfs dolls, velvet cloth bodies jointed at shoulders & hips, cloth mask faces w/painted features, Snow White w/yarn wig, Dwarfs w/white plush beards, Snow White wearing original yellow organdy dress w/pale blue velvet bodice & original underclothing, Dwarfs clothing part of the body w/separate velvet hats, unmarked, late 1930s, Dwarfs 12" h., Snow White 19" h., the set (ILLUS.) **2,200**

Snow White & the Seven Dwarfs animation sketch, graphite & colored pencil on paper, the Evil Hag offers Snow White the poisoned apple, 1937, 7 3/4 x 9 1/2" ... **1,150**

Snow White & the Seven Dwarfs art stamp set, 1937, w/box **85-125**

Snow White & the Seven Dwarfs blocks, "Safety Blocks," painted wood, a different character on each block, Halsam, 1938, in original box, the set **275**

Snow White & the Seven Dwarfs child's chair, leather & plush, lithograph of Snow White & the Dwarfs on front trim below the seat, lithograph of forest animals on the back, marked by Walt Disney Enterprises, 1938, 12" w., 15" h. **795**

Snow White & the Seven Dwarfs dolls, felt, each doll w/a painted felt face, wearing clothes w/felt shoes, each w/original paper label w/name except for Sleepy who had a control number, each Dwarf w/original box, Chad Valley, England, Snow White,16"h. Dwarfs,6"h. set of 8 .... **3,500**

Snow White & the Seven Dwarfs dolls, stuffed cloth w/painted composition faces, each Dwarf named on his cap, w/original boxes for dwarfs, Ideal, Snow White 15 1/2" h, each Dwarf 7" h., set of 8 .... **2,860**

Snow White & the Seven Dwarfs figures, bisque, Dwarfs' names on their hats, backs marked "Walt Disney," Dwarfs 3 1/2" h., Snow White 4 1/4" h., set of 8 .... **725**

Snow White & the Seven Dwarfs figures, bisque, figures range from 2" to 2 3/4" h., 1930s, set of 8 .... **525**

Snow White & the Seven Dwarfs lamps, figural, one depicting Snow White holding the hem of her skirt up, the other Dopey w/his name on the base, one shade pictures Doc & the other shows the seven Dwarfs outside their house, "Walt Disney Enterprise" seal on bottom, 1938, pr. **1,200**

Snow White & the Seven Dwarfs lunch pail, lithographed tin, rectangular w/double swing handles on top, colorful scenes around the sides & top, 1940s (light wear) **2,500**

Snow White & the Seven Dwarfs napkin ring, Bakelite, Plastic Novelties of New York, late 1930s, 2 1/2" h. **95**

Snow White & the Seven Dwarfs sheet music, "Heigh Ho" **17**

Snow White & the Seven Dwarfs soap figures, Schultz, original package, the set **295**

Snow White & the Seven Dwarfs tea set, aluminum, Aluminum Goods Company produced for Walt Disney Enterprises, 1937, w/box **425**

Snow White toothbrush or toothpick holder, china, figural, S. Maw & Sons, England, ca. 1938, 6" h. **450**

Three Caballeros sheet music, "Saludos Amigos," early 1940s **18**

Three Caballeros sheet music, "Three Caballeros," 1943 .... **18**

Three Little Pigs ashtray, ceramic, consisting of the three pigs, all wearing suits, perched on one end of the triangular ashtray, Japan, 1930s, 4 1/2" w. **145**

Three Little Pigs ashtray, china w/lustre finish, figures of the three pigs on the back edge of the ashtray, Japan, 1930s, 4 1/2" w., 3" h. **140**

Three Little Pigs drum, lithographed tin, Ohio Art Co., 6 1/2" **210**

Three Little Pigs figure, bisque, pig playing flute, 1930s, 4 1/2" h. **58**

Three Little Pigs figure, bisque, pig playing violin, 1930s, 3 1/2" h. **58**

Three Little Pigs plate, Salem China, 1930s **45**

Three Little Pigs playing cards, "Silly Symphony," Walt Disney Enterprises, 1932 .... **95**

Three Little Pigs sand pail, Ohio Art, 1930s, 3" h. **125**

Three Little Pigs toy top, lithographed tin, Chein 65

Three Little Pigs & Big Bad Wolf pocket watch, w/fob, Ingersoll 1,250

Three Little Pigs & Big Bad Wolf wall plaques, figurals in original box marked, "Walt Disney Character Plaq-Ettes," unused, 7 x 15" box, the set............................... 105

Three Little Wolves book, Whitman, copyright 1937, 9 1/2 x 13"....................................... 65

Thumper (from Bambi) & girlfriend figures, ceramic, American Pottery Co., pr. 65

Thumper (from Bambi) cookie jar, cov., ceramic.. 165

Thumper (from Bambi) figure, ceramic, American Pottery 65

Thumper (from Bambi) figure, ceramic, w/original paper label, American Pottery, 4" h... 70

Thumper Movie Cel

Thumper (from Bambi) movie cel, gouache on trimmed celluloid applied to a Courvoisier background, Thumper stands & wrinkles his nose, stamped "W.D.P." in lower right corner, 5 1/2 x 6 1/2" (ILLUS.) 1,955

Thumper (from Bambi) planter, ceramic, Leeds China Company 35

Thumper (from Bambi) salt & pepper shakers, ceramic, Leeds China, pr. 60

Ugly Duckling animation cel, trimmed celluloid applied to an airbrushed Courvoisier background, the Ugly Duckling ponders a frog in a pond, partial Disney label on back, 1939, 7 x 8" 1,150

Chapter 4
GAMES & GAME BOARDS

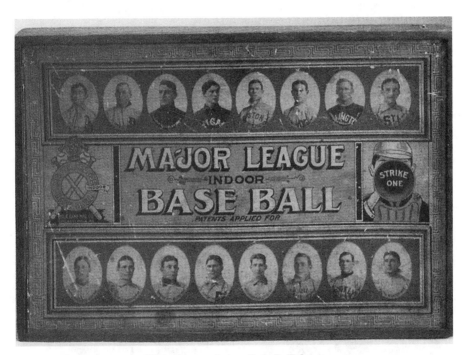

"Major League Indoor Base Ball" Game

Domino set, miniature painted bone, the set in a marbleized wooden egg-shaped case, 19th c., egg 2 1/2" l., the set (paint wear, very minor losses) **345**

Domino set, whalebone & exotic wood, the 28 pieces in a slide-top rectangular box, 19th c., each piece 7/8 x 1 13/16", the set (lacking slide top) **288**

Donald Duck game, "Bean Bag Party," Parker Bros., original box, dated 1939 .... **135**

Game board, folding-type, painted & decorated wood, pine dovetailed & glued folding box w/smoke-decorated & painted exterior in black & white checkerboard, interior painted w/a black, red & yellow backgammon board, trimmed w/abstract floral designs, 19th c., closed 7 1/2 x 15 3/4", 3" h. (old repairs, some paint loss, dirt) **863**

Game board, marquetry inlay, nearly square form w/the top inlaid w/an intricate design, the center large square filled w/bands of alternating light & dark squares, the dark squares each w/inlaid wheels, a wide outer border band w/inlaid fans at the corners of the inner square & scattered small inlaid stars & chevrons, the reverse inlaid w/a horse & "F.C.B." along w/the pencil inscription "2000 pieces Jan. 17, 1911," old alligatored varnish finish, 16 5/8 x 17 1/4" **688**

Game board, painted wood, bean bag toss board w/square opening, decorated in greens, orange, pink & yellow, stenciled w/the name "Bessie," along w/two bean bags, hinged support on the back, 19th c., 15 x 30" (minor surface abrasion, areas of repaint)... **575**

Game board, painted wood, hinged in the center, decorated in each corner w/a large round hex-style design w/painted bars between each & a large square w/half-circles of color in the center, painted green w/red, yellow, blue & black, late 19th - early 20th c., 19 1/4" sq. (minor paint loss).. **2,645**

Game board, painted wood, nearly square, painted in pink, light blue & orange on a creamy white ground outlined in black, early 20th c., 20 1/2 x 21" (cracks, minor paint wear).. **920**

Game board, painted wood, square, one side painted in black & red w/a checkerboard, the reverse w/a geometric pattern within a circle, both on a dark green ground, 19th c., 14" w. (some edge wear).. **7,475**

"Game of Auto Race," board-type, graphic racing game w/six early 1" die-cast vehicles, including Saxon & Maxwell, manufacturer's name on roof, box includes dice & instructions, Orotech Co., USA............ **58**

Decorated Two-sided Game Board

Game board, painted & decorated wood, board w/molded edge painted green, brown, black, red & yellow on one side, black & red checkerboard on the other, late 19th - early 20th c., paint wear, minor losses to edge, 18 1/2 x 18 3/4" (ILLUS.).. **1,495**

Game board, painted poplar, square w/large bull's-eyes in each corner w/a six-arm starburst in the center, tripleband block bands forming central cross design, original black, yellow & red paint, back initialed "S.W." & "A.W.," from Ohio, 19th c., 24 3/4" sq... **1,265**

"Game of Boy Scouts"

"Game of Boy Scouts," board-type, lithographed paper, missing all but two playing pieces, ca. 1910, No. 4405, Milton Bradley Company, 10 1/2 x 22", minor staining & some edge wear to box, torn interior strip (ILLUS.) **288**

"Game of Merry Christmas," board-type, folding game board, three wooden tokens, rules & spinner card, J.H. Singer (New York, New York), box 7 x 13 1/2", 1 1/2" h. (box & bottom w/edge damage) **920**

"Game of Robbing the Miller," board-type, McLoughlin Bros., 1888, box 8 x 15 1/2" (missing some playing pieces) **374**

"Games of John Gilpin - Rainbow Backgammon - Bewildered Travelers," board-type, w/book-form boards, instruction booklet, spinner, various pieces & folding wooden case, McLoughlin Bros., ca. 1900 (worn).................................... **115**

"Going to Market," card game, 52 cards advertising real products from 13 companies of the era, 1915 (box in poor condition) **75**

"Golfers," including figures on long shafts, clubs, balls, boundary markers, bunkers, sand traps, felt putting greens, tee area, instruction manual, Schoenhut, 1910, clubs 36" l., the set **3,500**

Lone Ranger card game, Parker Bros., 1938,, box 3 1/2 x 5" **87**

Lone Ranger game, board-type, "Lone Ranger Game - Hi-Yooo Silver!," Parker Bros., 1938 .... **60-85**

Lone Ranger game, target-type, tin stand-up Silver & Lone Ranger, Marx, 1938, box 9 1/2" sq... **225-300**

Mickey Mouse card game, "Mickey & Beanstalk," complete in original box, ca. 1940s **95**

Mickey Mouse game, "Pin the Tail on Mickey," includes 16 linen-like tails numbered consecutively & the MIckey target w/his back turned, in colorful box picturing Mickey, Minnie & the Three Pigs, marked "Walt Disney Enterprises," Marx Bros., target 17 1/2 x 22, box 9 1/2 x 10 1/2" (pinkish tinge to upper quarter of target, 2 small splits in box)................................. **350**

"Military Ten Pins," painted wood & lithographed paper, five soldiers w/red uniforms & blue legs & hats, five w/blue uniforms & red legs & hats, patented May 5, 1885, w/original wood box, 8" h. (some paper loss, box missing lid, major label loss, ball missing) **978**

"Major League Indoor Base Ball" Game

Neck & Neck Horse Race Game

"Major League Indoor Base Ball," board-type, the oak case w/color-printed front w/photographs of league players including H. Wagner & Ty Cobb, the interior w/a colored field, spinner & instructions, fifteen of sixteen team line-up cards, eighteen of twenty wood players, six score pegs & one of two play pegs, Philadelphia Game Manufacturing Co., considerable wear especially to field, early 20th c. (ILLUS.) **1,725**

"Mansion of Happiness (The)," board-type, color lithographed figures & Ives label, dated 1864, the set **259**

Marble game, includes one light sapphire blue w/mica, six green micas & twenty-seven clear glass mica marbles, round finished hard wood board w/34 holes, marbles 11/16" d. **210**

"Neck & Neck Horse Race," lithographed tin, a long narrow rectangular low platform w/racing lanes, small cast metal horses & riders, w/original box, Wolverine, Model 142, very good condition (ILLUS.)... **100**

"Picture Lotto," chromolithographed cards & colored & numbered disks, w/a set of chromolithographed paper on wood alphabet-nursery rhyme blocks, a group of alphabet-picture cards & a set of faces, McLoughlin Bros., 1888, the set................... **316**

Pinocchio card game, complete w/instructions & original box, ca. 1940 .... **60**

Pinocchio game, marble-type, "Pitfall" box cover colorfully illustrated, 1939................... **135**

Popeye game, "Pin the Pipe" party game, 1937 .... **95**

Roy Rogers Rodeo Game

Roy Rogers game, "Roy Rogers Rodeo Game," Dee McCann, 1939 (ILLUS.) **100-150**

"Siege of Manila," board-type, playing board on bottom of box, w/spinner, drawer w/four metal ships, dice, cup & shells, w/a book "The Life Story of The Hero of Manila for Our Boys and Girls," Parker Bros., ca. 1898, the set (missing lid) **288**

"Six Day Bike Race," board-type, by Lindstrom Tool & Toy Co., Bridgeport, Connecticut, late 19th - early 20th c., boxed, 9 1/2 x 15 1/4" **303**

Skittles, "Chief & Braves," nine papiermaché figures on wood bases, German, maker unknown, ca. 1890s, 9 x 9 1/2" h., the set **8,500**

Skittles, "Hens & Chicks," painted wood & papier-maché, Germany, maker unknowns **1,500**

Skittles, "Sailors," hand-painted composition w/wood base, large wood ball, probably German, ca. 1890s, 10 1/2" h., the set **2,600**

Sunray DX Getaway Chase Game

"Sunray DX Getaway Chase Game," board-type, cardboard & plastic, two auto play pieces, board & accessory sheets, w/original box, created by AMF for Sunray DX Oil Company, ca. 1940s, new in box, soiling & tears to box, 20 x 24 1/2", 3 1/2" h. (ILLUS.) **110**

Superman game, Quoit set, ca. 1940s, in original box **65**

Target, lithographed paper on wood, pop gun & "harmless" ammunition, nine targets of people, animals, clay pipes, rubber ball, ca. 1910, 15" l., the set **600**

Target game, "Trick Mule," W.S. Reed, 1880 .... **850**

"The Game of Jack and the Beanstalk"

"The Game of Jack and the Beanstalk," board-type, ca. 1898, McLoughlin Bros., edge wear & minor staining to box, 10 1/2 x 19 3/4" (ILLUS.) **863**

"The New Howard H. Jones Collegiate Football Game," board-type, folding board, instructions, goal posts, two play cards, play indicators, etc., ca. 1927-31, box 13 x 26", 2" h. (slight edge wear on box) **86**

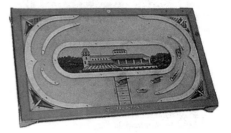

Tudor Tru-Action Horse Race Game

"Tudor Tru-Action Electric Horse Race Game," cardboard & metal board-type, rectangular w/red border & center printed overhead view of a racetrack w/a front view of a grandstand in the oval center, metal playing pieces, Model No. 525, minor scratches to board (ILLUS.) **303**

Uncle Sam, lithographed paper on wood figures on bases, ca. 1890s, 11 3/4" h., the set **850**

Chapter 5
GUNS

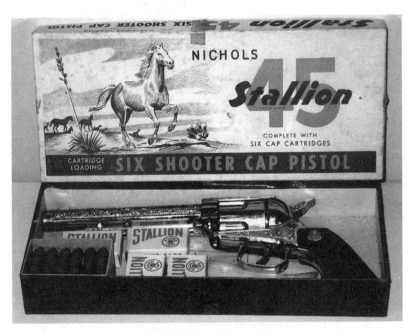

Nichols Stallion 45 Cap Pistol

BB gun, Daisy Model 25, pump w/plastic grip & forearm, w/operation manual, original box **$50**

Cap pistol, cast iron, automatic-shape, patent-dated 6-29-09, Champion Hardware Co., 4" l. **66**

Small Victorian Cap Pistol

Cap pistol, cast iron, one side marked "Pluck," the other side w/"Patent March 22nd 1880 - June 17th 1898," 3 1/2" l. (ILLUS.) **50**

Cap pistol, cast iron, "Pirate," Hubley **125**

Cap pistol, cast iron & plastic, "The American," metal body w/white plastic molded grips, leather holster, Kilgore Mfg. Co. (Westerville, Ohio), No. 105, complete w/original box, very good condition, gun 10" l. (small chip on right handle, box flaps loose) **385**

Cap pistol, cast iron, single shot w/spur trigger cap well on top, 3 1/2" l. **44**

Nichols Stallion 45 Cap Pistol

Hubley Texan 38 Cap Pistol

Cap pistol, cast metal & plastic, Nichols Stallion 45 Six Shooter Cap Pistol, 1950, complete in box (ILLUS.)................................ 275

Cap pistol, cast metal & plastic, "Texan 38," silvered trigger & barrel, white plastic grips w/embossed black longhorn heads, Hubley, ca. 1950s, very good condition (ILLUS.) 110

Machine gun, lithographed tin, "No.100 'Mac' Machine Gun," shoots paper, McDowell, ca. 1920s, original box 44

Pistol, "The Hubley Pirate Pistol," metal long-barreled antique-style w/ivory-colored plastic grips, marked on handle, w/original box w/colorfully printed picture of a pirate & treasure map, No. 265, Hubley Mfg. Co. (Lancaster, Pennsylvania), minor rust on pistol, flap on box torn off, pistol 9" l. (ILLUS.)... 94

Popeye pirate pistol, clicker-type gun, Marx, 1920s.. 360

Rifle, "My Pet Sparking Rifle," metal rifle in original cardboard long box printed on the top w/a color scene of the Cavalry chasing Indians, Model No. 2731, Made in Japan, ca. 1950s, 27" l...................... 44

Superman raygun, Krypto raygun, pressed steel projector pistol, able to flash pictures on wall, embossed design features Superman, original rolls in box, Daisy, 7 1/2" x 10" (minor pitting on gun) 550

Texan, Jr. cap gun, ca. 1950s 55

Water pistol, "Daisy #9" 65

Hubley Pirate Pistol

Chapter 6
PLUSH TOYS

Two Large Steiff Teddy Bears

Steiff Toys & Dolls

Bambi Steiff Toy

Bambi, stuffed plush, standing Bambi w/tan white-spotted fur, Steiff, button in ear, ca. 1950s, mint, 6" h. (ILLUS.) **$99**

Bear on wheels, brown mohair, embroidered nose, excelsior stuffing, steel frame & wheels, early 20th c., 9 1/4" l., 6 1/2" h. (eyes & button missing, fur loss on muzzle & front feet, nose embroidery worn) **201**

Bear on wheels, grey mohair w/glass eyes & leather collar, standing on a steel frame w/cast-iron wheels, unmarked, 22" l., 14" h. (wear) **825**

Bear on wheels, brown mohair, steel eyes, embroidered nose, mouth & claws, moveable head, excelsior stuffing, steel frame & wheels, ca. 1920, 21" l., 15" h. (fabric loss on head & back) **345**

Bear on wheels, large standing animal w/brown mohair coat & glass eyes, mounted on a steel frame w/sheet metal wheels w/black rubber treads, ring pull voice box, added leather collar & rope pull, button in ear w/ribbon, 31" l., 24" h. **2,090**

Cat, crouching pose w/front paws in a cylindrical pink muff, beige velvet w/black paint trim, faded red neck ribbon, button in ear, 7" l. (wear, tail sewn back) **550**

Cat on wheels, standing w/white mohair coat w/grey stripes, glass eyes, worn pink neck ribbon w/bell, pink felt ear linings, on small cast-iron wheels, original ear button, 14" l. (wear) **980**

Cat on wheels, very worn light mohair w/bead eyes, worn pink neck ribbon w/brass bell, standing w/front legs on tiny cast-iron wheels, original button in ear, 7 1/2" h. (repair, voice box silent) **413**

Clown, life-size, dressed in white polka dot shirt & suspendered pants, includes proof of authenticity, 17 x 50" **575**

Cow on wheels, brown & white mohair standing animal w/bead eyes, Steiff button in ear, on tiny cast-iron wheels, 10 1/4" l. (felt horns very worn & wrapped w/string) **578**

Dachshund on wheels, standing dog w/tan felt coat & glass eyes, leather collar, original button in ear, on tiny cast-iron wheels, 16 1/2" l. (wear, moth holes, damaged & repaired tail) **385**

Dog, seated, light brown mohair, button in ear, 8 1/2" h. **110**

Dog, seated, yellow mohair, glass eyes, black embroidered nose, mouth & claws, 1913, 5 1/2" h. (spotty fur loss, button missing) **173**

Dog on rockers, St. Bernard, synthetic dark brown & white fur, plastic eyes, black embroidered nose, ear button, steel frame & rocker base, mid-20th c., 50" l., 23" h. (fur matted on back) **173**

Dog on wheels, German Shepherd, cream & ginger mohair w/glass eyes, embroidered nose, mouth & claws, steel frame, wooden wheels, ca. 1920s, 20" l., 16 3/8" h. (button & left ear missing, some fur & fiber loss, voice box not working) **288**

Dog on wheels, Spitz, standing position, white mohair w/glass eyes, embroidered nose & mouth, excelsior stuffing, steel frame, small spoked metal wheels, 1908, 22" l., 18 1/2" h. (button missing, some fur & fiber loss, voice silent) **690**

Dog on wheels, cream & ginger fur, embroidered nose & mouth, cast iron frame & wheels, ca. 1910, 13" l., 10" h. (extensive fur loss) **86**

Doll, "Hellen" or "Helma," center face seam, black steel eyes, light brown hair, original Dutch costume w/Dutch cap, ca. 1913, 13 3/4" h. (slight fabric fading, back of left sabot damaged, button missing) **1,150**

Donkey, standing, tan body w/black trim, original red leather harness, button in ear, mint, 5" h. **88**

Elephant, "Jumbo," grey mohair, yes-no type, standing on hind legs, jointed at head & shoulders, jersey pads, glass eyes, felt tusks, ear button & chest tag, 1970s, 10" h. **201**

Elephant, pull toy, mohair, button eyes, on cast-iron wheels, excelsior stuffing, early 20th c., 21 1/2" l., 11 1/2" h. (wear & loss to stuffing) **288**

Large Steiff Elephant on Platform

Elephant on platform, large grey mohair elephant w/long curved trunk standing on a rectangular wooden platform w/wooden wheels, original button in the ear, small repair to back of head, overall 9' l., 3 1/2' h. (ILLUS.) **385**

Elephant on wheels, grey mohair, white felt tusks, red leather harness, red & yellow felt blanket, glass eyes, steel frame, rubber-tired metal wheels, ear button & tag, mid-20th c., 24 1/2" l. **431**

Fox terrier, riding-type, plush mohair, glass eyes, ear button, all on steel frame & wheels, ca. 1910, 21" l., 20 3/4" h. (moth & fiber loss & damage, voice not functioning) **546**

Giraffe, button in ear & tag, 11" h. **633**

Lamb, pull toy, curly wool, felt face, ears & legs, glass eyes, ear button, excelsior stuffing, all on metal frame & wheels, ca. 1913, 12 1/2" l., 11 1/8" h. (some moth damage) **1,610**

Lamb, pull toy, curly mohair, glass eyes, felt face & legs, on steel frame & wheels, 1913-20, 20" l., 15 3/4" h. (fiber loss & moth damage to felt, ear button missing, one non-matching wheel) **748**

Mallard drake, "Stanic," airbrushed Draylon fur, black plastic eyes, yellow felt bill, button in wing, ca. 1973, 13 1/2" l., 10 1/2" h. **230**

Okapi, velveteen, airbrushed coat, glass eyes, mohair mane & accents on ears & tail, ear button, 1960s, 11" h. **288**

Steiff Wittie Owl

Owl, "Wittie," dark brown & black plush, large green glass eyes, felt talons, original tag, very good condition, 4" h. (ILLUS.) **33**
Palomino colt, standing, blond mohair, button in ear, 11" h. (wear) **330**

Giant Panda Steiff Toy

Panda, standing upright, button in ear, ca. 1960s, 70" h. (ILLUS.) **1,870**

Steiff Peggy Penguin

Penguin, "Peggy," black & white plush w/orange bill & yellow & black head, 19" h. (ILLUS.) **242**

Steiff Jolanthe the Pig

Pig, "Jolanthe," plush, tan w/glass eyes, red cord around neck, original tag, mint, 6" l. (ILLUS.) **94**
Rabbit, tan plush, mother rabbit standing wearing a green felt dress w/red buttons & white apron, original tag, excellent condition, 10" h. **110**
Rabbit, blond mohair, fully jointed, pink glass eyes, excelsior stuffing, ca. 1913, 12" (slight moth damage) **805**
Sheep on wheels, standing animal w/wooly mohair coat, felt legs & face w/button eyes, worn neck ribbon w/bell, head turns, on small cast-iron wheels, 12 1/2" l. (one ear incomplete w/missing button) **935**
Snail, multicolored velvet, vinyl shell, rubber antennae, button & cloth tag, paper tag, 1960s, 6 1/2" l. **316**
Spider, multicolored plush back, gold furry underbody, legs, antenna & mouth, black glass eyes, 1960s, 9" l. (button & tag missing) **403**
Squirrel, blond mohair, black steel eyes w/felt backing, embroidered nose, mouth & claws, excelsior stuffing, ca. 1920, 7 1/2" **402**
Stegosaurus, "Dinos," yellow mohair belly, blue, emerald green, brown, magenta & yellow airbrushed body, green & black glass eyes, pink felt open mouth, green, blue & orchid felt back plates, yellow felt ears, 1960, 11" l. (one ear damaged, button missing) **403**
Teddy bear, blond mohair, fully jointed, black steel eyes, brown embroidered nose, mouth & claws, felt pad, blank ear button, right foot pad autographed by Steiff executive, "J.R. Junginger" (spotty fur loss, slight fiber loss) **863**

Two Large Steiff Teddy Bears

Teddy bear, curly blond mohair, black steel eyes, blank ear button, tan embroidered nose, mouth & claws, blonde felt pads, excelsior stuffing, w/original photo of bear & friends in a garden, some fur loss on muzzle, spotty moth damage on pad, ca. 1905, 20" h. (ILLUS. right) **9,200**

Teddy bear, ginger mohair, fully jointed, black steel eyes, embroidered nose, mouth & claws, tan pads, excelsior stuffing, button missing, fur worn & fiber loss on muzzle, moth damage on pads, ca. 1905, 24" h. (ILLUS. left)............................ **5,750**

Teddy bear, Polar bear, white mohair, 6' h. .. **4,370**

Teddy bear, miniature, beige mohair w/fully-jointed body, black bead eyes, embroidered nose & mouth, ear button, ca. 1905, 3 1/2" h. (some fur loss) **805**

Teddy bear, miniature, black mohair & glass eyes, original tags & ear button, 4" h. **165**

Teddy bear, yellow mohair, glass eyes, embroidered nose, mouth & claws, ear button, fully jointed, no-pads-style, excelsior stuffing, ca. 1910, 7" h. (spotty fur loss)........ **748**

Teddy bear, cinnamon mohair, black steel eyes, embroidered nose, mouth & claws, felt pads, fully jointed, ear button, ca. 1906, 9" h. (slight fur loss on muzzle, needs more stuffing) **2,990**

Steiff Teddy Bear with Long Ear Button

Teddy bear, brown mohair w/felt paws, glass eyes, jointed, long ear button, early, excellent condition, 10" h. (ILLUS.) **193**

Teddy bear, golden mohair, shoe button eyes, black embroidered nose, mouth & claws, felt pads, fully jointed, excelsior stuffing, early, 10" h. (slight fur wear)........ **1,035**

Teddy bear, marked w/silver button w/raised script in left ear, beige mohair body w/swivel head, excelsior stuffing, brown glass eyes, shaved muzzle w/dark brown floss nose & mouth, felt pads, 11" h.. **225**

Teddy bear, "Teddy Baby," cream mohair, glass eyes, open mouth, embroidered nose & claws, synthetic suede pads, fully jointed, 11 1/4" h. (ear button missing) **1,150**

Teddy bear, blond mohair, fully jointed, black steel eyes, very pointed nose, yellow felt pads, embroidered claws, excelsior stuffing, ca. 1907, 12" h. (traces of nose embroidery, some moth damage & fiber loss, excelsior needs replacing on left leg, button missing)................................. **288**

Teddy bear, blond mohair, fully jointed, glass eyes, embroidered nose, mouth & claws, felt pads, 12" h. (some fur loss) **1,495**

Teddy bear, ginger mohair, fully jointed, black steel eyes, black embroidered features & claws, ca. 1905, 12" h. (needs stuffing, pads replaced, some fur loss, fabric damaged on muzzle)............................ **288**

Teddy bear, light yellow mohair, black eyes, embroidered nose, mouth & claws, felt pads, fully jointed, excelsior stuffing, ca. 1906, 12" h. (button missing, fur & fiber damage, needs stuffing) **1,725**

Teddy bear, gold mohair, black shoe button eyes, embroidered nose, mouth & claws, tan feet pads, fully jointed, ca. 1905, 12 1/2" h. (some spotty fur loss, body needs some stuffing)................................... **1,725**

Teddy bear, light yellow mohair, black steel eyes, embroidered nose, mouth & claws, felt pads, fully jointed, excelsior stuffing, blank button, ca. 1905, 12 1/2" h. (extensive fur & pad loss, needs restuffing) **1,265**

Teddy bear, beige mohair, glass eyes, embroidered nose, mouth & claws, felt pads, fully jointed, 13" h. (button missing, some fur & fiber loss).. **230**

Teddy bear, blond mohair, glass eyes, embroidered nose, mouth & claws, fully jointed, excelsior stuffing, 1950s, 13" h. (button missing, slight fur loss & matting) **288**

Teddy bear, golden mohair, fully jointed, black embroidered nose, mouth & claws, black steel eyes, blank button, felt pads, excelsior stuffing, ca. 1905-09, 14" h. (spotty fur loss mostly on back side of bear & head)... **1,380**

Teddy bear, blond mohair, fully jointed, black shoe button eyes, embroidered nose, mouth & claws, nose stitched over black felt, felt pads, excelsior stuffing, ca. 1906, 15" (moth damage, fiber loss, red felt shoes bled on lower body)....................... **978**

Teddy bear, "Feed Me," rust mohair, glass eyes, unjointed, metal ring pulled on back of head opens mouth, metal box catches dry food, oil cloth bib, excelsior-stuffed head, ca. 1937, 15" h....................... **288**

Teddy bear, gold mohair, black steel eyes, embroidered nose, mouth & claws, beige felt pads, fully jointed, excelsior stuffing, ca. 1905, 16" h. (button missing, some fur & fiber loss, moth damage on pads)... **2,415**

Teddy bear, golden mohair, fully jointed, brown embroidered nose, mouth & claws, felt pads, black steel eyes, excelsior stuffing, ca. 1905, 16" h. (button missing, spotty fur & fiber loss, left ear needs restitching) **1,955**

Steiff Cinnamon Teddy Bear

Teddy bear, cinnamon mohair body w/swivel head & center seam, black shoe button eyes, black floss nose & mouth, excelsior stuffing, felt paws, four black floss claws, 17" h. (ILLUS.) 7,200

Teddy bear, cinnamon mohair, plush swivel head w/center seam, black shoe button eyes, black floss nose & mouth, excelsior stuffing, felt pads on paws, four black floss claws on each paw, 17" h. 7,200

Teddy bear, golden mohair, fully jointed, black embroidered nose, mouth & claws, black steel eyes, felt pads, excelsior stuffing, ear button, growler, ca. 1905, 17" h. (moth damage) 2,990

Steiff Golden Teddy Bear

Teddy bear, marked w/blank button in left ear, pale golden mohair plush swivel head w/center seam, black shoe button eyes, black floss mouth & nose w/vertical stitching, excelsior stuffing, applied ears, jointed shoulders & hips, felt pads on paws, four black claws, hump on back, 17" h. (ILLUS.) 7,000

Steiff Golden Teddy Bear

Teddy bear, pale golden mohair, plush swivel head w/center seam, black shoe button eyes, black floss mouth & nose w/vertical stitching, excelsior stuffing, applied ears, jointed shoulders & hips, felt pads on paws, four black claws, hump on back, marked w/blank button in left ear, 17" (ILLUS.) 7,000

Teddy Bear, marked w/silver button w/raised script, gold tag #0202/51, beige mohair body w/swivel head, excelsior stuffing, brown glass eyes, shaved muzzle w/dark brown floss nose & mouth, felt pads, 18" h. 350

Teddy bear, curly mohair, fully jointed, shoe button eyes, excelsior stuffing, ca. 1910, 19" h. (ear, nose & pads replaced w/corduroy, fiber & stuffing loss) 862

Teddy bear, ginger mohair, black steel eyes, embroidered nose, mouth & claws, fully jointed, excelsior stuffing, ca. 1905, 19" h. (fur & fiber loss on muzzle & ears, slight overall fur loss, replaced pads, button missing) 8,050

Teddy bear, blond mohair, center-seam style, embroidered nose, mouth & claws, felt pads, fully jointed, excelsior stuffing, ca. 1905, 20" h. (spotty fur & fiber loss, fur soiled, button missing) 11,500

Teddy bear, blond mohair, jointed shoulders & hips, hump on back, black shoe button eyes, cloth pads on paws, black floss nose & mouth, excelsior-stuffed, unmarked, 20" h. (worn, especially on face, eye replaced, some mending, pads replaced) 575

Teddy bear, blond mohair, glass eyes, re-embroidered nose, mouth & claws, felt pads, excelsior stuffing, fully jointed, blank ear button, ca. 1910, 21" h. (button missing, extensive fur & fiber loss) **805**

Rare Early Steiff Teddy Bear

Teddy bear, golden mohair, early center seam-type w/black steel eyes, embroidered nose, mouth & claws, fully jointed, excelsior stuffing, felt pads, button in ear, spotty moth damage on fur & pads, fiber unstable at ankles, needs stuffing, ca. 1905, 22" h. (ILLUS.) **10,063**

Teddy bear, "Heins," light yellow mohair, fully jointed, black embroidered nose, mouth & claws, glass eyes, excelsior stuffing, ear button, ca. 1920s, 24" h. (slight fiber loss, pads replaced) **2,760**

Twin Steiff Teddy Bears

Teddy bears, twin light yellow mohair, fully jointed, black steel eyes, tan embroidered nose, mouth & claws, cream pads, excelsior stuffing, ca. 1905, moth damage, spotty fur loss, ear buttons missing,10" h., pr. (ILLUS.) **2,530**

Weasel, marked "Wiggy," synthetic white winter fur, black plastic eyes, embroidered nose & mouth, felt pads, ear button & chest tag, ca. 1970s, 7 5/8" l. **259**

Wolf hand puppet, tan mohair w/black highlights, glass eyes, red tongue, excellent condition, 10" l. **83**

Teddy Bears (Non-Steiff)

1920s Mohair Teddy Bear

Teddy bear, brown short mohair stuffed w/straw, jointed limbs, hump on back, glass eyes, ca. 1920s, 20" h. (ILLUS.).......... **330**

Teddy bear, gold mohair plush, excelsior stuffed, amber glass eyes, shaved muzzle w/floss nose & mouth, swivel head, jointed at shoulders & hips, shaved mohair paw pads, non-working squeaker in torso, 13" h., (mohair thin, bottom of torso mended, mohair worn on end of paws, small tear on front of ankle on right leg) **170**

Early German Teddy Bear

Teddy bear, straw-filled tan mohair, button eyes, fully jointed, tail moves the head, Germany, early 20th c., very good condition, 10" h. (ILLUS.) 605

Teddy bear, miniature, ginger mohair, two-faced, black steel eyes, embroidered nose & mouth, comic face w/plastic tongue, metal nose, metal eyes, backed w/plastiform ringlets, fully jointed, Schuco, 1955, 3 1/2" h. 518

Teddy bear, yellow mohair, black steel eyes, eye glasses, Schuco "yes/no," ca. early 1900s, 4 3/4" (minor fur loss) 432

Teddy bear, golden mohair, embroidered nose & mouth, arms jointed at shoulders, red felt beret & trousers, black metal feet, includes key, Schuco "dancing bear," ca. 1930, 5" (slight fur loss) 288

Teddy bear, brown wool, black shoe button eyes, embroidered nose & mouth, tan felt pads, jointed at shoulders & hips, excelsior stuffing, exterior metal joints, early, 9 1/2" h. (fiber damage on top of head & pads)... 115

Teddy bear, cinnamon mohair body w/swivel head, excelsior stuffing, black shoe button eyes, brown cotton floss nose, oversized feet, hump back, felt pads, four floss claws, fully jointed, non-working squeeze-type growler, unmarked, w/Steiff characteristics, 10" 2,700

Teddy bear, light golden mohair, felt pads, black embroidered nose & mouth, dark brown claws, excelsior stuffing, unmarked, 10" (spotty overall fur loss) 748

Teddy bear, golden mohair, black shoe button eyes, black embroidered nose, mouth & claws, beige pads, jointed excelsior stuffing, Ideal Toy Co., ca. 1910, 10 1/2" (remnants of red felt tongue, minor fur loss)... 403

Teddy bear, brown woven mohair, black shoe button eyes, embroidered nose, mouth & claws, fully jointed, felt pads, 11" (some fur wear, moth damage) 115

Teddy bear, blond mohair, black shoe button eyes, embroidered nose & mouth, fully jointed, excelsior stuffing, ca. 1910, 12" (extensive fur loss) 259

Teddy bear, blond mohair body w/swivel head, excelsior stuffing in arms & legs, beige felt pads, kapok stuffing in torso, squeaker, unmarked, 12" 130

Teddy bear, light yellow mohair, blue shoe button eyes, embroidered nose, mouth & claws, beige felt pads, fully jointed, early, possibly Aetna, 12" h. (fiber & fur loss, repairs on muzzle & limbs) 345

Teddy bear, white mohair, black shoe button eyes, tan embroidered nose, mouth & claws, felt pads, fully jointed, includes pink dress & floral coat, ca. 1905, 12" (wear, two replaced pads).............................. 575

Teddy bear, black mohair body w/swivel head, excelsior stuffing, amber glass eyes, shaved muzzle w/black floss nose & mouth, beige felt pads, fully jointed, unmarked, 13"... 400

Teddy bear, golden mohair body w/swivel head, excelsior stuffing, white shoe button eyes w/metal centers, black floss pointed nose, low applied ears, squeeze-type squeaker, long felt pads, floss claws, fully jointed, unmarked, 14" 230

Teddy bear, blond mohair, glass eyes, embroidered nose, mouth & claws, velveteen pads, fully jointed, excelsior & kapok stuffing, possibly Joy Toy, Australia, 1920s, 14 1/2" h. (fur & fiber loss) 115

Teddy bear, white mohair, black shoe button eyes, fully jointed, rust embroidered nose, mouth & claws, includes X-ray of joints, Bing, ca. 1910, 15" 1,265

Teddy bear, orange mohair, fully jointed, glass eyes, mouth opens to reveal white glass teeth, long oval body, straight short arms & legs, early 20th c., 16 1/2" (one tooth broken, moth damage & fiber loss)...... 460

Teddy bear, blond mohair, black steel eyes, embroidered nose, mouth & claws, felt pads, fully jointed, ca. 1910, 17" (spotty fur loss, arms damaged at shoulders) 518

Teddy bear, golden mohair body w/swivel head, excelsior stuffing, brown glass eyes, shaved muzzle w/black floss nose, long arms w/felt pads & three floss claws, large oversized feet w/felt pads, & three floss claws, fully jointed, unmarked, 17" 325

Teddy bear, light yellow mohair, black steel eyes, re-embroidered mouth, nose & claws, fully jointed, excelsior stuffing, probably Ideal, ca. 1919, 17" h. (spotty overall fur loss).. 374

Teddy bear, yellow long mohair, glass eyes, embroidered nose & mouth, felt pads, kapok stuffing, fully jointed, 1930s, England, 17" (some fiber loss & moth damage) 200

Teddy bear, beige mohair, glass eyes, embroidered nose, mouth & claws, shaved mohair pads, fully jointed, Schuco, mid-20th c., 18" h. (fur somewhat matted) 288

Teddy bear, blond mohair, shoe button eyes, black embroidered nose, mouth & claws, felt pads, excelsior stuffing, fully jointed, possibly Ideal, ca. 1910, 18" (small patches of fur loss, loose joints) 1,035

Teddy bear, golden mohair body w/swivel head, black floss mouth & nose, shaved mohair muzzle, brown glass eyes, felt pads, small back hump, unmarked, 18"........ 375

Teddy bear, golden mohair body w/swivel head, excelsior stuffing, black shoe button eyes, hump, beige felt pads, four rust floss claws, fully jointed, unmarked, 18" 2,500

Teddy bear, light golden long mohair, swivel head, large brown glass eyes, black floss nose, black floss mouth, excelsior stuffing in head & body, fully jointed, small lump on back, mohair pads on paws, unmarked, 18" 365

Teddy bear, beige mohair w/dark brown tips, swivel head w/excelsior stuffing, dark brown glass eyes, red felt open-close mouth, black floss claws, unmarked, 19".. 110

Teddy bear, golden mohair, black steel eyes, fully jointed, tan felt pads, black embroidered nose, mouth & claws, Ideal Toy Co., ca. 1905, 19" 5,750

Teddy bear, ginger mohair, fully jointed, black shoe button eyes, black embroidered nose, mouth & claws, excelsior stuffing, felt pads, ca. 1919, 20" h. (some pad damage, slight fur loss mostly on face)... 460

Teddy bear, gold mohair, glass eyes, applied twill nose, embroidered mouth & claws, beige felt pads, fully jointed, excelsior stuffing, Ideal, ca. 1919, 20" h. (minor fur loss) 575

Teddy bear, pink mohair, glass eyes, embroidered nose, mouth & claws, felt pads, fully jointed, excelsior stuffing, possibly Stevans Mfg. Co., ca. 1920s, 20" h. (two pads replaced, some fading, spotty fur loss) 431

Teddy bear, golden mohair, glass eyes, embroidered nose, mouth & claws, velveteen pads, fully jointed, excelsior & kapok stuffing, Chiltern, ca. 1958, 21" h. (some spotty fur loss).................................... 173

Teddy bear, pink mohair body w/swivel head, five-piece excelsior body, brown glass eyes, pink felt pads, three black felt claws, unmarked, 21".. 575

Teddy bear, yellow mohair, glass eyes, embroidered nose & mouth, football-shaped body, short arms & straight legs, Ideal, ca. 1920, 21 3/4" h. (spotty fur loss) 575

Teddy bear, brown mohair, center seam sewn body, jointed limbs, stitched nose & mouth, large rounded ears, glass eyes, ivory felt paw pads, 23" h. (wear, ears loose)... 358

Teddy bear, golden mohair body w/swivel head, excelsior stuffing, glass eyes, brown floss nose, shaved muzzle, large oversized ears, cloth pads, no stitched claws, fully jointed, unmarked, 23"............... 295

Teddy bear, worn gold mohair, jointed limbs, sewn mouth & nose w/glass eyes, felt paw pads, early 20th c., 23 1/2" h. (damage, repair) 220

Teddy bear, dark golden mohair, fully jointed, shoe button eyes, hump on back, possibly early Ideal, 24" 875

Teddy bear, gold mohair, embroidered nose, mouth & claws, beige felt pads, fully jointed, excelsior stuffing, Ideal, ca. 1919, 25" h. (minor fur loss, ears need restitching) 546

Teddy bear, golden mohair, center-seam sewn body & jointed limbs, stitched nose & mouth on upturned snout, glass eyes, ivory felt paw pads, first half 20th c., 25" h. (worn, one paw pad worn & one replaced)... 523

Teddy bear, light yellow mohair, black shoe button eyes, black knit fabric nose, embroidered mouth & claws, felt pads, fully jointed, ca. 1905, w/owner provenance & early photo, Ideal Toy Co., 25" (very slight pad damage & fur loss) 13,800

Teddy bear, light yellow mohair, black shoe button eyes, brown knit fabric nose, embroidered mouth & claws, felt pads, fully jointed, ca. 1905, w/provenance & early photo, Ideal Toy Co., 25" (some pad damage & fur loss, left ear needs reattaching, fur somewhat greyed) 10,925

Teddy bear, golden mohair, jointed limbs, glass eyes, stitched nose & mouth, pink felt paw pads, first half 20th c., 26 1/2" h. (some wear & repair) 550

Teddy bear, light gold mohair, jointed limbs, stitched nose & mouth, glass eyes, ivory felt paw pads, squeak voice box, 27" h. (pads very worn).. 358

Teddy bear, golden mohair, glass eyes, tan felt pads, fully jointed, excelsior stuffing, detached partial cloth label, pink silk & mohair jacket, early Bruin, 28" (traces of nose, mouth & claw embroidery, slight fur loss, settled stuffing in limbs) 6,325

Teddy bear on wheels, light brown velveteen, glass eyes, on wooden platform w/metal wheels, ca. early 1900s, 7 1/2" l., 5 3/4" 202

Teddy bear on wheels, brown mohair, black shoe button eyes, embroidered nose, felt pads, excelsior stuffing, unjointed, "Teddy B" leather collar, steel frame w/wooden wheels, ca. 1920, 19 1/2" l., 12 1/2" (fur bare in spots, some fabric loss) 288

Teddy bear on wheels, ginger mohair, black embroidered nose, mouth & claws, glass eyes, steel frame, solid wooden wheels, ca. 1920s, 17" l. (some spotty fur loss) 748

Teddy bear on wheels, light brown mohair, glass eyes, open mouth, remnants of embroidered nose, felt pads, excelsior stuffing, metal frame & cast iron wheels, ca. 1913, 20 1/2" l. (wear around mouth & nose)... 230

Chapter 7

PULL TOYS

Teddy Bear Parade Pull Toy

Airplane, pressed steel, single engine plane, two decals "Little Jim Playthings," Army Airforce signs on wings, clicker, J.C. Penney, Steel Craft #NX107, 22 1/2" wing span (gearing for propeller missing) **$550**

Early Fisher-Price Pull Toy Set

Animals, lithographed paper on wood, includes a goat, pig, cow, mule & cart all in original colorfully lithographed box, Fisher-Price No. 207, minor paper separations & creasing, box edge wear & staining, ca. 1931, box 9 x 11", 2" h., the set (ILLUS.) **863**

Bunny Cart, No. 472, Fisher-Price **99**

Disney characters toy, "Disney Easter Parade," Fisher-Price No. 205, 1936, complete set with five figures, set **1,600**

Donald Duck toy, pull-type, "Donald Duck Choo Choo," Fisher-Price No. 450, 1942 ..... **125**

Donald Duck toy, pull-type, "Donald Duck Choo Choo," Fisher-Price No. 450, early version, 1940 .... **350**

Donald Duck toy, pull-type, "Donald Duck Xylophone," Fisher-Price, No. 185, 1938 ..... **275**

Donkey on wheels, the standing animal w/an amber velvet body, glass eyes & black mohair tail & mane raised on a thin rectangular board platform w/tiny tin wheels, late 19th - early 20th c., 13" l. **303**

"Dr. Doodle" Pull Toy

Duck, "Dr. Doodle," Fisher-Price No. 132, 1957 (ILLUS.) **143**
Elmer Elephant toy, pull-type, "Elmer Elephant," Fisher-Price No. 206A, 1936 .... **295**

Rare Ferdinand the Bull Toy

Ferdinand the Bull toy, pull-type, lithographed paper on wood, seated cut-out of Ferdinand on a green wood platform w/red metal wheels, Fisher-Price No. 34, 1939, minor wear (ILLUS.) **715**
Four men riding beams, lithographed tin, up & down movement from cammed axle, Germany, early 20th c., 10" l. **193**
Fred Flintstone toy, Fred plays xylophone, Fisher-Price, 1962 .... **85-150**

Horse & cart, painted wood, a silhouetted horse on small front wheel & w/hinged rear legs painted in original white & black w/red, black & green detail, pulling a cart w/canted sides nailed to the axle w/large spoked wheels, branded mark "Made by the S.A. Smith Mfg. Co. Battleboro, Vt. U.S.A.," first half 20th c., 20 1/2" l. (cart renailed to axle, corner of cart damaged) **275**
Horse on platform, mohair & burlap covering, black metal eyes, leather ears, fur mane, composition muzzle w/open-closed mouth, horsehair tail, leather bridle & saddle, marked "Made in Germany" on underside of wheeled platform, 18" l., 19" h. **450**
Horse on platform, papier-maché & wood, mounted on platform w/tiny tin wheels, late 19th - early 20th c., 8" l., 10" h. **193**
Horse on platform, the body covered in real horse hair, straw-filled, most of leather bridle & harness remains, on a rectangular red board wheeled base, late 19th c., 9 1/2" l., 9" h. **495**
Horse on platform, unmarked, papier-maché covered w/beige dappled flannel, brown glass eyes, leather ears w/real hair, mohair mane & tail, leatherette bridle & saddle, blue felt blanket, metal wheels, 8 1/2" h. **125**
Horse on platform, wood & composition, the standing animal w/a brown hair cloth covering, tack eyes & old colorful harness, on a narrow rectangular wood platform on tiny metal wheels, roach fur mane & bristle tail possibly old replacements, 19th c., 12 1/4" h. **220**
Horse on platform, wood & composition w/original dark brown mohair coat, fur mane & tail, fairly complete saddle & harness, thin rectangular wood platform w/tiny cast-iron wheels, late 19th c., 11" l., 12" h. (legs loose) **358**
"Kiddie-Kar-Kid," composition boy doll w/molded head & painted features on a straw-filled cloth body w/composition hands, sitting astride a wooden three-wheeled kiddy car & wearing a cotton suit & hat, natural finish on car w/original label & red wheels, H.C. White Co., North Bennington, Vermont, patented in 1924, 9 1/4" l., 10" h. (paint damage on doll's head & hands, clothes faded) **288**
Lamb on platform, lambskin coat w/wool pile fabric face & glass eyes, loud "baa" when head is pressed down, on a narrow, thin green-painted rectangular wood platform w/tiny cast-iron wheels, 19th c., 16" l., 13 7/8" h. (felt damage on body, wool pile around left eye & upper forelegs) **1,840**
Lion on platform, molded tin body in gold on green platform, early 20th c., 4 1/2" l. **121**
Mickey Mouse toy, "Mickey Mouse Safety Patrol," Fisher-Price, No. 733, ca. 1956 .... **175**
Mickey Mouse toy, pull-type, wooden, Mickey Mouse Xylophone, Fisher-Price, 1939, 9 x 11" **360**

Early Noah's Ark Pull Toy

Noah's Ark, lithographed paper on wood, building-shaped w/colored panels around the sides of animals & plants, narrow board base pointed at each end on small wooden wheels, ca. 1900 (ILLUS.) **495**

Pinocchio toy, "Plucky Pinocchio," Pinocchio on donkey w/bell, Fisher-Price No. 494 .... **275-325**

Pinocchio toy, pull-type lithographed wood, "Pinocchio Express," Fisher-Price No. 7, 1939, good (ILLUS. bottom page) **375**

Roy Rogers on Trigger, wood & metal, musical-type, late 1940s, 8 1/2" l. **125-175**

Rare Santa & Sleigh Pull Toy

Santa Claus in sled w/reindeer, cast iron, Santa dressed in red sitting in a fancy white sleigh pulled by two white reindeer on a red wheel, Hubley, early 20th c., excellent paint, 16 1/2" l. (ILLUS.) **1,925**

Teddy Bear Parade Pull Toy

"Teddy Bear Parade," lithographed paper on wood, Fisher-Price No. 195, 1938 (ILLUS.) **891**

Pinocchio Express Toy

Chapter 8
PUZZLES

"In Conference" Puzzle

Jigsaw-type, "A Chip off the Old Block,"
Johnward Dunsmore, 300 pcs., 1933....... **$20-30**

Jigsaw-type, "A Council of War," Gordon
Coutts, 280 pcs., 1940.................................. **20-40**

Jigsaw-type, "A Matter of State," Clyde De
Land, 300 pcs., 1933..................................... **20-30**

Jigsaw-type, "Advance Guard," Charles
Russell, 252 pcs., 1936 .... **35-40**

Jigsaw-type, "At Twilight," Frank Harper,
252 pcs., 1938.. **20-30**

Jigsaw-type, "Buffalo Hunt," Frederic
Remington, 300 pcs., 1933 .... **35-40**

Jigsaw-type, "Canyon Sunrise," Stanley
Walker, 378 pcs., 1937 .... **5-15**

Jigsaw-type, "Collected From Rainbow's
Rim," Hy Whitroy, 378 pcs., 1938 .... **5-15**

Jigsaw-type, "Colonial Days in Virginia,"
Charles M. Reylea, 357 pcs., 1933............. **20-30**

Jigsaw-type, "Come on Up," Leon Lippert,
192 pcs., 1933.. **20-30**

Jigsaw-type, "Country Vista," Walter M.
Thompson, 252 pcs., 1939............................ **5-15**

Jigsaw-type, "Dinner for Six," Mabel Roll-
ins Harris, 378 pcs., 1934............................ **20-30**

Jigsaw-type, "Doctors of Science," Harold
Mott-Smith, 300 pcs., 1933 .... **20-30**

Jigsaw-type, "Dreams Come True," Stan-
ley Walker, 140 pcs., 1940............................ **5-15**

"Electric Ship" Puzzle

Jigsaw-type, "Electric Ship," Walter
Greene, 300 pcs., 1933 (ILLUS.)................. **5-15**

"Fair Treasures" Puzzle

Jigsaw-type, "Fair Treasures," Charles M.
Relyea, 120 pcs., 1933 (ILLUS.) **35-40**
Jigsaw-type, "Farm Workers," Anthony
Cucchi, 2562 pcs., 1943 .... **20-30**

"Flushed" Puzzle

Jigsaw-type, "Flushed," Arthur Tait, 252
pcs., 1938 (ILLUS.) **20-30**
Jigsaw-type, "Found," Edward Eggleston,
140 pcs., 1938 .... **20-30**
Jigsaw-type, "Golden Galleon," Frederic
Grant, 168 pcs., 1936 .... **5-15**

"Green River Buttes" Puzzle

Jigsaw-type, "Green River Buttes," Dey
Deribcowsky, 400 pcs., 1937 (ILLUS.) **5-15**

Jigsaw-type, "Guardians All," H.H.
Walters, 252 pcs., 1940 .... **35-40**
Jigsaw-type, "Guardians of Freedom,"
Robert Skemp, 378 pcs., 1940 .... **35-40**
Jigsaw-type, "Hood's Double-Sided Rainy
Day and Balloon Puzzle," lithographed,
framed, original box, ca. 1891 (wear,
staining to box) **109**
Jigsaw-type, "Hooking a Big One," Charles
M. Reylea, 120 pcs., 1933 .... **35-40**
Jigsaw-type, "Hunter's Paradise," R.
Atkinson Fox, 357 pcs., 1933 .... **75-85**
Jigsaw-type, "Hunting Pals," Anthony
Cucci, 300 pcs., 1941 .... **20-30**
Jigsaw-type, "Hydro Project," Walter
Greene, 300 pcs., 1933 .... **5-15**

"In Conference" Puzzle

Jigsaw-type, "In Conference," Ray Mor-
gan, 216 pcs., 1933 (ILLUS.) **35-40**
Jigsaw-type, "Indian Summer," William
Chandler, 168 pcs., 1936 .... **5-15**
Jigsaw-type, "Jack Ashore," Henry Bacon,
300 pcs., 1933 .... **20-30**
Jigsaw-type, "Keeping the Tryst," Frank
Harper, 300 pcs., 1933 .... **35-40**
Jigsaw-type, "Let Me At 'Em," R. James
Stuart, 378 pcs., 1942 .... **35-40**
Jigsaw-type, "Menace of the Air," Lynn
Bogue Hunt, 165 pcs., 1933 .... **20-30**
Jigsaw-type, "Mother Love," Gene
Pressler, 125 pcs., 1933 .... **50-60**

"Mountain Chief" Puzzle

Jigsaw-type, "Mountain Chief," W. Lang-
don Kihn, 252 pcs., 1938 (ILLUS.) **20-30**

"The Bell's First Note" Puzzle

Jigsaw-type, "Mountain Hues," Robert Wood, 378 pcs., 1937 .... **5-15**

Jigsaw-type, "Mt. Moran," May Ferris Smith, 140 pcs., 1940 .... **5-15**

Jigsaw-type, "Nature's Power," Henry Lewis, 140 pcs., 1939 .... **5-15**

Jigsaw-type, "Off for the West," Wallace Robinson, 280 pcs., 1940 .... **5-15**

Jigsaw-type, "Old Fashioned Garden," William M. Thompson, 252 pcs., 1939 .... **5-15**

Jigsaw-type, "Part of Heart's Desire," R. Atkinson Fox, 209 pcs., 1933 .... **75-85**

Jigsaw-type, "Red Demon of the Forest," Philip Goodwin, 465 pcs., 1933 .... **75-85**

"Remembrance" Puzzle

Jigsaw-type, "Remembrance," Carle Blenner, 204 pcs., 1937 (ILLUS.) **5-15**

Jigsaw-type, "Spanish Dancer," Edward Eggleston, 140 pcs., 1940 .... **35-40**

"Spirit of the U.S.A." Puzzle

Jigsaw-type, "Spirit of the U.S.A.," Harold Anderson, 376 pcs., 1941 (ILLUS.) **35-40**

Jigsaw-type, "Springtime," George Ames Aldrich, 220 pcs., 1933 .... **5-15**

Jigsaw-type, "Star Light-Star Bright," R. James Stuart, 378 pcs., 1943 .... **35-40**

Jigsaw-type, "Starlight Trail," Walter Haskell Hinton, 252 pcs., 1941 .... **20-30**

Jigsaw-type, "Summer Pleasures," Annie Benson Muller, 252 pcs., 1937 .... **20-30**

Jigsaw-type, "Sunshine and Shadows," Rudolph Weber, 300 pcs., 1933 .... **5-15**

Jigsaw-type, "Sweethearts," Mabel Rollins Harris, 262 pcs., 1937 .... **20-30**

Jigsaw-type, "Tender Care," Frank Van Vreeland, 308 pcs., 1933 .... **5-15**

Jigsaw-type, "The Bell's First Note," J.L.G. Ferris, 465 pcs., 1936 (ILLUS. above) **20-30**

Jigsaw-type, "The Foundling," Hy Hintermeister, 378 pcs., 1939 .... **5-15**

"The Little Rogue" Puzzle

Jigsaw-type, "The Little Rogue," Maud Tousey Fangel, 300 pcs., 1933 (ILLUS.) ... **20-30**

Jigsaw-type, "The Pack Train," Phillip Goodwin, 252 pcs., 1937 .... **75-85**

Jigsaw-type, "The Part O' Heart's Desire," George McCord, 120 pcs., 1933 .... **5-15**

Jigsaw-type, "The Ship that Sank in Victory-1779," 465 pcs., 1936 .... **20-30**

Jigsaw-type, "The Touchdown," Hy Hintermeister, 252 pcs., 1937 .... **20-30**

Jigsaw-type, "Thoroughbreds," Gustave Muss-Arnolt, 378 pcs., 1937 .... **35-40**

Jigsaw-type, "To the Rescue," Walter Wilwerding, 378 pcs., 1940 .... **20-30**

Jigsaw-type, "Trophy of the Hunt," J.L.G. Ferris, 465 pcs., 1936 .... **20-30**

Jigsaw-type, "Trouble on the Trail," Frank Hoffman, 378 pcs., 1938 .... **20-30**

Jigsaw-type, "Unfinished Painting," 378 pcs., 1942 .... **5-15**

"Well-Hooked" Puzzle

Jigsaw-type, "Well-Hooked," William Harnden Foster, 336 pcs., 1933 (ILLUS.).. **20-30**

Jigsaw-type, "Winning of the West," Frank Tenney Johnson, 375 pcs., 1939 .... **20-30**

Puzzle blocks, each side produces a different view, one shows a large reclining white & black dog, matching view on box cover, late 19th c., minor wear, original box, each block 1 3/4" sq., set of 20 (ILLUS. below) **165**

Puzzle blocks, lithographed paper on wood, one view shows scene of Snow White & the Seven Dwarfs (non-Disney), eight other scenes possible, early 20th c., each block 1 1/4" sq., set of 20 .... **99**

Puzzle blocks, lithographed paper on wood, "The Young Ship Builder's Picture Puzzle Blocks," makes eight different early ship scenes, McCloughlin Brothers, 1892, near mint in near mint box, each block 2 1/2" sq., set of 12 .... **600**

Puzzle cubes, "Yankee Doodle," six Thomas Nast images on all sides, forms six various images of Uncle Sam, in original wood box, McLoughlin Bros., ca. 1890s, 10 x 11 1/2" **950**

Late Victorian Picture Puzzle Blocks

Chapter 9
VEHICLES

Schieble Tri-motor No. 30 Plane

Airplane, die-cast metal, "Autogyro," Tootsietoy (Dowst Bros., Chicago, Illinois), painted white w/blue prop, ca. 1930s, wingspan 4 1/4" w. **$150**

Airplane, die-cast metal, P-38 fighter, #81, folding wheels, yellow & green combat camouflage, Hubley Mfg. Co. (Lancaster, Pennsylvania) **248**

Airplane, lithographed tin, biplane, wooden cylinders & wheels, clicks & prop turns when pulled, stenciled designs on wings, attributed to Schieble, Z65 (repainted) **105**

Keystone Airmail Airplane

Steelcraft Army Scout Plane

Airplane, pressed steel, airmail model, single-engine, dark yellow body w/red metal wheels & red tail fin, complete, good labels, Keystone Mfg. Co. (Boston, Massachusetts), ca. 1930, 24" wingspan (ILLUS.) 963

Airplane, pressed steel, single-engine monoplane, blue body, orange wings, Wyandotte Toys (Wyandotte, Michigan), 1930s, 18" wingspan, very good condition 197

Airplane, pressed steel, single-engine monoplane, Boycraft, all-original, near perfect decals, ca. 1930, 24" l. 743

Airplane, pressed steel, Super Titan Liner, four-engine, silver & blue body, Wyandotte Toys 303

Airplane, pressed steel, "Tri Motor Mail Plane," wheel-driven propellers, 18" wing span (repainted).. 176

Airplane, pressed steel, tri-motor Army Scout Plane, silver w/red trim & rubber-rimmed metal tires, Steelcraft, late 1920s (ILLUS. above)... **2,475**

Army lift truck, pressed steel, Structo Mfg. Co., (Freeport, Illinois),12" l. (repainted)......... **28**

Automobile, 1930s Coupe, pressed steel, Wyandotte Toys, 13" (repainted) **77**

Automobile, boat-tailed Cabriolet, windup tin, "#8" on the side, ca. 1930s, 4 1/2" l. **121**

Automobile, boat-tailed racer, cast iron, orange w/chrome driver & wheel front axle, 6" l. (two rubber tires missing)...................... **165**

Unusual Airplane Toy

Schieble Tri-motor No. 30 Plane

Airplane, pressed steel, Tri-motor No. 30, worn red, white & light blue paint, metal wheels, Schieble, ca. 1930 (ILLUS.) **1,705**

Airplane, pressed steel, twin-motor airplane body w/four-blade helicopter rotor on top, pale yellow wings, green body, unmarked, ca. 1940 (ILLUS.)........................... **300**

Airplane, pressed steel, two-motor passenger plane, silver body, red wings, wooden wheels, Wyandotte Toys, 9 1/2" wing span **193**

Hubley Town Car Coupe

Automobile, cast iron, Town Car Coupe, worn light blue painted body, white hard rubber tires & spare, Hubley, 1930s (ILLUS.).. **523**

Automobile, coupe, cast iron, w/chrome rumble seat, rubber tires, painted red, Kenton Hardware (Kenton, Ohio), 7" l........... **330**

Automobile, Model A Ford, cast metal, made from hobby kit, Hubley Mfg. Co., 8" l. **61**

Automobile, Model T 4-door sedan, cast iron, Arcade Mfg. Co. (Freeport, Illinois), 6 1/4" l. (some rust, one wheel replaced) **220**

Buddy L Model T Ford

Automobile, Model T Ford, cast metal, original black paint in excellent condition, red & silver metal wheels, sticker on the bottom, Buddy L (Moline Pressed Steel Co., E. Moline, Illinois), minimal wear (ILLUS.) **1,128**

Kingsbury Pressed Steel Sedan

Automobile, pressed steel, sedan, black body w/orange bands, white rubber tires w/orange hubs, Kingsbury, ca. 1929, 14" l. (ILLUS.) **605**

Automobile, sedan, pressed steel, "Toy Town Sedan," Wyandotte Toys, 21" l. (replacement doors) **55**

Large Wyandotte Spring-Driven Auto

Automobile, sedan, spring-driven, pressed steel, the long yellow sedan w/green roof & red-hubbed tires, pull-back spring motor, all original, very good condition, Wyandotte, 13 1/4" l. (ILLUS.) **935**

Automobile set, "Build and Paint Auto Set," three pot metal cars & paints, Barclay Mfg. Co. (Hoboken, New Jersey), 1930s, original box **110**

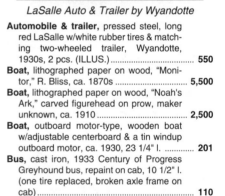

LaSalle Auto & Trailer by Wyandotte

Automobile & trailer, pressed steel, long red LaSalle w/white rubber tires & matching two-wheeled trailer, Wyandotte, 1930s, 2 pcs. (ILLUS.) **550**

Boat, lithographed paper on wood, "Monitor," R. Bliss, ca. 1870s **5,500**

Boat, lithographed paper on wood, "Noah's Ark," carved figurehead on prow, maker unknown, ca. 1910 .... **2,500**

Boat, outboard motor-type, wooden boat w/adjustable centerboard & a tin windup outboard motor, ca. 1930, 23 1/4" l. **201**

Bus, cast iron, 1933 Century of Progress Greyhound bus, repaint on cab, 10 1/2" l. (one tire replaced, broken axle frame on cab) **110**

Arcade Double-Decker Bus

Bus, cast iron, double-decker, green w/silver metal trim & black & silver tires, original sticker intact, Arcade Mfg. Co. (Freeport, Illinois), very good condition, 7 3/4" l. (ILLUS.) **330**

Kenton Hardware Double-Decker Bus

Bus, cast iron, double-decker w/seven riders on top, bright red & green paint, white rubber tires, Kenton Hardware, 1930s, 12" l. (ILLUS.) **1,485**
Bus, cast iron, Faegol, "Made by Arcade Mfg. Freeport, Ill.," steel wheels (repaint) **220**
Bus, cast iron, painted blue w/nickel-plated wheels, Arcade, 1920s, 4 5/8" l. **144**

Early Friction-type Sight-Seeing Bus

Bus, friction-type, sight-seeing style, pressed steel, long flat-topped model w/projecting hood, metal wheels w/hard rubber tires, dark yellow body & black roof, red & gold oval "Wanamaker's Toy Store" decal on the side, paint chips & scratches, mechanism not working, ca. 1930s, 26" l. (ILLUS.) **1,320**

Lion in Cage Wagon

Cage wagon, wooden cage on wheels w/jointed wood lion, Albert Schoenhut, (ILLUS.) **3,500**

Cement mixer, painted cast iron, in orange, light blue & nickel-plate, four small pierced metal wheels, embossed "Jaeger" on side of engine hood, Kenton Hardware (Kenton, Ohio), ca. 1930, 6 5/8" l. **374**

"Humpty Dumpty Circus Bandwagon"

Circus bandwagon, "Humpty Dumpty Circus Bandwagon," embossed wood, w/six bandsmen, driver, pair of horses on wheeled platform, donkey drawn clown in chariot, Albert Schoenhut (ILLUS.) **5,500**
Circus cage wagon, cast iron, "Overland Circus," wagon w/two white horses w/riders & driver, pulling a polar bear cage, Kenton Hardware, unused w/original box, 14" l. (ILLUS. below left) **358**
Circus cage wagon, cast iron, painted in polychrome w/a red cage wagon holding a white polar bear, on yellow wheels, a driver on top & pulled by two white horses without riders, Kenton Hardware, early 20th c., unused in original box, 14" l. **550**
Circus cage wagon, lithographed paper on wood, "Crandall's Happy Family," w/15 wild animals, pull cord, ca. 1870s **3,000**

"The Polar Bear"

Circus cage wagon, lithographed paper on wood, "The Polar Bear," cage wagon w/trainer & polar bear figures, drawn by two dappled horses on wood wheels, R. Bliss, ca. 1880s (ILLUS) **2,500**

Various Cast Iron Vehicles

Sheffield Farms Dairy Wagon

Circus wagon, cast iron, Overland Circus Calliope wagon, original paint, Kenton Hardware.. **688**

Coach, lithographed paper on wood, "Pansy" Tally Ho Coach, R. Bliss, 1900, 31" w. **3,500**

Covered wagon, open buckboard w/driver & two horses, cloth top sealed in original envelope, unused w/original box, Kenton Hardware, 15" l. (ILLUS. center w/circus wagon).. **350-450**

Dairy wagon, painted wood, a silhouetted white house w/string tail hinged to pull the closed wagon printed on the side w/"Sheffield Farms Company - The National Dairy Milk...," w/six tiny glass milk bottles in a tin carrier, Rich & Co. (Clinton, Iowa), ca. 1930, 20 1/2" l. (ILLUS. above) **633**

Schoenhut Dairy Wagon Set

Dairy wagon, painted wood, the white cloth-covered horse on a platform wheeled base pulling the closed wooden wagon w/a sign across the top "Hood's Grade 'A' Milk" & a company logo on the side, original driver, wooden crate & seven milk bottles, Schoenhut, early 20th c., horse missing tail, damage to driver's head, 25" l., the set (ILLUS.)........................ **3,105**

Arcade Baby Dump Truck

Dump truck, cast iron, "Baby Dump Truck No. 2," metal wheels, original worn red paint, worn white decal on cab door, Arcade, 1920s (ILLUS.) **457**

Dump truck, cast iron, finished in greenish grey, Mack-style front, C-cab, driver, red spoked metal wheels, spring-operated bed w/swinging tailgate, possibly by Dent, ca. 1920s, 7" l. (paint loss) **316**

Metalcraft Sand-Gravel Truck

Dump truck, pressed steel, black body w/red box w/yellow lettering reading "Sand-Gravel - Metalcraft St. Louis," silver all-metal wheels, late 1920s - early 1930s, restored (ILLUS.) **248**

Large Buddy L Dump Truck

Dump truck, pressed steel, black cab & red rear box, red & black tires, complete w/all stickers, Buddy L, ca. 1930s, 24" l. (ILLUS.).. **2,475**

Dump truck, pressed steel, black w/red chassis & wheels, Keystone Mfg. Co. (Boston, Massachusetts), Model #38, ca. 1927, 26 1/2" l. (overall wear) **345**

Dump truck, pressed steel, finished in black w/red chassis & wheels, open cab, front steering, decal on dashboard, hinged tailgate, Buddy L No. 201, ca. 1930s, 25" l. (lacks chain to winch, some scratches) **1,150**

Dump truck, pressed steel, highway maintenance truck, Buddy L, 14" l. **110**

Dump truck, pressed steel, hydraulic-type, dual rear wheels, rubber tires, headlight & bumper, Buddy L (Moline Pressed Steel Co., E. Moline, Illinois), Model #201A, ca. 1930, 24 1/2" l. (poor condition, some overpaint) **1,093**

Tonka Dump Truck

Dump truck, pressed steel, large plow attachment on the front, sign on side of door "State Highway Dept.," side dump-type, Tonka Toys, 1950s, 17" l. (ILLUS.)...... **248**

Dump truck, pressed steel, Mack, dark red paint, open cab w/lever action dump for back, metal tires w/hard rubber rims, worn Mack truck decal, Steelcraft, ca. 1930s, 25 1/2" l., 10 1/2" h. (paint loss, scratches) **440**

Buddy L Dump Truck

Dump truck, pressed steel, open cab, old worn black & red paint, worn label, Buddy L, some repair, 1930s, 24" l. (ILLUS.) **660**

Dump truck, pressed steel, yellow cab, red dump body, electric headlights, Buddy L, Model #434, ca. 1935, 19 1/2" l. **288**

Dump wagon, cast iron, contractors' horse-drawn style, two white horses pulling a deep wagon molded on the side w/"Contractors' Dump Wagon," body in black paint, large rear & smaller front yellow-painted wheels, Arcade Mfg. Co. (Freeport, Illinois), ca. 1920, 14" l. **173**

Earthmover, pressed steel, Heiliner Earth-mover, William Doepke Mfg. Co., 29" l. **143**

Early Wooden Express Wagon

Express wagon, painted wood, two carved horses on wheeled platform pulling a wooden flatbed wagon w/metal wheels, red wagon w/gold striping & the word "Express," black horses on red platform, some paint wear, late 19th c., 31" l. (ILLUS.) **920**

Farm wagon, cast iron, one horse & driver, worn paint, marked "Kenton Toys, Made in USA," 15" l. **275**

Fire ladder wagon, cast iron, Kingsbury Mfg. Co. (Keene, New Hampshire)............ **2,090**

Early Cast-Iron Fire Ladder Wagon

Fire ladder wagon, cast iron, the long red wagon w/gold striping, blue ladder racks & yellow wheels pulled by a black & a white horse on wheels, two drivers & wooden ladders, early 20th c., 24 1/2" l. (ILLUS.) **978**

Fire pumper, cast iron, chrome & red paint, unmatched, two-horse hitch w/gold trimmed harness, connecting rods simulate a gallop, early 20th c., 15" l. **770**

Early Cast Iron Fire Pumper

Fire pumper, cast iron, steam-type, worn red paint on body & driver, silver metal wheels, early 20th c., 5" l. (ILLUS.) **182**

Fire pumper, lithographed paper on wood, horse-drawn, detachable wood steam stacks & posts, W.S. Reed, ca. 1877, smaller than 15" l. **3,500**

Fire pumper, lithographed paper on wood, horse-drawn, detachable wood steam stacks & posts, W.S. Reed, ca. 1877, 15" l. **4,500**

Fire pumper wagon, horse-drawn, painted cast iron, one black horse & one nickel-plated horse, Ives & Blakeslee Company, ca. 1890, 20" l.(missing driver) **920**

Arcade Fire Pumper Truck

Fire truck, cast iron, fire pumper in red w/six cast blue & red firemen, rubber tires, Arcade, 1930s,13" l. (ILLUS.) **770**

Buddy L Fire Aerial Truck

Fire truck, pressed steel, fire aerial truck, worn original red paint, Buddy L, 1930s, 30" l. (ILLUS.) **1,210**

Buddy L Hook & Ladder Fire Truck

Fire truck, pressed steel, hook & ladder model No. 205, original worn red paint, solid metal wheels, w/ladders, missing the hook, Buddy L, 1930s, approximately 2' l. (ILLUS.) **550**

Kenton Fire Wagon Set

Fire wagon, cast iron, horse-drawn, a black & a white horse on a single small wheel pulling a fire wagon filled w/seven firemen, red wagon embossed "Fire Patrol," worn yellow wheels, Kenton Hardware Co., 1920s (ILLUS.) **440**

Fire water tower truck, pressed steel, red chassis w/open cab, long adjustable crane in back, black rubber tires w/red hubs, American LaFrance model, all decals, minimal paint wear, Sturditoys (Sturdy Corp., Providence, Rhode Island), 1920s, 34" l. **1,073**

Gyrocopter, pressed steel, Wyandotte Toys, ca. 1930s, 12 1/2" wingspan (one blade missing) **127**

Hansom cab, cast iron, w/driver & one white prancing horse, passenger inside, Kenton Hardware, original box, passenger damaged, 15 1/4" l. (ILLUS. right w/Circus wagon) **330**

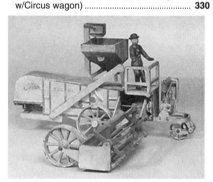

Early Cast-Iron Harvester

Harvester, cast iron, John Deere model, painted silver w/green blades & yellow wheels, original standing driver, Vindex, early 20th c. (ILLUS.) **7,150**

Hook & ladder, lithographed paper on wood, double horses, two firemen, W.S. Reed, ca. 1890s **4,000**

Horse-drawn carriage, lithographed paper on wood, "Cinderella Coach," possibly Bliss, ca. 1890s, 10" l **5,500**

Milk wagon, lithographed tin & wood, tin enclosed wagon body lithographed in color & marked "Rich's 1922" & "Rich's" on sides, wooden wheels & flat printed horse on front small wheels, the saddle printed "A Rich Toy," Rich & Co., 1930s, 20" l. **288**

Police Motorcycle with Sidecar

Motorcycle, cast iron, police motorcycle w/sidecar, red paint, rubber tires, driver replaced, Hubley, 1930s (ILLUS.).................. **715**

Hubley "Indian Crash Car" Motorcycle

Motorcycle, cast iron, three-wheeled "Indian Crash Car," red body & driver, gold wheels, Hubley Mfg. Co. (Lancaster, Pennsylvania), ca. 1930s, 80% paint, 6 1/2" l. (ILLUS.) **330**

Old Cast-Iron Motorcycle

Motorcycle, cast iron w/rubber tires, driver in uniform, painted orange w/"Patrol" embossed on the side, worn paint, rust spotting, 6 1/2" l. (ILLUS.)...................................... **182**

Motorcycle, cast metal w/rider, blue paint w/gold accent, rubber tires, Champion Hardware Co.(Geneva, Ohio), 7" l. **385**

Motorcycle w/side car, cast iron, w/driver & passenger, olive green, black, silver & pink, wheels marked "Harley Davidson," 9" l. (some wear).. **605**

Keystone Moving Van

Moving van, pressed steel, worn orange-painted van w/applied oval label reading "Keystone Moving Van - Long Distance Moving," black cab w/moving steering wheel, orange metal wheels w/rubber tires, back door opens, stop signal flag, springs at back wheels, paint chips & scratches, Keystone Mfg. Co. (Boston, Massachusetts), large (ILLUS.) **1,100**

Late 1930s Pedal Car

Pedal car, pressed steel body w/rubber tires & chrome hubcaps, original red paint, unmarked, late 1930s, 16 x 38", 22" h. (ILLUS.) **900**

Pile driver, "Panama Pile Driver," pressed steel, gravity toy, w/falling ball-operated driver, patent-dated in December 1905, w/seven clay balls, Wolverine, 15 1/2" h. (paint flaking).. **230**

Restored Silver Dash Racer

Race car, pressed steel, sleek silver body w/large red metal wheels, two drivers, Silver Dash Racer, Buffalo Toys, 1925, restored, 13 3/4" l. (ILLUS.) **226**

Ship, lithographed paper on wood, "Terror," Coast Defense Monitor, R. Bliss, ca. 1910, 20" l., 10" h. **1,200**

Steam roller, painted cast iron, early tractor-style w/driver & cab at rear above large pierced rear wheels, small front roller wheel, embossed "Huber" under driver's compartment, original driver, painted green, Hubley Mfg. Co. (Lancaster, Pennsylvania), ca. 1930, 7 1/2" l. (some surface rust) **345**

Steamboat, side-wheeler, lithographed paper on wood, marked "Providence," W.S. Reed Toy Co. (Leominster, Massachusetts), late 19th c., 20" l. (tears, edge wear) **690**

Steamboat, side-wheeler, painted cast iron, name "Puritan" raised across side-wheel frame, Wilkins Toy Co. (Keene, New Hampshire), ca. 1900, 11" l. (fair condition, some flaking) **431**

Steamshovel truck, lithographed tin, green open cab w/red & blue stripings, red shovel cab w/green roof, boom arm & bucket, Mack truck marked "Hercules," J. Chein & Co. (New York, New York), 1920s, 27 1/2" l. **2,530**

Taxi cab, cast iron, Arcade, No. 2 Yellow Cab, w/driver, 7 3/4" l. **800**

Arcade Fordson Tractor

Tractor, cast iron, Fordson model, green chassis & driver, red metal wheels, never played with, Arcade, ca. 1930, 6" l. (ILLUS.) **297**

Train, lithographed paper on wood, "Central Park" trolley, W.S. Reed, 1878 .... **6,500**

Train, lithographed paper on wood, "Empire Express," two engines, tender, two cars, alphabet blocks, R. Bliss, ca. 1890, overall 52" l. **3,500**

Train, lithographed paper on wood, "Hercules Atlantic & Pacific," engine, tender, Milton Bradley, 1880 .... **2,500**

Train, lithographed paper on wood, "Jackson Park Trolley," R. Bliss, ca. 1890s, 18" l. **4,000**

Train, lithographed paper on wood, "(The) Reindeer Train," engine, tender, four wooden cage cars, displays various wild animals, made to be assembled in puzzle fashion, Milton Bradley, 1900, 45" l. **1,500**

"U.S. Grant" Train

Train, lithographed paper on wood, "U.S.Grant," engine & two parlor cars, attributed to R. Bliss, ca. 1880s (ILLUS.)...... **2,500**

Train accessory, Lionel No. 124A railway station, tinplate w/two exterior & one interior light, grey base, two car arrivals signs (one sign replaced)... **288**

Train Street Light

Train accessory, street light, Lionel Lines, double bulb, painted dark green, 1929, 9" (ILLUS.) **65**

Train caboose, Lionel Lines, No. 517, standard gauge, 1927-40 .... **100**

Rare Lionel Santa Car

Train car, "Lionel Santa Car," Santa pumping handcar w/Christmas tree at opposite end, Mickey Mouse in Santa's backpack, mint in box, 1930s (ILLUS.) **2,310**

Train cattle car, Lionel No. 513, standard gauge, 1927-38 .... **175**

Train engine, brass, B & O "Tom Thumb" engine, non-standard gauge, runs on coal or bench top propane, manufactured by R. Ebert, 7 1/4" l. **138**

Train engine, brass, copper & steel, Welsh narrow gauge engine "Y DDRAIG," dark green & black enamel, manufactured by Gilbert Lindsey (England), 13 7/8 x 28" **1,155**

Train engine, brass, electric, Great Northern class Y-1 locomotive, "O" gauge, fine w/original box,18 1/2" l. **770**

Train engine, brass, electric, Pennsylvania GG-1 locomotive, "O" gauge, manufactured by Samhongsa, fine, 20 1/2" l. **825**

Train engine, brass, electric, Union Pacific #9000 4-12-2 locomotive, "O" gauge, manufactured by Samhongsa, mint in box, 25 1/2" l. **1,210**

Train engine, brass, live steam, "Dickens" locomotive, "O" gauge, manufactured by R. Ebert, good, 5 3/4" l. **413**

Train engine, brass, NY Central J1 4-6-4 "O" gauge locomotive, manufactured by Katsumi Moskeiten, mint w/box, 24 1/4" l., ... **1,155**

Train engine, brass, NY Central Niagara 4-8-4 locomotive, "O" gauge, manufactured by Katsumi Mokeiten, mint w/original box, 29 1/4" l. **1,155**

Train engine, brass & steel, Richard Trevithick's 1804 locomotive, wooden coal car, manufactured by R. Ebert, 19 1/2" l. **715**

Train engine, brass, three truck Shay locomotive & tender, "O" gauge, manufactured by Katsumi Mokeiten, good with original box, 16 1/2" l. **1,375**

Train engine, brass, Union Pacific 4-8-8-4 "Big Boy" locomotive, manufactured by Katsumi Mokeiten, fine w/original box, 34" l. **2,255**

Train engine, brass, Virginian triplex 2-8-8-8-4 locomotive & tender, "O" gauge, manufactured by Samhongsa, fine, 25 1/2" l. **1,293**

Train engine, electric, Southern Pacific 4-8-8-4 cab forward locomotive, gauge one, manufactured by Samhongsa, mint w/carrying case, ... **11,000**

Ives No. 1122 Locomotive & Tender

Train engine, Ives No. 1122 steam locomotive & tender, original black paint, tag on tender reads "The Ives Railway Lines," ca. 1920-30 (ILLUS.) **385**

Train engine, Lionel Lines 2-4-2 locomotive, No. 390/390E, standard gauge, 1929-33 .... **800**

Train engine, Lionel Lines locomotive, No. 256, "O" gauge, electric, 1924-30 .... **800**

Train engine, Lionel Lines locomotive, No. 8/8E, standard gauge, electric, 1925-32 .... **250**

Lionel Train Engine with AA Unit

Train engine, Lionel "Santa Fe" model w/AA unit, electric, grey & red w/gold striping (ILLUS.) **660**

Train engine, live steam, Union Pacific 4-8-8-4 "Big Boy," gauge one, manufactured by Samhongsa, mint w/carrying case **7,150**

Lionel Locomotive & Coal Tender

Train engine & coal tender, Lionel Lines, Locomotive No. 224E w/coal tender, 2-6-2 wheels, both black, 1940-1942 (ILLUS. previous page) **400**

Train engine & tender, Lionel No. 384 (B) standard guage 2-4-0 locomotive & No. 384-T tender, tinplate w/green lining (some retouching to tender top rail) **633**

Train gondola car, Lionel Lines, No. 212, standard gauge, 1926-40 .... **175**

Train handcar, Lionel Lines, Mickey & Minnie Mouse, No. 1100, "O" gauge, 1935-37 .... **1,000**

Train hopper, Lionel Lines, No. 216, standard gauge, 1926-38 .... **400**

Train operating crossing gate, Lionel Lines, No. 77/077, "O" gauge, 1923-35 .... **50**

Train set, "American Flyer S Gauge," tinplate, No. 290 steam locomotive, No. 370 diesel locomotive, eight freight cars, two transformers, ten original boxes of track, instructions, a Marx street light & Keystone buildings, some original boxes, the set (various conditions) **316**

American Flyer Train Set

Train set: American Flyer standard gauge No. 4644 0-4-0 electric locomotive in red & grey & No. 4151 Eagle & No. 4152 Eagle observation cars in red w/printed features, rear car w/observation platform, New York department store carton, ca. 1930s, very slight wear, the set (ILLUS.) **920**

Train set, "Hafner O Gauge Overland Flyer," including cast-iron windup locomotive, lithographed tin tender & blue passenger car, original box, the set (box in poor condition) **489**

Train set, Ives standard gauge passenger set, includes motor No. 3236 locomotive in green, No. 184 Pullman club car & No. 186 observation cars in tan, the set (chips & scratches especially on cars) **575**

Train set, Ives standard gauge passenger set, including No. 3241 NYC & HR electric locomotive, No. 184 buffet car & No. 186 observation car, finished in green, the set (roofs repainted, touch-ups on all pieces) **288**

Train set, Lionel No. 294 outfit, electric, "O" gauge, all cars & transformer in original boxes, all very good condition, early 20th c., the set **935**

Train set, "Lionel O Gauge," freight set, includes No. 224E steam locomotive, No. 224W tender, No. 2680 shell tanker, No. 2654 shell tank car, No. 2652 gondola car & No. 2657 caboose, the set **288**

Train set, Lionel O-gauge Outfit No. 92, electric 152 New York Central 0-4-0 locomotive, 629 Pullman car, 630 observation carriages, No. 57 lamp post, No. 58 lamp post, No. 68 crossing sign, No. 89 flag pole, instructions & quantity of track, the set **230**

Train set, lithographed paper on wood, a locomotive, tender & passenger car w/removable roof, marked "Buffalo" on the sides, Bliss Mfg. Co. (Pawtucket, Rhode Island), ca. 1900, minor paper loss, missing alphabet blocks, one connecting rod & pull cord eyelet, overall 45" l. (ILLUS. below) **7,188**

Train set, lithographed tin, Ives electric standard guage, engine No. 3242, club car No. 184, parlor car No. 185, observation car No. 186, complete w/track & box, all-original, ca. 1930s, the set **1,430**

Train set, pressed steel, Buddy L, 26" l. engine, 18" l. coal car, two 20" l. cattle cars & 19" l. caboose, original paint except on coal car, caboose marked "Built by Moline Pressed Steel Co., East Moline, Ill.," each piece marked w/"Buddy L," the set (paint chips, scratches, ragged edges on bottom of caboose) **3,685**

Train tank car, Lionel Lines, No. 815, "O" gauge, 1926-42 .... **100**

Tootsietoy Delivery Van

Truck, delivery moving van, cast metal, red cab & red & silver trailer, black wheels, "Tootsietoys - Coast to Coast," Tootsietoy (Dowst Bros., Chicago, Illinois), excellent condition, 9 1/4" l. (ILLUS.) **110**

Truck, delivery, pressed steel, "Hiway Express" on sides, Marx, ca. 1930s, 16" l. **165**

Rare Early Bliss Toy Train

Kenton Oil & Gas Tank Truck

Truck, die-cast, gasoline tanker, "Sinclair," Tootsietoy **66**

Truck, die-cast metal, Mack Auto Transport, yellow cab & trailer w/four autos, Tootsietoy, ca. 1930s, w/original box, 10 3/4" l. (missing one box flap) **230**

Truck, die-cast, oil tanker, "Mobil," Tootsietoy **45**

Truck, die-cast, tow truck, Tootsietoy **40**

Wyandotte Flatbed Truck

Truck, flatbed-type, pressed steel, red chassis w/gold grills, blue flatbed w/yellow interior, w/tilting ramp, Wyandotte, very good condition, ca. 1930s, 18" l. (ILLUS.) **506**

Truck, gasoline tanker, pressed steel, "Texaco" on sides, ca. 1950s, Buddy L, 23" l. **187**

Truck, low-boy type, pressed steel, Smith-Miller Toy Co., 23" l. (repainted) **248**

Truck, oil & gas tanker, cast iron, painted green w/raised words "Oil" & "Gas" along the sides in gold w/further gold trim, solid stamped steel wheels, minor painted chips, minor surface rust on wheel, missing driver, Kenton Hardware, 10" h., 4 3/4" h. (ILLUS. above) **2,750**

Truck, oil tanker, tin friction-type, open cab, squatty oval tank marked "Dan-Dee Oil Truck," all-metal wheels, marked "J. Chein & Co. - Made in U.S.A.," 9" l. (paint chips, rust spotting, denting, scratches & soiling) **413**

Buddy L Truck with Steam Shovel

Truck, pressed steel, flatbed truck w/steam shovel in back, dark blue, orange & grey paint, Buddy L, original labels, rubber wheels, 1930s (ILLUS.) **1,100**

Heinz Delivery Truck by Metalcraft

Truck, pressed steel, Heinz delivery truck, white w/closed cab & slatted back, rubber wheels, original labels on the back, Metalcraft, ca. 1930s (ILLUS.) **440**

Keystone Police Patrol Truck

Truck, pressed steel, "Keystone City Patrol," police van w/mesh sides & open cab, on rubber & metal tires, black body w/white print & red tires, marked on the side, Keystone, 1920s (ILLUS.) **1,100**

Sheffield Farms Milk Truck

Truck, pressed steel, milk truck w/stake back, red body w/rubber wheels on yellow hubs, printed on cab door "Sheffield Farms Company" & labeled on back "Sheffield Farms Sealect Milk," w/four original metal milk cans, late 1920s - early 1930s (ILLUS. above) **2,200**

Buddy L Model T Truck

Truck, pressed steel, Model T pick-up model, metal wheels trimmed in red, original black body paint, partial label, Buddy L (ILLUS.) **825**

Buddy L Railway Express Truck

Truck, pressed steel, semi-truck & trailer, "Railway Express Agency" w/red, yellow, green & black Wrigley's Spearmint advertisement on the trailer, green & yellow cab & trailer, black rubber tires w/red hubs, Buddy L, 1930s, some paint wear & light rust (ILLUS.) **715**

Buddy L Junior Tank Truck

Truck, pressed steel, tank truck, flattened green tank on red rack, black cab, rubber-rimmed red wheels, decal on tank, Buddy L Junior, 1930 (ILLUS.) **1,320**

Buddy L Tanker Truck

Truck, pressed steel, tanker truck, open cab, all-metal wheels, old worn black, blue & red paint & worn label, Buddy L, 1930s, 24" l. (ILLUS.) **715**

Truck, stake-type, cast iron, marked on cab "5 Ton Truck," Hubley Mfg. Co., 16" l. (old replacement driver & headlight) **1,760**

Truck set, cast iron, auto carrier & four autos including three coupes & one sedan, green truck cab & autos in red or blue, metal wheels, Arcade, late 1920s, the set (ILLUS. below) **3,520**

Arcade Auto Carrier & Four Autos

Early Tootsietoy Vehicle Set

Vehicle set, cast metal, "Tootsietoy Playtime Toys - No. 7005," set w/planes, cars & trucks, fitted in colorful original box, 1930s, the set (ILLUS.)................................. **1,155**

Early Tootsietoy Playtime Set

Vehicle set, "Playtime," set of original cast metal vehicles & airplanes, all mint in original colorful box, Tootsietoy, ca. 1930s, 10 pcs. (ILLUS.)................................... **633**

Wagon, wooden, advertisement type, Alderney Dairy, painted wood, replication of actual working dairy wagon, logos on side panels, pulled by dappled white horse on small wheeled platform, Albert Schoenhut, 1929-32, 11 1/2" h. x 12" l. **3,500**

Wagon, wooden, advertisement type, Hood's Grade "A" Milk, logos on side panels, white horse on wheeled platform, Albert Schoenhut, 1929-31, 12" l., 12 1/2" h.. **3,500**

Wagon, wooden, advertisement type, Sheffield Dairy, logos on sides, horse on wheeled platform, 1929-32, Albert Schoenhut, 12" l., 12 1/2" h. **3,500**

Water pump & round tank, cast iron, gold pump, blue tank, Arcade Mfg. Co., early 20th c., 8 1/2" h.. **138**

Early Steelcraft Zeppelin

Zeppelin, pressed steel, red body & red metal wheels, "Graf Zeppelin" on side & Sundial Shoes decal advertisement on the top front, Steelcraft, ca. 1930s, very good condition, 26" l. (ILLUS.)........................ **770**

Zeppelin, cast iron, marked "Zep," painted silver, ca. 1930s, 4 3/4" l. **86**

Chapter 10
WINDUP TIN & CLOCKWORK

Charlie McCarthy & His Benzine Buggy

Marx U.S. Army Bomber

Airplane, windup tin, U.S. Army Bomber, dark green w/yellow, red, white & blue trim, metal wheels, Marx, ca. 1940, 18" wingspan (ILLUS.) **$281**

Airplane, windup tin, "Wood's Mechanical Airplane," silver body on yellow wheels, single-engine monoplane, Girard-Marx, ca. 1930, excellent condition w/box, 12" l. **605**

Amos 'N' Andy Fresh Air Taxicab

Amos & Andy toy, "Fresh-Air Taxi," windup tin, ca. 1930s, Marx, very good, 8" l. (ILLUS.) **825**

Windup Tin Andy Walking Toy

Andy (Amos & Andy) toy, windup tin walker, good, Marx, 1930s, near mint (ILLUS.) **825**

Aquaplane, windup tin, color lithographed monoplane in silver, blue & red w/a large red propeller, on oblong half-round red & green pontoons, No. 38, J. Chein, mint toy w/original box **385**

Girard Fire Chief Siren Coupe

Automobile, windup tin, "Fire Chief Siren Coupe," red body w/decal on door, Girard, ca. 1940, battery conversion, 14 1/2" l. (ILLUS.) **450**

Automobile, windup tin, long sleek red body w/looped metal front & rear bumpers, Marx, 1930s (ILLUS.) **500**

"Balky Mule," windup tin, a cut-out colorful mule pulls a two-wheeled cart w/driver,

Marx, w/original box, 8 3/8" l. (minor wear) **275**

"Balky Mule," windup tin, lithographed in color, Lehmann (Germany), Model #425, early 20th c., 7 1/4" l. **230**

Barnacle Bill Walking Toy

Barnacle Bill toy, windup tin walker, J. Chein, very good condition, 7 1/2" h. (ILLUS.) **385**

Beetle, windup tin, "A Souvenir from the Universal Theatres Concession CO. Chicago, Ill.," made in Germany, "GRDM," legs move when pulled or pushed, 2 1/2" l. **99**

Boy riding tricycle, windup tin, Unique Art, runs, 9" h. (some paint missing across mouth & on stomach) **138**

Buck Rogers toy windup tin, "Buck Rogers Space Ship," Marx, 1934, 12" **400-800**

Bus, windup tin, "Inter-State Bus," double-decker, lithographed primarily in orange & yellow, right-hand driver, open top deck, rear staircase, metal wheels, model 109, Strauss, 10 1/2" l. (some scratches) **805**

Buttercup toy, windup tin, the crawling baby lithographed in color, Germany, mid-1920s, 7 1/2" l. (paint loss to right side) **259**

Captain America toy, windup tin, Captain America on tricycle, excellent original condition **330**

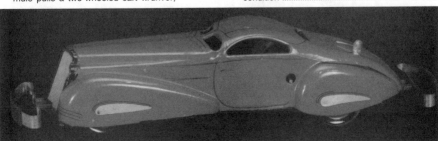

Sleek Marx Windup Automobile

Very Rare Ernst Plank Airship

Charlie McCarthy & His Benzine Buggy

Charlie McCarthy toy, windup tin, color lithographed, Charlie McCarthy & His Benzine Buggy, Louis Marx, excellent, 7" l. (ILLUS.) **578**

Circus cage wagon, windup tin, circus cage wagon pulled by an elephant, the articulated elephant pulls a box-style cage on large solid metal wheels, one side of cage w/hinged opening doors, colorfully lithographed, possibly Ferdi-nand Strauss Corp. (New York, New York), ca. 1930 (possibly incomplete) **173**

Clockwork airship, a shaded mustard-colored superstructure & tubular fins, twin-bladed celluloid propeller, each embossed w/E.P. trademark, steel-blue colored gondola w/a captain holding telescope, airman standing by the engine, ventilator, rubber & tinplate forward propeller, w/cloth-covered suspension wire & cast-metal winding key, Ernst Plank, Germany, early 20th c., w/excelsior-filled maker's carton w/lithographed comic label, torn triangular label, dent & chipping around suspension eyelet, chip to nose & rear propeller shaft, motor shifted within body, damages to box (ILLUS.) **23,000**

Clockwork buckboard, painted tin, red wagon w/driver pulled by a black horse, most original paint, Stevens & Brown (New York, New York), late 19th c., works (ILLUS.) **2,420**

Clockwork figure of gardener, pushing cart, black face, probably Lehman, late 19th - early 20th c... **440**

Clockwork fire engine house, complete w/bell which rang when fire pumper rushed through the door, Ives Corp., (Bridgeport, Connecticut) **2,970**

Rare Stevens & Brown Clockwork Toy

Early Clockwork Velocipede Toy

Clockwork girl on velocipede, papier-maché, cloth & tin, the rider w/a papier-maché head & jointed cloth body pedaling a velocipede, Stevens & Brown, girl's head missing paint, clothes soiled & tattered, ca. 1880, 10 3/4" l. (ILLUS.)......... **1,485**

Early Carrette Limosine

Clockwork limosine, lithographed tin, open cab w/driver, closed rear, original dark green body w/red & yellow trim, metal & hard rubber tires, Carrette, Germany, early 20th c. (ILLUS.).............................. **4,950**

German Clockwork Limousine

Clockwork limousine, lithographed tin, green & black chassis on green metal wheels, hood & doors open, forward, neutral & reverse action, real working pistons, complete, all-original, Moko (Germany), early 20th c., minimal fading, 9 1/2" l. (ILLUS.) **935**

Rare Bing Clockwork Limousine

Clockwork limousine, tinplate, hand-painted w/beveled glass windows, kilometer taxi meter, nickel-plated carriage lights, rubber wheels, original key & box built for storage, minor flaking, missing windshield, driver & rear luggage rack, damage to roof luggage rack, Bing (Germany), ca. 1910, 14 1/4" l. (ILLUS.).. **21,850**

Victorian Clockwork Locomotive

Clockwork locomotive, painted tin, early locomotive w/four small pierced front wheels & two large rear wheels, closed cab w/pointed arch windows, bell, smokestack & cowcatcher, worn black, gold & red paint w/faint stenciled "Union" on side, last quarter 19th c. (ILLUS.)......... **2,475**

Clockwork motorcycle & rider, lithographed tin, driver in red, black motocycle, Germany, complete, works, early **1,100**

Clockwork polar bear, off-white mohair, glass eyes, composition nose & open mouth w/teeth, French clockwork mechanism, Distler key, 12" l. (nose rubbed) **978**

Clockwork roadster, lithographed tin, "7" on side, Marklin (Germany), ca. 1930s, works, 15 1/2" l. (replaced fenders) **1,210**

Clockwork touring car, w/driver, lithographed tin, doors open, adjustable steering, Bing (Germany) **523**

Clockwork truck, "Kingsbury Army Truck USA Defense" on original canvas cover, Kingsbury Mfg. Co. (Keene, New Hampshire), ca. 1930s-40s, 14" l. **160**

Gunthermann Clockwork Windmill

Clockwork windmill, lithographed tin, tall upright open-sided mill on a round stepped base, yellow & red printed decoration, Gunthermann, Germany, early 20th c., 14 1/2" h. (ILLUS.) **303**

Clown toy, windup celluloid, figure, C.K., Japan, 1930s, w/original box, 8" h. **230**

Marx Coo Coo Car Windup Toy

"Coo Coo Car," windup tin, red crazy car w/black & white driver, w/original color box, L. Marx, ca. 1930s (ILLUS.) **605**

"Cowboy Rider," windup tin, cowboy twirling a lasso while astride a rearing horse, lithographed in color, Louis Marx & Co. (New York, New York), 1930s, w/original box, 7" h. **431**

Delivery wagon, windup tin, "New Milk Wagon & Horse," lithographed tin w/closed wagon on metal wheels pulled by a brown horse, side of wagon reads "Toyland's Farm Products - Milk & Cream," original box, Louis Marx, toy 10 1/4" l. (slight wear to box & one flap detached) **489**

Dick Tracy police car, windup tin, color lithographed, good condition, w/instructions, Marx **250**

Strauss "Dizzie Lizzie" Car

"Dizzie Lizzie," windup tin, black sedan w/various slang slogans of the 1920s written in white around the body, metal wheels, w/driver, Strauss, 1926, 8" l. (ILLUS.) **330**

Donald Duck toy, carousel, windup celluloid, long-billed Donald on wheeled metal base rolls forward as the carousel turns, Japan, ca. 1930s, 7" h. (arms glued in place) **1,250**

Windup Celluloid Drummer Boy

"Drummer Boy," windup celluloid, boy wearing a pink hat & outfit, drum at front, w/original box, Japan, 10" h. (ILLUS.).......... **660**

Dwarf Dopey toy, windup tin, eyes moving up & down as he walks from side to side, Louis Marx & Co., ca. 1938, 8" h. 375

Figaro (Pinocchio's cat) toy, windup tin, rolls over, good, Marx 140

G.I. Joe & K-9 Pups Windup Toy

"G.I. Joe & the K-9 Pups," windup tin, light green w/red & yellow trim, Unique Art Mfg. Co., ca. 1930s, 9" h. (ILLUS.) **175-225**

Goofy toy, windup celluloid, cat on tail, Louis Marx & Co. **225-250**

"Hercules Ferris Wheel," windup tin, color lithographed, six gondolas in double wheels above a rectangular base, J. Chein, complete w/original box, excellent condition **495**

Horse & cart, windup tin, driver in open cart, wire spoke wheels, trotting horse, paint excellent, early 20th c., 9" l. **743**

Humphreymobile Windup Toy

Humphrey (Joe Palooka) toy, windup tin, color lithographed, Humphreymobile, Wyandotte, original box, near mint, 8 1/2" l. (ILLUS.) **553**

Jackie Coogan toy, windup tin "The Kid," Jackie Googan walker, young boy w/cap, eyes move from side to side, 7 1/4" h. **440**

Joe Penner toy, windup tin, color lithographed, Joe Penner & his duck, Louis Marx, pristine, 8 1/2" l. **490**

"Kiddy Cyclist," windup tin, boy on a tricycle, Unique Art Mfg. Co., ca. 1930s **165**

Marx Knockout Champs Toy

"Knockout Champs," windup tin & celluloid, raised square platform w/printed figures supports two celluloid boxers, Marx, ca. 1940 (ILLUS.) **413**

Li'l Abner & His Dogpatch Band Toy

Li'l Abner toy, "Li'l Abner & His Dogpatch Band," windup tin, 1945, Unique Art, w/original box, 5 3/4" x 9" (ILLUS.) **825**

Lone Ranger & Silver toy, windup tin, the Lone Ranger riding a rearing Silver, a lariat in one hand, L. Marx, 1938, boxed, 7" l. **350-700**

Maggie & Jiggs Windup Toy

Maggie & Jiggs (Bringing Up Father) toy, windup tin, figures of Maggie & Jiggs on facing wheeled platforms joined by a slender rod, good paint, Nifty (ILLUS.) **1,100**

Fine Marx Merrymakers Toy

"Marx Merrymakers," windup tin, upright piano w/four Mickey Mouse-like mice around it, original marquee on the top, Marx, 1930s (ILLUS.).................................. **1,760**

Mary & her little lamb, windup celluloid & tin the celluloid figure of Mary in a long blue dress & bonnet standing on a metal wheeled platform above the mechanism, the lamb on a smaller wheeled platform pulled behind, Japan, excellent condition..... **605**

Mickey & Minnie Acrobats

Mickey & Minnie Mouse toy, windup celluloid & tin acrobats, George Borgfeldt, very good, w/original box, 13" h. (ILLUS.)..... **691**

Mickey Mouse & Boy Windup Toy

Mickey Mouse toy, windup celluloid, figure of boy dressed like Pinocchio lifting a jointed plastic figure of Mickey Mouse, early Schuco (ILLUS.).................................... **880**

Mickey Mouse toy, windup celluloid, Mickey riding a bucking bronco, ca. 1930s, 5 1/2" l. **2,800**

Mickey Mouse Jazz Drummer

Mickey Mouse toy, windup tin, "Jazz Drummer," plunger causes a lithographed two-dimensional Mickey to play the drum, by Nifty, Germany, ca. 1931, 6 3/4" h., good (ILLUS.).. **2,100**

Mickey Mouse Dipsy Car Toy

Mickey Mouse toy, windup tin, "Mickey Mouse Dipsy Car," colorful, Marx, Walt Disney Productions, excellent working condition, 6" h. (ILLUS.).................................. **458**

Mickey Musician Toy

Mickey Mouse toy, windup tin, "Mickey Musician," standing Mickey playing the xylophone, Marx, working, complete w/box (ILLUS.)... **660**

Mickey Mouse toy set, windup tin, "Mickey Mouse Meteor Express," five-piece train set w/track, excellent condition, the set **595**
Minnie Mouse toy, windup celluloid, Minnie on a trapeze, Borgfeldt, 1930s, w/box........ **1,800**

Moon Mullins & Kayo on Handcar

Moon Mullins toy, windup tin, "Moon Mullins & Kayo on Handcar," ca. 1930s, mint w/original box, 6" l. (ILLUS.) **880**

Marx Motorcycle Cop Windup Variation

Motorcycle, windup tin, police officer in white & red uniform on a yellow cycle, black & white windup button on side, L. Marx, ca. 1930s (ILLUS.) **220**

Marx Motorcycle Cop Windup

Motorcycle, windup tin, police officer in white & red uniform on a yellow cycle, black windup button on side, L. Marx, ca. 1930s, slight wear (ILLUS. previous page).. **209**

"Oh-My Alabama Coon Jigger," windup tin, lithographed in color w/a black dancer, Model 685, Lehmann (Germany), early 20th c., 10" h. (wear to top of base) **403**

Pinocchio toy, windup tin, acrobat, Marx, 16 1/2" h. **495**

Pinocchio Windup Tin Walking Toy

Pinocchio toy, windup tin, figure of a walking Pinocchio carrying buckets, moving eyes, marked "Walt Disney Ent. copyright 1939, Marx," 8 1/2" h. (ILLUS.).............. **525**

Pluto toy, windup tin, "Musical Pluto," lithographed tin square platform w/crouching figure of Pluto going around in a circle passing through a doghouse & other structure, good condition **440**

Popeye toy, lithographed tin, drummer, squeeze-type, Chein, 7" h., very good (missing drum head) **1,210**

Popeye Carrying Parrot Cages Toy

Popeye toy, windup tin, color lithographed, Popeye carrying parrot cages, Marx, 1930s, w/damaged box, 8 1/2" h. (ILLUS.)... **440**

Popeye toy, windup tin, color lithographed, Popeye in rowboat, figure in pressed steel, aluminum rowboat, ca. 1935, Hoge, pristine condition, 14 1/2" l. **4,620**

Popeye toy, windup tin, color lithographed, Popeye the Pilot in airplane, red, white & blue, excellent condition, Louis Marx **695**

Popeye with Punching Bag Toy

Popeye toy, windup tin, color lithographed, Popeye w/punching bag, tin platform w/overhead suspended celluloid punching bag, J. Chein, very good, works, 7" h. (ILLUS.)... **770**

Popeye Express

Early Lehmann Windup Tin Racer

Popeye toy, windup tin, "Popeye Express," Popeye pushing a wheelbarrow w/trunk on it & parrot on trunk, Louis Marx, excellent, 8 1/2" l. (ILLUS. previous page).......... **1,293**

Powerful Katrinka toy, windup tin, color lithographed, Powerful Katrinka lifting Jimmy in cart, Nifty, very good condition, 6 1/2" l.. **1,350-1,650**

"Quack Quack" Windup toy

"Quack Quack," windup tin, mother duck pulling basket cart w/three ducklings, good color, Lehmann, Germany, early 20th c. (ILLUS.).. **413**

Racer, wndup tin, painted yellow w/blue & cream trim & white & red metal wheels, marked "D-R Patent, Patd. USA Az Dec. 1913 - Made in Germany," Lehmann Co. (Germany), very minor scratches, 6" l. (ILLUS. above)... **1,045**

Racer, windup tin, red chassis w/black & white number, white fenders & pale green side pipe & grill, black rubber wheels, Marklin (Germany), missing driver, repainted fenders (ILLUS. below)........ **1,650**

"Rodeo Joe," windup tin, crazy car w/cowboy driver, lithographed in color, Unique Art Mfg. Co., Inc. (New York City & also Newark, New Jersey), 1930s, 7" l. **201**

"Sky Rangers," windup tin, lithographed in color w/a monoplane & naval dirigible at opposite ends of a long bar atop a lighthouse & circling it when wound, dirigible & lighthouse decorated w/scenes of sailors, Unique, w/original box, 10" h. (scratches to toy, water stains on box)........ **345**

Steamroller, windup tin, corrugated metal roof, large smokestack, large rear wheels & smaller diameter roller at front, ca. 1930, 11 1/2" l. **230**

Early Marklin Windup Racer

Toonerville Trolley Windup Toy

Three Little Pigs toy, windup celluloid, acrobat-type w/three celluloid figures of pigs swinging on a trapeze, in original box w/decorative label on the lid, Japan, 10" h. **275**

Toonerville Trolley toy, windup tin, color lithographed model of the trolley, Fischer, ca. 1922, pristine, 5" l. (ILLUS. above) **825**

Uncle Wiggly toy, windup tin car, 1935, excellent condition, 8" l. **770**

Uncle Wiggly toy, windup tin, color lithographed, Uncle Wiggly Crazy Car, Distler, excellent, 9 1/2" l., ... **3,520**

"Whoopie Car," windup tin, comic character driving a jalopy, orange chassis w/black wording, Marx, Model No. 150,

rarer version, works well, complete w/box, 1930s **935**

"Whoopie Car," windup tin, lithographed in color, Model No. 150, Marx, 1930s, w/original box, 7" l. (box fair to good condition) **748**

Zeppelin, windup tin, silver-colored body w/propeller at the tail, Ferdinand Strauss Corp., 1930s, 9 1/2" l. **201**

Zilotone, windup tin, clown standing on mechanism playing curved xylophone keyboard, w/seven metal disks, Wolverine, 1930s (ILLUS. below) **413**

"Zippo - The Climbing Monkey," windup tin, colorful monkey figure climbs string, Louis Marx, original box, 9 1/4" h. (minor wear) **193**

Windup Tin Zilotone Toy

Chapter 11
MISCELLANEOUS

Early Child's Push Toy

Accordion, paper w/three reeds, colorful scene of a carnival & a clown playing an accordion, marked "Made in Germany," 6 1/4" l. **$33**

African Chief, Teddy Roosevelt Adventure in Africa Series, jointed wood, wearing a top hat, coat, vest, hound's tooth pants, ca. 1912, 9" h. (some holes & restitching on coat, top hat bit worn) **575**

African native beater, Teddy Roosevelt Adventure in Africa Series, jointed wood, cloth robe, carrying wooden spear, 1910, Albert Schoenhut (ILLUS. w/Safari set) **1,500**

Alligator, wooden, glass eyes, Style I, Albert Schoenhut, 7" l. **650**

Alligator, wooden, hand-painted eyes, Albert Schoenhut, 12" l. **400**

Animals, lithographed paper on wood, "Crandall's Menagerie," w/elephant, gorilla, toucan, camel, zebra, etc., in box w/paper label, patented 1867, 12 1/2 x 17 1/2" **1,500**

Arabian camel, wooden, glass eyes, Style II, w/open mouth, ca. 1910-20, Albert Schoenhut, 7" l. **400**

Arcadia Airport, wooden, Arcade Mfg. Co. (Freeport, Illinois) **660**

Baby elephant, wooden w/cloth ears, Albert Schoenhut, 3 3/4" l., 3" h **700**

Bactrian camel, wooden, glass eyes, Albert Schoenhut, ca. 1910-20, 7" l. **850**

Balance toy, w/aluminum cowboy on horse, weight at end of bent rod, ca.1940s, 24" l. **77**

Barn, wooden, brick design on exterior, Morton E. Converse Co. (stalls gone) **22**

Bell ringer toy, cast wheels w/bell between them, pulled by a tin horse, brown w/gold trim & red saddle, 5 1/2" l. **198**

Bell ringer toy, tin & cast metal, four-wheeled platform w/each wheel mounted w/three round bells, pulled by two running horses on small wheels, late 19th c.,11" l. **193**

Blocks, building-type, wood, "Crandall's Building Blocks," w/original box & instructions, ca. 1880, the set (no box lid, fair to good condition) **58**

Blocks, educational-type, lithographed paper on wood, one side features animals & letters of the alphabet, the other side shows various horse-drawn early fire vehicles, one end features a fireman, the other end shows soldiers, very good condition, late 19th c., each block 2 1/2 x 4", set of 12 .... **413**

Blocks, wooden, light stacking type, lithographed pictures of children except largest w/animals, tops w/numbers or alphabet except largest, sized 4" x 4" x 3 1/2" to 1 1/2" x 1 1/2", set of seven........................ **275**

Bowling set: 10 pins & 2 balls; wooden, turned design, the set **28**

Bridge, lithographed paper on wood, "(The) New York & Brooklyn Bridge," w/operable bridge cars which move on pulley & string, ca. 1890, 49" overall, 1 x 4" w., 9 3/4" h. **4,500**

Buffalo, wooden, painted eyes, Style IV, w/molded head, Albert Schoenhut, 8" l. **800**

Bulldog, leather tail, collar & ears, painted eyes, brindle color, Albert Schoenhut, 6 1/4" l., 3 3/4" h. **550**

Bulldog, leather tail, collar & ears, painted eyes, white, Albert Schoenhut, 6 1/4" l., 3 3/4" h. **475**

Bulldog, Rolly Dolly, hand-painted jointed wood on rounded base, Albert Schoenhut, 6 1/4" h. **2,500**

Cane, wooden, cap firing w/lead weight on bottom holding firing points, black & gold cast metal duck head handle, 34" l. **105**

Cat, wooden, painted eyes, ca. 1910-20, Albert Schoenhut, 5 1/2" l. **950**

Chauffeur, Rolly Dolly, w/goggles & matching hat, Albert Schoenhut, 10 1/2" h. **1,700**

Circus animal, alligator, jointed wood, painted body & eyes, leather feet, standard size, Schoenhut & Co., 12" l. (two feet damaged, needs restringing) **230**

Circus animal, elephant, jointed wood, painted w/painted eyes, leather ears & tusks, hemp tail & rubber trunk, standard size, Schoenhut & Co., w/original color-lithographed cardboard box, elephant 10 3/8" l. (some paint wear on head, trunk damaged, box w/edge wear) **633**

Circus animal, giraffe, jointed wood, realistically painted body w/painted eyes, leather ears & cotton tail, standard size, Schoenhut & Co., 11 5/8" h. (normal paint wear, needs restringing) **316**

Circus animal, lion in wooden cage, jointed wood, Schoenhut & Co. **990**

Circus animal, tiger, jointed wood, realistically painted w/painted eyes, cloth tail, standard size, Schoenhut & Co. (some paint wear, needs restringing) **230**

Circus set, "Humpty Dumpty Circus," reduced size, includes tent w/flags & base, two clowns, donkey, elephant, two chairs, two ladders & center ring, Schoenhut & Co., base 9 x 18", the set (fabric wear & staining, paint fair to good, figures need restringing) **863**

Circus set, "Humpty Dumpty Circus," tent w/cloth backdrops & grouping of circus animals & performers, Albert Schoenhut, the set.. **7,500**

Clown, Rolly Dolly, painted papier-maché, black, Albert Schoenhut, 11 1/2" h. **900**

Clown, roly-poly, composition material, blue & white, early 20th c., 4 1/2" h...................... **138**

Clown on Horse

Clown on horse, Rolly Dolly, Albert Schoenhut, 6 1/8" h. (ILLUS.)................................. **1,200**

Clowns, Rolly Dollies, five, painted composition, Albert Schoenhut, 6 1/4 to 15" h. (ILLUS. below) **1,100**

Coloring book, "Spot Planes," Merrill Publishing Co., 1944, 10 x 15" **17**

Construction toy, lithographed paper on wood, "New Cathedral Construction Toy," self-contained case for parts, books, blocks inscribed w/scriptual references, W.S. Reed, ca. 1870s..................... **3,500**

Cow, nodder-type, composition, model of a realistic cow w/worn brown & white hide covering, small natural horns & glass eyes in nodding head, late 19th c., 12" l. (some wear & damage, tail missing) **193**

Deer, wooden, painted eyes, Albert Schoenhut, 6 1/2" l. **550**

Clown Rollies

Donkey w/blanket, wooden, glass eyes, ca. 1910-20, Albert Schoenhut, 9 1/2" l. 250

Drum, child's size, embossed tin w/eagle & banner in red, gold & blue japanning, wooden bands around sides, 10" d., 7 3/4" h. (heads damaged)............................. 440

Drum, child's size, tin, decorated w/flags in red, white, blue & gold-stenciled japanning, wooden bands, 6" d., 5 1/4" h. (heads worn).. 275

Drum, metal, w/parchment top & bottom, Ohio Art Co., 10" h. (some rust spots) 17

Dutch couple Jolly Jiggers, papier-maché & wood, cloth outfits, couple suspended on hooks dance on platform when board is compressed, Albert Schoenhut, 21" l., 16" h. 5,500

Elephant w/blanket, wooden, glass eyes, ca. 1910-20, Albert Schoenhut, 9" l. 250

Erector Master Builder Set

Erector set, "Erector Master Builder Set #10092," metal carrying case, overall excellent (ILLUS.) 770

Erector set, Gilbert Model #4-1/2, w/manual, 1951, original box 22

Erector set, No. 8, w/locomotive parts, shovel, electric motor & instruction books, in wood case w/color lithographed label in lid, early 20th c., the set (rust, bending, other wear) 1,093

Farm set, chromolithographed pressed cardboard, a house, family, animals & trees, No. 744/2, Herolin (Germany), early 20th c., in maker's box w/label, box 12 3/4" w., the set (box bottom missing part of rim)... 173

Farm set, die-cast metal, African "Farm No. 1398," comprised of two mounted elephants, various European & native workers, horses, cattle, poultry, trees, fencing & hut, in original box w/cover, Heyde Miniatures (Dresden, Germany), 20th c., the set (incomplete, electrical tape on box) 1,725

Farm set: wooden barn & nine pieces of livestock; "Red Robin Farm," sliding doors, stenciled brick front & ends, 18" l., 17" h., the set 220

Farmer, molded face w/wooden rake, Albert Schoenhut, 8" h. 600

Figure, lithographed paper on wood, "Quaker in Rocking Chair," attributed to R. Bliss, ca. 1890, 13" h. 650

Figure, lithographed paper on wood, "Ye Hero of '76," figure of Revolutionary patriot set in groove on wooden stand, Charles M. Crandall, ca. 1876 (U.S. Centennial related) 3,500

Figures, lithographed paper on wood, American Twin-Animal Ark, painted animals, R. Bliss, 1890, 17" l. (also came in 13" & 24" sizes).. 2,000

Figures, lithographed paper on wood, Boy & Girl at School Desk, R. Bliss, ca. 1890s, figures 5 1/4" h., desk 5 1/4" w., the set.. 2,500

Fire engine house, wooden, Arcade............. 1,375

Rare Coaster Fire Patrol Wagon

Fire patrol wagon, coaster-type, painted wood, rectangular painted red platform w/side rails & front seat marked along sides in large letters "Fire Patrol," two large & two smaller wooden wheels w/iron rims, w/auxiliary set of sled runners, late 19th - early 20th c. (ILLUS.) 2,090

Early French Flip-toy

Flip-toy, lithographed paper on wood, four blocks forming figure of Napoleon II of France, each block double-sided, the Emperor in two naval uniforms, w/turned wood handle, w/torn slipcase, ca. 1850, 7 1/4" h. (ILLUS.)... 690

Gazelle, wooden, Albert Schoenhut (ILLUS. w/lion)... 1,800

Giraffe, wooden, glass eyes, Style II, w/closed mouth, Albert Schoenhut, 1910, 11" h. 450

Goose, wooden, painted eyes, Style I, Albert Schoenhut, 1910, 6 1/2" h. 450

Circus Lion, Rhino, Gazelle & Hippo

Gorilla, wooden, painted eyes, molded head, Teddy Roosevelt "Adventure in Africa Series," Albert Schoenhut, 9" h. **3,000**

Gravity toy, lithographed tin & wood, two blades m ounted on a wire spiral, one blade w/a lithographed tin boy at each end & the other w/wood & paper fans, wood & metal stand on each end of the wire, the blades rotate as they descend, early 20th c. **220**

Hippopotamus, wooden, Albert Schoenhut (ILLUS. w/lion).............................. **850**

Hippopotamus, wooden, glass eyes, one-piece head & neck, Style II, Albert Schoenhut, 9 1/2" l. **850**

Historioscope, lithographed paper on wood, "Panorama and History of America," w/hand crank to scroll pictures, views of Columbus landing through the Civil War era, Milton Bradley, ca. 1870s.... **1,100**

Historioscope, lithographed paper on wood, "Panorama of Visit of Santa Claus to the Happy Children," w/hand crank to scroll pictures, Milton Bradley, ca. 1900 .... **1,200**

Historiscope, "Bradley's Historiscope," panoramic history of America & the United States including poster, tickets, lecture & instructions, case w/metal handle, early 20th c., case 6 5/16 x 11 7/16", 2" h. (case w/imperfections) **489**

Hunter on horseback, rider wearing green hat & red jacket, pointing his rifle, brown horse on narrow rectangular base, Elastolin, early, 5 1/4" h.. **44**

Hyena, wooden, painted eyes, Teddy Roosevelt "Adventure in Africa Series," Albert Schoenhut, 6" l. (ILLUS. w/set)........... **350**

Jig toy, painted wood, early flat hinged figure of Harlequin in a costume painted in red, blue & yellow triangles, tall rounded dark paper hat, reverse painted green, yellow & cream, pull string to move arms & legs, composition collar, hand-written on the back "Harry K. 1876," 12" h. **121**

Keystone Cop, Rolly Dolly, Albert Schoenhut, 10 1/4" h. **750**

"Favorite" Toy Kitchen Range

Kitchen range, cast iron, "Favorite," greenish blue paint & nickel trim, warming oven above, complete w/skillet, pot & coal bucket, small break where top hooks into bottom, good paint, early 20th c., 8" w., 9 1/2" h. (ILLUS.).. **259**

Lamb (Mary's), wooden, glass eyes, Style I, tiny bell on collar, Albert Schoenhut, 8" h. **400**

Leopard, wooden, glass eyes, Style I, Albert Schoenhut, ca. 1910, 7" l. **650**

Lion, wooden, Albert Schoenhut (ILLUS. far left w/group) **500**

Lion, wooden, painted eyes, Albert Schoenhut, ca. 1910, 8" l. (ILLUS. above)... **500**

Magic lantern, "Triumph Lantern Magic" metal, bulbous lens section on a flaring metal base, w/six slides & paper describing it, made in Germany, original box, early 20th c. **165**

Marionette, carved wood & stuffed cloth, the realistically-carved man's head w/articulated mouth & glass eyes, carved wood torso, stuffed cloth arms & carved wood hands, jointed carved wood legs w/painted shoes, remnants of wig, 25" h. **495**

Marionette, carved wood & stuffed cloth, the wooden head carved realistically as a dark-haired man w/mustache, the waisted body of straw-stuffed cloth, cloth upper arms & carved wood lower arms, jointed carved wood legs w/carved & painted boots, undressed, includes a "Theatrical Date Book - 1886-87-88" also signed "Lew Morton of Three Ronaldos," marionette 33" h., the group **715**

Mary, wooden, Style I, w/two-part head, original clothing, Albert Schoenhut, 8" h. **650**

Mary & Lamb

Mary & lamb, wooden, w/wood feed crib, Albert Schoenhut, the set (ILLUS.)............. **1,400**

Movie camera, child-sized, painted wood, Schoenhut & Co... **935**

Musical Rabbit Rolly

Musical rabbit, Rolly Dolly, Albert Schoenhut, Germany, 8 1/4" h. (ILLUS.).................. **350**
Noah's Ark set, painted wood, painted
wooden ark accompanied by some 183
finely carved & painted small animals, fine
overall quality & conditioin, American-
made, 19th c., the set (ILLUS. below)......... **16,675**
Ostrich, wooden, painted eyes, Style III,
flat-sided head, Albert Schoenhut,
9 1/2" h. **450**
Penny toy, lithographed tin, black dancer,
hand-cranked mechanism, Distler (Ger-
many), early 20th c., 3 3/8" h. **201**
Penny toy, lithographed tin, flatbed truck,
yellow cab & flatbed on red frame w/red
tin wheels, Germany, early 20th c., very
good condition, 4" l. **275**

Early German Penny Toy

Penny toy, lithographed tin, motorcycle
w/side car & two figures, Germany, early
20th c. (ILLUS.)... **633**
Penny toy, lithographed tin, single yellow
horse pulling a shell-form two-wheeled
chariot, Germany, early 20th c., 5 1/4" l.
(paint wear).. **242**

Child's Piano with Dancing Dolls

Piano, wooden w/ornate cast-iron legs &
base, eight wooden white keys w/eleven
black keys, eight tiny "dancing" Flat Top
china dolls inside mirrored display area,
14" h. (ILLUS.) **2,900**
Pig, wooden, glass eyes, ball-jointed neck,
Style I, Albert Schoenhut, 7" l....................... **700**

"African Safari" complete set

Play set, Teddy Roosevelt "Adventure in
Africa Series," complete w/25 wooden
jungle denizens & Teddy Roosevelt,
cameraman & native beaters, w/colorful
lithographed paper on wood jungle
backdrop, ca. 1910, Albert Schoenhut,
the set (ILLUS.)... **15,000**
Polar bear, wooden, glass eyes, Style I,
Albert Schoenhut, 8" l. **1,700**

Fine Noah's Ark Set

Early Pond Yacht Toy

Pond yacht, wood & canvas, model of a single-masted sailboat w/wooden hull & canvas, string & brass rigging, worn paint, late 19th c., 64" l., 80" h. (ILLUS.)....... **880**

Poodle, wooden, glass eyes, cloth ruffle collar, Style II, Albert Schoenhut, 8" l. **450**

Pop-up toy, cowboy & horse, wooden jointed figures on wood block base, collapses when bottom is pressed.................................... **28**

Puppet, Joe Louis hand puppet, vinyl head & gloves, cloth costume, JVZ Co., 10" l. (small hole in one glove)................................... **72**

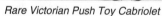

Rare Victorian Push Toy Cabriolet

Push toy, cabriolet & horse, the small hide-covered horse w/mane & tail above a small front wire-spoked wheel attached to rails supporting the seat w/low back w/turned spindles above two large wire-spoked wheels, upright curled iron bars w/turned wood handle at the back, late 19th c. (ILLUS.)... **2,750**

Early Cat Push Toy

Push toy, painted wood & cast iron, a flat grey-painted model of a jointed cat raised on a two-wheeled base, wooden push rod behind, late 19th c., cat 10" l. (ILLUS.)... **358**

Early Child's Push Toy

Push toy, steel & wood, "Trot-a-way King," jointed wood dappled horse w/mane & tail raised on large red metal wheel w/rubber rim w/metal seat platform & smaller wheels at the back, patent-dated 1889 (ILLUS.)... **1,100**

Record player, windup tin, "Bing Pygmy Phone," tin horn above the rectangular box holding the works, the base in green printed in red, white & black around the sides w/figures of the Seven Dwarfs, a black child, Little Red Riding Hood & the Big Bad Wolf, Bing (Germany), works well, early 20th c... **413**

Reindeer, wooden w/leather antlers, glass eyes, Albert Schoenhut, 7" sq. **600**

Rhino, wooden, Albert Schoenhut (ILLUS. w/lion) **550**

Rocking horse on platform, carved & painted wood, the crudely carved animal decorated w/dapple grey paint w/darkened brown varnish, glass eyes, worn original saddle & harness, raised on board cross braces & suspended from swinging iron bands above a trestle-form platform base w/old red paint, 19th c., 40" l., 34" h. **578**

Rocking horse on platform, carved & painted wood, the horse painted brown w/leather saddle & ears, glass eyes, on cast iron rockers & painted stand, 19th c., 37" l., 28" h. (paint wear, losses)................... **345**

Fine Victorian Platform Rocking Horse

Rocking horse on platform, painted wood, the rearing dapple grey horse w/painted mane & real hair long tail, leather bridle, leather saddle & stirrups, raised on a long angled spring-hinged tapering board on a slightly arched platform base, fine painted base decoration, England or America, late 19th c., minor paint loss, other minor losses, 47 " l., 43 1/4" h. (ILLUS.)....................................... **3,450**

Nice Rocking Horse on Platform

Rocking horse on platform, painted wood, well-carved animal w/a dapple grey coat, glass eyes, horse hair mane & tail, leather ears, red base w/yellow & black striping, remnants of leather saddle, some paint loss, late 19th - early 20th c., 38 3/4" l. (ILLUS.)... **460**

Rocking horse on rockers, carved & painted wood, the carved body w/old worn dapple grey paint raised on long, slender red rockers, old leather saddle & stirrups,

incomplete harness & traces of mane & tail, 19th c., 42 1/2" l. **440**

Rocking horse on rockers, carved & painted wood, the full-bodied primitive horse mounted on long curved rockers w/crossbars near the tips & a wooden platform under the horse, the horse in worn old dapple grey paint w/traces of red on the rockers, worn remains of saddle, missing mane & tail, rocker platform incomplete, 19th c., 45" l., 24 1/2" h............. **495**

Rocking horse on rockers, carved & painted wood, the well-carved horse in white w/original leather saddle & collar, long curved red-painted rockers, mid-19th c., 65" l., 34" h. (saddle slightly deteriorated).. **2,750**

Early Rocking Horse on Rockers

Rocking horse on rockers, painted wood, well-carved animal painted off-white w/leather saddle & reins, hair mane & tail, on long curved rocker base, repairs, minor losses, old repaint, 19th c., 48 1/2" l., 27 1/4" h. (ILLUS.)......................... **920**

Rocking horse on stationary base, painted wood, old red & brown repaint w/black trim, mane & tail replaced, harness replaced & saddle incomplete, paint wear, 19th c., 35" l...................................... **330**

Russian peasant woman, roly-poly, painted wood, Russia, pre-War, 3 1/2" h................. **22**

Safari cameraman, wooden, in cloth outfit w/small wooden camera around neck, Teddy Roosevelt "Adventure in Africa Series," 1910, Albert Schoenhut **1,500**

Sand toy, lithographed paper on wood, "Black Musicians," pasteboard figures on wood, three black minstrels, activated by shifting sands, glass enclosed case, Henry Menche patent, 1875 .... **2,500**

Sand toy, lithographed paper on wood, "General," animated General swings saber when sand-activated, German maker unknown, 1870s.. **750**

Sand toy, painted tin, hand-cranked wire chain belt carries six buckets that dump into bin cart which dumps when full, painted red & green, ca. 1930s, small.......... **242**

Various Santa Claus Rollies

Santa Clauses, Rolly Dollies, in various sizes, Albert Schoenhut, the set (ILLUS. above) **7,700**

Seesaw, painted tin, boy & girl wire frame mounted on a wooden base, 7" h. (minor paint loss on figures) **121**

Wooden Service Station Set

Service station, lithographed paper on wood, rectangular building in red & white w/black & green trim, w/chute opening, car rack & air pump all on rectangular base, ca. 1940, unmarked (ILLUS.) **180**

The American Girl Toy Sewing Machine

Sewing machine, "The American Girl," cast metal, black body w/nickel plate trim, National Sewing Machine Company, w/original box, very good condition, early 20th c. (ILLUS.) **138**

Sewing machine, "The Little Comfort Automatic Hand Sewing Machine," metal frame, chain-drive mechanism, original wooden box w/paper label, ca. 1897, machine 6 1/2" h., box 7 1/16 x 7 3/4", 3 3/l6" h. **518**

Sled, child's push-type, wood, painted black & red w/cherry red upholstery, late 19th c., 50" l. (some edge paint wear) **288**

Sled, child's size, decorated wood & iron, the board platform curved at each end & decorated w/original red & green w/yellow striping & black printed designs of looping scrolls at each end & a bird on branch in the center, raised on curved steel-tipped runners w/wooden braces, late 19th - early 20th c., 32" l. **220**

Sled, child's size, painted wood, long wooden platform w/rounded rear & incurved scalloped front end, on bentwood runners, the platform decorated w/a square lake & mountain landscape w/stenciled colored band, sprig bands & a starburst on the ends, 40" l. (damage, old repair) **385**

Sled, child's size, painted wood, the platform painted red w/a stag & foliage decoration, on metal runners, probably northern Europe, 19th c., 12 1/8 x 45" (paint wear, surface abrasion) **173**

Sleigh, lithographed paper on wood, "Santa Claus Sleigh," pulled by reindeer, R. Bliss, ca. 1890, 12 3/4" l. **2,500**

"Santa Pulling Sleigh"

Sleigh, lithographed paper on wood, "Santa Pulling Sleigh," sleigh in painted wood, Santa in composition w/cloth outfit, German maker unknown, 8" l., 7" h. (ILLUS.) **1,200**

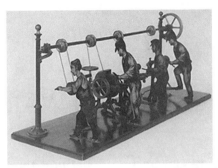

Unique Steam Engine Accessory

Steam engine accessory, lithographed & painted metal, a row of silhouette-cut lithographed hinged lathe workers standing in a line w/pulleys & crank shaft above supported between slender metal poles, all mounted on a thin rectangular wooden base, late 19th - early 20th c., 13" l. (ILLUS. above) **2,090**

Teddy Roosevelt, wooden, individual figure in cloth outfit, kepi, rifle, Teddy Roosevelt "Adventure in Africa Series," Albert Schoenhut, 1910 (ILLUS. w/set) **2,500**

Victorian Ten Pins Set

Ten pins set, turned wood, the tall tapering & pointed wood pins w/pointed tops, black trim bands, original turned balls, late 19th c., excellent condition, each pin 12" h., the set (ILLUS.) **220**

Theater, lithographed paper on wood, "Lime Kiln Club Theater," w/four minstrel players in box-like stage setting, R. Bliss, ca. 1870s **8,500**

Tiger, wooden, glass eyes, Style I, Albert Schoenhut, 1910, 7 1/2" l. **550**

Velocipede, carved & painted wood, a carved & white-painted leaping horse w/hair mane & tail, leather saddle, raised on three large wooden wheels w/crank shaft for front wheels through the horse's head, worn paint & split in horse's body, late 19th c. (ILLUS. left) **550**

Two Victorian Velocipedes

Velocipede, carved & painted wood, a dapple-painted leaping horse w/white hair mane & tail raised on three large wooden wheels w/a turn handle through the body, leather saddle & reins, turned wood hand grips, late 19th c. (ILLUS. right) **1,000**

Wagon, coaster-type, painted wood, rectangular platform painted red on mustard yellow wheels, black lettering on the sides "The Flyer," 19th c., 22" l., 8" h. (paint wear, repairs) **173**

Wagon, coaster-type, painted wood & steel, the low-sided rectangular bed w/old worn red & green paint w/"Pioneer" stenciled in small yellow letters, long hinged wooden handle w/steel grip & hinge, small wooden-spoked front wheels & larger rear wheels, late 19th - early 20th c., bed 34" l. **715**

Wagon, coaster-type, "Peerless No. 400," painted & decorated wood, the pine body w/stenciled & painted decoration, long handle, red disk wheels w/solid rubber tires, Paris Mfg. Co. (South Paris, Maine), early 20th c., body 36" l. **173**

Wagon, coaster-type, steel, "My Pal," oval shallow carriage on four metal wheels w/hard rubber rims & high half-round modernistic hub caps, long hinged handle w/grip, worn dark red paint on body & wheels, marked "Manufactured in U.S.A. Pines Winterfront Co. Chicago, Ill.," 23 1/2" l. (minor denting, rust spotting, scratches & soiling) **1,210**

Wagon driver, wooden, advertisement type, separate figures from wagon set, Albert Schoenhut, 1929-31, 7 1/2" h. **750**

Wolf, wooden, painted eyes, Albert Schoenhut, 7" l. **650**

Zebra, wooden, glass eyes, Albert Schoenhut, 8" l. **750**

Zebu, wooden, Teddy Roosevelt "Adventure in Africa Series," Albert Schoenhut, 1910, 7 1/2" h. **1,650**

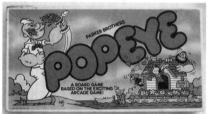

Chapter 12
BATTERY-OPS & WINDUPS

"Fishing Monkey on Whales"

Godzilla Battery-operated Toy

Battery-operated, "Action Walking Godzilla," walks & roars, Trendmasters, 1994 (ILLUS.) **$20-75**

Two Battery-operated Toys

Battery-operated, "Arthur A Go-Go," long-haired fellow playing drums, cloth & metal (ILLUS. left) **143**

Battery-operated, "Blasting Attack Godzilla," walks, fins light up, Bandai **150-200**

"Blushing Frankenstein"
Battery-operated Toy

Battery-operated, "Blushing Franken-stein," plastic figure w/shirt & pants, on tin base, Rosko, 1960s, 13" h. (ILLUS.).. **175-350**

Battery-operated, boat, outboard motor-boat, cruiser-type w/canvas top, front light, motor in box, Schuco Toy Co. (Nuremberg, Germany), motor in box **175**

Battery-operated Power Yacht

Battery-operated, boat, "Phillips 66" power yacht, hard plastic w/red upper decks & roof & white hull & trim, small Phillips sticker near the stern, w/original box w/lid forming marina dock, tear in box lid, takes 2 D-size batteries, ca. 1950s, 17 1/2" l., 5" h. (ILLUS.).................................. **209**

Battery-operated, bunny reading while standing & turning pages in book, w/magnet in hand, Japan, 1950s, 8" h............ **61**

Battery-operated, Charlie Weaver bartend-er, mixes drinks, smoke comes out his ears, mint in box.. **95**

Battery-operated, Dalek (Doctor Who) figure, boxed, Marx, 1965 .... **200-350**

Battery-operated, duck w/popcorn vendor **72**

Battery-operated, "DX Godzilla," moving version of 1992 Godzilla, Bandai **75-100**

E.T. Finger Light

Battery-operated, E.T., the Extra-Terrestri-al finger light, wearable, glows when pressed, Knickerbocker, 1982, 5" l. (ILLUS.).. **12-20**

Battery-operated, "Electro Submarino," Schuco, w/original instructions, in origi-nal rare box.. **250**

Battery-operated Fishing Bear

Battery-operated, "Fishing Bear," seated furry bear w/pink straw hat & blue & black checked outfit holding a fishing pole, w/original box w/small tear in front, Japan, ca. 1950s (ILLUS.) **330**

Battery-operated, flying saucer w/astronaut, Japan, 8" d... **209**

Battery-operated Fred Flintstone riding dinosaur, fur-coated tin, Marx, 1962, 22" l... **250-400**

Battery-operated, Fred Flintstones Bedrock Band, lithographed tin & plush & vinyl, ALPS, Japan, 1962 .... **300-450**

Battery-operated, Godzilla, boxed, Bandai Real Hobby Series..................... **325-375**

Battery-operated, Godzilla, rubber body, vinyl tail, walks & roars, Bandai, 1994, 11" h................................ **100-150**

Lost in Space Battery-operated Robot

Battery-operated, Lost in Space robot, plastic w/wired control box, Toy Island, 1998, 10 1/4" h. (ILLUS.)............................ **25-45**

Battery-operated, "Magic Man," smoking clown in tinplate & cloth, w/controller & packing, w/original box, Marsuan (Japan), ca. 1960... **316**

Battery-operated, "Mighty King Kong," tin, Marx **200-350**

Battery-operated, "Professor Owl," tinplate, w/two disks & instructions, original box, Etco (Japan) **431**

Battery-operated, "Rabbits Carriage (The)," plush grey mother rabbit in red checked skirt pushing a tin baby carriage w/little pink baby, w/original box, Japan, ca. 1950s, very good working order (slight fur discoloration).............................. **99**

Godzilla Battery-operated Toy

Battery-operated, Godzilla, tin w/wire remote control, Marusan, 1966, 11" h. (ILLUS.).................................. **1,000-3,500**

Battery-operated, Guitar playing Chimp, standing furry chimp at a microphone w/guitar, one leg raised on step, cloth & metal (ILLUS. right w/"Arthur a Go-Go) **121**

Battery-operated, "Hy-Que the Amazing Monkey," tinplate, rubber & cloth, original box, T.N. (Japan), ca. 1960 (box damaged)... **219**

Battery-operated, Lost in Space robot, plastic, made in various colors, Remco, 1966, 12" h., each...................... **400-800**

Rare Battery-Operated Santa Toy

Battery-operated, "Santa Claus Phone Bank," cloth & plastic Santa seated at a tin desk w/a phone, connected to a wall-style phone-bank, never used, w/original box, ca. 1950s (ILLUS.)................................. **605**

Battery-operated, Santa Claus sitting on a roof next to a chimney, holds gifts & drums, mint in box **150**

Battery-operated, Santa Claus walking & playing drums & cymbals **35**

Battery-operated, Scooby-Doo Mystery Machine, 'funny rumble action,' Boley, 1998 .... **18-25**

Shoe Shine Joe Battery-Operated Toy

Battery-operated, "Shoe Shine Joe," hair-covered monkey-like figure seated polishing shoe & smoking a pipe, mint in original box, Japan, ca. 1950s (ILLUS.)....... **220**

Battery-operated, "Snake Charmer," seated Indian man wearing turban & playing pipe w/jar & snake in front of him on the rectangular tin platform, cloth clothing, Line Mar, w/original box.................................. **403**

Battery-operated, "Squawky the Parrot," tinplate & cloth parrot on a perch, w/tag, packing & original box, Louis Marx, ca. 1960 (wear to toy, box damaged) **173**

Battery-operated, talking Dalek (Doctor Who), British import, Politoy Co., 1975, 7" h... **200-300**

Battery-operated, "Teddy the Artist," a plastic & cloth bear wearing a plaid jacket seated at a tin table & drawing, w/nine templates, two crayons, sketch book, packing & original box, Yonezawa (Japan), ca. 1960... **403**

Battery-operated, "Tric-Cycling Clown," tinplate, rubber, plastic & cloth, w/packing & original box, Cragston (Japan), ca. 1960 .... **374**

Walking Frankenstein Battery-operated Toy

Battery-operated, walking Frankenstein, tin, Marx, 1963, 12 1/2" h. (ILLUS.)... **1,000-1,600**

Battery-operated, "Walking Meltdown Godzilla," (Heat Walk Godzilla), glows, Bandai, 1995 .... **125-175**

Battery-operated, "Whistling Spooky Kooky Tree," lithographed tin, tree-trunk form w/plastic moving arms, leaves on top, moving eyes & mouth, Louis Marx, ca. 1960, 14 1/2" h. (some wear)........ **690**

Windy Elephant Battery-Operated Toy

Battery-operated, "Windy - Juggling Elephant," grey plush rearing elephant w/a tin umbrella above his trunk, atop a square tin base, T.N. (Japan), ca. 1950s, mint toy in original box (ILLUS.).................... **176**

Bullwinkle toy, windup tin & vinyl, Bullwinkle in car, KO, Japan, Flare Import, 1962 .... **300-500**
Bus, windup tin "Greyhound," dark blue horizontally ribbed body w/silver greyhound logo, movable front wheels, ca.1950s, Keystone Mfg. Co. (Boston, Massachusetts), 18" l. (some spotting, scratches & soiling) **358**
Captain Marvel toy, windup tin, Captain Marvel Lightning Race Car, Automatic Toy Co., 1947, 4" l. **100-200**
Casper the Friendly Ghost toy, windup tin, Line Mar, Japan, 1950s **70-450**
Cinderella toy, wind-up plastic, dancing w/the prince, Irwin Mfg. Box, Inc. **225**
Cinderella toy, windup tin "Cinderella Railcar," a handcar driven by the composition figures of Gus & Jaq, complete w/track, Well-Brimtoy, England, in original box **1,500**
"Circus Monkey," windup tin, tin monkey covered w/mohair & felt, Bestmaid, Japan, w/original box, ca. 1950s, 4 5/8" h. **110**

Creature from the Black Lagoon Windup Toy

Creature from the Black Lagoon, windup tin, Robot House, 1992, 9" h. (ILLUS.).... **85-115**
Creature from the Black Lagoon walking toy, windup plastic w/red winder, Hong Kong, 3" h. **15-25**

Dick Tracy Police Station Toy

Dick Tracy toy, windup tin, Dick Tracy Police Station w/car, Marx, 1950s, 3 1/2 x 8" (ILLUS.) **300-600**

Disneyland toy, Express train set, windup tin, Marx, set, in original box **500**
Donald Duck & Goofy toy, windup tin, Donald & Goofy duet, 1946, Marx, 10 1/4" h., very good (Goofy missing one ear)... **556**
Donald Duck & Nephews toy, windup tin, "Marching Soldiers," a fat Donald on two small wheels carrying a rubber rifle over his shoulder & towing in a row his three nephews each w/a rubber rifle & on two small wheels, Line Mar, 1950s, 11 1/2" l. (scratches)... **374**
Donald Duck toy, friction-type, "Disney Flivver" car, features a long-necked Donald Duck driver in a yellow convertible lithographed w/Mickey Mouse, Thumper, Dopey & others **605**
Donald Duck toy, friction-type, tinplate rocket, features Donald steering a friction-drive wheeled missile, w/original box, 7" l. **775**
Donald Duck toy, keywind tinplate, waddling figure covered in plush sailor suit w/bobbing head, Line Mar, Japan, w/original box, 6" h. **660**
Donald Duck toy, windup tin, Donald on motorcycle, Line Mar, Walt Disney Productions, colorful, bright, clean, 3 1/2" long **220**
E.T., windup walker, glowing heart, carded, LJN, 1982... **10-15**
E.T., The Extra-Terrestrial, windup walker, dressed in scarf, robe or dress & hat, LJN, 1982, each... **10-15**

"Fishing Monkey on Whales"

"Fishing Monkey on Whales," windup tin, TPS (ILLUS.).. **440**
Flintstone toy, windup tin, Barney Rubble hops when wound, Marx, early 1960s, 3 1/2" h. **100-180**
Flintstone toy, windup tin, Dino hops when wound, Marx, early 1960s, 3 1/2" h. **100-180**
Flintstone toy, windup tin, Fred hops when wound, Marx, early 1960s, 3 1/2" h. **100-180**

Fred & Dino Windup Toy

Flintstone toy, windup tin w/vinyl head, Fred rides Dino, Marx, 1962, 5 1/4" h. (ILLUS.) **155-225**

Flintstones toy, windup plastic, Bedrock Express, train & track through Bedrock, Marx, 1962.. **175-250**

Frankenstein toy, windup tin, Marx, 1960, 6" h.. **150-350**

Frankenstein toy, windup tin, Robot House, 1991, 9" h...................................... **85-115**

Godzilla toy, windup plastic, blue, walker, Go series, Bandai, 1994................................. **8-15**

Godzilla toy, windup tin, brown version, walks, swings arms, boxed, Billiken, 1990s, 7" h.. **75-125**

Godzilla toy, windup tin, Godzilla w/Mothra at his tail, Billiken, 1990s **100-150**

Godzilla toy, windup tin, green version, walks, swings arms, boxed, Billiken, 1990s, 7" h.. **100-150**

Godzilla toy, windup walker, Japan, 1970s?, 2" h. **12-20**

Trendmasters Godzilla Toy

Godzilla toy, windup walker, Trendmasters, 1994 (ILLUS.) **4-8**

Goofy toy, windup plastic, Goofy being bitten by a chipmunk, Marx, very good.............. **110**

Goofy toy, windup plastic, Goofy in a convertible automobile, 5" l. **75**

Goofy toy, windup plastic, standing figure of Goofy w/a little dog biting the seat of the pants, Marx **105**

Goofy toy, windup tin, Goofy w/twirling tail, brightly lithographed figure hobbles & hops in circles when wound, w/original lithographed box, Line Mar, Japan, 5 1/2" h. **695**

Gremlins toy, windup, Gizmo, LJN, 1984 ..... **12-30**

Gremlins toy, windup, Stripe on stool, smoking cigar, LJN, 1984, 3 3/4" h............. **12-30**

Hopalong Cassidy on Topper, windup tin, rocking base motion, colorfully lithographed, Marx, 1946, 11" l. **450-750**

Howdy Doody toy, windup tin, Howdy w/banjo, Marx, early 1950s, 5" h. **250-500**

Huckleberry Hound Toy

Huckleberry Hound toy, windup tin, Huckleberry walker w/large feet, blue body w/pink snout & yellow hat, Line Mar, ca. 1960, 3 3/4" h. (ILLUS.)................................ **303**

Jetsons toy, windup tin, hopping Astro, Marx - Line Mar, early 1960s, 4" h. **100-200**

Jetsons toy, windup tin, hopping George, Marx - Line Mar, early 1960s, 4" h. **100-200**

Jiminy Cricket (from Pinocchio) toy, windup tin, a smiling Jiminy Cricket wearing a black & white tuxedo w/blue top hat bobs up & down when wound, Line Mar, ca. 1960, 6" h. **400**

King Kong Toy

King Kong, windup plastic, walks, red winder, 3 1/2" h. (ILLUS.) **15-25**

Mary Poppins Whirling Toy

Lost in Space robot, windup plastic, Masu-
daya, 1985, 4" h. **25-40**

Ludwig Von Drake toy, friction-type, Ludwig seated on an open car carriage, Marx **300**

Ludwig Von Drake toy, windup tin walker,
figure wearing cap, jacket & checked
vest & carrying a cane, Line Mar,
Japan, ca. 1961 .... **220**

Mary Poppins toy, windup plastic, figure
holding umbrella, whirling action, w/origi-
nal box, ca. 1964, Marx (ILLUS. above) **220**

Mickey Mouse toy, battery-operated,
"Loop the Loop," mint in box **155**

Mickey Mouse toy, battery-operated, Mickey the drummer, lighted eyes, Line Mar **375**

Mickey Mouse toy, lithographed tin, friction-type, Mickey on motorcycle, very
good, Line Mar **175**

Mickey Mouse toy, windup tin, "Mickey Musician," standing Mickey playing the xylophone, Line Mar, working, complete
w/box, 7" h. (chips to xylophone, box lid
torn at corners & top) **748**

Mickey Mouse toy, windup tin, Mickey
w/twirling tail, very good, Line Mar **230**

Minnie Mouse toy, mechanical, Minnie
dressed in white go-go boots, black fish-
net hose, gold miniskirt & white lace
gloves, human-like hair in ponytail, large
head compared to body, head turns as
she dances, ... **485**

Minnie Mouse toy, windup tin, "Minnie
Mouse Knitter," Line Mar, w/box **1,000**

Mummy (The) toy, windup tin, Robot
House, 1992, 9" h. **85-115**

Phantom of the Opera toy, windup nodder,
Japan, 1963 .... **75-100**

Pink Panther toy, windup plastic walker,
3" h. **12-20**

Pinocchio toy, battery-operated, "Pinocchio Playing Xylophone," Rosko, w/box **275**

Planet of the Apes toy, windup, Galen or
Zaius, AHI, 1974, each **50-90**

Pluto toy, friction-type, Pluto driving a four-
wheel car w/lever action handlebars,
Marx, Japan, 6" l. **395**

Pluto on Tricycle Toy

Pluto toy, windup celluloid & tin, Pluto on
tricycle, celluloid Pluto on tin tricycle
w/rear bell, colorful, Line Mar, Japan
(ILLUS.) **413**

Pluto toy, windup plastic, Pluto w/twirling
tail, good, Walt Disney Productions **55**

Pluto toy, windup tin & celluloid, celluloid
Pluto performing on a high bar w/"Gym
Toy" pennant, Line Mar, in original box,
13" h. **505**

Pluto toy, windup tin, "Drum Major," Line Mar, Japan, 5 1/2" h. **525**

Pluto toy, windup tin, "Roll-Over Pluto," when wound the lithographed pooch bounds forward & rolls over, w/original ears, Marx, w/original box, 8" l. **272**

Popeye toy, windup tin, color lithographed, Popeye roller skater, w/cloth pants, Line Mar, ca. 1950s, very good condition, 6 3/4" h. **935**

Popeye on Tricycle Toy

Popeye toy, windup tin, Popeye riding a tricycle w/bell on the back, Line Mar, Japan (ILLUS.) **495**

Popeye Speedboat Toy

Popeye toy, windup tin, Popeye Tin Speedboat, special edition, Richard Johnson Toys, 1996, w/box (ILLUS.) **25-40**

Attacking Martian Robot

Robot, battery-operated, "Attacking Martian," lithographed tin, black body & red feet w/printed controls on front, ca. 1950s, excellent condition, 11 3/4" h. (ILLUS.) **148**

Rare Mechanized Robot Toy

Robot, battery-operated, "Mechanized Robot," lithographed tin w/black body, red arms & feet & domed clear plastic over the head, T.N. (Japan), ca. 1950s, near mint w/damaged box, robot 13" h. (ILLUS.) **1,843**

Robot, battery-operated, "Mr. Atom - The Electronic Walking Robot," angular silver & red body, excellent condition w/original box, ca. 1950s **825**

Cragston's Mr. Robot Toy

Robot, battery-operated, "Mr. Robot," lithographed tin w/clear plastic dome head w/red bubbles, red body w/black arms & controls on front, Cragston (Japan), near mint w/original cardboard headguard, original box w/minor damage, ca. 1950s (ILLUS.) **1,155**

Robot, battery-operated, Piston robot, see-through body w/lighted pistons, realistic sounds, mint in box **145**

Robot, battery-operated, "Roto-Robot," open door, shooting & blinking guns, rotating body, walks, mint in box **145**

"Spaceman Robot"

Robot, battery-operated, "Spaceman Robot," (TV), 1960s (ILLUS.) **330**

TV Robot Toy

Robot, battery-operated, "TV Robot," the squared torso in the form of a TV screen, battery compartment clean, 11 1/2" h. (ILLUS.) **248**

Robot, "Mego Man," windup tin, Sy, Japan, 7" l. (windup not working) **193**

"Planet Robot"

Robot, windup tin, "Planet Robot," black, red & silver, together w/original box (ILLUS.) **358**

Line Mar Windup Robot

Robot, windup tin, silver w/red & black trim, Line Mar, 6" h. (ILLUS.) **330**

Rodeo Joe Windup Toy

"Rodeo Joe," windup tin, color lithographed, cowboy driving a jalopy, Unique Art Mfg. Co. (New York, New York), complete, very good condition (ILLUS.) **187**

Friction Toy Animal Satellite

Satellite, friction-type, lithographed tin, a spherical form in grey w/red trim & a design of a dog on the side, a little dog pops out of the top, marked "MS-7" on side, Japan, 1950s, excellent condition, 4 1/4" d. (ILLUS.) **165**

Windup Plastic Smurf Walking Toy

Smurfs toy, windup plastic Smurf walker, Wallace Berry Co., 1980, 3" h. (ILLUS.) **8-12**

Gargamel Plastic Walker Toy

Smurfs toy, windup plastic, Gargamel walker, Galoob, 1982, 3 3/4" h. (ILLUS.) **8-12**

Windup Plastic Smurfette Walker Toy

Smurfs toy, windup plastic walking Smurfette, 3" h. (ILLUS.) **8-12**

Tom Corbet Windup Spaceship

Superman toy, windup tin, from Tim Burton's film, Billiken, 1989 .... **50-75**

Superman toy, windup tin Superman Rollover Airplane, bronze tone, Marx, 1940s, 6 1/2" l. **750-1,500**

Superman toy, windup tin, Superman Rollover Airplane, red or blue, Marx, 1940s, 6 1/2" l., each **1,200-2,000**

Superman toy, windup tin, Superman Turnover Tank, Marx, 3 x 4" **400-800**

Tom Corbet Space Cadet toy, windup tin, spaceship on wheels, dark blue w/red, yellow & white trim, L. Marx, 1950s, missing tail fin (ILLUS. above) **253**

Tom Corbett toy, windup tin, "Tom Corbett Space Cadet Polaris Rocket," Marx, 1952, 12 1/2" h. **300-650**

Tom Corbett toy, windup tin, "Tom Corbett Space Cadet Sparkling Space Ship" Marx, 1950s **350-700**

Windup Celluloid Occupied Japan Toy

Windup celluloid & tin traveling boy, celluloid figure of a boy w/pink cap & blue jacket w/hinged arms & legs on a crankshaft extending from a rectangular tin suitcase, made in Occupied Japan, ca. 1950, excellent working condition, 4" h. (ILLUS.) **138**

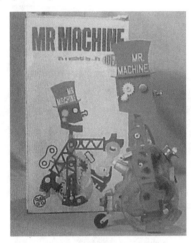

Mr. Machine Windup Toy

Windup plastic "Mr. Machine," flattened plastic sections w/hinged head & arms, on mechanized base, red & yellow, w/original box, 1960s, excellent working condition, Ideal (ILLUS.) **413**

Wolfman Toy

Wolfman, windup tin, Robot House, 1992, 9" h. (ILLUS.) **85-115**

Zorro toy, windup tin, masked figure of Zorro riding his horse, Marx, w/original box **225**

Chapter 13
CHARACTER TOYS

Bullwinkle Stamp Pad Toy

Alice Cooper action figure, plastic, Alice w/14-piece diorama, Todd McFarlane, 2000, 6" h. **$14-20**

Alice Cooper Christmas Ornament

Alice Cooper Christmas ornament, shows Alice in top hat w/name, Santa's Rockshop, 1990s, 3" d. (ILLUS.).................. **8-12**

Alice Cooper Model Kit

Alice Cooper model kit, resin, unlicensed, unmarked, 1990s, box 10 1/2" l. (ILLUS.)... **30-50**

Alice Cooper toy, diecast metal car, Trash
Mobile, limited edition, Racing Champi-
ons, 1999 .... **8-15**

Alice Cooper Plush Bear

Alice Cooper toy, plush bear, white w/Alice
eye make-up & T-shirt, Steven Smith,
2000, 10" h. (ILLUS.) **20-25**

Annie Oakley badge, Post cereal premium **18**

Annie Oakley lunch box & thermos, steel,
Aladdin Industries, 1955, the set **160**

*Annie Oakley Neckerchief
& Hanky Embroidery Set*

**Annie Oakley Neckerchief & Hanky Em-
broidery Set,** ST, 1955 (ILLUS.) **60-75**

Archie & friends coloring book, The
Archies, Whitman, No. 1135 .... **12-20**

Annie Oakley & horse figures, hard
plastic, Hartland, pr. **275**

Archie & friends costume, Archie, cloth
w/plastic string mask, Ben Cooper, 1969 .... **30-70**

Archie Doll by Marx

Archie & friends doll, Archie, plastic, carded w/removable clothes, Marx, 1976
(ILLUS.) **40-75**

Archie & friends doll, Betty, plastic w/re-
movable clothes, carded, Marx, 1976 .... **40-75**

Jughead Doll by Marx

Archie & friends doll, Jughead, plastic
w/removable clothes, carded, Marx,
1976 (ILLUS.) **40-75**

Archie & friends doll, Sabrina, plastic
w/removable clothes, carded, Marx,
1977 .... **45-85**

Veronica Doll by Marx

Archie & friends doll, Veronica, plastic
w/removable clothes, carded, Marx,
1977 (ILLUS.) **40-75**

Archie & friends lunch box & thermos,
The Archies, steel box & plastic thermos,
Aladdin, 1969 .... **75-125**

Archie & friends paper dolls, Whitman,
1969, the set... **25-50**

Austin Powers Action Figure

Austin Powers action figure, plastic, "Do I
make you horny baby, do I?," McFarlane,
1999, carded, 6" h. (ILLUS.) **6-12**

The Archies Cardboard Record

Archie & friends phonograph record,
cardboard, "The Archies," cereal box cut-
out, 33 1/3 rpm, 1970s (ILLUS.) **15-35**

Austin Powers Nodder Figure

Austin Powers figure, plastic, nodder-
type, "Wacky Wobbler," Funko, 1998-99,
7 1/2" h. (ILLUS.) **8-15**

Austin Powers Silly Slammer Toy

Austin Powers toy, Silly Slammer, plush bean bag bust of Austin, says various phrases, GGI, 1999, 5 1/2" h. (ILLUS.) **5-8**

Baby Huey puppet, hand-type, cloth body, vinyl head, Gund **15-35**

Banana Splits coloring book, "Hanna Barbera's Banana Splits," Whitman, 1960s **20-50**

Banana Splits costume, child's, plastic mask of any character, cloth costume shows the group, Ben Cooper, 1968, each **75-150**

Banana Splits Character Cup

Banana Splits cup, plastic, figural face of any one of four characters, painted, vitamin promo, F&F Plastics, 1969, 3 1/4" h., each (ILLUS. of one) **20-35**

Banana Splits figure, articulated plastic, one of any four, Sutton & Sons, 1971, bagged, 7" h., each **50-120**

Banana Splits figure, plush, any of the four characters, Sutton & Sons, w/string tag, 1970, each **60-80**

Banana Splits harmonica, figural yellow plastic banana, carded, 1973, 6" l. **15-25**

Banana Splits lunch kit, white vinyl w/color graphics of the band, King Seeley Thermos, 1969 .... **300-450**

Banana Splits lunch kit & thermos, steel & glass, 1969 .... **75-125**

Banana Splits model kit, "Banana Buggy," yellow plastic, 1/25 scale, Aurora, 1969 .... **250-400**

Banana Splits paint-by-number set, Hasbro, 1969 .... **50-100**

Banana Splits pennant, felt, Banana Splits & other Hanna Barbera characters **50-70**

Banana Splits puppet, soft plastic, any of the four characters, premium from inside Kellogg's cereal, 1968, 8 x 9", each **15-25**

Banana Splits ring, adjustable band, gold w/round picture of the group under plastic **5-8**

Banana Splits ring, silver-colored metal, figural faces of each character, adjustable band, 1990s, each **3-5**

Banana Splits tambourine, plastic & cardboard w/graphic design in the center, 1973 .... **30-40**

Banana Splits toy, plastic, Banana Band, toy instruments, Larami, 1973 .... **35-65**

Banana Splits toy, "Talking Telephone," Hasbro, 1969 .... **150-250**

Banana Splits View-Master reel packet, set of three, No. B 502, the set **12-20**

Barney Rubble Friction Toy

Barney Rubble toy, "Rubble's Wreck from The Flintstones," friction action, Marx, 1960s, mint w/original box (ILLUS.) **770**

Bat Masterson wallet, Croyder, 1950s, unused, mint in box **99**

Batgirl Lunchbox

Batgirl lunchbox, steel, pictures Batgirl, Flash & Green Arrow on one side above "Super Friends," pink border, Aladdin, 1976 (ILLUS.) **40-80**

Rare Batgirl & Robin Tumbler

Batgirl & Robin tumbler, glass w/red, blue, yellow & black decoration, Pepsi premium, 1977 (ILLUS.) **1,792**

Batman action figure, Mego Comic Action Heroes, 1975, 3" h. **50-275**

Batman costume, plastic cowl w/cape, Ideal, 1965 .... **45-90**

Batman costume, suit, cape & plastic string mask, Ben Cooper, 1965 .... **40-80**

Batman figure, Mego, 1974, 12" h. **75-175**

Batman paint-by-number book, Whitman, 1966 .... **30-70**

Batman playset, plastic, Batman, Robin & others in display box, Ideal, 1966, box 14 x 22" **600-1,200**

Batman puppet, soft vinyl head, plastic body, Batman or Robin, Ideal, mid-1960s, each **50-100**

Batman toy, Flying Copter, remote-controlled plastic helicopter, Batman decals, Remco, 1966, 12" l. **60-125**

Batman toy set, slot car set w/Batmobile, Magicar, England, 1966 .... **200-400**

Batman toy set, "Switch 'N' Go Set," w/a 9" l. plastic three-speed Batmobile, track, figures, etc., Mattel, 1966, the set **250-500**

Batman toy set, Thingmaker mold set, Mattel, 1960s, the set **60-120**

Batman utility belt, yellow plastic w/gadgets attached, Ideal, 1966 .... **400-1,000**

Beany Talking Plush Doll

Beany (Beany & Cecil) doll, plush talking-type, vinyl head, hands & shoes, Mattel, 1963, 17" h. (ILLUS.) **80-300**

Beany & Cecil carrying case, round vinyl w/strap handle, 1960s, 9" d. **45-75**

Beany & Cecil coloring book, Whitman, 1960s **30-60**

Beany & Cecil costume, Cecil, Ben Cooper, 1960s **75-150**

Beany & Cecil lunch kit & thermos, vinyl w/metal thermos, King Seeley Thermos, 1963 .... **350-500**

Beany & Cecil record player, Beany & Cecil & their pals, nice graphics on case, Vanity Fair, 1961 .... **150-300**

Beany & Cecil toy, boat, plastic & wood Leakin' Lena, Irwin, 1962 .... **100-200**

Beany & Cecil toy, Colorforms, Beany & Cecil Cartoon Kit, early 1960s **60-120**

Beany-Copter Cap

Beany & Cecil toy, plastic, Beany-Copter, red cap w/rotating blue propeller, Mattel, 1961 (ILLUS.) **125-200**

Beatles action figure, Yellow Submarine Beatles, w/accessories, McFarlane, 1999, 8" h., each **6-12**

Beatles bubble bath container, plastic, Paul or Ringo, Soaky, Colgate Palmolive, 1965, each **100-250**

Beatles coloring book, Saalfield, 1964 ...... **50-100**

Beatles doll, vinyl w/large head & rooted hair, any of the four, w/instruments, Remco, each **100-250**

Beatles model kit, plastic, John or George, Revell, 1965, each **100-250**

Ringo Revell Model Kit

Beatles model kit, plastic, Paul or Ringo, Revell, 1965, each (ILLUS. of Ringo).... **100-200**

Benny the Ball Plush Toy

Benny the Ball (Top Cat) toy, plush w/vinyl head, Ideal, 1962, 5" h. (ILLUS.) **25-60**

Rare Betty Tumbler

Betty (from Archie comic) tumbler, glass w/picture of Betty in blue, yellow & flesh-tone, Pepsi premium, ca. 1970s (ILLUS.) **807**

Billy Baloney (Pee-Wee Herman) doll, Matchbox, 1988, 18" h. **50-80**

Bingo Rubber Figure

Bingo (Banana Splits) figure, rubber, orange w/painted highlights, hanger string, 1968, 4 1/2" l. (ILLUS.) **60-120**

Bonanza model kit, Revell, 1965, assembled **35-40**

Bonanza Model Kit

Bonanza model kit, Revell, 1965, unused (ILLUS.) **75-125**

Boo Boo Bear toy, plush, Knickerbocker, 1960s, 9 1/2" h. **50-85**

Brave Eagle & horse figures, hard plastic, Hartland, pr. **250**

Bret Maverick figure, plastic, Hartland, 1958, w/box & tag **350-450**

Bret Maverick Hartland Figure

Bret Maverick figure, plastic, Hartland, 1958, without box (ILLUS.) **150-200**

Bret Maverick Hartland Figure, Hartland, 1958, w/box, no tag **350-400**

Bugs Bunny alarm clock, battery-operated, Janex, 1974 .... **40-80**

Bugs Bunny bank, metal, Bugs w/barrel on base, 1940s, 5 1/2" h. **75-150**

Bugs Bunny bank, plastic, Bugs on carrot box, Dakin, 1971 .... **30-50**

Bugs Bunny Soaky Container

Bugs Bunny bubble bath bottle, figural plastic Bugs, Soaky, Colgate-Palmolive, 1960s, 10" h. (ILLUS.) **15-40**

Bugs Bunny Clothes Rack

Bugs Bunny clothes rack, painted wood, flat figure of Bugs w/pegs, reads "Hang It Up, Doc!," on base, Brachs, 1991, 54" h. (ILLUS.) **35-55**

Bugs Bunny comic book, Bugs Bunny No. 46, Dell, 1956 .... **2-5**

Bugs Bunny comic book, Looney Tunes No. 157, Bugs paints Elmer on cover, Dell, 1954 .... **2-8**

Bugs Bunny Vinyl Figure

Bugs Bunny figure, articulated vinyl, Dakin, 1971, 10 1/2" h. (ILLUS.) **15-30**

Bugs Bunny figure, bendable, Applause, 1980s, 4" l. **5-12**

Bugs Bunny figure, talking-type, plastic w/pull string, "Chatter Chum," Mattel, 1982 .... **20-40**

Bugs Bunny Pez dispenser, plastic, no feet **15-20**

Talking Bugs Bunny Doll

Bugs Bunny doll, talking-type, plush w/rubber mask face & hands, Mattel, 1971, 22" h. (ILLUS.) **35-65**

Bugs Bunny Pez Dispenser

Bugs Bunny Pez dispenser, plastic, yellow body w/feet, 1978, 5" h. (ILLUS.) **1-4**

Bugs Bunny puppet, hand-type, cloth
w/rubber head, Zany, 1940s 50-100

Bugs Bunny puppet, plush w/pull string,
Talking Bugs Bunny, Mattel, 1962, 13" h. ... 35-75

Bugs Bunny ring, plastic flicker-type, Ar-
by's premium, 1987 20-35

Bugs Bunny toy, Magic Slate, Golden,
1987 5-9

Bugs Bunny wrist watch, Lafayette, 1978... 30-60

Bullet (Roy Rogers' dog) figure,
molded plastic, Hartland, 1950s 65

Bullwinkle & friends bank, ceramic Bull-
winkle, 1960s, 6" h. 200-300

Bullwinkle & friends bank, ceramic
Mr. Peabody, 1960s, 6" h. 300-400

Bullwinkle & friends bank, plastic
Bullwinkle, Play Pal, 1972, 11 1/2" h. 45-75

Bullwinkle & friends bank, plastic Rocky
w/tree, Play Pal, 1973 45-75

Bullwinkle Soaky Container

Bullwinkle & friends bubble bath bottle,
plastic, figural Bullwinkle, Soaky, Colgate-Palmolive, 1960s, 11" h. (ILLUS.) 30-60

Rocky the Squirrel Soaky Container

Bullwinkle & friends bubble bath bottle,
plastic, figural Rocky, Soaky, Colgate-
Palmolive, 1960s, 9" h. (ILLUS.) 30-60

Bullwinkle & friends coloring book, Bullwinkle the Moose, Whitman, 1960 25-50

Bullwinkle & friends coloring book,
Rocky & Bullwinkle, Watkins-Strathmore,
1962 25-45

Bullwinkle & friends coloring book,
Rocky the Flying Squirrel, Whitman,
1960 25-50

Bullwinkle & friends doll, Bullwinkle, talking-type, cloth & vinyl w/pull string, Mat-
tel, 1971, 11" h. 100-200

Bullwinkle & friends figure, bendable
Boris, Wham-O, 1972, 3 1/2" h. 15-30

Bendable Bullwinkle Figure

Bullwinkle & friends figure, bendable Bullwinkle w/letter sweater, Jesco, 1985, on
9" card (ILLUS.) 12-20

Bullwinkle & friends figure, bendable Bullwinkle, Wham-O, 1972, 6" h. 15-30

Bullwinkle & friends figure, bendable Mr.
Peabody, Jesco, 1985, carded, 3 1/2" h. 12-20

Mr. Peabody Bendable Figure

Bullwinkle & friends figure, bendable Mr. Peabody, Wham-O, 1972, on card, 4" h. (ILLUS.) **20-40**

Natasha Bendable Figure

Bullwinkle & friends figure, bendable Natasha, 'fat' version, Jesco, on card, 1980s, 5 1/2" h. (ILLUS.) **12-20**

Bullwinkle & friends figure, bendable Natasha, 'thin' version, Wham-O, 1972, 3" h. **15-30**

Bendable Rocky Figure

Bullwinkle & friends figure, bendable Rocky, Wham-O, 1972, 3" h. (ILLUS.) **15-30**

Bullwinkle & Rocky Rubber Figures

Bullwinkle & friends figure, Bullwinkle, flat rubber, cereal premium, 1960s, 2" h. (ILLUS. right) **12-20**

Bullwinkle & friends figure, Rocky, flat rubber, cereal premium, 1960s, 2" h. (ILLUS. left with Bullwinkle) **12-20**

Bullwinkle & friends lunch box, steel box, Bullwinkle & Rocky, Universal, 1962 ..... **500-750**

Bullwinkle & friends lunch kit & thermos, blue vinyl w/metal bottle, Bullwinkle, King Seeley Thermos, 1963 .... **500-750**

Bullwinkle & friends lunch kit & thermos, yellow vinyl w/generic metal bottle, Bullwinkle, King Seeley Thermos, 1963 ...... **300-500**

Bullwinkle & friends Pez dispenser, plastic, Bullwinkle, brown & yellow, no feet **200-250**

Bullwinkle & friends thermos bottle, metal, Bullwinkle & Rocky, Universal, 1962 .... **150-200**

Bullwinkle Stamp Pad Toy

Bullwinkle & friends toy, "Bullwinkle's Stamp Pad - 4 Colors," picture of Bullwinkle, Larami, 1970 (ILLUS.) **20-35**

Bullwinkle & friends toy, Colorforms, Bullwinkle Cartoon Kit, 1962 .... **50-125**

Bullwinkle & friends toy, Magic Slate, 1963 .... **40-65**

Bullwinkle & friends View-Master reels, Bullwinkle, three-reel set, No. 515 .... **12-20**

Captain Marvel paint set, w/five chalkware figures, 1940s **300-600**

Fine Captain Marvel Club Button

Captain Marvel pinback button, "Captain Marvel Club - Shazam," lithographed metal, half-length portrait of Captain Marvel in the center, wording around border, in red, white & blue, pristine condition, 7/8" d. (ILLUS.) **99**

**Casper the Friendly Ghost bubble bath
bottle,** plastic, figural Casper, Soaky,
Colgate-Palmolive, 1960s **35-50**

**Casper the Friendly Ghost bubble bath
bottle,** plastic, figural Wendy, Soaky,
Colgate-Palmolive, 1960s **40-60**

Casper the Friendly Ghost costume,
Casper, Collegeville, 1960s **25-50**

Casper the Friendly Ghost costume, Herman or Katnip, Collegeville, 1960s, each .. **30-70**

Casper the Friendly Ghost doll, Casper
holding a puppy, 8" h. **45-75**

Casper the Friendly Ghost doll, cloth
body, Mattel, 1960s, 15" h. **50-85**

Casper the Ghost Talking Doll

Casper the Friendly Ghost doll, talking-
type, terry cloth w/plastic face, pull string,
Mattel, 1961, 15" h. (ILLUS.) **45-125**

Casper the Friendly Ghost figure, Casper
on a stack of books, Tyco, 1994, 3" h. **1-4**

Casper the Friendly Ghost lamp, figural
Casper, Archlamp, 1950, 17" h. **75-95**

Casper the Friendly Ghost lunch box,
blue vinyl, color scene of Casper, Wendy
& other ghosts near haunted house, King
Seeley Thermos, 1966.......................... **300-500**

**Casper the Friendly Ghost Pez dispens-
er,** plastic, no feet **120-200**

Casper the Friendly Ghost puppet,
Casper, cloth body, plastic head, Gund,
1960s, 8" h... **25-50**

Casper the Friendly Ghost puppet, hand-
type, Katnip, cloth body w/soft vinyl head,
Gund, 1960s **15-40**

Spooky Ghost Hand Puppet

Casper the Friendly Ghost puppet, hand-
type, Spooky w/top hat, cloth body, vinyl
head, Gund, 1962, 11" h. (ILLUS.) **25-50**

Wendy Witch Hand Puppet

Casper the Friendly Ghost puppet, hand-
type, Wendy, cloth body, vinyl head,
Gund, 1960s, 9 1/2" h. (ILLUS.)................. **25-50**

Casper the Friendly Ghost squeak toy,
rubber Casper w/logo, Sutton & Sons,
1972... **25-50**

Casper Thermos Bottle

Casper the Friendly Ghost thermos bottle, orange steel w/haunted house scene, goes w/blue vinyl lunch box, King Seeley Thermos, 1966 (ILLUS.) **50-75**

Casper the Friendly Ghost toy, Casper jack-in-the-box, metal box, plays theme song, Mattel, 1960 .... **40-70**

Casper the Friendly Ghost toy, "Casper the Talking Ghost," plush w/hard plastic face & talking mechanism, Mattel, 1960s, works, in original box, 14" h. **193**

Casper the Friendly Ghost toy, top, blue w/Casper inside, 1960s **30-45**

Casper the Friendly Ghost View-Master reels, series of three reels, 1960s, the set **5-12**

Cecil Plush Talking Doll

Cecil (Beany & Cecil) doll, plush talking-type, plastic eyes, Mattel, 1963 (ILLUS.) **75-250**

Cecil Soap Container

Cecil (Beany & Cecil) soap container, figural plastic Cecil head & neck, Roclar Distributors, late 1950s - early 1960s, 8" h. (ILLUS.) **30-60**

Cecil Jack-in-the-Box Toy

Cecil (Beany & Cecile) toy, metal & cloth musical jack-in-the-box, Mattel, 1961 (ILLUS.) **200-300**

Charlie's Angels doll, Farrah Fawcett, Mattel, 1977, 12" h. **50-100**

Charlie's Angels Dolls

Charlie's Angels doll, Jill, Hasbro, 1977, 8" h. (ILLUS.) **35-75**

Charlie's Angels doll, Kelly, Hasbro, 1977, 8" h. (ILLUS.) **35-70**

Charlie's Angels doll, Kris, Hasbro, 1977, 8" h. **35-70**

Charlie's Angels doll, Sabrina, Hasbro, 1977, 8" h. (ILLUS.) **40-85**

Farrah's Glamour Center Toy

Charlie's Angels toy, plastic styling head, "Farrah's Glamour Center," Mego, 1977, 10" h. (ILLUS.)... **50-100**

Mego Cher Doll

Cher doll, articulated plastic, original pink dress, Mego, 1976, 12" h. (ILLUS.) **40-80**

Cindy Bear Push Puppet

Cindy Bear (Yogi Bear's girlfriend) puppet, push-type, plastic, on round base, Kohner, 1960s, 4" h. (ILLUS.) **15-35**

Col. Ronald Mackenzie & horse, hard plastic, black rearing horse, Hartland, mint w/original hang tag............................... **1,950**

Daffy Duck bank, metal, Daffy w/barrel on base, 1940s, 5 1/2" h. **75-150**

Daffy Duck figure, bendable Daffy, Applause, 1980s, 4" h...................................... **12-20**

Daffy Duck Vinyl Figure

Daffy Duck figure, hollow vinyl, articulated Daffy, Dakin, 1968, 8 1/2" h. (ILLUS.)........ **15-35**

Daffy Duck Pez dispenser, no feet, removable eyes **10-15**

Daffy Duck Pez dispenser, w/feet **1-4**

Daffy Duck ring, plastic flicker-type, Arby's premium, 1987 .... **20-35**

Daffy Duck tumbler, glass w/picture of Daffy, Pepsi series, 1973, 6 1/2" h. **8-15**

Dale Evans wristwatch **140**

Dennis the Menace book, "Babysitter's Guide," paperback, 1954 .... **15**

Dick Tracy Model

Dick Tracy model kit, plastic, Dick Tracy hanging on fire escape firing his gun, 1/16 scale, Aurora, painted by Even Stuart, 1968 (ILLUS.) **300-600**

Dick Tracy toy, squad car, friction-type, blue, machine gun in window, 1950s, Marx, 6 1/2" l. **150**

Dick Tracy toy set, cap gun, handcuffs, badge & more, Hubley, 1970s, the set.... **70-140**

Dick Tracy water pistol, plastic, Larami, 1971 .... **30-60**

Ding-A-Ling figure, hard plastic, TV-Tinykin, Marx, 1960s, 1" h. **10-20**

Dixie & Pixie TV-Tinykins Figures

Dixie figure, hard plastic, TV-Tinykin, Marx, 1960s, 1" h. (ILLUS. left) **25-35**

"Snoopy" Astronaut Dolls

Dolls, "Snoopy" astronauts, one inscribed & signed by Tom Stafford on back of helmet w/"'Snoopy' LM-4 Call Sign, Tom Stafford, Apollo X Cdr, May 69" & the second w/"'Snoopy' LM-4, Gene Cernan, Apollo X LMP," Determined Productions, 1969, 10" h., set of two (ILLUS.) **2,530**

Dr. Evil & Mini Me (Austin Powers movie) action figures, plastic, two-pack, w/scooter, McFarlane, 1999, 6" h. **10-20**

Dropper (Banana Splits) figure, rubber, yellow w/pink painted highlights, hanger string, 1968, 4 1/2" l. **60-120**

Fat Albert Figure

Fat Albert figure, soft PVC plastic, any character, Hong Kong, early 1970s, about 3 1/4" h. (ILLUS. of Fat Albert) **12-20**

Fat Albert lunch box, steel, King Seeley Thermos, 1973... **25-45**

Fat Albert Thermos Bottle

Fat Albert thermos bottle, plastic, King
Seeley Thermos, 1973 (ILLUS.)................... 8-20

Fat Albert View-Master reels, Fat Albert
and the Cosby Kids, three-reel packet,
No. B554, 1970s, the set.............................. 7-12

Fat Bastard (Austin Powers movie) action figure, plastic, McFarlane, 1999,
carded, 6" h. 15-30

Fembot (Austin Powers movie) action
figure, plastic, Trendmasters, 1999,
9" h. 8-20

Flintstones bank, ceramic, "Fred Loves
Wilma," 1960s, 8" h. 65-95

Flintstones bank, chalkware, large figural
Fred or Barney, each 60-85

Flintstones bank, china, figural Dino w/golf
bag, 8 1/2" h. 75-100

Flintstones bank, figural plastic, Barney
w/Bamm-Bamm, 1971, 19" h. 15-30

Bamm-Bamm Bubble Bath Bottle

Flintstones bubble bath bottle, figural
plastic Bamm-Bamm, Purex, 1960s,
8 1/2" h. (ILLUS.) 15-30

Pebbles Figural Plastic Bank

Flintstones bank, figural plastic, Pebbles,
Transogram, 1963, 10 1/4" h. (ILLUS.) 40-65

Flintstones Beach Ball

Flintstones beach ball, inflatable plastic,
color graphics of Flintstones characters,
1973 (ILLUS.) 10-20

Barney Rubble Bubble Bath Bottle

Flintstones bubble bath bottle, figural
plastic Barney Rubble, Roclar, 1960s,
6 1/2" h. (ILLUS.) 15-30

Fred Flintstone Bubble Bath Bottle

Flintstones bubble bath bottle, figural plastic Fred, Milvern Co., 1960s, 7 1/2" h. (ILLUS.) **20-40**

Flintstones cereal premiums, colorful figural plastic dinosaurs, from Pebbles Cereal, 1980s, each **2-5**

Flintstones Circus set, Kohner, 1965, the set **75-150**

Flintstones coloring book, "The Flintstones," Whitman, 1960 .... **15-25**

Flintstones costume, Fred Flintstone, Ben Cooper, 1962 .... **30-45**

Flintstones doll, Baby Pebbles, leopard print outfit, bone in hair, Ideal, 1962, 16" h. **125-200**

Flintstones doll, Bamm-Bamm, Ideal, No. BB17, 1962, 17" h. **75-150**

Flintstones doll, Pebbles, cloth body, vinyl head, arms & legs, Mighty Star, 1982, 12" h. **25-40**

Flintstones doll, Pebbles & her cradle, 12" l. doll in plastic log cradle, Ideal, 1964, boxed **175-300**

Flintstones doll, Tiny Bamm-Bamm, Ideal, 1963, in window box, 12" h. **80-150**

Flintstones doll, Tiny Pebbles, Ideal, 1964, in window box, 12" h. **85-160**

Fred Flintstone Figure on Card

Flintstones figure, bendable Fred, carded, Giant Vallue, 1960s, 4" h. (ILLUS.) **15-35**

Wilma Flintstone Bendable Figure

Flintstones figure, bendable Wilma, Giant Value, 1960s, 4" h. (ILLUS.) **15-35**

Plastic Fred Flintstone Figure

Flintstones figure, hollow plastic Fred Flintstone, painted, 5 1/2" h. (ILLUS.) **5-8**

Flintstones figure, hollow plastic Hoppity, Dakin, 1971, 8 1/2" h. **40-65**

Flintstones figure, plastic Dino, Dakin, 1970, 8" h. **40-60**

Flintstones figure, soft vinyl Baby Puss, Knickerbocker, 1961, in window box, 10" h. **75-125**

Flintstones figure, soft vinyl Fred Flintstone, Knickerbockers, 1960, in window box, 15" h. **20-30**

Flintstones figures, hard plastic, TV-Tinykins, various characters, Marx, 1960s, about 1 1/2" h., each **10-20**

Dakin Fred Flintstone Figure

Flintstones figure, vinyl Fred Flintstone, cloth outfit, on base, Dakin, 1970, 8" h. (ILLUS.) **15-30**

Denny's The Flintstones Lunch Box

Flintstones lunch box, red plastic w/color decal of 'The Dinos,' Pebbles, Bamm-Bamm & Dino, for Denny's Restaurants (ILLUS.) **12-20**

Flintstones Aladdin Lunch Box

Flintstones lunch box, steel, color scene of Flintstones & Dino, red border, Aladdin, 1962 (ILLUS.) **150-225**

Flintstones lunch box, vinyl, Pebbles & Bamm-Bamm, Aladdin, 1971................... **75-125**

Flintstones model kit, Flintstones Motorized Sports Car & Trailer, Remco, 1961.. **50-150**

Flintstones model kit, Flintstones Motorized Yacht, Remco, 1961 .... **50-150**

Flintstones model kit, Flintstones Mototrized Paddy Wago, Remco, 1961 .... **50-150**

Flintstones paper doll book, Great Big Punch-Out Book, w/dolls, Whitman, 1961, 11 x 22, complete **25-40**

Flintstones paper dolls, Pebbles & Bamm-Bamm, Whitman, 1965 .... **20-30**

Pebbles & Bamm-Bamm Figures

Flintstones figures, bendable Pebbles & Bamm-Bamm, carded together, Giant Value, 1960s, 2 1/2" h. (ILLUS.)................. **15-35**

Flintstones figures, colored plastic, Fred, Barney, Wilma or Betty, Empire, 1976, 3" h., each.. **15-25**

Flintstones puppet, push-type, Dino on round base, Kohner, 1960s (ILLUS.).......... **25-50**

Fred Push Puppet by Arco

Flintstones puppet, push-type, Fred, Arco Industries, 1976, 4 1/2" h. (ILLUS.) **12-25**

Fred Flintstone Push Button Puppet

Flintstones puppet, push-type, Fred, Kohner, 1960s, 4" h. (ILLUS.) **20-45**

Dino Pez Dispenser

Flintstones Pez dispenser, plastic Dino, 4 1/2" h. (ILLUS.) **3-5**

Flintstones playset, Bedrock Village, TV-Tinykins, No. 5948, Marx, 1962, the set.. **400-650**

Flintstones playset, Flintstones, 50 pieces, Marx, No. 4672, 1961, the set.......... **150-300**

Flintstones playset, Flintstones Hunting Party, w/three dinosaurs, Marx, early 1960s, rare, the set **150-300**

Flintstones playset, Flintstones small Marx set No. 2670, the set...................... **150-300**

Flintstones playset, TV-Tinykins, smaller versions, 1960s, the set............................ **75-150**

Flintstones projector set, Flintstones Give-A-Show Projector Set, box w/Flintstone & other Hanna-Barbera characters, Kenner, 1963, the set........................... **40-60**

Flintstones puppet, finger-type, Pebbles, made in Taiwan, 3 1/2" h................................ **4-10**

Flintstones puppet, push-type, Bamm - Bamm, Kohner, 1960s, 4" h....................... **20-45**

Dino Push Button Puppet

Hoppity Push-type Puppet

Flintstones puppet, push-type, Hoppity, Kohner, 1960s (ILLUS.) **30-60**

Pebbles Push-type Puppet

Flintstones puppet, push-type, Pebbles, Kohner, 1960s, 4" h. (ILLUS.) **20-45**

Flintstones puppet, push-type, Wilma, Kohner, 1960s, 4" h. **20-45**

Flintstones thermos, steel, first issue, orange, Aladdin, 1962 .... **30-35**

Flintstones thermos, steel, second issue, yellow, Aladdin, 1963 .... **25-30**

Dino & Pebbles Ramp Walker Toy

Flintstones toy, plastic ramp walker, Dino & Pebbles, painted, Marx, 1962, 2 3/4" h. (ILLUS.) **40-75**

Fred & Barney Ramp Walker Toy

Flintstones toy, plastic ramp walker, Fred & Barney, painted, Marx, 1962, 2 3/4" h. (ILLUS.) **40-75**

Flintstones toy, plush Barney, Nanco, 1989-90, 14" h. **8-15**

Flintstones toy, plush Dino begging, 9 1/2" h. **10-20**

Flintstones toy, plush Fred w/blue tie, Nanco, 1989-90, 14" h. **8-15**

Barney Rubble Spinikin Toy

Flintstones toy, spin-action-type, plastic Barney Rubble as fireman, Spinikin by Kohner, 1960s, 4 1/2" h. (ILLUS.) **20-45**

Flintstones toy, squeak-type, soft rubber Dino, Sanatoy, 1979, 9 1/2" h...................... **15-35**

Flintstones toy, Wilma driving car, friction-action, lithographed tin car w/soft vinyl head, Marx, 1962, 3 1/2" h........................ **50-100**

Foghorn Leghorn Vinyl Figure

Foghorn Leghorn figure, soft vinyl, articulated, Dakin, 1970, 8 1/2" h. (ILLUS.)......... **25-50**

Foghorn Leghorn Pez dispenser, plastic, no feet... **65-95**

Foghorn Leghorn Pez dispenser, w/feet, brown head, yellow beak, red wattle **50-75**

Foghorn Leghorn puppet, hand-type, cloth w/rubber head, Zany, 1940s **50-100**

Foghorn Leghorn puppet, hand-type, cloth w/vinyl head, 1960s, 9" h................... **50-80**

Foghorn Leghorn Ace Plush Toy

Foghorn Leghorn toy, plush, Ace, 1997, 15" h. (ILLUS.) **15-25**

Foghorn Leghorn 1995 Plush Toy

Foghorn Leghorn toy, plush, string hanger on head, Ace, 1995, 12" h. (ILLUS.)........... **10-15**

Gabby Hayes accessory set, set of hand-cuffs, jailer keys & badge on original graphic display card, the set 125

Gene Autry bicycle horn, pistol-shaped,"Rootin' Tootin' Pistol Horn," metal flaring barrel w/handlebar attach-ment & rubber squeeze handle, 1950s, boxed, 7" l. 95

Gene Autry billfold, picture of Gene & Champ on the front & Gene playing gui-tar on the back, original star badge inside 120

Gene Autry chaps, children's, fine graphics & Gene's name on the front, ca. 1950s 175

Rare Gene Autry Doll

Gene Autry doll, composition, portrait-style wearing all-original tagged cowboy outfit including boots, belt, hat & kerchief (ILLUS.) 3,100

Gene Autry flashlight 65

Gene Autry Guitar and Case

Gene Autry guitar, plastic w/relief decora-tion in white, Emenee, 1950s, w/original decorative case, near mint, 2 pcs. (ILLUS.) 200

Gene Autry handkerchief 32

Gene Autry lunch box & thermos, steel, Melody Ranch design, Universal, 1950s 300-350

Gene Autry pistol, gold-washed metal, Le-slie Henry, mint in box 550

Gene Autry toy, Magic Slate, "Gene Autry's Champion Slate," Lowe Co., 1950s 30-40

General Custer & horse figures, hard plastic, Hartland, pr. 200

Greenie Meenie doll, Kosmic Kiddle, green curl w/attached pink plastic cap, blue coat w/two buttons, black & white remov-able disc eyes, purple plastic stand & spaceship (one antenna missing) 115

Gunsmoke book, 1963, contains eight sto-ries w/text, cartoon strip & James Arness pictures, hard cover, colored, 93 pp. 60

Gunsmoke coloring book, Whitman, 1959, fine 36

Gunsmoke lamp, figural, Hartline, 1950s, very fine (one spur broken) 636

Have Gun Will Travel vest, Togs, mint in packet w/cards, 1950s 110

Hokey Wolf figure, hard plastic, TV-Ti-nykin, Marx, 1960s, 1 1/2" h. 10-20

Hopalong Cassidy bedspread, full-size, chenille, scene of Hoppy riding Topper, beige,1950s 175

Hopalong Cassidy bedspread & curtain panels, chenile, 3 pcs. 250

Hopalong Cassidy billfold, brown leather, Hoppy riding Topper, w/zipper, 1950 50-90

Hopalong Cassidy billfold, head shots of Hoppy & Topper, black w/zipper, 1950 40-80

Hopalong Cassidy Binoculars

Hopalong Cassidy binoculars, black w/yellow decal of Hoppy on horseback, original yellow, red & black box marked "Hopalong Cassidy Field Glasses," mint toy in excellent box, ca. 1940 (ILLUS.) 330

Hopalong Cassidy & Topper Binoculars

Hopalong Cassidy binoculars, silvered
metal w/yellow decal of Hoppy & Topper,
flaring red plastic eye sockets
(ILLUS.) **75-100**

Hopalong Cassidy book, pop-up-type,
"Hopalong Cassidy at the Double X
Ranch," Garden City Publishing, 1950,
fine **116**

Hopalong Cassidy Camera

Hopalong Cassidy camera, box-style
w/flash attachment, black w/silver front
printed w/pictures of Hoppy & his facsimile signature, ca. 1950s, very good condi-
tion (ILLUS.) **193**

Hopalong Cassidy coloring book, 1951,
8 1/2 x 11" **55**

Hopalong Cassidy compass, wrist watch-
style w/round compass decorated
w/Hoppy's face on top & two crossed
guns on the bottom, original black leather
band w/Hoppy & Western scenes, mint **195**

Hopalong Cassidy dinnerware set, ceramic, creamy white w/colored decals,
1950s, each piece **35-50**

Hoppy Dinnerware Set

Hopalong Cassidy dinnerware set, ceramic, creamy white w/colored
decals, 1950s, set w/box (ILLUS.) **200-300**

Hopalong Cassidy domino set,
Milton Bradley, 1950 .... **150-200**

Hopalong Cassidy figures, hard plastic,
Hoppy on Topper, chain reins, Ideal,
1950s, boxed, 5" h., 2 pcs **125-200**

Hopalong Cassidy fork & spoon,
metal, the set **50**

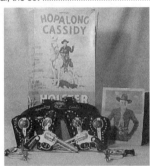

Very Rare Hoppy Gun & Holster Set

Hopalong Cassidy gun & holster set, a
pair of cast metal gold-washed revolvers,
black leather holster, pair of spurs &
booklet, mint in original box w/some tape
damage, the set (ILLUS.) **2,750**

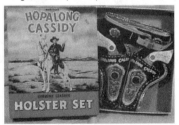

Hoppy Wyandotte & R & S Holster Set

Hopalong Cassidy gun & holster set, pair
of cast-metal revolvers w/white plastic
grips by Wyandotte, in black leather hol-
sters w/silvered metal trim w/jewels by R
& S Toy Company, in original box w/pic-
ture of Hoppy & Topper & "Hopalong
Cassidy - Genuine Leather Holster Set,"
mint toys in excellent box, the set
(ILLUS.) **1,540**

Hopalong Cassidy hair barrette 75
Hopalong Cassidy lunch box & thermos,
steel, Hoppy riding Topper,
Aladdin, 1954 .... **225-300**

Hopalong Cassidy Night Light

Hopalong Cassidy night light, plastic, cylindrical body w/domed red top & red
ringed base, clear sides around color-
printed inner cylinder that turns as the
light bulb heats up, scenes of Hoppy
riding w/signpost "Hopalong Cassidy Bar
20 Ranch," 1950s, 9" h. (ILLUS.) **825**
Hopalong Cassidy pen knife, miniature,
black plastic handle w/his name on one
side & picture of Hoppy & Topper on the
other side, single blade, end ring, excel-
lent condition, extended 3 3/4" l. **77**

Hopalong Cassidy Felt Pennant

Hopalong Cassidy pennant, triangular felt,
black w/picture of Hoppy & Topper & a
rope-style Hopalong facsimile signature,
Casey Premium Merchandise Company,
Chicago, mint (ILLUS.) **30-45**
Hopalong Cassidy pocket knife, three-
blade, black & white sides w/picture of
Hoppy & Topper, steel ends & ring, very
good condition, closed 3 1/2" l. **127**

Hopalong Cassidy Radio

Hopalong Cassidy radio, Arvin, 1950,
near mint (ILLUS.) **458**
Hopalong Cassidy record & story album,
"Hopalong Cassidy and the Square
Dance Holdup," two-record set w/story
& photos, the set.. **75-100**
Hopalong Cassidy record & story album,
"Hopalong Cassidy & the Singing
Bandit"... **75-100**
Hopalong Cassidy ring, w/compartment,
advertising premium............................. **50**
Hopalong Cassidy rocking chair, child
size, chrome & vinyl, scene of Hoppy &
Topper, Comfort Lines, 1950s............... **100-175**

Hopalong Cassidy Rug

Hopalong Cassidy rug, chenille, white
ground w/outlined colored horsehead &
fence w/"Hopalong Cassidy" in thin colored letters, ca. 1950s, very good condi-
tion (ILLUS.) **66**

Hopalong Cassidy Spurs

Hopalong Cassidy spurs, child's, silvered
& gilt-metal w/leather straps, bust portrait
of Hopalong w/his name on side
rondels, ca. 1950s, pr. (ILLUS.) **198**

Hopalong Cassidy thermos, Aladdin, 1950, near mint **61**

Hoppy Wave-lid Aladdin Thermos

Hopalong Cassidy thermos, steel, yellow ground w/red lettering, color scene of Hoppy standing beside Topper, wave design red lid, Aladdin, 1950-52 (ILLUS.) **40-60**

Hopalong Cassidy toy, inflatable Topper figure, barrel-shaped body w/painted legs, early 1950s, 19" h. **100-150**

Hopalong Cassidy toy, "Shooting Gallery," wind-up, Automatic Toy Co., in original decorated box, the set **295**

Hopalong Cassidy Tumbler

Hopalong Cassidy tumbler, milk glass, gently flaring cylindrical sides, black printed half-length picture of Hoppy w/a lasso above his name, ca. 1950s, 5" h. (ILLUS.) **33**

Hopalong Cassidy View-Master reel, scenes of Hoppy & Topper, 1950s **8-12**

Hopalong Cassidy woodburning set, electric burning tool & wooden plaques, American Toy Co., Chicago, 1950, complete in original box **275**

Hopalong Cassidy wristwatch, U.S. Time, 1950, fine **119**

Howdy Doody doll, composition, jointed arms & legs, copyright Bob Smith, ca. 1950s, 12 1/2" h... **1,500**

Howdy Doody Push Puppet Toy

Howdy Doody toy, push-type puppet, Howdy w/microphone on red round base, Kohner, No. 180, 1950s-60s (ILLUS.)........ **45-80**

Huckleberry Hound bank, figural vinyl, Huckleberry sitting, Dakin, 1980, 5" h. **20-40**

Huckleberry Hound Bank-Soap Bottle

Huckleberry Hound bank-soap bottle, figural plastic, red, black & tan, Knickerbocker, 1960s, 9 1/2" h. (ILLUS.) **15-30**

Huckleberry Hound TV-Tinykin Figure

Huckleberry Hound figure, hard plastic, TV-Tinykin, Marx, 1960s, 1 1/2" h. (ILLUS.) **10-20**

Huckleberry Hound Rubber Figure

Huckleberry Hound figure, soft rubber, figural Huckleberry in black & white, Dell Rubber Co., early 1960s, 6" h. (ILLUS.) **30-60**

Huckleberry Hound lunch box & thermos, metal box & thermos, Aladdin, 1971 .... **150-200**

Huckleberry Hound playset, "Huckleberry Hound Presents...," TV-Tinykins miniature size, Marx, late 1950s - early 1960s, the set...................... **100-150**

Huckleberry Hound puppet, push-type, Kohner, 1960s... **20-45**

Huckleberry Hound spoon, metal, figural handle, Old Company Plate, 1960s, 6 1/4" l. **20-35**

Huckleberry Hound toy, Colorforms, Huckleberry Hound Cartoon Kit, 1962 .... **75-125**

Huckleberry Hound toy, plush Huckleberry w/vinyl face & hands, Knickerbocker, 1959, 18" h. **40-65**

Huckleberry Hound Wiggle Blocks

Huckleberry Hound toy, wiggle blocks, plastic TV sets w/various characters, Vari-Vue, Kohner, 1960s, 1 1/2" h., each (ILLUS. of two) **4-8**

Huckleberry Hound View-Master Set

Huckleberry Hound View-Master reels, Huckleberry & Yogi Bear on color cover, three-reel set, No. B512, 1960 (ILLUS.) **10-18**

James Bond 007 action figure, James Bond 007, w/complete set of accessories, all in original packages, excellent, Gilbert **2,933**

James Bond 007 action figures, vinyl, from "Moon Raker," lot of 4, all in original boxes, Mego, 1979... **776**

James Bond Aston Martin DB5, w/original box, autographed by Desmond Llewelyn, Corgi, 1965 .... **1,208**

James Bond gun, ricochet-type, James Bond "Thunderball Secret Agent 007," Lone Star Tada, good w/fair box, 23" l. **863**

James Bond spy watch, excellent w/display card & fair case, Gilbert **1,035**

Jet Patrol lunch box & thermos, metal, 1957, Aladdin **201**

Jetsons (The) bank, ceramic, shows Elroy, Astro & Orbity asleep, Giftique, 1986, boxed, 6 1/2" **125-175**

Jetsons (The) coloring book, Whitman, 1962 .... **30-50**

Jetsons (The) coloring book, Whitman, 1963 .... **20-35**

Jetsons (The) costume, any character, Ben Cooper, 1960s **50-100**

Jetsons (The) figure, bendable, any character, JusToys, carded, 1990s, each **8-15**

Jetsons (The) lunch box, plastic 3-D style, Servo, 1987 .... **50-100**

Jetsons (The) lunch box, plastic w/paper decal scene, Servo, 1987 .... **75-125**

Jetsons (The) lunch box, steel w/domed top, Aladdin, 1963 .... **450-650**

Jetsons (The) puppet, hand-type, cloth & rubber Rosie, Knickerbocker, 1960s **75-125**

Jetsons (The) thermos bottle, metal, Aladdin, 1963 .... **100-150**

Jetsons (The) toy, Colorforms set, 1963.... **60-100**

Astro Wendy's Premium Toy

Jetsons (The) toy, plastic Astro in spacecraft, Wendy's premium, one of six characters, 1989, each (ILLUS.) **3-5**

George Jetson Wendy's Premium Toy

Jetsons (The) toy, plastic, George in flying disk, Wendy's premium, one of six characters, 1989, each (ILLUS.) **3-5**

Astro Pull Toy without Wheels

Jetsons (The) toy, pull-type, hollow plastic figure of Astro, Transogram, early 1960s (ILLUS. without wheels) **125-200**

Astro & George Jetson Ramp Walker

Jetsons (The) toy, ramp walker, hard plastic, figural Astro & George, painted, Marx, early 1960s, 3" h. (ILLUS.) **50-80**

Jonny Quest coloring book, Whitman, 1960s **40-80**

Jonny Quest model kit, Bandit, cold-cast porcelain, 1990s, boxed, 6" h. **40-65**

Jonny Quest model kit, cold-cast porcelain, Jonny, Hadji, Race or Dr. Quest, 1994, each **50-75**

Jonny Quest paint-by-number set, Transogram, 1964 .... **30-50**

Jonny Quest toy, plush Bandit, 1979 .... **30-45**

Kermit the Frog telephone, mint in original decorative box, 1970s **225**

Kiss action figure, any of the four members, w/gold or black record, McFarlane, 1997, 6" h., each **5-15**

Kiss action figure, any of the four members, w/stands, McFarlane, 1997, 6" h., each **5-12**

Kiss doll, vinyl, any of the four, Mego, 1978, 12" h., each **100-225**

Kiss lunch kit, metal w/plastic thermos, King Seeley Thermos, 1977 .... **65-130**

Kiss model kit, "KISS Custom Chevy Van," AMT, 1977 .... **25-75**

Lassie Billfold

Lassie billfold, black plastic w/color photo of Lassie, Campbell's Soup mail-order give-away, 1959 (ILLUS.) **25-35**

Lassie Coloring Book from 1960

Lassie coloring book, Lassie w/black lamb on cover, Whitman, 1960 (ILLUS.) **12-18**

Lassie coloring book, Lassie w/helicopter on cover, Whitman, 1969 .... **10-15**

Lassie coloring book, Lassie w/Ranger Corey on cover, Western Publishing, 1966 .... **10-15**

Lassie coloring book, Timmy & Lassie on cover, Whitman, 1958 .... **20-30**

Lassie costume, Halloween-type, costume, mask & hood in box, Collegeville, 1956 .... **65-80**

Hollow Vinyl Lassie Figure

Lassie figure, hollow vinyl, mottled gold, "Lassie" on the collar, unmarked, 6" l. (ILLUS.) **8-12**

Breyer Lassie Figure

Lassie figure, plastic, brown & white w/red tongue, Breyer, unmarked, 1950s, 6" h. (ILLUS.) **85-100**

Lassie figure, plastic, fully articulated, from "Lassie and her Friends" playset, Gabriel, 1976 .... **50-85**

Lassie figure, plush, Animal Planet promotion, w/three tags, Golden Books Family Entertainment, 1997, 11" h. **20-35**

California Stuffed Toys Lassie

Lassie figure, plush, brown & white, sitting, California Stuffed Toys, Lassie Television, 1982, 21" h. (ILLUS. Page 122)........ **40-65**

Knickerbocker Two-foot Long Lassie

Lassie figure, plush, flocked plastic face, Knickerbocker, Wrather Corp., 1965, 2' l. (ILLUS.)... **50-65**

Lassie figure, plush, fur face w/plastic nose, limited edition, Gund, 1989 Palladium, 2' l. **40-50**

Knickerbocker Short Hair Lassie

Lassie figure, plush, plastic face w/felt ears, short hair, Knickerbocker, Wrather Corp. 1965, 1' long (ILLUS.) **25-35**

Lassie figure, plush, plastic face, yellow photo ribbon, Knickerbocker, Wrather Corp., 1965, 1 1/2' l. **35-45**

Lassie figure, plush, red collar w/plastic Gravy Train tag, Gravy Train promotion, Dakin, 1993, 15" h. **18-25**

Lassie figure, soft rubber, squeak-type, Rempel, 1955, 9 x 13" display stand-box, figure 8" h.. **100-150**

Lassie Lunch Box & Thermos

Lassie lunch box, steel w/blue border, "The Magic of Lassie," King-Seeley Thermos, 1978 (ILLUS. left)................................ **50-65**

Lassie playset, plastic, "Heartland Farm Playset," 21 pieces including, Jeff, Gramps, Lassie, Marx, 1955, the set... **200-400**

Lassie playset, reissue of Heartland Farm Playset starring Lassie, Marx, 1993, the set... **60-85**

Lassie thermos, blue plastic, from the "The Magic of Lassie" kit, King-Seeley Thermos, 1978 (ILLUS. right with lunch box).... **10-15**

Lassie toy kit, "Forest Ranger Kit," photos, handbook, wallet, ID cards, badge, etc., mail-order, 1960s, the set **65-95**

Lassie View-Master reels, "Lassie Look Homeward," three-reel set, GAF Corp., No. B480, 1965.. **15-20**

Lassie View-Master reels, "Lassie Rides the Log Flume," three-reel set, GAF Corp., No. B489, 1968................................ **10-15**

Lassie View-Master Reel Set

Lassie View-Master reels, Lassie & Timmy, three-reel set, Sawyers, No. B474, 1959 (ILLUS.)... **15-20**

Li'l Audrey squeak toy, soft hollow vinyl, late 1950s - early 1960s, 13 1/2" h. **25-50**

Lone Ranger belt & holster, leather **85**

Lone Ranger billfold, Lone Ranger sign & "Hi-Yo Silver," brown vinyl, color artwork, 1953... **65-95**

Lone Ranger boots, child's, brown leather...... **175**

Lone Ranger coloring book, Hi-Yo Silver, Whitman, 1955, 6 1/2 x 7 1/2" **20-30**

Lone Ranger figure, chalkware carnival-type, Lone Ranger on Silver, 1940s, 11" h. **75-125**

Lone Ranger guitar, pressed wood, reads "Hi-Yo Silver - Lone Ranger," Superior Musical Instruments, 1940s **150-200**

Reproduction Lone Ranger Lunch Box

Lone Ranger lunch box, steel, scene of Lone Ranger riding Silver, red sides, 1990s reproduction by G Whiz (ILLUS.) **20-30**

Lone Ranger lunch box, steel, scene of Lone Ranger & Silver, reads "Hi-Yo Silver," blue sides version, ADCO Liberty, 1954 .... **250-400**

Lone Ranger lunch box, steel, scene of Lone Ranger & Silver, reads "Hi-Yo Silver," red sides version, ADCO Liberty, 1954 .... **200-300**

Legend of the Lone Ranger Set

Lone Ranger lunch box & thermos, steel, color scene of Lone Ranger on Silver & Tonto on Scout, black trim, marked "The Legend of the Lone Ranger," Aladdin, 1980 (ILLUS.) **30-55**

Lone Ranger model kit, plastic, Lone Ranger on a rearing Silver, 1/10 scale, Aurora, 1967 .... **20-150**

Lone Ranger 1974 Model Kit

Lone Ranger model kit, plastic, Lone Ranger on a rearing Silver, comic scenes series, re-release of 1967 kit, Aurora, 1974 (ILLUS.) **20-25**

Lone Ranger paint book, scene of Lone Ranger w/"Hi-Yo Silver," Whitman, 1938, 11 x 14" **65-95**

Lone Ranger paint box, lithographed tin w/paints inside, Milton Bradley, 1950s **35-60**

Lone Ranger picture printing kit, rubber stamps & booklet, Staperkraft, 1939, the set **80-120**

Lone Ranger play suit, w/original box, unused, size 12, 1950s **110**

Lone Ranger push puppet, Lone Ranger on Silver, 1968, on a 2" d. round base **40-65**

Lone Ranger rocking horse, painted wood, Lone Ranger & Silver w/"Hi-Yo Silver," 1940s, 21" h. **250-350**

Lone Ranger school bag, green fabric & vinyl, colorful flap scene of the Lone Ranger & Tonto on horseback, w/shoulder strap, 1950s, 10 1/2 x 12" **175**

Gabriel Lone Ranger & Silver Figures

Lone Ranger toy, paddle-ball, Hi-Yo Silver Lone Ranger Bat-O-Ball, from Tom's Toasted Peanuts, 1939 ...... **100-150**

Lone Ranger View-Master packet, The Legend of the Lone Ranger, three-reel set, 1981 .... **10-15**

Lone Ranger View-Master packet, The Lone Ranger, three-reel set, GAF, 1956 ... **25-35**

Long Ranger playset, "Lone Ranger Rodeo," Marx, 1950, box 13 x 15" **150-250**

Lone Ranger & Silver figures, articulated plastic figures w/accessories, Gabriel, 1977, 12" h., 2 pcs. (ILLUS. above) **40-75**

Lone Ranger & Silver figures, hard plastic, half-rearing pose, Hartland, 1950s, boxed, 9 1/2" h., pr. **150-250**

Lone Ranger & Silver figures, hard plastic, Hartland, 1960, 5 1/2" h., pr. **40-100**

Hartland Lone Ranger & Silver

Lone Ranger & Silver figures, hard plastic, rearing horse, Hartland, 1954, boxed, 9 1/2" h., pr. (ILLUS.) **200-300**

Lone Ranger & Silver figures, hard plastic, standing pose, Hartland, 1950s, boxed, 9 1/2" h., pr. **200-300**

Lone Ranger tattoo transfers, sold w/bubble gum, Swell, 1970s **12-20**

Man from U.N.C.L.E. doll, Napoleon or Illya, Gilbert, 1966, 12" h., each **75-250**

Man from U.N.C.L.E. gun set, "Napoleon Solo Gun," window box holds pistol, rifle conversion & more, Ideal, 1965, the set... **300-700**

Man from U.N.C.L.E. Illya Kit

Man from U.N.C.L.E. model kit, Illya, two kits combine to make diorama, Aurora, 1966 (ILLUS. of Illya) **75-225**

Napoleon Solo Model Kit

Man from U.N.C.L.E. model kit, Napoleon Solo, two kits combined make a diorama, Aurora, 1966, each (ILLUS. of Napoleon) **75-225**

Marvin the Martian Alarm Clock

Marvin the Martian alarm clock, plastic, 1998, 10" h. (ILLUS.) **20-40**

Marvin the Martian figure, bobbing-head type, resin, Warner Bros. Store exclusive, 1996, 7" h. **20-30**

Marvin the Martian figure, PVC, Marvin w/flag, 1988, 2" h.. **5-10**

Marvin the Martian figure, resin, Marvin w/dog in hinged rocket, Warner Bros. Store exclusive, 1996, 6" h. **20-30**

Marvin the Martian Pez dispenser, plastic, figure of Marvin & rocket, carded, 1998, 6 1/2" h. **8-15**

Marvin the Martian toy, plush, Ace, 1997, 15" h. **15-25**

Marvin the Martian toy, plush, w/tag, Ace, 1998, 23" h. **20-35**

Marvin the Martian toy, Subway Kids' Pak, Marvin's 50th Birthday, 1998, four different, each **5-10**

Maverick coin, silver, premium for Kaiser Foil, 1950s, near mint **25**

Maverick Oil Painting Set

Maverick oil painting set, "Maverick Oil Painting by Numbers," Hasbro, 1958 (ILLUS.) **60-75**

Mighty Mouse charm bracelet, metal, Mighty Mouse & other Terrytoons characters, 1950s **60-100**

Mighty Mouse figure, articulated vinyl, Dakin, 1977 .... **45-75**

Mighty Mouse PVC Plastic Figure

Mighty Mouse figure, PVC plastic, Mighty Mouse flying over clouds, Presents, 1988, 2 1/4" h. (ILLUS.) **3-6**

Mighty Mouse Rubbery Figure

Mighty Mouse figure, yellow rubbery plastic w/cloth cape, Terrytoons, 1950s, 9 1/2" h. (ILLUS.) **20-50**

Mighty Mouse figures, plastic, Mighty Mouse, Bat Bat, Cow, Petey, Scrappy, Pearl Pureheart, Wendy's premium set, 1989, each **5-10**

Mighty Mouse flashlight, figural, Dyno, 1979, 3 1/2" l. **45-75**

Mighty Mouse toy, plush, Ideal, 1950s-60s, 14" h. **75-125**

Mighty Mouse & Space Mouse Tumbler

Mighty Mouse tumbler, clear w/red, yellow, black & white image of Mighty Mouse, Terrytoons series, Pepsi premium, 1977 (ILLUS. left) **660**

Mighty Mouse View-Master reels, packet of three, No. B526, the set **15-20**

Miss Piggy Muppet Puppet

Miss Piggy puppet, plush & vinyl, mouth
moves, Fisher-Price, 1979 (ILLUS.) **10-30**

Mr. Bigglesworth Talking Cat Toy

**Mr. Bigglesworth (Austin Powers movie)
toy,** plush talking cat figure, Blockbuster
exclusive, Trendmasters, 1999, 9" l.
(ILLUS.) **15-30**

**Mr. Jinks holding Pixie & Dixie bubble
bath bottle,** figural plastic, Purex, 1960s,
10" h... **30-45**

Mr. Jinks figure, hard plastic, TV-Tinykin,
Marx, 1960s, 2" h.
(ILLUS .) **10-20**

Mr. Jinks TV-Tinykin Figure

Mr. Jinks puppet, push-type, Kohner,
1960s, 4" h.. **20-45**

Mr. Jinks toy, plush figure w/vinyl face,
Knickerbocker, 1959, 13" h...................... **65-125**

Muppets doll, plush, "Dress-Up Muppet
Doll," Kermit or Miss Piggy, Fisher-Price,
1981, each **20-35**

Gobo Fraggle Rock Muppets Doll

Muppets doll, plush, Fraggle Rock series,
Gobo, Tomy, 1980s, 17" h. (ILLUS.) **30-50**

Red Fraggle Muppet Doll

Muppets doll, plush, Fraggle Rock series,
Red Fraggle, Hasbro Softies, 1985,
16 1/2" h. (ILLUS.).. **30-60**

Uncle Traveling Matt Muppet Doll

Muppets doll, plush, Fraggle Rock series, Uncle Traveling Matt, Hasbro Softies, 1985, 16" h. (ILLUS.) **35-70**

Muppets doll clothes, "Dress-Up Muppet Doll Fashions," various outfits in packages, Fisher-Price, 1981-82, each **10-25**

Pigs in Space Muppet Lunch Box

Muppets lunch box & thermos, metal w/plastic thermos, "Pigs in Space," color grouping of Miss Piggy & other characters, King Seeley Thermos, 1977 (ILLUS.) **30-60**

Muppets Pez container, plastic, Kermit, Miss Piggy or Fozzy, w/feet, each **1-3**

Muppets Pez container, plastic, Miss Piggy w/eyelashes.. **10-15**

Nancy & Sluggo (comics) sewing set, 1949, original box, box 16" l. **100**

Northwest Passage coloring book, Lowe, 1959, unused...................................... **35**

Oddjob (James Bond) action figure, good w/fair box, Gilbert, 10 1/2" h. **1,035**

Olive Oyl Articulated Figure

Olive Oyl figure, articulated vinyl, Dakin, early 1970s, 9 1/4" h. (ILLUS.) **35-50**

Gund Olive Oyl Marionette

Olive Oyl marionette, vinyl & cloth, vinyl head & hands w/cloth costume in red, green & yellow, Gund, 11" h. (ILLUS.) **165**

Olive Oyl Hand Puppet by Gund

Olive Oyl puppet, hand-type, cloth w/soft vinyl head, Gund, 1957, 10" l. (ILLUS.)...... **20-45**

Oscar the Grouch (Muppets) costume, vinyl costume w/string mask, Ben Cooper, 1979 .... **10-30**

Paladin (Have Gun - Will Travel, TV) & horse figures, hard plastic, Hartland, pr. **350**

Pee-Wee Herman action figure, plastic, Chairy, Matchbox, 1988, about 5" h. **15-30**

Pee-Wee Herman action figure, plastic, Conky, windup-type, Matchbox, 1988, about 5" h. **20-35**

Cowboy Curtis Action Figure

Pee-Wee Herman action figure, plastic, Cowboy Curtis, Matchbox, 1988, about 5" h. (ILLUS.).. **15-35**

Pee-Wee Herman action figure, plastic, Globey & Randy, Matchbox, 1988, about 5" h. **15-35**

Jambi & Puppet Land Band Figure

Pee-Wee Herman action figure, plastic, Jambi & the Puppet Land Band, Matchbox, 1988, about 5" h. (ILLUS.).................. **15-35**

Pee-Wee Herman Action Figure

Pee-Wee Herman action figure, plastic, jointed, Pee Wee Herman, Matchbox, 1988, 6" h. (ILLUS.)..................................... **10-15**

King of Cartoons Action Figure

Pee-Wee Herman action figure, plastic,
King of Cartoons, Matchbox, 1998, about
5" h. (ILLUS.).. **10-25**

Magic Screen Action Figure

Pee-Wee Herman action figure, plastic,
Magic Screen, Matchbox, 1988, 3 1/2" h.
(ILLUS.).. **10-20**

Pee-Wee Herman action figure, plastic,
Miss Yvonne, Matchbox, 1988, about
5" h.. **25-45**

Pee-Wee Herman & Scooter Figure

Pee-Wee Herman action figure, plastic,
Pee Wee Herman & Scooter, Matchbox,
1988 (ILLUS.).. **10-25**

Reba Action Figure

Pee-Wee Herman action figure, plastic,
Reba, Matchbox, 1988, about 5" h.
(ILLUS.).. **15-30**

Pee-Wee Herman action figure, plastic,
Ricardo, Matchbox, 1988, about 5" h......... **15-25**

Pee-Wee Herman bicycle, child's **150-300**

Pee-Wee Herman costume, child's size,
1980s.. **25-40**

Pee-Wee Herman costume, deluxe adult
size w/plastic mask, 1980s **30-50**

Pee-Wee Herman doll, Matchbox, 3' h..... **450-650**

Plush Pterri Talking Doll

Pee-Wee Herman doll, plush Pterri, talk-ing-type, Matchbox, 1988, 13" h. (ILLUS.) **35-70**

Pee-Wee Herman Talking Doll

Pee-Wee Herman doll, vinyl, large talking version, Matchbox, 17" h. (ILLUS.) **40-90**

Pee-Wee Herman doll, vinyl, large version, Matchbox, 18" h. **30-65**

Pee-Wee Herman lunch box & thermos, red or pink plastic, "Pee-Wee's Play-house," Thermos, 1987, each **25-40**

Pee-Wee Herman phonograph record, LP, Allee Willis & Pee-Wee Herman, "Big Adventure" special edition, picture disk **25-45**

Pee-Wee Herman phonograph record, "Surfin' Bird," 45 rpm, picture sleeve, Back to the Beach **3-5**

Pee-Wee Herman playset, "Pee-Wee's Playhouse," Matchbox, 1989, boxed, 20 x 28" **50-120**

Pee-Wee Herman scooter, life-size, Matchbox, 1980s, boxed **100-175**

Pee-Wee Herman sleeping bag, Match-box, 1988 .... **15-35**

Pee-Wee Herman toy, Colorforms set, 1980s.. **20-40**

Pee-Wee Herman toy, kite, w/cartoon Pee Wee logo, 1980s.. **10-18**

Pee-Wee Herman toy, plush Chairy, Matchbox, 1988, 12" h. **35-60**

Chairy Plush Chair Toy

Pee-Wee Herman toy, plush, child's sit-upon chair, Chairy, w/tag, Matchbox, 1988 (ILLUS.).. **200-350**

Pee-Wee Herman toy, plush, Vance the Talking Pig, Matchbox, 1988, 12" h. **50-80**

Pee-Wee Herman toy, Shrinky Dinks, boxed set **12-20**

Pee-Wee Herman Slap-Stix

Pee-Wee Herman toy, Slap-Stix, re-usable static stickers, Colorforms, 1987 (ILLUS.) .. **15-35**

Pee-Wee Herman toy, yo-yo, w/Pee-Wee graphics, 1980s.. **4-10**

Pee-Wee Herman ventriloquist dummy **40-150**

Pee-Wee Herman View-Master reels, gift set of boxed reels, Pee-Wee box, 1980s, the set **12-20**

Pee-Wee Herman View-Master reels, "Pee-Wee's Playhouse," packet of three, No. 4074, 1980s **8-12**

Pink Panther coloring book, Pink Panther weenie roast scene on cover, Whitman, 1976 .... **12-20**

Pink Panther costume, Ben Cooper, 1964 .... **40-80**

Pink Panther Vinyl Figure

Pink Panther figure, articulated vinyl, Dakin, 1971, 8" h. (ILLUS.) **30-65**

Pink Panther figure, bendable Pink Panther, United Artists, Hong Kong, 1988, 4" h. **8-15**

Pink Panther & Sons Lunch Box

Pink Panther lunch box, metal, color scene of "Pink Panther and Sons - and All Their Friends," red border, King Seeley Thermos, 1984 (ILLUS.) **25-50**

Pink Panther & Kids Lunch Box

Pink Panther lunch box, red plastic w/color decal of Pink Panther & his children, King Seeley Thermos, 1984 (ILLUS) **12-25**

Pink Panther lunch box, vinyl, Aladdin, 1980 .... **65-95**

Pink Panther music box, limited edition, Royal Orleans, 1982, 1983 or 1984, each **50-100**

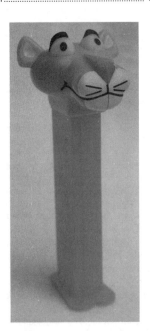

Pink Panther Pez Dispenser

Pink Panther Pez dispenser, plastic, base w/feet (ILLUS.) **4-10**

"Trot-a-way King" child's push car, late 19th c., $1,100.
Courtesy of Slawinski Auction Company.

Noah's Ark lithographed paper on wood
pull toy, ca. 1900, $495. Courtesy of
International Toy Collectors
Association Auction.

Fisher-Price #132 Dr. Doodle
pull toy, ca. 1957, $143.
Courtesy of International Toy
Collectors Association Auction.

Fisher-Price #195 Teddy Bear Parade
pull toy, $891. Courtesy of International
Toy Collectors Association Auction.

Wolverine windup tin Zilotone toy
with seven metal disks, $413. Courtesy
of International Toy Collectors
Association Auction.

Left: Early Hubley cast-iron Santa Claus Sleigh pull toy, original paint, 17" long, $1,238. Courtesy of International Toy Collectors Association Auction.

Right: Victorian child's cabriolet with hide-covered horse, last quarter 19th century, fine original condition, $2,750. Courtesy of York Town Auction, Inc.

Left: Battery-operated Cragstan's Mr. Robot toy and box, $1,155. Courtesy of International Toy Collectors Association Auction. **Center:** A 1960s Television Spaceman Robot battery-operated toy, $330. Courtesy of International Toy Collectors Association Auction. **Right:** A Line-Mar windup tin toy robot, 6" high, $330. Courtesy of International Toy Collectors Association Auction.

Right: Windup tin and celluloid "Knockout Champs" by Marx, $413. Courtesy of International Toy Collectors Association Auction.

An Ives No. 1122 electric steam locomotive and tender, $385. Courtesy of International Toy Collectors Association Auction.

Above: An electric Lionel "Santa Car" with original box, $2,310. Courtesy of International Toy Collectors Association Auction. **Below:** Victorian painted tin locomotive with a clockwork mechanism, $2,475. Courtesy of Mt. Morris Auction, Mt. Morris, New York.

Top: A Marx windup tin U.S. Army bomber, ca. 1940, $281. Courtesy of International Toy Collectors Association Auction. **Bottom:** Schieble's Tri-motor No. 30 pressed steel airplane, ca. 1930, $1,705. Courtesy of International Toy Collectors Association Auction.

Left: Early wood "Fire Patrol" wagon with auxillary sled runners, $2,090. Courtesy of Gene Harris Antique Auction Center. **Right:** Large "Atom Racer" car, ca. 1950s, $1,320. Courtesy of International Toy Collectors Association Auction.

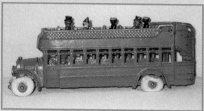

A 13" long cast-iron fire pumper by Arcade, $770. Courtesy of International Toy Collectors Association Auction.

Cast-iron double-decker bus with passengers by Kenton Hardware, 12" long, $1,485. Courtesy of International Toy Collectors Association Auction.

Right: A Metalcraft pressed steel Sand-Gravel dump truck, restored, $248. Courtesy of International Toy Collectors Association Auction.

Pressed steel late 1920s "Keystone City Patrol" police truck, $1,100. Courtesy of the Paine Auction Service.

Early Arcade cast-iron Baby Dump Truck, $220. Courtesy of International Toy Collectors Association Auction.

Above: A pressed steel battery-operated Girard "Fire Chief Siren Coupe," ca. 1940, $450. Courtesy of DuMouchelles, Detroit, Michigan. **Right:** Pressed steel unmarked pedal car from the late 1930s, 38" long, $900. Courtesy of Kenneth S. Hays & Associates Auction.

Cast-iron Arcade car transport truck with original trailer and cars, the set $3,520. Courtesy of Gene Harris Antique Auction Center.

MISCELLANEOUS NEWER TOYS

George Jetson Wendy's premium toy, 1989, $3-5. Courtesy of Dana Cain.

Beany and Cecil "Beany-Copter" cap with flying propeller, Mattel, 1961, $125-200. Courtesy of Dana Cain.

Left: Bugs Bunny articulated vinyl figure by Dakin, 1971, 10 1/2" high, $15-30. Courtesy of Dana Cain.

Cardboard cereal box cut-out record for "The Archies," 1970s, $15-35. Courtesy of Dana Cain.

Bullwinkle's Stamp Pad set, Larami, 1970, $20-35. Courtesy of Dana Cain.

Figural plastic Pebbles Flintstone bank, Transogram, 1963, $40-65. Courtesy of Dana Cain.

MISCELLANEOUS NEWER TOYS

Left: Marvin the Martian plush toy with tag, Ace, 1998, 23" high, $20-35. Courtesy of Dana Cain. **Center:** Mighty Mouse flying in clouds PVC plastic figure by Presents, 1988, $3-6. Courtesy of Dana Cain. **Right:** Popeye and Wimpy ramp walker plastic toy with nodding heads, Marx, 1964, $60-100. Courtesy of Dana Cain.

Left: Plastic Huckleberry Hound soap bottle-bank by Knickerbocker, 1960s, $15-30. Courtesy of Dana Cain. **Center:** Popeye articulated vinyl squeak toy by Cameo, 1950s, no pipe, $80-160. Courtesy of Dana Cain. **Right:** Olive Oyl hand puppet by Gund, 1957, 10" long, $20-45. Courtesy of Dana Cain.

Left: Top Cat plastic Soaky bubble bath bottle, Colgate-Palmolive, 1960s, 9 1/2" high, $30-60. Courtesy of Dana Cain. **Center:** Tweety Bird coloring book, No. 2946 by Whitman, $10-30. Courtesy of Dana Cain. **Right:** Tweety Bird articulated vinyl figure by Dakin, 1976, 4" high, $12-25. Courtesy of Dana Cain.

Left: Dick Tracy windup tin "Dick Tracy Police Station" with car, Marx, 1950s, $300-600. Courtesy of Dana Cain. **Below center:** Smurf head radio with carrying strap, 4 1/2" long, $12-20. Courtesy of Dana Cain.

Tasmanian Devil in leopard jungle suit plush toy by 24K Co./Mighty Star, 1993, 8 1/2" high, $6-12. Courtesy of Dana Cain.

Li'l Abner & The Dogpatch 4 Band windup tin toy by Unique Art, 1945, $600-1,200. Courtesy of Dana Cain.

MISCELLANEOUS NEWER TOYS

Left: Cher articulated plastic doll in original dress, Mego, 1976, 12" high, $40-80.
Courtesy of Dana Cain. **Center:** Lassie plush toy by California Stuffed Toys, 1982,
21" high, $40-65. Courtesy of Dana Cain. **Right:** Red Raggle plush toy from Fraggle Rock,
Hasbro Softies, 1985, 16 1/2" high, $30-60. Courtesy of Dana Cain.

Left: Yogi Bear "Magic Slate" toy,
Whitman, 1960, $30-50. Courtesy
of Dana Cain.

Left: Wile E. Coyote plush toy by Mighty Star, 19" high, $12-25. Courtesy of Dana Cain.
Center: Yogi Bear articulated vinyl figure by Dakin, 1970, 8" high, $25-45. Courtesy of
Dana Cain. **Right:** Howdy Doody push puppet toy, Kohner No. 180,
1950s-60s, $45-80. Courtesy of Dana Cain.

Smurfs plastic lunch box with thermos, King Seeley Thermos, 1984, $12-20. Courtesy of Dana Cain.

Lone Ranger reproduction steel lunch box by G Whiz, 1990s, $20-30. Courtesy of Dana Cain.

Left: Super Friends lunch box with Batgirl & others, Aladdin, 1976, $40-80. Courtesy of Dana Cain.

"Porky's Lunch Wagon" dome-top lunch box, King Seeley Thermos, 1959, $100-350. Courtesy of Dana Cain.

"Roy Rogers and Dale Evans" steel lunch box and thermos, 1950s, $150-250. Courtesy of Dana Cain.

"Pigs in Space" metal lunch box with plastic thermos, King Seeley Thermos, 1977, $30-60. Courtesy of Dana Cain.

The Flintstones and Dino steel lunch box, Aladdin, 1962, $150-225. Courtesy of Dana Cain.

Left: Casper The Friendly Ghost blue vinyl lunch box, King Seeley Thermos, 1966, $300-500. Courtesy of Dana Cain.

E.T. lunch box with thermos, Aladdin, 1982, $30-50. Courtesy of Dana Cain.

Pink Panther and Sons plastic lunch box with decal, King Seeley Thermos, 1984, $12-25. Courtesy of Dana Cain.

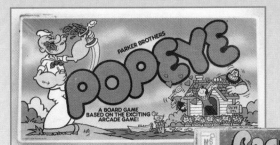

Left: Popeye Board Game, Parker Brothers, 1983, $10-25. Courtesy of Dana Cain.
Below: Casper The Friendly Ghost Game, Milton Bradley, 1959, $10-20. Courtesy of Dana Cain.

The Flintstones Stoneage Game, Transogram, 1961, $30-50. Courtesy of Dana Cain.

Planet of the Apes Game, Milton Bradley, 1974, $35-75. Courtesy of Dana Cain.

Above: The Road Runner Game, Whitman, 1975, $8-15. Courtesy of Dana Cain.
Right: Yogi Bear Game, Milton Bradley, 1971, $20-40. Courtesy of Dana Cain.

Left: Superman 100-piece jigsaw puzzle, Golden, 1983, $4-10. Courtesy of Dana Cain.
Center: "4 Flinstones Children's Puzzles," each 10 pieces, in box, Warren, 1976, $10-18.
Courtesy of Dana Cain. **Right:** Bullwinkle Jr. Jigsaw Puzzle, Whitman, 1950s-60s,
63-piece, $25-50. Courtesy of Dana Cain.

Left: Smurfs on sled 100-piece jigsaw
puzzle, Milton Bradley, 1983, $4-8.
Courtesy of Dana Cain.

Left: Huckleberry Hound three-reel View-Master packet No. B512, 1960, $10-18.
Courtesy of Dana Cain. **Center:** "Lassie and Timmy" three-reel View-Master packet No.
B474, Sawyers, 1959, $15-20. Courtesy of Dana Cain. **Right:** "The Woody Woodpecker
Show" three-reel View-Master packet No. B508, 1964, $8-15. Courtesy of Dana Cain.

From Left: The Incredible Hulk model kit, Aurora, 1966, $75-250. Courtesy of Joe Fex; Dick Tracy model kit, Aurora, 1968, $75-150. Courtesy of Dana Cain; Robin The Boy Wonder model kit, Aurora, 1966, $45-85. Courtesy of Joe Fex; Superman plastic model kit with painting-style box art, Aurora, 1963, $50-300. Courtesy of Dana Cain; The Man From U.N.C.L.E. Napoleon Solo model kit, Aurora, 1966, $75-225. Courtesy of Dana Cain.

Left: Halcyon Movie Classics "Attacking Alien" model kit, $25-40. Courtesy of Joe Fex. **Center:** Star Trek U.S.S. Enterprise Command Bridge model kit, AMT, 1975, $20-50. Courtesy of Joe Fex. **Right:** Beatles "Ringo" model kit, Revell, 1965, $100-200. Courtesy of Dana Cain.

Right: Batmobile plastic model kit, Aurora, 1966, $100-275. Courtesy of Joe Fex.

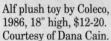

Alf plush toy by Coleco, 1986, 18" high, $12-20. Courtesy of Dana Cain.

Above: Dracula figure with patch and ring, Remco, 1980, 8" high, $100-200. Courtesy of Dana Cain.
Left: E.T. Shrinky Dinks Activity Set, Colorforms, 1982, $15-25. Courtesy of Dana Cain.

Godzilla tin wire remote-control toy, Marusan, 1966, 11" high, $1,000-3,500. Courtesy of Dana Cain.

Assembled "Lost in Space Robot" model kit, shooting lightning bolt, Aurora, 1968, $400-800. Courtesy of Dana Cain.

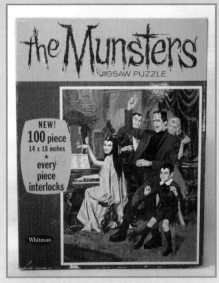

"The Munsters Jigsaw Puzzle,"
100-piece, Whitman, 1964, $30-45.
Courtesy of Dana Cain.

Herman Munster stuffed cloth talking doll,
Mattel, 1964, 20" high, $200-400.
Courtesy of Dana Cain.

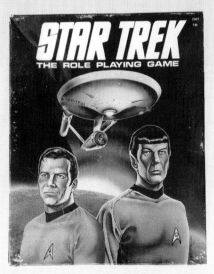

"Star Trek - The Role Playing Game," Fasa,
1983, $20-45. Courtesy of Dana Cain.

Planet of the Apes Dr. Zaius action figure,
Hasbro Signature Series, 1998, 12" high,
$10-25. Courtesy of Dana Cain.

Left: Roy Rogers on standing Trigger plastic figures, Hartland Plastics, boxed with tag, late 1950s, $125-250. Courtesy of Dana Cain. **Center:** Hopalong Cassidy metal thermos, Hoppy beside Topper, wave design lid, Aladdin, 1950-52, $40-60. Courtesy of Dana Cain. **Right:** Hopalong Cassidy silvered metal binoculars with color decals, 1950s, $75-100. Courtesy of Dana Cain.

Left: Lone Ranger model kit, comic scenes series, Aurora, 1974, $20-25. Courtesy of Dana Cain.

Lone Ranger on rearing Silver plastic figures, Hartland Plastics, boxed, 1954, 9 1/2" high, $200-300. Courtesy of Dana Cain.

Nichols Stallion 45 Six Shooter Cap Pistol in original box, 1950, complete, $275. Courtesy of International Toy Collectors Association Auction.

Pink Panther Hand Puppet

Pink Panther puppet, hand-type, plush,
1980s-90s, 11" h. (ILLUS.) **12-20**

Pink Panther thermos bottle, plastic, for
steel lunch box, King Seeley Thermos,
1984 .... **10-20**

Pink Panther thermos bottle, plastic, for
vinyl box, Aladdin, 1980 .... **15-35**

Pink Panther toy, plush, 24K Company,
1990, 16" h. **8-15**

Pink Panther toy, plush, interior wires for
support, Mighty Star, 36" h. **20-45**

Pink Panther toy, plush, interior wires for
support, Mighty Star, 41" h. **25-50**

Pink Panther toy, plush, Mighty Star, 15" h. **8-15**

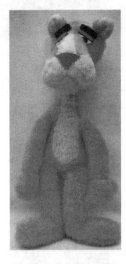

Pink Panther Plush Toy

Pink Panther toy, plush, Mighty Star, 18" h.
(ILLUS.) **8-15**

Pink Panther Plush Toy with Shirt

Pink Panther toy, plush, Pink Panther
wearing "Think Pink" shirt, Mighty Star,
25" h. (ILLUS.) **18-28**

Pink Panther View-Master reels, three-
reel packet, No. J12, the set **5-8**

Pixie, Dixie & Mr. Jinks toy, Magic Slate,
1959 .... **30-50**

Pixie figure, hard plastic, TV-Tinykin, Marx,
1960s, 1" h. (ILLUS. right w/Dixie figure) **15-25**

Popeye bank, ceramic, figural, Vandor,
1980 .... **250-450**

Popeye bubble pipe, 1950s, mint in pack-
age **50**

Popeye coloring book, Lowe, 1958 .... **25-45**

Popeye Cookie Jar

Popeye cookie jar, cov., ceramic, figural
head, American Bisque (ILLUS.) **825**

Popeye costume, w/plastic string mask,
Ben Cooper, 1984, the set **12-25**

Articulated Vinyl Popeye Figure

Popeye figure, articulated vinyl, squeak head, Cameo, 1950s, 13 1/2" h. (ILLUS. without pipe) **80-160**

Popeye figure, bendable vinyl, Jesco, 1988 .... **5-10**

Popeye flicker ring **10**

Popeye lunch box & thermos, metal box & bottle, Popeye & boat, King Seeley Thermos, 1964 .... **100-150**

Popeye lunch box & thermos, Popeye & Bluto, Universal, 1962............................. **400-700**

Popeye lunch box & thermos, steel box & plastic thermos, Aladdin, 1980 .... **75-125**

Popeye Pez dispenser, plastic, no feet, painted hat **75-125**

Popeye Pez dispenser, plastic, no feet, removable hat **50-75**

Popeye Pez dispenser, plastic, no feet, removable hat & pipe.. **50-75**

Popeye Push Puppet

Popeye puppet, push-type, Kohner, 1960s, 4" h. (ILLUS.).. **20-45**

Popeye toy, Colorforms, Popeye TV Kit, 1966, the set.. **35-70**

Popeye toy, jack-in-the-box, Mattel, 1961 .. **75-125**

Popeye & Spinach Can Ramp Walker

Popeye toy, plastic, ramp walker, Popeye pushing spinach can, painted, Marx, early 1960s, 3" h. (ILLUS.)................................. **50-80**

Popeye Gund Hand Puppet

Popeye puppet, hand-type, cloth w/soft vinyl head, Gund, 1957, 10" l. (ILLUS.) **20-45**

Popeye & Wimpy Ramp Walker

Popeye toy, plastic, ramp walker, Popeye &
Wimpy, heads nod, Marx, early 1964,
boxed, 4 1/2" h. (ILLUS.) **60-100**

Porky Pig Soaky Bottle

Porky Pig bubble bath bottle, figural plastic, Soaky, Colgate-Palmolive, 1960s,
9 1/2" h. (ILLUS.) **30-60**

Vinyl Porky Pig Figure

Porky Pig figure, articulated vinyl, Dakin,
1976, 6" h. (ILLUS.) **12-25**

Porky Pig figure, rubber, Sun Rubber,
1950s, boxed, 6" h. **50-150**

Porky's Lunch Wagon Lunch Box

Porky Pig lunch box, steel w/dome top,
"Porky's Lunch Wagon," various characters shown, King Seeley Thermos, 1959
(ILLUS.) **100-350**
Porky Pig ring, plastic flicker-type, Arby's
premium, 1987 .... **20-35**

Porky Pig Thermos Bottle

Porky Pig thermos bottle, metal, various
characters shown, for Porky's Lunch
Wagon, King Seeley Thermos, 1959
(ILLUS.) **20-35**
Porky Pig toy, plush, cloth w/vinyl head,
Mattel, 1960s, 18" h. **30-45**
Porky Pig toy, squeak-type, Dakin,
5 1/2" h. **8-15**

Prince Valiant Dime Bank

Prince Valliant dime bank, lithographed tin, the front printed in red, black & white on yellow w/title & scene of the Prince charging on his horse & wielding his sword, King Features trademark, 1954, very good condition (ILLUS.) **83**

The Rebel Game

Rebel Game (The), board-type, Ideal, 1961 (ILLUS.).. **75-125**

The Restless Gun Game

Restless Gun Game (The), board-type, Milton Bradley, 1960 (ILLUS.) **50-65**
Rifleman rifle, Hubley, 1960, very fine............. **220**
Road Runner action figures, plastic, Road Runner & Wile E. Coyote two-pack, w/accessories, Playmates, 1990s........................ **8-15**

Road Runner costume, w/plastic string mask, Collegeville, 1960s **35-50**
Road Runner figure, articulated vinyl, Dakin, 1968, 9" h. **20-45**
Road Runner figure, plastic, Royal Crown, 1979, 7" h.. **20-30**
Road Runner lunch box & thermos, steel box w/either steel or plastic thermos, King Seeley Thermos, 1970, each............. **50-75**
Road Runner model kit, plastic, MPC **45-75**
Road Runner Pez dispenser, plastic, no feet... **20-40**
Road Runner Pez dispenser, plastic, w/feet... **7-12**
Road Runner toy, plush, Mighty Star, 13" h. **12-25**
Road Runner tumbler, glass, color scene of Road Runner running from Wile E., Pepsi series, 1976, 6 1/4" h. **8-12**
Road Runner tumbler, glass, picture of Road Runner, Pepsi series, 1973, 6 1/2" h. **8-12**
Roy Rogers alarm clock, very good, Ingraham, 1950s.. **170**
Roy Rogers bath towel **125**
Roy Rogers billfold, leather, zip-around closure, scene of Roy on rearing Trigger, mint **145**
Roy Rogers binoculars **98**

Roy Rogers Camera

Roy Rogers camera, black plastic & silver metal, scene of Roy & Trigger on front w/their names, late 1940s, boxed, 4" h. (ILLUS.).. **100-200**
Roy Rogers cowboy hat, green felt **100**
Roy Rogers curtains, scenes of Roy, Dale Evans & Pat Brady, grey ground, two panels, the set... **225**

Roy Rogers Guitar

Cardboard Roy Rogers Playset

Roy Rogers guitar, cardboard & wood, bust portrait of Roy & Trigger, Range Rhythm toys, 1950s, 28" l. (ILLUS.) **75-175**

Roy Rogers Lantern

Roy Rogers lantern, "Roy Rogers Ranch Lantern," lithographed tin, battery-operated, red, blue & yellow, wire bail handle, Ohio Art Co., mint original box, 12" h. (ILLUS.) **275**

Roy Rogers lunch box, saddle bag **157**

Roy Rogers pants, boy's, heavy brown cotton w/colorful Roy Rogers patch sewn on pocket, near mint **95**

Roy Rogers playing cards, marked "Happy Trails," Victorville, California, in plastic box, the deck **8-15**

Roy Rogers playset, cardboard fold-out type, shows Roy Rogers Double R Bar Ranch, 1950s (ILLUS. above) **100-175**

Roy Rogers playset, plastic, Roy Rogers Double R Bar Ranch, w/figures, Marx, 1950s, 24" l. box, the set **250-350**

Roy Rogers playset, plastic, Roy Rogers Rodeo, w/figures, Marx, early 1950s, 15" l. box, the set **250-350**

Roy Rogers riding toy, plastic on metal base w/wheels, skinny model of Trigger, 1950s, 18 1/2" h. **150-225**

Roy Rogers riding toy, plush on metal base w/wheels, model of Trigger, early 1950s, 18" h. **200-300**

Roy Rogers token, round copper-tone metal, "Roy Rogers Riders Lucky Piece" **25**

Roy Rogers toy, horse trailer & jeep w/figures of Roy, Trigger & Pat, Ideal, 1950s, box 15" l., the set **200-300**

Roy Rogers - Dale Evans Lunch Box

Roy Rogers & Dale Evans lunch box & thermos, pressed steel, box-style, color picture of Roy on rearing Trigger on one side, vignette scenes on the other side, "Roy Rogers and Dale Evans - Double R Bar Ranch," red border band, some paint wear on edges, American Thermos, 1955 (ILLUS.) **220**

Roy Rogers Semi-Truck & Trailer

Roy & Dale with Pets Lunch Box

Roy Rogers toy, semi-truck & trailer, lithographed tin, yellow, red & blue w/Roy on rearing Trigger on side & "Roy Rogers - Trigger - Trigger Jr. - King of the Cowboys - Smartest Horses in the Movies" on the side, holds figures, early 1950s, the set (ILLUS. page 137) **250-350**

Roy Rogers yo-yo, plastic, photo of Roy & Trigger on the side, Western Plastics, 1950s **15-25**

Roy Rogers & Dale Evans lunch box & thermos, steel, names in oval center reserve surrounded by color scene of Roy & Dale w/various pets, yellow border, 1950s (ILLUS. above) **150-250**

Roy & Dale at Ranch Lunch Box

Roy Rogers & Dale Evans lunch box & thermos, steel, Roy riding Trigger w/Dale standing in background near gateway to the ranch, wood grain backing, 1953 (ILLUS.) **150-250**

Roy Rogers & Dale Evans w/Trigger coloring book, 1951, 64 pp., 2 pages slightly colored in, excellent condition **125**

Roy Rogers & Trigger figures, hard plastic, small size on card, Hartland, late 1950s **60-100**

Roy Rogers & Trigger Figures

Roy Rogers & Trigger figures, hard plastic, Trigger standing, half-rearing or rearing, Hartland, 1950s, each pr. (ILLUS. of one)... **150-250**

Roy & Standing Trigger Figures

Roy Rogers & Trigger figures, hard plastic, Trigger standing, Hartland, late 1950s, boxed w/tag (ILLUS.).. **125-250**

Scooby-Doo Bubble Gum Bank

Scooby-Doo bubble gum bank, plastic,
model of Scooby-Doo's head on base,
1970s, 9 1/2" h. (ILLUS.) **40-65**

Scooby-Doo candy dispenser, plastic,
Pocket Pop, Flix, 1999 .... **3-5**

Scooby-Doo coloring-activity book,
Scooby dancing on the cover, Cartoon
Network, Landolls Fun Books, 1990s **2-5**

Scooby-Doo coloring-activity book,
Scooby & Shaggy on the cover, Cartoon
Network, Landools Fun Books, 1990s **2-5**

Scooby-Doo Plastic Cup

Scooby-Doo cup, plastic, tall cylindrical
handled form, red w/color picture of
Scooby, 1971, 4 1/4" h. (ILLUS.) **15-25**

Scooby-Doo Lite-Brite Picture Refill

Scooby-Doo Lite-Brite Picture Refill, 12
Scooby picture designs, Hasbro, 1978
(ILLUS.) **8-15**

Scooby-Doo lunch box, blue plastic
w/scene of Scooby & Scrappy, King See-
ley Thermos, 1980 .... **20-35**

Scooby-Doo lunch box, plastic, "Pup
Named Scooby-Doo," Aladdin, 1984 .... **20-40**

Scooby-Doo lunch box, plastic, Scooby-
Doo on front, Aladdin, 1984 .... **40-65**

Scooby-Doo lunch box & thermos, green
plastic box w/decal, green plastic ther-
mos, King Seeley Thermos, 1973 .... **25-40**

Scooby-Doo lunch box & thermos, steel
box & green plastic thermos, King Seeley
Thermos, 1973 .... **50-70**

Scooby-Doo phonograph record, LP, Deluxe Peter Pan Book & Record set, 1978,
12" w. **20-40**

Scooby-Doo playset, plastic, Haunted
House Playset, Warner Bros., 1998,
boxed **12-20**

Scooby-Doo playset, Shaker Maker, Ideal,
1970s, the set **25-65**

Scooby-Doo radio, plastic, model of Scoo-
by's head, Sutton, 1972, 6 1/2" h. **30-50**

Scooby-Doo toy, bean bag-type, Cartoon
Network-Oscar Meyer mail-away promo-
tion, 1998 .... **20-30**

Scooby-Doo toy, plastic parachuters, "Sky-
diving Scooby-Doo,"1978 .... **25-35**

Scooby-Doo toy, plush, Floppies, Warner
Bros., 1998 .... **20-25**

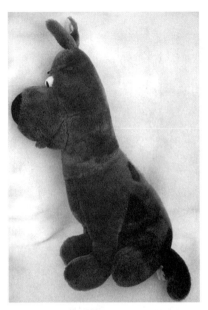

Scooby-Doo Plush Toy

Scooby-Doo toy, plush, Knickerbocker, 20" h. (ILLUS.)... **20-35**

Scooby-Doo toy, plush, Scooby in beach gear, Warner Bros., 1997 .... **20-25**

Scooby-Doo toy, plush, Scooby in raincoat & boots, Warner Bros., 1997 .... **20-25**

Scooby-Doo toy, plush, Scooby w/heart, "I Woof You," Warner Bros., 1997 .... **20-25**

Scooby-Doo toy, yo-yo, white w/Scooby decal, carded, late 1970s **8-15**

Scooby-Doo toys, plastic, fast-food type, several produced for Burger King, 1996, each **3-6**

Scooby-Doo toys, plastic, fast-food type, Wendy's Zombie Island series, 1990s, each **4-7**

Dairy Queen Scooby-Doo Toy

Scooby-Doo toys, plastic, series of six vehicle-related toys, produced for Dairy Queen, 1999, each (ILLUS. of one)............... **4-6**

Scooby-Doo View-Master reels, three-reel packet, No. 1079, the set **4-8**

Scooby-Doo View-Master reels, three-reel packet, No. B553, the set.............................. **5-10**

Sergeant Preston & horse, hard plastic, black horse, carrying silk flag, Hartland, mint w/original hang tag................................ **1,250**

Sesame Street Playset

Sesame Street playset, plastic, houses, figures & furniture, Play Family series, Fisher-Price, 26-pieces, 1975-76, the set (ILLUS.)... **40-80**

Shari Lewis & Friends chalkboard, Bar-Zim, 1950s, 16 x 24" **25-50**

Shari Lewis & Friends coloring book, Shari Lewis on cover, Saalfield, No. 5335.. **20-30**

Shari Lewis & Friends coloring book, Shari Lewis & puppets on the cover, Saalfield **25-35**

Hush Puppy Plush Doll

Shari Lewis & Friends doll, plush, Hush Puppy wearing felt tee-shirt, Direct Connect International - Amerawell Products, 1993, 9" h. (ILLUS.)...................................... **8-15**

Shari Lewis & Friends lunch kit & thermos, vinyl w/steel thermos, Aladdin, 1963 .... **400-600**

Shari Lewis & Friends paper dolls, Saalfield, 1958 .... **40-80**

Shari Lewis & Friends puppet, Baby Lamb Chop w/velcro angel wings, bell, Target exclusive, 1993, 16 1/2" h. **12-20**

Charlie Horse & Hush Puppy Puppets

Shari Lewis & Friends puppet, Charlie Horse, cloth w/vinyl head, Tarcher, 1960, 11" l. (ILLUS. right) **20-35**

Shari Lewis & Friends puppet, Hush Puppy, cloth w/vinyl head, Tarcher, 1960, 9" l. (ILLUS. left) **20-35**

Shotgun Slade game, board-type, Milton Bradley, 1960, unused **85**

Shotgun Slade Jigsaw Puzzle

Shotgun Slade jigsaw puzzle, Milton Bradley, 1960 (ILLUS.) **25-30**

Silver Figure Sealed on Card

Silver (Lone Ranger's horse) figure, plastic, jointed legs, from "The Legend of the Lone Ranger" movie, sealed on original card, Gabriel, 1979 (ILLUS.) **30-45**

Hubley Model of Silver

Silver (Lone Ranger's horse) model, hard plastic, jointed standing figure w/separate harness, color insert card of the Lone Ranger & Silver, mint condition in mint box, Hubley, 1950s (ILLUS.) **110**

Smokey the Bear record, 45 rpm, w/original folder, ca. 1959 .... **38**

Baby Smurf Doll

Smurf doll, cloth & vinyl, Baby Smurf, 12 1/2" h. (ILLUS.) **18-32**

Smurf figures, plastic, Surfin' Smurfs, four
styles, Hardees premium, 1990, each............ **2-4**

Plastic Smurf Figure

Smurf figures, PVC plastic, wide variety of
characters & styles, Schleich, 1970s-
80s, 2" h., each (ILLUS. of one) **2-5**

Smurf lunch box & thermos, plastic,
Smurf dome, King Seeley Thermos,
1981 .... **15-25**

Smurf lunch box & thermos, plastic,
Smurfette, King Seeley Thermos, 1984 ..... **10-18**

Smurf lunch box & thermos, plastic,
Smurfs fishing, King Seeley Thermos,
1984 .... **10-18**

Smurfs Lunch Box

Smurf lunch box & thermos, plastic,
Smurfs in landscape, King Seeley Ther-
mos, 1984 (ILLUS.) **12-20**

Smurf lunch box & thermos, steel box &
plastic thermos, Smurfs, King Seeley
Thermos, 1984... **35-65**

Smurf Pez dispenser, plastic, Gargamel,
Papa Smurf or Smurfette, w/feet, each.......... **4-9**

Smurf Pez dispenser, plastic, Smurf, no
feet **12-20**

Smurf Head Plastic Radio

Smurf radio, plastic, flattened model of a
Smurf head, w/carrying strap, 4 1/2" h.
(ILLUS.) **12-20**

Smurf Radio with Singing Smurf

Smurf radio, plastic, rectangular w/picture
of Smurf singing, 5" l. (ILLUS.) **12-20**

Smurf toy, plastic, talking Smurf, pull string,
head moves, 7" h.. **25-40**

Smurf toy, plastic, talking Smurfette, pull
string, head moves, 7" h............................... **25-40**

Smurf toy, plush Papa Smurf, Wallace Ber-
ry, 1979, 10 1/2" h. **12-20**

Smurf toy, plush Papa Smurf, Wallace Ber-
ry, 1981 .... **8-15**

Smurf Toy with Tee-shirt

Smurf toy, plush, Smurf w/football tee-shirt, Velcro on hands, Wallace Berry, 1981, 13" h. (ILLUS.) **15-25**

Smurf Plush Toy

Smurf toy, plush, Smurf w/white hat & pants, Wallace Berry, 1981, 10 1/2" h. (ILLUS.) **12-20**

Smurf View-Master reels, three-reel packet, Baby Smurf, No. BD 246, the set **5-10**

Smurf View-Master reels, three-reel packet, No. BD172, the set................................... **5-10**

Space Mouse tumbler, clear w/pink, grey, black & white image of Space Mouse, Walter Lantz, Pepsi premium, ca. 1970s (ILLUS. right with Mighty Mouse)................. **375**

Spider-Man toy, pogo stick, ca. 1960s, excellent original condition **450**

Super Hero Express Toy

Super Hero toy, wind-up tin train, "Super Hero Express," lithographed in color, a two-wheeled locomotive & three hinged cars featuring scenes of the various Marvel characters, 1960s, mint in box (ILLUS.)... **9,075**

Superman bicycle siren, in original box, 1950s... **75**

Superman lunch box & thermos, Aladdin, 1978... **50-85**

Superman lunch box & thermos, metal box & thermos, King Seeley Thermos, 1967.. **150-300**

Superman lunch box & thermos, steel, Universal, 1954 .... **350-500**

Superman Aurora Model Kit

Superman model kit, plastic, painting-style box cover art, Aurora, 1963, 4 x 13" box (ILLUS.).. **50-300**

Superman movie viewer, #800, w/three movies, Acme, very good w/good box, ... **205**

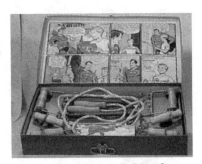

Superman Muscle Building Set

Superman muscle building set, "Superman Golden Muscle Building Set No. 1001," complete w/equipment & progress chart, by Peter Puppet Playthings, original box 11 1/4 x 18" (ILLUS.) **990**

Superman pinback button, "Superman of America Club," ca 1948 .... **60**

Superman playset, plastic, cast w/three backdrops & cardboard figures, Ideal, 1973, the set **50-100**

Superman puppet, hand-type, soft vinyl head, cloth or plastic body, Ideal, mid-1960s, 12" h. **30-60**

Superman puzzle, in cylinder box, ca. 1950s **45**

Superman toy, metal, pogo stick, plastic Superman head on top, 1977 .... **50-100**

Swee Pea Gund Hand Puppet

Swee Pea puppet, hand-type, cloth w/soft vinyl head, Gund, 1957, 10" l. (ILLUS.)...... **20-45**

Tarzan action figure, 1984, Dakin, 4" h. **75**

Tarzan action figure, 1972, Mego, 8" h. **350**

Tarzan action figure, Tarzan, The Epic Adventures "Kerchak" action figure, 1995, Trendmasters, 12" h. **25**

Tarzan action figures, young Tarzan & Kala, 1984, Dakin **25**

Tarzan Aurora kit, #181, 1974 .... **100**

Tarzan Belt Buckle

Tarzan belt buckle, limited edition, #233 of 1,000, Smokey Mountain Knife Works, 1995 (ILLUS.) **7**

Tarzan Big Little Book

Tarzan Big Little Book, #2005, "Tarzan and the Mark of the Red Hyena," 1967 (ILLUS.) **5**

Tarzan book, "Tarzan and the Amazons," cover by Burne Hogarth, Superscope Story Teller, 1977 .... **6**

Tarzan book, "Tarzan of the Apes/Return of Tarzan," hardcover, 1995, Book of the Month Club **15**

Tarzan book, "Tarzan of the Movies," Gabe Essoe, hard cover, Cadillac Publishing, 1968 .... **20**

Tarzan calendar, artwork by Boris Vallego, Ballantine Books, 1978 .... **15**

Tarzan card #1, Banner Prods., 1966 .... **2**

Tarzan comic book, "Dell #1," February 1948, cover by Jesse March **600**

Tarzan comic book, "Dell #21," June 1951, Lex Barker photo cover **100**

Tarzan comic book, "Jungle Tales of Tarzan #3," May 1965, Charlton Comics **7**

Tarzan comic book, "Korak #9" July 1965, Gold Key **9**

Tarzan comic book, "Korak, Son of Tarzan," #22, Gold Key, April, 1968 2

Tarzan comic book, "Limited Collectors Edition (large format) #C-22," 1973, DC, cover by Joe Kubert 8

Tarzan comic book, "Love, Lies and the Lost City," #1 of 3, 1992, Malibu Comics 2

Tarzan comic book, "March of Comics #114," 1954, K.K. Publications 15

Tarzan comic book, "Sparkler Comics #42," March 1945, cover by Burne Hogarth 150

Tarzan comic book, "Tarzan #138," October 1963, Gold Key 9

Tarzan comic book, "Tarzan #16," September 1978, Marvel 2

Tarzan comic book, "Tarzan," #168, June, 1967, signed by Ron Ely (Tarzan), Gold Key 20

Tarzan comic book, "Tarzan #2," August 1996, Dark Horse Comics, cover by Art Suydam 3

Tarzan comic book, "Tarzan #224," October 1973, DC 4

Tarzan comic book, "Tarzan Family #60," November-December 1975, DC......................... 4

Tarzan British Comic Book

Tarzan comic book, "Tarzan Summer Special," British, 1979 (ILLUS.) 5

Tarzan comic book, "Tarzan, The Lost Adventure," #2 of 4, by ERB and Joe Lansdale, 1995, Dark Horse Comics 3

Tarzan comic book, "Tarzan's Jungle World," Dell #25, 1959 20

Tarzan comic book, "Weird Worlds #1," DC, September 1972 2

Tarzan Flicker Ring

Tarzan flicker ring, Vari Vue, 1960s (ILLUS.).. 12

Tarzan Knife Set

Tarzan knife set, Smokey Mountain Knifeworks, boxed, 1995 (ILLUS.) 25

Tarzan movie lobby card, "Greystoke," 1984, Warner Bros. 5

Tarzan movie lobby card, "Tarzan and the Huntress," 1947, RKO 275

Tarzan Movie Lobby Card

Tarzan movie lobby card, "Tarzan Goes to India," Jock Mahoney in title role, MGM, 1962, set of 8 (ILLUS.)...................................... 15

Tarzan movie lobby card, "Tarzan The Magnificent," 1960, Paramount Pictures......... 10

Tarzan movie lobby card, "Tarzan's Hidden Jungle," 1955, RKO **35**

Tarzan movie lobby card, "Tarzan's Jungle Rebellion," 1970, National General Pictures **25**

Tarzan movie poster, "Tarzan and the Slave Girl," 1950, RKO **75**

Tarzan movie poster, "Tarzan the Ape Man," 1981, MGM.. **40**

Tarzan movie poster, "Tarzan's Greatest Adventure," 1959, Paramount **35**

Tarzan Movie Pressbook

Tarzan movie pressbook, "Tarzan and the Valley of Gold," Mike Henry in title role, American International Pictures, 1966 (ILLUS.) **15**

Tarzan Movie Pressbook Repro

Tarzan movie pressbook (repro), "The New Adventrues of Tarzan," 1965 autographed by Bruce Bennett (Herman Brix) (ILLUS.) **50**

Tarzan paperback book, "King of the Apes," by Joan Vinge, 1983, Random House **2**

Tarzan Paperback Book

Tarzan paperback book, "Tarzan and the Castaways," 1978, Ballantine, cover by Boris Vallejo (ILLUS.)... **4**

Tarzan paperback book, "Tarzan and the Cave City," by Barton Werper, 1964, Gold Star.. **15**

Tarzan paperback book, "Tarzan and the City of Gold," Ace #F-205, cover by Frank Frazetta... **5**

Tarzan paperback book, "Tarzan and the Jewels of Opar," 1984, Ballantine, cover by Neal Adams...................................... **3**

Tarzan paperback book, "Tarzan and the Jewels of Opar," Ballantine, 19th printing, May 1991, cover by Barclay Shaw (signed) **10**

Tarzan paperback book, "Tarzan and the Lion Man," Ace f-#212, cover by Frank Frazetta **5**

Tarzan paperback book, "Tarzan and the Lion Man," Mark Goulden, Ltd. (British), 1950 .... **5**

Tarzan paperback book, "Tarzan and the Lost Empire," 1949 Dell, #436.......................... **65**

Tarzan paperback book, "Tarzan and the Tower of Diamonds," by Richard Reinsmith, TSR Inc., 1985 .... **3**

Tarzan paperback book, "Tarzan and the Valley of Gold," by Fritz Leiber, 1966, Ballantine **8**

Tarzan paperback book, "Tarzan Lord of the Jungle," 1963, Ballantine, cover by Dick Powers.. **4**

Tarzan paperback book, "Tarzan of the Apes," adapted by Harold & Geraldine Woods, 1982, Random House **3**

Tarzan paperback book, "Tarzan Triumphant," Ballantine, cover by Dick Powers, 1964 .... **5**

Tarzan photo, then and now, signed by Denny Miller (Tarzan, 1959) 15

Tarzan picture puzzle, H-G Toys Inc., 1975 10

Tarzan toy, plastic knife, Japan............................ 65

Tarzan toy, Tarzan bow & arrow play set, 1976, Fleetwood 75

Tarzan toy, Tarzan & gorilla clicker, Japan 30

Tarzan toy, Tarzan Thingmaker accessory Kit, 1966, Mattel.. 125

Tarzan toy, "Tarzan and the Giant Ape," 1977, Mattel, 15" h. 300

Tarzan video 4 pack, Glenn Morris on cover, 1995, Madacy Music Group 25

Tasmanian Devil (Taz) bank, ceramics, Goad, 1990, 5 1/2" h. 30-50

Tasmanian Devil (Taz) bank, plastic, Applause, 1980s... 12-20

Tasmanian Devil (Taz) figure, plastic, on base, Superior, 1989, 7" h. 5-10

Tasmanian Devil (Taz) lunch box & thermos, plastic, Looney Tunes Tasmanian Devil, generic thermos, Thermos, 1988..... 12-20

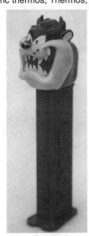

Tasmanian Devil Pez Dispenser

Tasmanian Devil (Taz) Pez dispenser, plastic, brown body, w/feet, 1995 (ILLUS.) 2-5

Tasmanian Devil (Taz) toy, Magic Slate, Golden, 1992.. 4-8

Taz Plush Toy with Large Mouth

Tasmanian Devil (Taz) toy, plush, figure mostly mouth, tag removed, 7" h. (ILLUS.)... 5-10

Tasmanian Devil (Taz) toy, plush, life-sized 75-125

Tasmanian Devil (Taz) toy, plush, Mighty Star, 13" h.. 15-25

Taz Plush Toy with Leopard Suit

Tasmanian Devil (Taz) toy, plush, wearing leopard jungle suit, 24K Co. - Mighty Star, 1993, 8 1/2" h. (ILLUS.) 6-12

The Jetsons (TV) lunch box w/thermos, metal, dome top, 1963, Aladdin 978

The Three Stooges coloring book, Lowe, 1959, fine 92

The Three Stooges display card, "Flying Cane," Empire, 1959, very good 35

The Three Stooges hand puppet, Curly, blue cloth, 1950s, very fine 150

The Three Stooges hand puppet, Larry, 1950s, very fine... 150

The Three Stooges hand puppet, Moe, pink cloth, 1950s, very fine 150

The Three Stooges ring, flasher-type, Curly, 1960s, near mint 15

The Three Stooges ring display card, 1960s, near mint... 40

Tom & Jerry "Tom" Pez Candy Container

Tom & Jerry Pez dispenser, "Tom," 1960s (ILLUS.)... 35-65

Tom & Jerry Transistor Radio

Tom & Jerry transistor radio, MI, 1960s (ILLUS.) **75-100**

Tonto & Scout figures, hard plastic, Hartland, boxed, 1954, 9 1/2" h., pr. **100-250**

Tonto & Scout figures, hard plastic, semirearing pose, Hartland, boxed, 1954, 9 1/2" h., pr. **200-350**

Gabriel Tonto & Scout Figures

Tonto & Scout figures, plastic w/articulated limbs, Gabriel, 1977, 12" h., 2 pcs. (ILLUS.) **40-75**

Top Cat Soaky Bottle

Top Cat bubble bath bottle, plastic, figural Top Cat, Soaky, Colgate-Palmolive, 1960s, 9 1/2" h. (ILLUS.) **30-60**

Top Cat Coloring Book

Top Cat coloring book, "Choo Choo Coloring Book," Watkins Strathmore Co., No. 1857, 1960s (ILLUS.) **20-35**

Top Cat coloring book, Top Cat, Whitman, 1961 .... **25-40**

Top Cat costume, Ben Cooper, 1965 .... **50-80**

Top Cat Plastic Figure

Top Cat figure, hollow vinyl, Top Cat or other character, no mark, about 7 1/2" h., each (ILLUS. of Top Cat) **12-30**

Top Cat figures, plastic, TV-Tinykins, various characters, Marx, 1960s, 1 1/2" h., each **10-20**

Top Cat playset, hard plastic, TV Tinkykins miniature set, Marx, 1960s, the set........ **100-200**

Top Cat toy, plastic, ramp walker, Top Cat & Benny, Marx, 1960s.................................. **40-70**

Top Cat View-Master reels, three-reel packet, No. B513 or BB513, each set **12-20**

Topper (Hopalong Cassidy's horse) rocking horse, plastic & wood, Rich Toys, early 1950s, 27" h.......................... **200-250**

Topper (Hopalong Cassidy's horse) soap figure, "Hopalong Cassidy's Horse "Topper" in Pure Castile Soap," figure in rectangular box w/illustrated cover featuring a cardboard cut-out of a Hopalong gun on the lid & bottom & targets, Daggett & Ramsdell, complete in original box, the set.. **95**

Trigger (Roy Rogers' horse) lunch box & thermos, steel, picture of Trigger, American Thermos, 1956................................. **175-300**

Georgene Tubby Tom Doll

Tubby Tom doll, stuffed cloth, marked on paper hang tag "Tubby Tom by Marge, © 1951 by Marjorie H. Buell, Tubby Tom by Marge, Georgene Novelties, Inc., New York City, Exclusive Licensed Manufacturers, Made in U.S.A.," large painted black eyes, closed smiling mouth, applied ears, black yarn tuft of hair in front, brown flannel back of head for hair, jointed body, red fabric on ankles for socks, black cloth feet for shoes, dressed in original white shirt, brown pants, black jacket, red ribbon tie, white sailor hat, including marked box, light age discoloration on edge of sailor hat, one bottom edge of box repaired inside, 13" (ILLUS.) **900**

Tweety Bird Vinyl Bank

Tweety Bird bank, figural vinyl, Tweety on cage, Dakin, 1969-71, 10" h. (ILLUS.) **15-35**

Tweety Bird bubble bath bottle, plastic, figural, Soaky, Colgate-Palmolive, 1960s, 8 1/2" h. **20-30**

Tweety Bird Coloring Book

Tweety Bird coloring book, Whitman, No. 2946 (ILLUS.)... **10-30**

Vinyl Tweety Bird Figure

Tweety Bird figure, articualted vinyl, Dakin, 1976, 4" h. (ILLUS.)..................................... **12-25**

Tweety Bird figure, vinyl, Tweety Goofy Gram, holding valentine, Dakin, 1971 .... **20-35**

Tweety Bird Pez dispenser, plastic, no feet, ... **12-20**

Tweety Bird puppet, hand-type, cloth w/rubber head, Zany, 1940s **50-100**

Twiggy clothing set, "Twiggy-Do's," No. 1725, yellow, green & white knit short dress, yellow socks, yellow pointed-toe shoes, yellow purse w/chain strap, two-strand white & green bead necklace, no fading or wear, the set **115**

Twiggy clothing set, "Twigster," No 1727, yellow & orange knit short dress, match-ing scarf w/fringe trim, orange cut-out shoes, no fading or wear, the set................... **95**

Boxed Twiggy Doll

Twiggy doll, 1967, blonde, never removed from box (ILLUS.) **330**

Underdog & Simon Action Figures

Underdog action figures, vinyl, two-page w/Underdog & Simon & Power Pill Ring, Limited Edition, Exclusive Premier, any one of four produced, 1998, each (ILLUS. of one).. **8-15**

Underdog alarm clock, yellow plastic, Un-derdog's arms move, Germany, 1970s, 3" h.. **120-200**

Underdog bank, figural plastic, Play Pal, 1973, 11 1/2" h... **25-40**

Underdog book, "Dot-to-Dot Book," Whit-man, 1980.. **15-35**

Underdog Cereal Premium

Underdog cereal premium, flat rubber fig-ure of Underdog, blue, 1960s, 2" l. (ILLUS.).. **12-20**

Underdog coloring book, Underdog flying w/helicopter on cover, Whitman, 1974....... **15-25**

Underdog costume, w/plastic string mask, Ben Cooper, 1969 .... **60-120**

Underdog figure, articulated plastic, w/cloth cape, Dakin & Co., 1976, 6" h..... **50-100**

Underdog Bendable Figure

Underdog figure, bendable vinyl, Jesco, 1985 (ILLUS.) **12-25**

Underdog lunch box, metal, 1990s, 6 x 7 1/2" **7-10**

Underdog lunch box, metal, miniature version, 1990s, 4 1/2 x 5 1/2" **7-10**

Underdog lunch box, vinyl, rare, 1972 .... **900-1,700**

Underdog lunch box & thermos, steel box & plastic thermos, Okay Industries, 1974 .... **700-1,200**

Underdog ring, silver colored metal w/round picture of Underdog **8-15**

Underdog ring, yellow plastic w/black paint, full picture of Underdog, 1970s...... **75-125**

Underdog toy, inflatable plastic flip-it balloon, lands on its feet,w/cardboard base, 1977, on 8 x 18" card **8-12**

Underdog toy, Magic Slate, Whitman, 1975, 8 1/2 x 13"..................................... **30-40**

Underdog toy, plush, large size **25-50**

Virginian record, Virginian - Men From Shilo 45 r.p.m. record, DJ copy, 1971, near mint **35**

Wagon Train Covered Wagon

Wagon Train covered wagon model, Marx, 1960, w/box (ILLUS.) **135-175**

Wagon Train Gun & Holster Set

Wagon Train gun & holster set, Hubley, 1959, w/box (ILLUS.) **175-250**

Wagon Train gun & holster set, Hubley, 1959, without box (ILLUS.) **40-50**

Wanted: Dead or Alive miniature gun, Marx, 1960, very fine **26**

Wanted: Dead or Alive Target Game

Wanted: Dead or Alive Target Game, Marx, 1960, w/box (ILLUS.) **250-350**

Wanted: Dead or Alive Target Game, Marx, 1960, without box **100-125**

Ward Bond & horse figures, hard plastic, Hartland, pr. **225**

Wild Bill Hickok badge, Post Raisin Bran premium, 1950s **18**

Wild Bill Hickok outfit, child's, ca. 1950s, mint in box **95**

Wild Wild West (TV) game, board-type, Transogram, 1966, unused, mint **666**

Wile E. Coyote Articulated Figure

Wile E. Coyote figure, articulated hollow vinyl, Dakin, 1968, 10" h. (ILLUS.)................ **20-45**

Wile E. Coyote model kit, plastic, MPC........ **45-75**

Wile E. Coyote Pez dispenser, plastic, no feet **40-60**

Wile E. Coyote Pez dispenser, plastic, w/feet **20-40**

Wile E. Coyote Hand Puppet

Wile E. Coyote puppet, hand-type, vinyl, 1970s (ILLUS.)... **12-20**

Wile E. Coyote Plush Toy

Wile E. Coyote toy, plush, Mighty Star, 19" h. (ILLUS.)... **12-25**

Wile E. Coyote tumbler, glass, picture of Wile E., Pepsi series, 1973, 6 1/4" h. **8-12**

Wimpy Hand Puppet by Gund

Wimpy puppet, hand-type, cloth w/soft vinyl head, Gund, 1957, 10" l. (ILLUS.) **20-45**

Woody Woodpecker alarm clock, plastic, Woody's Cafe, Columbia Time, 1959.... **100-150**

Woody Woodpecker Soaky Bottle

Woody Woodpecker bubble bath bottle, plastic, figural Woody, Soaky, Colgate-Palmolive, 1960s, 9" h. (ILLUS.)................ **15-35**

Woody Woodpecker cap, cloth, 1950s **60**

Woody Woodpecker coloring book, Whitman, 1950s... **30-50**

Woody Woodpecker Costume

Woody Woodpecker costume, one-piece cloth suit w/large red & white Woody on the chest, w/a molded plastic face mask, Collegeville, in original box (ILLUS.)............... **33**

Woody Woodpecker figure, plastic nodder-type, 1950s.. **75-150**

Woody Woodpecker lunch box, yellow plastic, Aladdin, 1972................................... **35-65**

Woody Woodpecker paper dolls, Woody & Andy Panda, Saalfield, 1968................... **30-50**

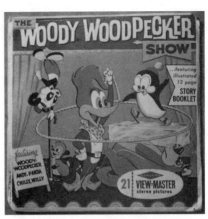

Woody Woodpecker View-Master Set

Woody Woodpecker View-Master reels, "The Woody Woodpecker Show," three-reel set, No. B508, 1964, the set (ILLUS.).... **8-15**

Woody Woodpecker View-Master reels, three-reel packet, No. B522, the set.......... **10-18**

Wyatt Earp & horse figures, hard plastic, Hartland, pr.. **200**

Wyatt Earp (TV) cap gun, original box **150**

Yogi Bear bank, figural plastic, Knickerbocker, 1960s, 22" h. **25-45**

Yogi Bear Plastic Bank

Yogi Bear bank, figural plastic, Knickerbocker, 1960s, 9 1/2" h. (ILLUS.)................. **8-15**

Yogi Bear bank, figural vinyl, Dakin, 1980, 7" h.. **12-20**

Woody Woodpecker Hand Puppet

Woody Woodpecker puppet, talking handtype, cloth w/vinyl head, pull string, Mattel, 1962, 12" l. (ILLUS.) **40-80**

Woody Woodpecker toy, jack-in-the-box, Mattel, 1960s... **50-100**

Yogi Bear Articulated Vinyl Figure

Yogi Bear figure, articulated vinyl, Dakin, 1970, 8" h. (ILLUS. above)......................... **25-45**

Rubber Yogi Bear Figure

Yogi Bear figure, figural rubber, Dell Rubber Co., early 1960s, 6" h. (ILLUS.) **30-60**

Yogi Bear figures, hard plastic, TV-Tinykins, any character, Marx, 1960s, about 1 1/2" h., each (ILLUS. of group below)............................. **10-20**

Yogi Bear guitar, plastic, Yogi Bear Ge-Tar, Mattel, 1960s............................... **75-125**

Yogi Bear lunch box, plastic 3-D version, Yogi's Treasure Hunt, Servo, 1987 .... **50-75**

Yogi Bear lunch box, plastic w/paper decal, Yogi's Treasure Hunt, Servo, 1987 ..... **15-30**

Yogi Bear lunch box, steel, Aladdin, 1974 **75-125**

Yogi Bear lunch box & thermos bottle, steel box & bottle, Yogi Bear & Friends, Aladdin, 1961 .... **100-200**

Yogi Bear playset, hard plastic, TV-Tinykins Jellystone Park Playset, Marx, figures 2 1/4" h., the set.......................... **100-200**

Yogi Bear TV-Tinykins Figures

Yogi Bear Push Puppet

Yogi Bear puppet, push-type, plastic, on round base, Kohner, 1960s, 4" h. (ILLUS.) **15-35**

Yogi Bear Magic Slate Toy

Yogi Bear toy, Magic Slate, Whitman, 1960 (ILLUS.) **30-50**

Yogi Bear toy, plush, Knickerbocker, 1960s, 19" h. **40-75**

Small Yogi Bear Plush Toy

Yogi Bear toy, plush, small size, 1980s-90s (ILLUS.)... **5-12**

Yogi Bear toy, plush w/vinyl face, Knickerbocker, 1959, 16" h. **50-100**

Yogi Bear toy, vinyl squeak-type, Sanitoy, 1979, 12" h. **15-25**

Zippy the Chimp Doll

Zippy the Chimp (Howdy Doody) doll, plush w/rubber face, ears, hands & shoes, Rushton Co., 1950s, 16" h. (ILLUS.)... **100-165**

Chapter 14
DISNEY TOYS & COLLECTIBLES

Disney Parade Roadster Toy

Abu (Aladdin) movie cel, gouache on celluloid applied to a matching production background, Abu steals a melon from a vendor for breakfast while swinging by his tail, 1992, 12 1/2 x 17" **$4,600**

Alice in Wonderland cookie jar, ceramic, marked "Walt Disney Productions," Regal China, 1950s 425

Alice in Wonderland doll, Alice, Duchess Doll Co., mint in box 145

Alice in Wonderland figure, ceramic, Alice, Evan K. Shaw Co., w/label 1,000

Alice in Wonderland figure, ceramic, The Mad Hatter, Evan K. Shaw 300

Alice in Wonderland figure, ceramic, The White Rabbit, Evan K. Shaw label 300

Alice in Wonderland figurines, "Tweedle Dum and Tweedle Dee" - Evan K. Shaw Co., pair 700

Alice in Wonderland marionette, Alice, wood, early 1950s, original box 145

Alice in Wonderland movie cel, reclining Cheshire Cat pointing, 1951, 4 3/4" x 7".... **5,750**

Alice in Wonderland movie cel, gouache on trimmed celluloid applied to a prepared background, Alice swings a paint brush brimming w/red paint, 1951, 10 x 12" 1,610

Alice in Wonderland paint box, 1950s 55

Alice in Wonderland sheet music, "I'm Late" 25

Alice in Wonderland wrist watch, U. S. Time, ca. 1950, w/teacup in box 450

Aristocats movie cel, "Amelia, Abigail & Uncle Waldo," Walt Disney Production seal, 6 x 1 1/2" 377

Aristocats mug, pottery, gold rim, 1970........... 45

Bambi candy container, PEZ 55

Bambi record album, three records, narrated by Shirley Temple, RCA, 1949............ 165

Big Al cookie jar, cov., Walt Disney Productions 130

Disney Bongo the Bear Doll

Bongo the Bear doll, stuffed plush, painted face, red jacket & blue bow tie, small hat, in original box w/small story book, 1948, 15" h. (ILLUS.).................................. 275

Brer Rabbit (from Song of the South) figure, ceramic, 7" h. 80

Cinderella & Prince planter, ceramic, Evan Shaw...................................... 400

Cinderella alarm clock, Bradley...................... 70

Cinderella apron, uncut J. C. Penney pattern, Disney copyright 40

Cinderella cookie jar, ceramic, Enesco 400

Cinderella hand puppet, Walt Disney Productions, 1956...................................... 28

Cinderella handkerchief, Walt Disney Productions, 8 1/2" square............................. 25

Cinderella marionette, Hazelle's Marionettes, mint in box 140

Cinderella paint set, tin box 85

Cinderella planter, ceramic, standing in rags w/white apron, Evan K. Shaw Co., sticker 500

Cinderella sheet music, "Bibbidi-Bobbidi-Boo" 38

Cinderella sheet music, "So This Is Love," France, 1958 19

Cinderella tea set: cov. teapot, sugar bowl, tray & six plates, cups & saucers; tin, Ohio Art Co., the set...................................... 260

Cinderella wrist watch, w/glass slipper case, U. S. Time, 1950, mint in box............... 480

Cinderella & Prince salt & pepper shakers, ceramic, Walt Disney Productions, pr. 105

Cruella De Vil (101 Dalmations) animation cel, gouache on celluloid, Cruella stands & shoots an evil glance over her shoulder, 1961, 9 x 9" 1,840

Daisy Duck wristwatch, 1948, w/original box 385

Davy Crockett bandana, yellow w/red & black graphics, 17" sq...................... 55

Davy Crockett bank, "Davy Crockett Shoot-A-Bear," metal, mechanical............... 400

Davy Crockett bank, embossed "Davy Crockett Pony Express," saddle bag-shaped, mint in package 65

Davy Crockett bedspread, chenille, pictures Davy fighting a bear............................. 205

Davy Crockett bedspread & rug, chenille, 2 pcs. 405

Davy Crockett billfold, vinyl...................... 22

Davy Crockett binoculars 45

Davy Crockett boots, high rubber-type w/fringe, in original frontiersman box, 1950s...................................... 225

Davy Crockett breakfast set: mug, bowl & plate, Oxford China, 3 pcs. 55

Davy Crockett candy dispenser, plastic, Pez...................................... 18

Davy Crockett chair, folding-type, aluminum w/canvas seat & back, illustration of Davy & signature in script on back 60

Davy Crockett charm bracelet, mint on original card...................................... 95

Davy Crockett clock, wall-type, Davy on face & pendulum, 1955, w/original box........ 400

Davy Crockett coloring book, colorful cover, Saalfield, 1955, unused, 16 pp. to color, 10 1/2 x 14"...................................... 20

Davy Crockett cookie jar, ceramic, standing boy, name on rifle, Brush........................ 500

Davy Crockett Cookie Jar by Regal

Davy Crockett cookie jar, cov., bust of Davy wearing coonskin cap & "Davy Crockett" embossed on his collar, base marked "Translucent Vitrified China, copyright, C. Miller 55-140 B," Regal China (ILLUS.)...................................... 600

Davy Crockett coonskin cap, mint in box, Walt Disney Productions 68

Davy Crockett costume & accessories, in original box w/picture of Fess Parker on cover...................................... 120

Davy Crockett equipment set, powder horn, belt & compass, colorful, mint in original box, the set 125

Davy Crockett figure, w/coonskin hat, rifle, powder horn & canteen, Remco, mint condition 120

Davy Crockett flashlight, original box 55

Davy Crockett hobby horse 350

Davy Crockett knife, "Davy Crockett's own Frontier Knife," Barlow 55

Davy Crockett lamp, composition, figure of Davy, w/original shade 175

Davy Crockett lamp, ceramic base w/figure of Davy & bear by tree, glossy green & brown-toned glaze, Premco Mfg. Co., Chicago, 1955, 8" h. 400

Davy Crockett lunch box w/thermos, official Walt Disney model, Kruger,1955 275

Davy Crockett movie projector, "Magic Picture," in the shape of a gun, battery-operated, unused in original box 140

Davy Crockett mug, milk white glass, red graphics 32

Davy Crockett pencil box, "Frontierland" 48

Davy Crockett play set, "Davy Crockett at the Alamo," Marx 325

Davy Crockett play suit, in original box, appears unused, by Ben Cooper 95

Davy Crockett poster, movie poster, "Davy Crockett And The River Pirates," 27 x 41" 185

Davy Crockett record, "The Ballad of Davy Crockett," 1955, yellow jacket 350

Davy Crockett records, "So Dear To My Heart," 78 rpm, set of 3 45

Davy Crockett revolver, click-gun-type, metal, picture of Davy holding a rifle 120

Davy Crockett scrapbook, all-wood hinged covers, fine design on the front cover, 9 x 12" 195

Davy Crockett sheet music, "Ballad of Davy Crockett," w/Fess Parker's picture on cover 40

Davy Crockett teaspoon, silver plate 17

Davy Crockett tray, tin, lithographed picture of Davy Crockett & scenes from Alamo & Congress around him 55

Davy Crockett tumblers, glass, ca. 1955, set of 6 125

Davy Crockett wallpocket, ceramic, model of a moccasin 100

Davy Crockett wristwatch, Bradley, 1956 130

Davy Crockett wristwatch, U.S. Time, 1954, w/powder horn case, mint in box 385

Disney characters book, "Previews of Pictures to Come," drawings include 101 Dalmations, etc., Vol. 13 60

Disney characters book, "Previews of Pictures to Come," drawings include Donald Duck & Ludwig Von Drake, Vol. 14 60

Disney characters ceiling globe, glass, illustration includes Mickey & Minnie Mouse, Donald Duck & Pluto 205

Disney characters chalkboards, Mickey Mouse, Donald Duck, Pinocchio & Ludwig Von Drake, child size, copyright Walt Disney Productions, 1961, unused, each, 16 x 23", set of 4 300

Disney Characters Chamber Pot

Disney characters chamber pot, child's, ceramic, molded in relief on one side w/Mickey & Minnie Mouse running off to Dreamland & Huey, Dewey & Louie on the reverse, trimmed in color, marked "141" on the bottom, 6" d. (ILLUS.) **3,000**

Disney characters Christmas card, Mickey Mouse & several other characters, 1949 45

Disney characters iron-on patches, Bondex, 1946, original package 60

Disney characters lunch box, school bus w/Disney characters, w/thermos bottle, Aladdin Industries 75

Disney characters nodders, celluloid, Mickey, Donald, Pluto & Goofy, ca. 1950s, 3" h., set of 4 75

Disney Character Party Baskets

Disney characters party baskets, molded plastic, each w/the silhouetted figure of a different character on the front & trimmed in color, on original color card, old stock (ILLUS.) 88

Disney characters phonograph record, "Little Toot," by Capitol Records, 1948 35

Disney characters pillow, pictures Mickey Mouse, Donald Duck, Goofy & others riding rocket ships 55

Disney characters poster, "How to catch & cure a cold," advertising Kleenex, 1951 17

Disney characters rug, Mickey & Minnie in airplane, Donald in parachute, label reads "Alexander Smith--Good Housekeeping," 27 x 45" 350

Disney characters rug, area-type, featuring a host of Disney characters including

Mickey & Minnie Mouse, Goofy, Lady, Tramp, Bambi, Thumper, Chip 'n Dale, Gus, Jaq, The Seven Dwarfs, Donald Duck & his nephews, ca. 1950s, 68 x 100" 700

Disney characters sand pail, pictures Donald, Mickey, Pluto & Goofy, Ohio Art Co... 150

Disney Parade Roadster Toy

Disney characters toy, windup tin, "Mechanical Disney Parade Roadster," colorfully lithographed long auto w/plastic figures of various characters in the front & back open seats, Louis Marx, ca. 1950, w/original box (ILLUS.) 633

Disneyland Melody Player, w/original box, near mint 600

Disneyland record set, "Your Trip To Disneyland," the set 50

Disneyland school bag, red plastic lettering, tan trim, 1960. 13"..................................... 100

Disneyland toy, tin jeep w/images of Mickey, Donald, Pluto & Goofy, good, Marx.......... 90

Donald Duck baby bottle warmer 125

Donald Duck baby food warming dish, figural, coral, American Pottery, large 225

Donald Duck bicycle, 1950s, restored.......... 1,500

Donald Duck book, "Donald Duck Bringing Up Boys," Whitman Publishing Co., 1948 40

Donald Duck book, "Donald Duck & Ghost Morgan's Treasure," Big Little Books, 1946 105

Donald Duck book, "Donald Duck & His Cat Troubles," 1948.. 40

Donald Duck book, "Donald Duck's Adventure," Little Golden Book, 1950....................... 60

Donald Duck camera, pictures Donald, Huey, Dewey & Louie, Walt Disney Productions & Herbert George Co., Chicago, Illinois, uses 127 film, 12 exp. 250

Donald Duck cartoon cel, gouache on celluloid applied to a Courvoisier background w/"W.D.P." stamped on the mat, shows Donald dressed as a Western hero twirling a gun on the index finger of his left hand, Walt Disney's signature on the lower right hand corner, 8" d. 2,185

Donald Duck Coffee bank, tin, "Donald Duck Coffee-Free Sample," short cylindrical can w/coin slot in lid, picture of Donald on the front, fine condition 205

Donald Duck Cola bottle, 1953, 7 oz............... 60

Donald Duck cookie jar, cov., ceramic, cylindrical, California Originals 130

Donald Duck lemonade pack, colorful cardboard pack w/Donald's face on the side, holds six 7-oz. full bottles..................... 125

Donald Duck phonograph record, "Donald Trick or Treat," 78 rpm, Golden Records, 1951, w/dust cover, 6" d.................. 30

Donald Duck projector, metal case, Stephens Products Co., Middletown, Connecticut, mint w/box 95

Donald Duck salt & pepper shakers, ceramic, figural, marked "McCoy," pr. 60

Donald Duck sand pail, tin, Disneyland candy-type, 1950s...................................... 125

Donald Duck sign, tin, "Donald Duck Bread" over picture of Donald & loaf of bread in colorful wrapper over "Oven Fresh Flavor".. 400

Donald Duck Jack-in-the-Box

Donald Duck toy, jack-in-the-box, composition & cloth Donald in a lithographed cardboard box, very good condition (ILLUS.).. 138

Donald Duck Bosco Tumbler

Donald Duck tumbler, clear glass tapering cylindrical form w/blue enameled decoration, Bosco premium (ILLUS.) 25

Donald Duck wrist watch, oblong or round, U. S. Time, 1948 250

Donald Duck & Goofy toy, a dancing figure of Goofy atop a round base lithographed w/Disney characters, w/a Donald Duck drummer playing on a smaller attached drum, Marx, ca. 1946, 10" h....................... **2,800**

Donald Duck & Ludwig Von Drake salt & pepper shakers, 1961, pr. 135

Donald Duck & Mickey Mouse book, "Donald Duck & Mickey Mouse Cub Scouts," Walt Disney Productions, 1950 45

Donald Duck & nephews billfold, plastic, dressed in Western garb roping a calf, Disney Productions, 3 x 7 1/2" 88

Donald Duck & nephews Huey, Louie & Dewey candy pail, Overland Candy Co., Chicago, 1949, 3 oz., 3 1/2" h. 65

Donald Duck & nephews rug, shows the nephews playing tricks.................... 95

Donald Duck & Pluto ceiling globe, Donald chasing butterflies on one side & Pluto chasing butterflies on the other side, 11" d., mint condition 400

Donald Duck & Pluto toy, automobile, hard rubber, Sun Rubber Co., Barberton, Ohio, 1940s, 6 1/2" l. 120

Dumbo cookie jar, cylindrical, picture of mouse on finial, California Originals............. 180

Dumbo salt & pepper shakers, Leeds China Co., 4" h., pr................................. 60

Dumbo & Pluto cookie jar, turnabout-type, Leeds China.................................... **150-175**

Dwarf Doc figure, porcelain, Goebel,1950s 45

Dwarf Dopey cookie jar, ceramic standing figure, Treasure Craft, mint in box, 11" h. 175

Dwarf Dopey puppet, hand-type, Gund........... 40

Dwarf Grumpy figure, porcelain, Goebel, 1950s.. 45

Dwarf Happy figure, porcelain, Goebel, 1950s.. 45

Dwarf Sleepy figure, porcelain, Goebel, 1960s.. 45

Eeyore (from Winnie the Pooh) cookie jar, cov., dark grey w/pink cover, ceramic, large, California Originals........................ 750

Figaro (Pinocchio's cat) figure, porcelain, rolling a ball, Goebel w/full Bee mark........... 350

Flora (good fairy from Sleeping Beauty) movie cel, gouache on celluloid, large cel of Flora w/out-stretched wand, 1959, 11 x 14" 460

Flower Salt & Pepper Shakers

Flower the Skunk (Bambi) salt & pepper shakers, china, figural, paper sticker "Walt Disney Flower Character W. D. P. F Fm copyright," marked on bottom "W. Goebel" w/full bee and (R) in parenthesis, also printed "Germany" mint condition w/cork stoppers, 2 2/3" h., pr. (ILLUS.).. 400

Goofy candy container, PEZ, Walt Disney Productions.. 40

Goofy flasher pin, red, from Disneyland, 2 1/2".. 80

Goofy rug, colorful scene of Goofy riding on a go-cart, fringed ends 185

Hades (from Hercules) movie cel, half-length portrait of Hades angered by the incompetence of his assistants, Pain & Panic, two-cel set-up, 1997, 12 1/2 x 17" .. **3,737**

Haley Mills paper doll, "Moon-Spinners," Whitman, 1964, very fine................................ 40

Hercules animation maquette, full-figure statuette of Hercules in action, hand-painted, numbered 36 of 40, 20 1/2" h....... **4,887**

Hercules movie cel, color scene w/half-length portraits of Zeus & Hera, Zeus holding the baby Hercules & the baby Pegasus hovering behind Hera, two-cell set-up, 1997, 19 1/2 x 30 3/4" **2,990**

Huey, Dewey & Louie (Donald Duck's nephews) sweater pins, in box, set of 3..... 140

Ichabod Crane (Adventures of Ichabod and Mr. Toad, The) cartoon cel, gouache on celluloid, Brom Bones leans over & beckons w/one finger, from "The Legend of Sleepy Hollow" sequence, 1949, 7 1/2 x 11 1/2"...................................... 575

Ichabod Crane (Adventures of Ichabod and Mr. Toad, The) cartoon cel, gouache on trimmed celluloid, scene of Ichabod bowing to the rich & beautiful Katrina Van Tassel in "The Legend of Sleepy Hollow" segment, 1949, 10 x 12" **1,150**

Jiminy Cricket (from Pinocchio) doll, wooden flex doll w/umbrella, Ideal Toy Co., copyright Walt Disney, ca. 1950s, 6" h... 500

Jiminy Cricket (from Pinocchio) Soaky container 15

Jiminy Cricket (from Pinocchio) wrist watch, U. S. Time, 1948 290

Johnny Appleseed record album, 1949.......... 36

Johnny Appleseed book, "Walt Disney's Johnny Appleseed," first edition..................... 36

Mowgli and Kaa Movie Cel

Jungle Book (The) movie cel, gouache on celluloid applied to a production background, a matching production set-up w/Mowgli scolding the snake Kaa, 1967, 12 1/2 x 16" (ILLUS.)..................................... 8,050

King Louie (from "The Jungle Book") doll, stuffed plush, Steiff, original button in ear, 12" h. 325

Lady and The Tramp movie cel, gouache on celluloid applied to a hand-prepared background, scene of Lady looking back at Tramp & two of their puppies, 1955, 9 1/2 x 13 1/2" 2,587

Lady and The Tramp Movie Cel

Lady and The Tramp movie cel, gouache on celluloid applied to a printed background, Joe & Tony look down & smile at the startled Lady, 1955, 13 1/2 x 17 1/2" (ILLUS.)... 3,450

Lady and The Tramp movie cel, gouache on celluloid applied to a printed background, Lady & Tramp sit side by side in anticipation of their romantic dinner, 1955, 8 1/4 x 10 1/4" 3,450

Lady and The Tramp movie cel, Tramp, gouache on celluloid applied to a printed background, Tramp smiles & walks forward, 1955, 12 1/2 x 14"................................. 920

Lady & The Tramp hand puppets, Gund, pr. 75

Lady & The Tramp tape dispenser, metal, 1950s.. 60

Ludwig Von Drake cookie jar, cov., pottery, bust portrait of Professor Von Drake, American Bisque, 1961...................... 250

Ludwig von Drake cookie jar, ceramic, American Bisque 500

Ludwig Von Drake doll, plush velveteen, Gund, 18" h... 60

Ludwig Von Drake lunch box, 1961 150

Ludwig Von Drake lunch box w/thermos, Aladdin, 1962 275

Ludwig Von Drake salt shaker, ceramic, Walt Disney Productions 30

Mad Hatter (from Alice in Wonderland) counter display, advertising hats & the movie "Alice in Wonderland," cardboard, 10 x 12" 85

Maleficent (witch from Sleeping Beauty) tumbler, clear glass, No.D2405 28

Mary Poppins Cookie Jar

Mary Poppins cookie jar, ceramic, figural Mary in a pink dress & parasol w/penguins dancing in front, unknown maker, 1960s (ILLUS.)... 1,350

Mary Poppins doll, vinyl, Hasbro, 1964, very fine... 40

Mary Poppins hair dryer, 1964, original box 85

Mary Poppins lunch box & thermos, depicting a flying Mary Poppins on both sides of the box, the thermos w/a carousel scene, near mint condition, 1965............ 275

Mary Poppins paint set, 1960s, unused......... 105

Mary Poppins pencil case, vinyl, 1964............. 25

Mary Poppins spoon, silver plate, figural handle depicting Mary w/open umbrella, International Silver, 1964, near mint condition 35

Meg (from Hercules) animation maquette, full-figure statuette of Meg, hand-painted, numbered 25 of 44, 13" h. .. 2,875

Mickey Mouse alarm clock, Ingersoll, ca. 1950, w/original box (stain on clock face, edge wear & staining on box) 230

Mickey Mouse blocks, picture-type, Germany, ca. 1950, in original carrying case 230

Mickey Mouse book ends, cast iron, seated Mickey leaning against a book, John Wright, Inc., Wrightsville, Pennsylvania, 1972, 5" h., pr... 176

Mickey Mouse camera, "Mick-A-Matic," ear-activated.. 60

Mickey Mouse candy container, composition Mickey head & molded cardboard body, w/original paper label, 1940s **305**

Mickey Mouse cartoon cel, gouache on celluloid, large image of Mickey standing smiling & holding an envelope, ca. 1950s, 9 x 10" **1,380**

Mickey Mouse clothes bag, cloth, shows Mickey pointing at a pair of pants on the clothes line w/"Mickey" on the pocket, Vogue Designs, 14 x 20" **125**

Mickey 60th Anniversary Cookie Jar

Mickey Mouse cookie jar, cov., ceramic, model of a tall birthday cake w/Mickey seated on top, made to celebrate his 60th Anniversary in 1988, Walt Disney Productions (ILLUS.) **650**

Mickey Mouse cookie jar, cov., Mickey Clock, pictures Mickey & "Mickey Mouse Cookie Time" on the clock face of a Big Ben-type alarm clock, marked "Enesco WDE-219" **450**

Mickey Mouse cookie jar, cov., pottery, figural Mickey wearing chef's outfit & holding a rolling pin, "Flour XXX" on his pocket, marked "Copyright The Walt Disney Co. by HOAN Ltd." **80**

Mickey Mouse costume, orange w/red pants, plastic mask, ca. 1950s, child's size large 12-14, original size paper tag sewn in (mask slightly pushed in, minor soil on one arm & leg) **75**

Mickey Mouse desk, school master-type w/flip-over blackboard, marked "Falcon Toy" **400**

Gund Mickey Mouse Doll

Mickey Mouse doll, plush w/painted face, red felt shorts, white felt gloves & orange felt shoes, red ribbon bow tie, Gund, ca. 1950s-60s, 14" h. (ILLUS.) **77**

Mickey Mouse flatware set: knife, fork & spoon; stainless steel, 1959, mint in original box, the set **400**

Mickey Mouse handkerchief, Mickey playing football, 1940s, 8 1/2" sq. **18**

Mickey Mouse lamp, table model, soft rubber figure of Mickey sits on the round base, paper shade decorated w/various Disney characters, ca. 1950s **275-350**

Mickey Mouse Mug

Mickey Mouse mug, ceramic, swelled cylindrical form w/embossed standing figure of Mickey in long blue pants & yellow shirt, name at bottom, pale blue angled handle, Walt Disney Productions, ca. 1950s (ILLUS.) **38**

Mickey Mouse paint book, "Mickey Mouse & The Beanstalk," 1948 60

Mickey Mouse pencil case, rocket-shaped, ca. 1960, 12" l. 25

Mickey Mouse record set, "Mickey Mouse's Birthday Party," 78 r.p.m., 1953 65

Mickey Mouse rocker, wooden, good, Walt Disney Productions 300

Mickey Mouse rug, pictures Mickey riding a donkey, ca. 1949, 21 x 39" 165

Mickey Mouse Straws Package

Mickey Mouse straws, unopened cardboard box w/large color picture of Mickey on the front, "Mickey Mouse Sunshine Straws," some wear & staining on box, ca. 1950s (ILLUS.) 20

Mickey Mouse toy, SIT-N-GO W-1 Astro-car, Mickey Mouse as driver, windup, Matchbox, mint 210

Mickey Mouse toy, train car, Lionel No. 69672, Mickey Mouse 50th Anniversary commemorative, mint in original box 400

Mickey Mouse wrist watch, 50th Birthday, Bradley, 1978, mint, w/original box 350

Mickey Mouse wrist watch, "America on Parade," limited edition Bicentennial watch, mint 235

Mickey Mouse & Donald Duck crayon box, tin, Transogram, 1946 90

Mickey Mouse & Donald Duck lunch box, scene of Pluto pulling a cart filled w/Donald's nephews & Mickey running behind, near mint condition, 1954 1,250

Mickey Mouse & Donald Duck Sunshine straw holder, holds 12 flat packages of straws, Walt Disney Productions 45

Mickey Mouse Club cap pistol w/holster, badge & other accessories, ca. 1965, original package 65

Mickey Mouse Club Clubhouse, heavy cardboard, never assembled, 1950s, w/original box, 50" h. 425

Mickey Mouse Club costume, Mouseketeer, 1950s, mint in box 185

Mickey Mouse Club letter & envelope, paper, large Disney letterhead & information on club magazine, dated 1956, the set 45

Mickey Mouse Club lunch box, w/metal thermos, excellent condition 65

Mickey Mouse Club Mouseketeer ears 1950s 28

Mickey Mouse Club toy, moving van, the red cab w/articulated trailer lithographed w/portraits of Mickey & friends, also marked "Mickey's Mousekemovers," friction action, Line Mar, w/original box, 12 1/2" l. 1,050

Mickey Mouse Club tray, tin, illustrates several Disney characters, 1950s, 12 1/2 x 17" 235

Minnie Mouse cookie cutter, aluminum, 4" 85

Minnie Mouse doll, plush & felt, Charlotte Clark, late 1940s, 20" h. 800

Minnie Mouse fork, stainless steel 30

Minnie Mouse wrist watch, Timex, 1968 125

Nana (nursemaid dog in Peter Pan) movie cel, gouache on trimmed celluloid applied to a prepared background, an agitated Nana straightens up blocks in the children's bedroom, 11 1/4 x 13 1/2" 920

Nightmare Before Christmas Bank

Pluto Child's Rocking Chair

Nightmare Before Christmas bank, ceramic, figural Mayor Schmid, Disney-authorized (ILLUS.).. **75**

101 Dalmatians book & record set, 1965........ **25**

101 Dalmatians puzzles, 1961, set of 4 .... **125**

Peter & the Wolf book, "Make Mine Music," Little Golden Book, published by Simon & Schuster, 1947 edition **25**

Peter & the Wolf candy mold, tin, marked "Belgium," 1946, 8 x 12" **175**

Peter Pan book, colorfully illustrated w/24 characters including Tinkerbell, die-cut cover w/plastic sword & feather, Spain, 1954 .... **45**

Peter Pan Christmas card, Disney Productions, 1953 .... **35**

Peter Pan hand puppet, Gund Mfg. Co., Walt Disney Productions **35**

Peter Pan handkerchief, Walt Disney Productions, 8 1/2" square **20**

Peter Pan marionette, Peter Puppet Playthings, ca. 1952....................................... **195**

Peter Pan movie drawing, graphite & colored pencil on paper, Peter Pan stretched out on his hammock holding his pan flute, 1953, 9 x 11"............................. **575**

Peter Pan phonograph record, 78 r.p.m., Golden Records, 1952, w/dust cover, 6" d. **8**

Pinocchio alarm clock, Bayard, France **195**

Pinocchio book, "Pinocchio," Little Golden Books, Walt Disney Productions, 1948.......... **20**

Pinocchio cookie jar, bust of Pinocchio, pottery, marked "CJ46-Copyright USA" on two lines, Doranne of California............... **650**

Pinocchio cookie jar, cov., ceramic, head of Pinocchio, Metlox, 11" h............................. **325**

Pinocchio doll, stuffed plush w/mask face, Gund, 1960s.. **38**

Pinocchio doll, jointed wood, composition, copyright Walt Disney, ca. 1950s, 7 1/2" h. **350**

Pinocchio lunch box, tin, cylindrical, Walt Disney Productions, Libbey Glass Co.......... **300**

Pinocchio & Jiminy Cricket puppets, hand-type, vinyl heads, Gund, 10" l., the set **55**

Pluto alarm clock, scene of Pluto in front of his doghouse surrounded by baby chicks, blue case, Bayard, France, 1964...... **195**

Pluto applique, iron-on type, Walt Disney Productions, 1946... **28**

Pluto bank, wooden, sits on haunches, 11" h. **110**

Pluto child's rocking chair w/arms, covered in white & yellow vinyl w/a color decal of Pluto by his doghouse on the back, Walt Disney Productions, ca. 1950s (ILLUS. above).. **248**

Pluto doll, plush velveteen, featuring a seated Pluto w/pie-cut eyes, stitched snout, black velveteen nose & red tongue, original Gund tag affixed to one long, droopy wire-framed ear, 17 1/2" h. **140**

Pluto hand puppet, Gund, 1950s...................... **65**

Pluto lamp, ceramic, figural, soft brown tones, Leeds, marked "Walt Disney Productions" on base, late 1940s, 4 x 4 x 6"...... **145**

Pluto mug, ceramic, Salem China **90**

Pluto wrist watch, Ingersoll, 1947................... **225**

Prince Charming (from Cinderella) planter, ceramic, gold sword, w/sticker, Shaw Pottery **400**

Robin Hood movie cel, gouache on celluloid applied to a production background, a key cel set-up of Lady Cluck charging toward Prince John's men during the battle/football game, 1973, 12 1/2 x 16"......... **1,610**

Robin Hood Movie Cel

Robin Hood movie cel, gouache on celluloid applied to a production background of three tents, Robin Hood defends himself w/his sword from the advances of Prince John's men, gouache on paper w/a photocopy line-on-cel overlay, 1973, 5 1/4 x 11" (ILLUS.) 2,300

Scamp & Jock (Lady and The Tramp) movie cel, gouache on celluloid applied to a printed background, Scamp the puppy pulls at Jock's sweater, 1955, 10 x 12" .. 1,840

Si & Am (Lady and The Tramp) movie cel, gouache on celluloid applied to a key production background, a key production set-up of Si and Am destroying the parlor, 1955, 12 x 19 1/2" 4,025

Sleeping Beauty Movie Cel

Sleeping Beauty movie cel, gouache on celluloid applied to printed background, Flora, Merryweather & Fauna contemplating Princess Aurora's fate, 12 3/4 x 14 12" (ILLUS.) 1,150

Sleeping Beauty movie cel, gouache on celluloid applied to a printed background, King Stefan & King Hubert duel w/a fish, 1959, 12 1/2 x 17" 1,035

Snow White animated alarm clock, Bayard, France, 1964, w/box.............................. 525

Snow White cookie jar, Walt Disney Productions, Enesco label................................. 450

Snow White figure, bisque, Goebel, Germany, full bee & crown mark 400

Snow White planter, ceramic, Leeds China Company, late 1940s, 6 1/2" h. 60

Snow White wristwatch, "Magic Mirror," U.S. Time, 1950, w/box 350

Snow White & the Seven Dwarfs figurines, porcelain, Goebel Full Bee mark, signed Disney, 1953, the set 1,050

Sword in the Stone animation cel, gouache on celluloid applied to a matching production background, Wart is held spellbound by an enchanted sugar bowl, 1963, 12 1/2 x 16" 2,185

Sword in the Stone bracelet charm, w/images of the owl, castle, etc., on card............. 120

That Darn Cat book, pictorial highlights of the movie w/shots of Hayley Mills & the cast, spiral-bound, 1965 45

Thumper (from Bambi) figure, china, Disney No. 131, Goebel, small.............................. 35

Thumper (from Bambi) figure, miniature, Hagen-Renaker....................................... 125

Thumper (from Bambi) salt & pepper shakers, ceramic, Goebel, w/label, pr......... 175

Thumper's girlfriend (from Bambi) ashtray, china, Disney No. 8, Goebel 325

Tinkerbell (from Peter Pan) bell, figural handle, ceramic, sold in Disneyland............. 275

Tinkerbell (from Peter Pan) figure, china, Goebel, Germany, 1959, 8" h. 285

Tinkerbell Movie Cel

Tinkerbell (from Peter Pan) movie cel, gouache on trimmed celluloid applied to a printed background, Tinkerbell looks to the side, stretches her arms & lifts one leg while standing beside a group of large thread spools, 1953, 8 1/2 x 11" (ILLUS.).. **3,162**

Tinkerbell (Peter Pan) movie drawing, graphite & colored pencil on paper, a large drawing of Tinkerbell, 1953, 7 1/2 x 9 1/2" **805**

Tweedle Dee & Tweedle Dum (from Alice in Wonderland) salt & pepper shakers, Walt Disney Productions, 1950s, pr. **375**

20,000 Leagues Under the Sea coloring book, 1953 .... **40**

20,000 Leagues Under the Sea toy, wind-up "Nautilus," actual working submarine, w/box **325-350**

Uncle Remus (from Song of the South) doll, stuffed cloth, 1940s, 14" h. **500**

Walt Disney World map, "Guide to the Magic Kingdom," in wooden frame, used at Disney World, 32 x 36" **275**

Wendy (from Peter Pan) hand puppet, Gund Mfg. Co., Walt Disney Productions **45**

White Rabbit (from Alice in Wonderland) creamer, ceramic, Regal China **195**

Who Framed Roger Rabbit Movie Cel

Who Framed Roger Rabbit movie cel, gouache on celluloid applied to a photographic background, Jessica's car has been smashed & Benny the Cab offers her a ride, 1988, 10 3/4 x 16 1/2" (ILLUS.).. **4,095**

Winnie the Pooh cookie jar, cov., Ransburg **125**

Winnie the Pooh toy, jack-in-the-box **38**

Winnie the Pooh toy, squeeze-type in original package, 1962, 5 1/2" h. **34**

Winnie the Pooh toy, "Tricky Trapeze," 1964, 5 1/2" h. **48**

Winnie the Pooh and Tigger Too production set-up, gouache on celluloid applied to a water-color production background, scene of Tigger asking Roo if he is "ready for some bouncin'," marked on bottom center "2518 VI sc. 212," 1974, 12 1/2 x 16"... **1,955**

Zorro coloring book, Whitman, 1958, very fine **31**

Zorro figures, Zorro on horse, Marx, 1958, very fine, 2 pcs.. **121**

Zorro gloves, w/original tag, mint, pr. **25**

Zorro half-mask & wrist flashlight, in original box, 2 pcs. **150**

Zorro Wrist Watch & Box

Zorro wrist watch, U. S. Time, 1957, original box (ILLUS.) **225-300**

Chapter 15
GAMES

Popeye Board Game

Addams Family (The) game, "Addams Family Creepy Mansion," Pressmen, 1992, 13" $18-25

Addams Family (The) game, board-type, Ideal, 1965 .... **65-175**

Addams Family (The) game, board-type, Milton Bradley, 1973 .... **40-125**

Addams Family Card Game

Addams Family (The) game, card-type, Milton Bradley, 1965, 6" h. (ILLUS.) **30-75**

Addams Family (The) game, target-type, Ideal, 1965 .... **125-175**

Alien game, board-type, Kenner, 1979 .... **65-95**

Alien game, computer-type, Commodore, 1985 .... **20-35**

Alien game, "Operation Aliens," British only .. **20-40**

Alley Oop game, original can, Royal Toy Co.. **300**

Banana Splits game, Hasbro **35-60**

Batman game, "Batman and Robin Game," Milton Bradley, 1966 .... **35-70**

Batman game, target-type, Batman and Robin, lithographed tin target w/Joker's face, Hasbro, 1966 .... **75-150**

Beany & Cecil game, "Beany and Cecil Match It," Mattel, 1960s **30-75**

Beatles game, "Flip Your Wig," Milton Bradley, 1964 .... **90-180**

Branded Game

Branded game, board-type, Milton Bradley, 1966 (ILLUS.) **35-40**

Bugs Bunny game, "Bugs Bunny Bagatelle Game," Ideal, 1975 .... **12-25**

Bugs Bunny game, "Bugs Bunny Under the Cawit Game," Whitman, 1972 .... **15-30**

Bullwinkle & Friends game, board-type, "Bullwinkle Hide and Seek Game," Milton Bradley, 1961 .... **25-75**

Bullwinkle & Friends game, board-type, "Bullwinkle Super Market Game," Whitman, 1970s **20-60**

Bullwinkle & Friends game, "Bullwinkle Card Game, Ed-U-Cards," 1962 .... **25-50**

Casper the Friendly Ghost game, bagatelle-type, Ja-Ru, 1988 .... **6-10**

Casper The Friendly Ghost Game

Casper the Friendly Ghost game, board-type, "Casper The Friendly Ghost Game," Milton Bradley, 1959 (ILLUS.) **10-20**

Casper the Friendly Ghost game, board-type, Schaper, 1974 .... **10-25**

Creature from the Black Lagoon game, "Creature from the Black Lagoon Mystery Game," Hasbro, 1963 .... **225-295**

Davy Crockett game, board-type, "Davy Crockett Indian Scouting Game," 1955, unused **75**

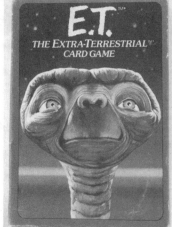

Dick Tracy Master Detective Game

Dick Tracy game, board-type, "Dick Tracy, Master Detective," Selright, 1960, excellent & complete (ILLUS.) **66**

Dick Tracy Board Game

Dick Tracy game, board-type, "Dick Tracy - The Master Detective Game," SeeRight - Selchow & Righter, 1961 (ILLUS.) **35-75**

Dick Tracy game, target-type, cardboard target w/dart gun, Marx, 1940s, target 17" w. **250-300**

Dick Tracy game, target-type, lithographed tin target, Marx, 1941, 10" w. target **100-200**

Disneyland game, board-type, "Adventureland," 1956 .... **35**

Disneyland game, board-type, "Pirates of the Caribbean" **40**

Doctor Who game, board-type, "Dalek Shooting Game," tin lithograph board, Marx, 1965, 8 x 20" **300-500**

Doctor Who game, board-type, "Doctor Who Daleks Oracle Question and Answer Board Game," 1965 .... **150-250**

Doctor Who game, Dalek bagatelle game, Denys Fisher, 1976 .... **100-150**

Dracula game, "Dracula Mystery Game," Hasbro, 1963 .... **175-225**

Dracula game, "I Vant to Bite Your Finger," Hasbro, 1981 .... **20-30**

E.T. game, board-type, Parker Brothers, 1982 .... **12-20**

E.T. Card Game

E.T. game, card-type, Parker Brothers, 1982, 4 1/4 x 6" box (ILLUS.) **10-20**

E.T. Preschool Game

E.T. game, "Touch & Tell," electronic preschool game, Texas Instruments, 1981, 10 x 14" (ILLUS.) **25-40**

E.T., the Extra-Terrestrial game, video-
type, Atari, 1982.. **5-10**

Fat Albert game, board-type, Milton Brad-
ley, 1973... **25-40**

Flintstones game, board-type, "Dino the
Dinosaur Game," Transogram, 1961......... **40-65**

Flintstones game, board-type, "Flintstones
Hoppy the Hopparoo Game," Tran-
sogram, 1965 .... **75-100**

Flintstones Stoneage Game

Flintstones game, board-type, "The Flintstones Stoneage Game," Transogram,
1961 (ILLUS.)... **30-50**

Flintstones game, card-type "Flintstones
Prehistoric Rummy, Ed-U-Card," 1960s,
box 3 1/2" sq... **25-40**

Flintstones game, "Flintstones Brake-Ball
Game," Whitman, 1960............................... **30-45**

Flintstones game, "Flintstones Cut-Ups
Game," Whitman, 1962............................... **35-50**

Flintstones game, target-type, lithographed tin, "Flintstones Mechanical
Shooting Gallery Target Game," Marx,
1962, 14" w. **200-275**

Gene Autry game, board-type, "Bandit
Trail"... **138**

Godzilla game, computer-type, for IBM,
1993... **75-100**

Godzilla game, Ideal, 1963...................... **200-400**

Gremlins game, board-type, International
Games, 1984... **20-30**

Gunsmoke game, Lowell, 1955, unused......... **125**

Hopalong Cassidy Canasta set, very good
w/good box **90**

Hopalong Cassidy game, "Hopalong
Cassidy Lasso Game," Transogram,
1950s... **125-175**

Huckleberry Hound game, board-type,
"Huckleberry Hound Western Game,"
Milton Bradley, 1959 .... **25-65**

Huckleberry Hound game, board-type,
Milton Bradley, 1981 .... **10-25**

Huckleberry Hound game, "Huckleberry
Hound Spin-O Game," 1959 .... **75-125**

Huckleberry Hound game, target-type,
"Huckleberry Hound's Huckle Chuck Tar-
get Game," Transogram, 1961 .... **40-80**

Huckleberry Hound game, "Tiddly Winks,"
Milton Bradley, 1959 .... **25-50**

James Bond Board Game

James Bond game, board-type, "James
Bond - Secret Agent 007 Game," Sean
Connery cover art, Milton Bradley, 1964
(ILLUS.)... **30-70**

Jetsons game, board-type, "Jetsons Out of
This World Game," Transogram, 1963 . **100-200**

Jetsons game, board-type, Milton Bradley,
1985... **12-20**

Jetsons game, board-type, "Rosey the Robot with Astro the Dog Game," Tran-
sogram, 1962 .... **65-95**

Jetsons game, "Jetsons Fun Pad Game,"
Milton Bradley, 1963 .... **65-125**

Jonny Quest game, board-type, Milton
Bradley, 1964 .... **45-85**

Jonny Quest game, board-type, Tran-
sogram, 1964, rare **300-500**

King Kong game, board-type, Ideal, 1963,
10 x 20" box... **40-65**

Ideal King Kong Game

King Kong game, board-type, Ideal, 1976
(ILLUS.)... **18-25**

Milton Bradley King Kong Game

King Kong game, board-type, Milton Bradley, 1966 (ILLUS.) **35-60**

Adventures of Lassie Game

Lassie game, board-type, "Adventures of Lassie," Lisbeth Whiting, 1955 (ILLUS.) **65-75**

Lassie game, board-type, "Lassie," Game Gems, 1965 .... **20-25**

Lone Ranger game, "Lone Ranger and the Silver Bullets," 1956, box 13 1/2 x 16" **60-80**

Lone Ranger game, target-type, square color cardboard target, Marx, 1946 .... **90-160**

Lost in Space game, board-type, Milton Bradley, 1965 .... **50-100**

Ludwig Von Drake card game, Walt Disney Productions, 1963, w/box **18**

Ludwig Von Drake game, "Tiddly Winks" **25**

Mary Poppins card game, Whitman, 1966, w/box **25**

Mickey Mouse card games, "Library of Games," five volumes of card games, 1946, the set **125**

Mickey Mouse game, "Mickey Mouse Target," includes target, guns & darts, Louis Marx Bros., in original box **575**

Mickey Mouse game, "Slugaroo," die-cut cardboard, 6 1/2" h. Mickey batter, 18" of fence, ca. 1950 .... **75**

Mighty Mouse game, board-type, Milton Bradley, 1978 .... **15-30**

Mighty Mouse game, "Mighty Mouse Rescue Game," Harett-Gilmar, 1960s **50-100**

Mummy (The) game, "Mummy Mystery Game," Hasbro, 1963 .... **150-225**

Munsters (The) game, board-type, "Munsters Drag Race," Hasbo, 1964..... **150-200**

Munsters (The) game, board-type, "Munsters Picnic Game," Hasbo, 1964 .... **100-150**

Munsters (The) game, board-type, "The Munsters," Milton Bradley, 1966 ... **100-150**

Munsters (The) game, bowling set, Ideal, 1965 .... **250-350**

Munsters (The) game, card-type, Milton Bradley, 1960s **45-75**

Munsters (The) game, "Masquerade Party Game," Hasbro, 1964 .... **50-95**

Munsters (The) game, target-type, Ideal, 1965 .... **125-175**

Muppets game, "The Dark Crystal Card Game," Milton Bradley, 1982, box 11 1/2" sq. **40-80**

Nightmare before Christmas game, video-type, hand-held, Tiger Electronics, 1993 .... **25-50**

Peter Pan game, board-type, Hunt Foods premium, 1969 .... **16**

Peter Pan game, "Peter Pan Adventure Game," Transogram **30**

Phantom of the Opera game, "Phantom of the Opera Mystery Game," Hasbro, 1963 .... **175-225**

Pink Panther game, board-type, Cadaco, 1981 .... **8-15**

Pink Panther game, board-type, Warren, 1977 .... **20-40**

Planet of the Apes Game

Planet of the Apes game, Milton Bradley, 1974 (ILLUS.) **35-75**

Popeye game, board-type, "Adventures of Popeye," Transogram, 1957 .... **50-100**

Popeye Board Game

Popeye game, board-type, Parker Brothers, 1983 (ILLUS.) **10-25**

Road Runner Race Game

Road Runner game, board-type, "Beep Beep - The Road Runner Race Game," Whitman, 1975 (ILLUS.) **8-12**

Road Runner game, board-type, Milton Bradley, 1968 .... **30-50**

Road Runner game, "Road Runner Pop-Up Game," Whitman, 1982 .... **20-35**

Roy Rogers game, "Horseshoe Set," two tin targets w/sticks & four vinyl horseshoes, Ohio Art Co., 7 1/4 x 14" box **175**

Scooby-Doo game, board-type, "Scooby-Doo Where Are You Game," Milton Bradley, 1975... **20-30**

Scooby-Doo game, "Scooby-Doo and Scrappy-Doo Game," Milton Bradley, early 1980s **12-20**

Scooby-Doo game, "Scooby-Doo Comic Game," Mattel, 1973 .... **15-25**

Scooby-Doo game, "Scooby-Doo Mystery," Super Nintendo, Akklaim Entertainment, 1995-96 .... **30-50**

Smurfs game, board-type, Milton Bradley, 1984 .... **8-12**

Star Trek Game

Star Trek game, "Star Trek the Role Playing Game," Fasa, 1983 (ILLUS.) **20-45**

Star Wars game, "Battle at Sarlacc's Pit" (Return of the Jedi), w/figures, Parker Bros., 1983 .... **15-30**

Superman game, board-type, "Calling Superman," 1954 .... **95**

Tarzan game, Tarzan, The Epic Adventures "City of Gold Tarzan," 1995, Trendmasters **10**

Man From U.N.C.L.E. Game

Smurf Spin-A-Round Game

Smurfs game, "Smurf Spin-A-Round Game," Milton Bradley, 1983 (ILLUS.) **10-18**

Star Trek game, board-type, Hasbro, 1974... **35-75**

The Man from U.N.C.L.E. game, board-type, "Napoleon Solo- The Man From U.N.C.L.E. Game," Ideal, 1965 (ILLUS.) ... **25-45**

Top Cat game, board-type, Transogram, 1962... **80-140**

(Twenty) 20,000 Leagues Under the Sea game, Jaymar Games, copyright Walt Disney Productions, w/box **65**

Uncle Wiggily Game

"Uncle Wiggily Game," board-type, color-printed box, Milton Bradley, little use, ca. 1950s (ILLUS.) **22**

Underdog game, board-type, Milton Bradley, 1964 boxed **50-90**

Underdog game, board-type, "Underdog to the Rescue Game," Whitman, 1975, boxed **12-20**

Underdog game, "Underdog Save Sweet Polly Game," Whitman, 1972 .... **45-75**

Wendy the Good Little Witch game, board-type, Milton Bradley, 1966 .... **120-200**

Woody Woodpecker game, board-type, Milton Bradley, 1959 .... **60-100**

Woody Woodpecker game, board-type, "Travel with Woody Woodpecker Game," Cadaco-Ellis, 1950s **45-75**

Woody Woodpecker game, board-type, "Woody Woodpecker's Crazy Mixed Up Color Factory Game," Whitman, 1972 .... **12-25**

Woody Woodpecker game, board-type, "Woody Woodpecker's Moon Dash Game," Whitman, 1976 .... **12-25**

X-Files (The), computer-type, Fox Interactive game, 1990s, 8 1/2 x 10" box (ILLUS. below) **25-35**

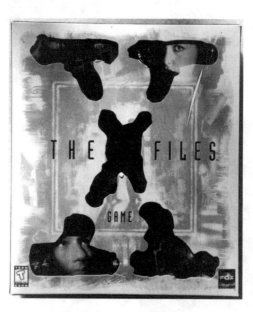

Yogi Bear Board Game

Yogi Bear game, board-type, Milton Bradley, 1971 (ILLUS.) **20-40**

Yogi Bear game, board-type, "Yogi Bear Break a Plate Game," Transogram, 1960s **50-90**

Yogi Bear game, board-type, "Yogi Bear Go Fly a Kite Game," Transogram, 1961 .. **25-65**

The X-Files Computer Game

Chapter 16
MODEL KITS

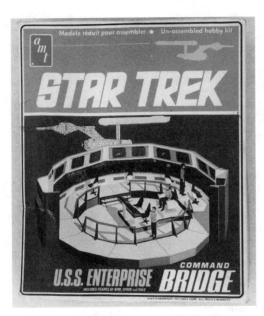

AMT Enterprise Command Bridge Kit

Addar - Plastic Kits, 1970s

Evel Knievel's Sky Cycle, 1974 .... **$30-75**

Jaws, based on Spielberg's shark film, 1975 .... **40-100**

Planet of the Apes, Caesar, 1/11 scale, 1974 .... **30-60**

Planet of the Apes, Cornelius, 1/11 scale, 1973 (ILLUS.) **20-45**

Planet of the Apes, Dr. Zaius, 1/11 scale, 1973 .... **25-50**

Planet of the Apes, Dr. Zira, 1/11 scale, 1974 .... **20-40**

Addar Cornelius Kit

Addar General Aldo Kit

Planet of the Apes, General Aldo, 1/11 scale, 1973 (ILLUS.) **20-40**

Addar General Ursus Kit

Planet of the Apes, General Ursus, 1/11
   scale, painted by Joe Fex, 1973 (ILLUS.) .. **30-60**
Planet of the Apes, Stallion & Soldier, 1/11
   scale, 1974 .... **40-80**
Prehistoric Dinosaurs, Super Scenes se-
   ries, 1976 .... **40-50**

**Airfix - Plastic Kits
(Britain/France), 1960s-1980s**

Airfix Corythosaurus Kit

Dinosaur, Corythosaurus, 1979 (ILLUS.) **30-40**
Dinosaur, Stegosaurus, 1979 .... **25-35**

Airfix Tyrannosaurus Rex Kit

Dinosaur, Tyrannosaurus Rex, 1976,
   14" h. (ILLUS.) **25-35**
Henry VIII, 1973 .... **5-10**
James Bond's Aston Martin DB-5, 1965.. **75-200**
Napoleon, 1978... **5-10**

AMT & AMT/Ertl - Plastic Kits - 1960s-
Bigfoot, 1/7 scale, 1978................................... **20-45**

AMT/Ertl Gigantics Tarantula Kit

Gigantics, Mantis, Scorpion or Tarantula
   Diorams (Fundimensions reissue), 1996,
   AMT/Ertl (ILLUS. of Tarantula)..................... **8-15**

AMT Kenworth Truck Tractor Kit

Movin' On, from NBC TV series, 1/25 scale
Kenworth truck tractor (ILLUS.)..................... **8-20**

AMT Munster Koach Kit

Munster Koach, 1964 (ILLUS.) **50-175**
Munster Koach & Dragula, reissued in one
package, 1991, MT/Ertl................................ **35-50**
Munsters (The), "Dragula" car, 1965........... **50-225**
Star Trek, Galileo 7 Shuttlecraft, 1/35 scale,
1974 .... **50-100**
Star Trek, Mr. Spock, shooting three-head-
ed monster, 1/12 scale, 1967 .... **40-125**
Star Trek, USS Enterprise, 18" h. w/lights,
1966 .... **75-200**

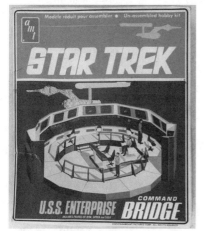

AMT Enterprise Command Bridge Kit

Star Trek, USS Enterprise Command
Bridge, 1/32 scale, 1975 (ILLUS.).............. **20-50**

Star Trek The Motion Picture, Klingon
Cruiser, 1984, AMT/Ertl **10-20**

Aurora - Plastic Kits,
1950s-70s -Animals

Aurora Big Horn Sheep Kit

Big Horn Sheep, 1/12 scale, 1963 (ILLUS.).. **25-60**

Aurora Cougar Kit

Cougar, 1/8 scale, 1962 (ILLUS.)................... **25-65**

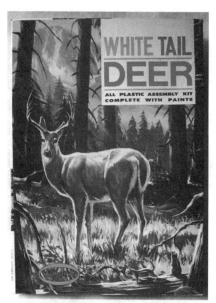

Aurora White-tailed Deer Kit

White-tailed Deer, 1/8 scale, 1962 (ILLUS.) .. **25-50**

Aurora - Plastic Kits, 1950s-70s - Historicals & Other Figures

Aurora Alfred E. Neuman Kit

Alfred E. Neuman (MAD Magazine), w/op-
tional signs & arms, 1965 (ILLUS.) **75-175**

Anzio Beach, World War II diorama,
1/87 scale, 1968... **10-50**

Black Knight of Nurnberg — 1580, 1/8
scale, 1956 .... **30-60**

Aurora Blackbeard Kit

Blackbeard, 1/10.5 scale, painted by Evan
Stuart, 1965 (ILLUS.) **75-200**

Aurora Blue Knight of Milan — 1520 Kit

Blue Knight of Milan — 1520, reissue,
1963, 9" h. (ILLUS.)...................................... **20-50**

Aurora Caballero Kit

Caballero, 1/8 scale, 1957 (ILLUS.) **35-95**

Aurora Dempsey vs Firpo Kit

Dempsy vs Firpo, Great Moments in Sport
series, 1/14 scale, 1965 (ILLUS.)............ **45-110**

Aurora Gladiator Kit

Gladiator, Adventure series, 1/8 scale,
1964 (ILLUS.).. **50-120**

Aurora Porthos Kit

Porthos, of "The Three Musketeers," 1/8
scale, 1958 (ILLUS.) **25-75**

Aurora Red Knight of Vienna Kit

Red Knight of Vienna (The), 1/8 scale,
1957 (ILLUS.)... **30-60**
Silver Knight of Augsburg — 1560, 1956,
9" h... **20-50**

Aurora Whoozis? Kit

Whoozis?, "So What if I Ain't Smart — I'M
LOVELY," 1968 (ILLUS.)............................. **25-75**

Aurora Willie Mays Kit

Willie Mays, Great Moments in Sport series, 1/10 scale, painted by Evan Stuart,
1965 (ILLUS.).. **100-200**

Aurora - Plastic Kits, 1950s-70s - Monsters (all series)

Aurora Addams Family Haunted House Kit

Addams Family Haunted House, 1965
(ILLUS.) **300-750**

Aurora Bride of Frankenstein Kit

Bride of Frankenstein, 1965 (ILLUS.) **300-850**

Aurora Chamber of Horrors, Le Guillotine Kit

Chamber of Horrors, Le Guillotine, 1964
(ILLUS.) **125-450**

1963 Creature from the Black Lagoon Kit

Creature from the Black Lagoon (The),
1963, 8 1/2" h. (ILLUS.) **125-400**

Creature from the Black Lagoon (The),
Frightening Lightning, glow version,
1969 .... **55-200**

Creature from the Black Lagoon (The),
glow version, 1972 .... **55-125**

1975 Creature from the Black Lagoon Kit

Creature from the Black Lagoon (The),
Monsters of the Movies series, painted
by Dennis Grimm, 1975, 7 1/4" h.
(ILLUS.) **75-225**

Aurora Customizing Monster Kit

Customizing Monster Kit, 1964
  (ILLUS.) **60-240**

Aurora Dr. Jekyll Kit

Dr. Jekyll, Monsters of the Movies series,
  glow pieces, 1975 (ILLUS.) **50-125**

Aurora Dr. Jekyll as Mr. Hyde Kit

Dr. Jekyll as Mr. Hyde, painted by
  Evan Stuart, 1964 (ILLUS.) **200-300**

Aurora Dracula Kit

Dracula, 1962 (ILLUS.) **25-300**
Dracula, Frightening Lightning, glow
  version, 1969 .... **150-325**

Dracula, glow version, 1972 .... **25-75**
Dracula's Dragster, 1965 .... **250-400**
**Forgotten Prisoner of Castel-Mare
  (The),** Frightening Lightning, glow
  revsion, 1969 .... **150-350**

Forgotten Prisoner of Castel-Mare Glow Kit

**Forgotten Prisoner of Castel-Mare
  (The),** glow version, 1972 (ILLUS.) **100-300**

Aurora Forgotten Prisoner of Castel-Mare Kit

**Forgotten Prisoner of Castel-Mare
  (The),** painted by Evan Stuart, 1966
  (ILLUS.) **150-400**
Frankenstein, 1961 .... **25-250**
Frankenstein, Frightening Lightning,
  glow version, 1969 .... **25-150**

Aurora Frankenstein Glow Kit

Frankenstein, glow version, 1972
  (ILLUS.) **25-75**
Frankenstein, Monster Scenes, 1971 .... **50-100**

Frankenstein, Monsters of the Movies
series, 1974 .... **150-250**
Frankenstein's Flivver, 1965 .... **300-400**
Ghidrah, Monsters of the Movies
series, 1975 .... **150-500**

Aurora "Big Frankie" Kit

Gigantic Frankenstein, "Big
Frankie," painted by Evan Stuart,
1964 (ILLUS) **700-1,200**
Godzilla, glow version, 1969 .... **75-300**

Aurora Godzilla Glow Kit

Godzilla, glow version, 1972 (ILLUS.) **75-175**

Aurora Godzilla Kit

Godzilla, painted by Evan Stuart, 1964
(ILLUS.) **85-500**

Godzilla's Go-Cart, 1966 .... **650-3,000**
Hunchback of Notre Dame, 1964 .... **85-300**
Hunchback of Notre Dame,
Frightening Lightning, glow version,
1969 .... **25-150**

Aurora Hunchback of Notre Dame Glow Kit

Hunchback of Notre Dame, glow version,
1972 (ILLUS.) **25-75**

Aurora King Kong Kit

King Kong, 1964, 10" h. (ILLUS.) **75-400**
King Kong, Frightening Lightning, glow
version, 1969, 10" h. **75-250**

Aurora King Kong Glow Kit

King Kong, glow version, painted by
Evan Stuart, 1972 (ILLUS.)........................ **75-175**
King Kong's Thronester, 1966 .... **350-1,000**

Aurora Mr. Hyde Kit

Mr. Hyde, Monsters of the Movies
series, glow pieces, 1975 (ILLUS.) **50-125**

Aurora Mummy Kit

Mummy (The), 1963 (ILLUS.) **25-300**

Aurora Mummy Glow Kit

Mummy (The), Frightening Lightning, glow
version, 1969 (ILLUS.).............................. **25-150**
Mummy (The), glow version, 1972 .... **25-60**

Mummy's (The) Chariot, 1965 .... **250-450**
Munsters (The), living room scene,
1964, rare... **400-900**
Phantom of the Opera, Frightening
Lightning series, 1969............................. **250-350**
Phantom of the Opera, glow version,
1969 .... **25-150**

Aurora Phantom of the Opera Kit

Phantom of the Opera, painted by Joe Fex,
1963 (ILLUS.)... **25-300**

Aurora Humorous Vampire Kit

Vampire, humorous design by William Castle, painted by Evan Stuart, 1966
(ILLUS.).. **50-150**

Aurora Vampirella Kit

Vampirella, w/optional poses, Monster
Scenes series, painted by Evan Stuart,
1971 (ILLUS.)... **75-200**

Aurora Wolfman Kit

Wolfman, 1962 (ILLUS.) **25-300**
Wolfman, Frightening Lightning, glow
version, 1969... **25-150**
Wolfman, glow version, 1972........................... **25-75**
Wolfman, Monsters of the Movies
series, 1974 .... **175-250**
Wolfman's Wagon, 1965 .... **300-400**
Wolfman's Wagon, reproduction,
unmarked, 1990s **40-95**

Aurora - Plastic Kits, 1950s-70s - Prehistoric Scenes, 1971

Allosaurus, No. 736, 1/13 scale, green
& yellow **90-125**
Armored Dinosaur (Ankylosaurus),
No. 744, 1/13 scale, orange..................... **90-125**

Aurora Cave Bear Kit

Cave Bear, No. 738, 1/13 scale, dark brown
(ILLUS.) **40-50**
Cave (The), No. 732, 1/13 scale, grey............ **40-50**

Aurora Cro-Magnon Man Kit

Cro-Magnon Man, No. 730, 1/13 scale, tan
(ILLUS.)... **20-30**

Aurora Cro-Magnon Woman Kit

Cro-Magnon Woman, No. 731, 1/13 scale,
tan (ILLUS.) **30-40**
Flying Reptile, No. 734, 1/13 scale,
orange **50-75**
Giant Bird, No. 739, 1/13 scale, blue-
silver **40-50**
Jungle Swamp, No. 740, 1/13 scale,
orange & green **50-75**

Aurora Saber Tooth Tiger Kit

Saber Tooth Tiger, No. 733, 1/13 scale,
yellow, painted by Evan Stuart (ILLUS.).... **30-40**
Sail Back Reptile (Dimetrodon), No.745,
1/13 scale, copper & green **50-75**

Spiked Dinosaur, No. 742, 1/13 scale,
tan & green **70-85**

Aurora Tar Pit Kit

Tar Pit, No. 735, 1/13 scale, orange
(ILLUS.) **40-50**

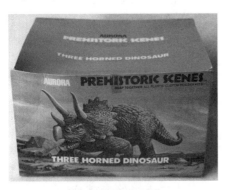

Aurora Three-Horned Dinosaur Kit

Three-Horned Dinosaur (Triceratops),
No. 741, 1/13 scale, silver (ILLUS.) **70-85**

Tyrannosaurus Rex, No. 746, 1/13
scale, red w/glow parts, 35" l. **150-200**

Aurora Wooly Mammoth Kit

Wooly Mammoth, No. 743, 1/13 scale,
green & cream, painted by Evan Stuart,
18" l. (ILLUS.) **90-125**

Aurora - Plastic Kits, 1950s-70s - Superheroes & Comic Scenes

Aurora Batman Kit

Batman, w/tree, bats & owl, 1/8 scale,
painted by Evan Stuart, 1964
(ILLUS.) **100-300**

Aurora Batmobile Kit

Batmobile, 1/32 scale, 1966
(ILLUS.) **100-275**

Aurora Captain America Kit

Captain America, 1/12 scale, 1966
(ILLUS.) **75-250**

Aurora Incredible Hulk Kit

Incredible Hulk (The), 1/12 scale, 1966
(ILLUS.) **75-250**

Penguin (Batman villain), w/umbrellas,
1/12 scale, 1967 .... **250-500**

Aurora Robin the Boy Wonder Kit

Robin the Boy Wonder, 1/12 scale,
1966 (ILLUS.) **45-85**

Aurora Superboy Kit

Superboy, w/eight page comic book,
1/8 scale, 1974 reissue (ILLUS.) **20-50**

Superman, 1/8 scale, in original painted
artwork box, 1963 .... **50-300**

Tarzan, 1/11 scale, in original long
box, 1967 .... **45-200**

Tarzan, 1/11 scale, w/eight page
comic book, 1974 .... **20-50**

Aurora Tonto Kit

Tonto, 1/10 scale, w/eight page
comic book, 1974 (ILLUS.) **15-35**

Aurora Wonder Woman Kit

Wonder Woman, 1/12 scale, 1965
(ILLUS.) **150-400**

Aurora - Plastic Kits, 1950s-70s - TV & Movie Tie-Ins

12 O'Clock High, B17 Bomber
Formation, w/three planes, 1965 .... **100-250**

**Banana Buggy (from Banana Splits
TV show),** 1/25 scale, yellow, 1969 ...... **250-400**

Doctor Dolittle, Good Ship Flounder,
1968 .... **30-75**

Land of the Giants, w/giant snake,
1/48 scale, 1968 .... **150-350**

Lost in Space, Cyclops w/rock, 1/42
scale, 1966 .... **200-800**

Rat Patrol, 1/87 scale, 1967............................ **20-70**

Billiken - Vinyl & Resin
Kits, 1980s-present

20 Million Miles to Earth, Ymir,
resin, 1980s.. **550-650**
Baragon, vinyl.. **75-100**

Billiken Beast from 20,000 Fathoms Kit

Beast from 20,000 Fathoms, red or green
vinyl, 1980s (ILLUS.)............................... **350-500**
Creature from the Black Lagoon, 1991 .... **50-100**
Dracula **130-200**
Frankenstein, 1991 .... **75-125**
Godzilla, vinyl, 1954 style............................... **65-95**
Godzilla, vinyl, 1962 style............................... **50-90**
Godzilla, vinyl, 1964 style............................... **65-95**
Godzilla, vinyl, 1992 style............................ **85-110**
Mummy (The), 1990.................................... **100-150**

Billiken Phantom of the Opera Kit

Phantom of the Opera, 1980s
(ILLUS.).. **200-250**

Predator, soft vinyl, 1991, 12" **35-75**

Dark Horse - Cold-cast
Porcelain Kits, 1990s-present

*Dark Horse Creature from
the Black Lagoon Kit*

Creature from the Black Lagoon,
1/8 scale, 1991 (ILLUS.)........................ **125-150**

Dark Horse Frankenstein Kit

Frankenstein, w/metal chains,
1991, 10 1/2" h. (ILLUS.)........................ **110-140**
King Kong, sculpted by Ray
Harryhausen.. **115-155**
King Kong bust **75-95**
Predator, 1/8 scale, limited edition of
1,000... **125-175**
S-Files, Flukeman, 1990s........................... **100-150**

Fundimensions - Plastic Kits, 1970s

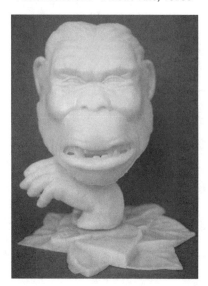

Fundimensions Ape Man Glo Head Kit

Haunted Glo-Head, Ape Man, undecorated, (decorated version shown w/Mummy box) 1975 (ILLUS.) **20-45**

Fundimensions Haunted Glo-Head Boxes

Haunted Glo-Head, Mummy, one of four versions, 1975 (ILLUS. of box) **20-45**

Haunted Glo-Head, Vampire, one of four versions, 1975 (ILLUS. w/Mummy) **20-45**

Haunted Glo-Head, Werewolf, one of four versions, 1975 (ILLUS. w/Mummy) **20-45**

Halcyon - Plastic & Vinyl Kits - 1990s

Halcyon Attacking Alien Kit

Alien, Attacking Alien w/base, 1/9 scale (ILLUS.) **25-40**

Alien, Tsukuda reissue, black vinyl, 16" **85-195**

Halcyon Alien Chestburster Kit

Alien Chestburster, 1/1 scale, tan vinyl, 1992, 10" h. (ILLUS.) **100-135**

Halcyon Alien 3 Dog Burster Kit

Alien Dog Burster, Alien 3, 1/1 scale, tan vinyl, 12" h. (ILLUS.) **100-150**

Alien Facehugger, tan vinyl, 1992,
   life-size, 50" l. **200-250**
Alien Queen, black vinyl, 1992, 14" h. **100-150**
Alien Queen Chestburster, tan
   vinyl, 10 1/2" **125-175**
Alien Queen Facehugger w/Fetus,
   vinyl, 46" h. **50-115**
Alien Warrior, Aliens, base & egg,
   plastic, 9"... **30-90**

Halcyon Predator 2 Creature Kit

Predator 2 Creature, Movie Classic series,
   plastic, painted by Joe Fex, 1990s
   (ILLUS.) **30-45**

Hawk - Plastic Kits, 1960s - Frantics, Designed by Reuben Klamer, 1965

Hawk Bopped Out Steel Pluckers Havin' a Bash Kit

**Bopped Out Steel Pluckers Havin'
a Bash** (ILLUS.)... **40-80**

Frantic Banana Punishing the Skins **40-80**

Hawk Totally Fab Kit

Totally Fab (ILLUS.)... **40-80**

Hawk - Plastic Kits, 1960s - Silly Surfers, 1964

Hawk Hodad Makin' the Scene with a Six-Pack

Hodad Makin' the Scene with a Six-Pack
   (ILLUS.)... **35-75**
**Hot Dogger and Surf Bunny Riding Tan-
   dem** **40-80**
Hot Dogger Hangin' Ten **30-60**
Woodie on a Surfari **35-75**

Hawk - Plastic Kits, 1960s - Weird-ohs, Designed by Bill Campbell, 1963-64

Daddy the Way-out Suburbanite, 1963 .... **40-90**
Davey the Way-out Cyclist, 1963................. **40-90**
Digger the Way-out Dragster, 1963.............. **40-90**
Drag Hag, 1963.. **40-90**

Endsville Eddy, 1963 .... **30-75**
Francis the Foul, 1963 .... **30-75**

Hawk Freddy Flameout Kit

Freddy Flameout, 1963 (ILLUS.) **30-75**
Huey's Hut Rod, 1963 .... **25-60**
Killer McBash, 1963 .... **60-140**
Leaky Boat Louie, 1963 .... **50-120**
Sling Rave Curvette, 1964 .... **15-40**
Wade A. Minit, 1964 .... **20-50**

Hawk Weird-ohs Glow Kit

Weird-ohs, Glows in the Dark versions,
1969-70, each (ILLUS. of Endsville
Eddie) **25-65**

Horizon - Vinyl Kits, 1980s-90s

Apatosaurus, 1/30 scale **35-45**

Horizon Bram Stoker's Dracula Bat Kit

Bram Stoker's Dracula, Dracula Bat ver-
sion, 1990s (ILLUS.) **35-65**

Horizon Bram Stoker's Dracula Wolf Kit

Bram Stoker's Dracula, Dracula Wolf ver-
sion, 1990s (ILLUS.) **35-65**

Horizon Bride of Frankenstein Kit

Bride of Frankenstein, w/optional gown,
Sci-Fi Art Kits, painted by Joe Fex, 1988
(ILLUS.) **25-40**
Creature from the Black Lagoon, 1993,
built-up 12" **40-65**
Elasmosaurus, 1/30 scale **35-45**

Horizon Frankenstein Kit

Frankenstein, painted by Joe Fex, 1993
(ILLUS.) **40-65**
Hunting Velociraptor, sculpted by Darga,
30" l. **65-75**

Horizon Invisible Man Kit

Invisible Man, w/optional poses, Sci-Fi Art
Kits, painted by Joe Fex, 1988 (ILLUS.) ... **25-40**
Jurassic Park, Brachiosaurus,
1/19 scale **100-135**
Jurassic Park, Spitter
(Dilophosaurus), 1990s **80-110**
Jurassic Park, Tyrannosaurus, 1990s **100-135**
Jurassic Park, Velociraptor, 1990s **80-110**
Life-size Hatchling T-Rex, sculpted by
Darga **55-70**

Horizon Mole People Kit

Mole People, Sci-Fi Art Kits, 1988 (ILLUS.) .. **25-40**

Horizon Mummy Kit

Mummy (The), Tom Tyler as the Mummy,
painted by Joe Fex, 1993 (ILLUS.) **40-65**
Phantom of the Opera, Sci-Fi Art Kits,
1988 .... **25-40**

Horizon Robocop 3 Figure

Robocop 3, 1/6 scale, 1989 (ILLUS. of
figure) **25-45**
Stegosaurus, 1/30 scale **35-45**

Horizon Tyrannosaurus Rex Kit

Tyrannosaurus Rex, 1/30 scale (ILLUS.) **40-60**

Lindberg - Plastic Kits, 1950s-present

Dinosaur, Brontosaurus, Pyro reissue,
1979 .... **10-18**

Dinosaur, Dimetrodon, Pyro reissue,
8 1/4" l., 1979 .... **10-18**

Dinosaur, Stegosaurus, Pyro reissue, 1979 .. **10-18**

Dinosaur, Tyrannosaurus, Pyro reissue,
1979 .... **10-18**

Lindberg Glo-Monster Fiend Kit

Glo-Monster Fiend, reissue of 1964 "Glob,"
1971 (ILLUS.) **25-45**

Lindberg Godzilla Kit

Godzilla, Super Detailed, snap-fit, painted
by Joe Fex, 1995, 7 1/2" h. (ILLUS.) **10-15**

Lindberg Goofy Klock Kit

Goofy Klock, motorized, 1965 (ILLUS.) **70-140**

Jurassic Park, Hadrosaurus
(Corythosaurus), 1993 .... **10-15**

Jurassic Park, Spitter, 1993 .... **15-22**

Jurassic Park, Stegosaurus, 1993 .... **10-15**

Jurassic Park, Tyrannosaurus, 1993 .... **20-25**

Lindberg Velociraptor Kit

Jurassic Park, Velociraptor, 1993 (ILLUS.) .. **15-22**

Lindberg - Plastic Kits -Lindy Loonys, "The Hep Model in the 'Square' Box," 1965

Bert's Bucket **35-80**

Big Wheeler **35-80**

Fat Max **35-80**

Road Hog **35-80**

Satan's Crate **35-80**

Scuttle Bucket **35-80**

Lindberg - Plastic Kits - Miscellaneous

UFO, classic saucer w/little green alien
inside, 1956 .... **125-175**

UFO, reissue of 1956 kit, glows in the
dark, 1972 .... **40-65**

Mad Lab - Resin Kits Sculpted by Michael Parks, 1990s-present

20 Million Miles to Earth, "Tiny Terrors" Ymir holding Dumbo.................................... **20-40**

Mad Lab Alien Kit

Alien, "Tiny Terrors" running alien, unmarked, 4 1/2" h. (ILLUS.)........................... **15-35**

Mad Lab Bart'nstein Kit

Bart'nstein, Bart Simpson as Frankenstein, limited edition, 9" h. (ILLUS.) **50-100**

Bride of Frankenstein & Frankenstein

Bride of Frankenstein, "Tiny Terrors," painted by Joe Fex, 4 1/2" h. (ILLUS.)....... **15-30**
Creature from the Black Lagoon, "Tiny Terrors," `1991, 4 1/4" h. **15-30**
Dead Elvis, "Tiny Terrors," zombie in Elvis jumpsuit... **15-30**

Mad Lab Dracula Kit

Dracula, "Tiny Terrors" (ILLUS.).................... **20-30**

Mad Lab Famous Monsters Cover Card

Famous Monsters cover card, Curse of the Werewolf, painted by Joe Fex, 4 1/2" h. (ILLUS.)... **10-25**

Mad Lab Frankenstein Kit

Frankenstein, "Tiny Terrors," holding a bottle marked "Hootch," painted by Joe Fex, 1991, 4" h. (ILLUS.)..................................... **15-25**

Frankenstein, "Tiny Terrors," painted by Joe Fex, 4 1/4" h. (ILLUS. w/Bride of Frankenstein) **15-25**

Frankenstein, "Tiny Terrors," wearing boxer shorts, 1992, 4 1/4" h. **15-25**

Frankenstein's Daughter, "Tiny Terrors," 4 1/2" h. **20-30**

Mad Lab Godzilla Kit

Godzilla, "Tiny Terrors," stomping Godzilla, 1991, 3 1/2" h. (ILLUS.) **20-40**

Mad Lab Gorgo Kit

Gorgo, "Tiny Terrors," 4" h. (ILLUS.) **15-35**

King Kong, "Stranglehold," Kong w/snake, 13" h. **100-130**

Mad Lab King Kong Kit

King Kong, "Tiny Terrors," including dead T-Rex (not shown), 3 1/2" h. (ILLUS.) **20-30**

Mad Lab Little Red & Big Bad Wolf Kit

Little Red & the Big Bad Wolf (werewolf), 1/6 scale (ILLUS.) **120-165**

Mad Lab Morlock Kit

Morlock, from The Time Machine, "Tiny Terrors," painted by Joe Fex (ILLUS.) **15-35**

Mummy (The), "Tiny Terrors," 1992, 4 1/2" h. **15-25**

Outer Limits, Sixth Toe, "Tiny Terrors," 1993 .... **15-25**

Teenage Frankenstein, "Tiny Terrors" **15-25**

Wolfman, "Tiny Terrors," marked "ML MP," 4" h. **15-25**

Marx - Paintable Plastic Figures, 1960s-70s

Army Men series, most in green, about
6" h., each **2-4**

Marx Campus Cuties Figures

Campus Cuties series, fleshtone, 6" h.,
each (ILLUS. of two) **3-5**

Disney character series, brightly colored,
about 6" h., each.. **2-6**

Monster Studio Set

Monster Studio set, six figures w/paints,
Marx molds, by Uncle Milton, 1991, the
set (ILLUS.).. **40-80**

Marx Prehistoric Times Caveman Figure

Prehistoric Times series, large caveman,
about 5-6" h., each (ILLUS.) **5-10**

Superhero series, each **4-9**

Marx Universal Monster Figure

Universal Monster series, about 5" h.,
each (ILLUS.) **5-10**

Monogram - Plastic Kits, 1970s-80s - Dinosaurs (re-issues from Aurora's Prehistoric Scenes line)

Allosaurus, 1/13 scale, 1979 & 1987 .... **25-35**
Ankylosaurus, 1/13 scale, 1979 & 1987 .... **20-30**
Dimetrodon, 1/13 scale, 1979 & 1987 .... **15-25**
Pteranodon, 1987.. **30-40**
Styracosauarus, 1987................................... **30-40**
Triceratops, 1987.. **30-40**

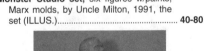

Monogram Tyrannosaurus Rex

Tyrannosaurus Rex, 1/13 scale,
1979 & 1987 (ILLUS.) **40-55**
Woolly Mammoth, 1/13 scale,
1979 & 1987 .... **30-40**

Monogram - Plastic Kits (most re-issued Aurora)

Creature from the Black Lagoon, 1994 .... **15-20**

Monogram Dracula Kit

Dracula, 1991 (ILLUS.) **20-45**

Monogram Elvira's Macabre Mobile Kit

Elvira's Macabre Mobile, 1988 (ILLUS.)....... **20-40**

Monogram Godzilla Kit

Godzilla, w/glow pieces,
  discontinued, 1978 ILLUS.)...................... **60-120**

Monogram Luminators Dracula Kit

Luminators, Dracula, glows in dark,
  1991 (ILLUS.).. **15-25**

Luminators, Frankenstein, glows in dark,
  1991.. **15-25**

Luminators, King Kong, glows in dark,
  1991.. **25-75**

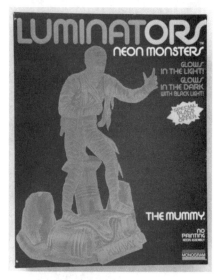

Monogram Luminators Mummy Kit

Luminators, Mummy, glows in dark,
  1991(ILLUS.).. **15-25**

Luminators, Phantom of the Opera,
  glows in dark, 1992 .... **15-25**

Mummy (The), 1983.. **20-35**

Passenger Rocket, 1/192 scale,
  Willy Ley on box art, 1950s...................... **75-225**

Monogram Superman Kit

Superman, blue, 1978 (ILLUS.)...................... **20-50**

Monogram Wolf Man Kit

Wolf Man, w/optional glow pieces, painted
by Joe Fex,1983 (ILLUS.) **20-45**

MPC - Plastic Kits, 1960s-present

Alien, 1979 .... **25-100**

Black Hole, Maximillian robot, from Disney
film, 1979, 11" h. **15-35**

Black Hole, V.I.N. Cent. robot, from Disney
film, 1979, 8 1/2" h.. **20-40**

Dark Shadows, Barnabas Vampire Van,
late 1960s **75-225**

Dark Shadows, Werewolf, 1969 .... **75-275**

Dinosaur, Brontosaurus, reissue of Airfix,
1982 .... **10-20**

Dinosaur, Tyrannosaurus, reissue of Airfix,
1982, 14" h. **10-20**

Night Crawler Wolf Man Car, 1971 .... **45-125**

Road Runner, Beep Beep Road Runner....... **45-75**

Road Runner, Wile E. Coyote **45-75**

Star Wars, Darth Vader Tie-fighter,
MPC/Ertl, 1989 reissue................................... **8-15**

Star Wars, Darth Vader w/glowing light saber, MPC/Ertl, 1989 reissue, 11 1/2" h. **8-15**

Palmer - Plastic Kits, late 1950s

American Mastodon skeleton, 10" h. **20-40**

Brontosaurus skeleton, 13" h. **20-40**

Polar Lights (primarily produce re-issues of Aurora, Addar, etc.)

Addams Family Haunted House, Aurora
reissue, glow version, 1995 .... **20-35**

Bride of Frankenstein, Aurora reissue,
1997.. **20-35**

Polar Lights Go Cart Kit

Go Cart (The), Aurora reissue of Godzilla's
Go Cart, box art modified, 1999 (ILLUS.).. **15-25**

Polar Lights Mummy's Chariot Kit

Mummy's (The) Chariot, Aurora reissue,
glow version, Frightening Lightning, 1995
(ILLUS.)... **15-25**

Polar Lights Munsters Living Room Kit

Munsters (The), living room scene,
Aurora reissue, 1997 (ILLUS.).................... **15-25**

Polar Lights Wolf Man Kit

Wolf Man (The), original model design, 1998 (ILLUS.) **15-25**

Pyro - Plastic Kits, late 1950s-late 1960s

Human Heart, life-size, 1960s **15-35**

Pyro - Plastic Kits, late 1950s-late 1960s - Dinosaurs

Dimetrodon, 1/10 scale **20-40**

Horned Dinosaur, Triceratops, 1/40 scale.... **20-40**

Pyro Plated Dinosaur Kit

Plated Dinosaur, Stegosaurus, 1/32 scale (ILLUS.) **20-40**

Protoceratops, 1/8 scale................................. **20-40**

Thunder Lizard, Brontosaurus, 1/72 scale, 11" h.. **20-40**

Tyrant King, Tyrannosaurus, 1/48 scale, 10" h.. **20-40**

Revell - Plastic Kits, 1950s-present - Custom Monsters Series, Designed by Ed"Big Daddy" Roth, 1963-65

Angel Fink, 1965.. **50-175**

Revell Brother Rat Fink Kit

Brother Rat Fink, painted by Evan Stuart, 1963 (ILLUS.).. **40-90**

Revell Drag Nut Kit

Drag Nut, 1963 (ILLUS.)................................ **45-150**

Fink-Eliminator, 1965.................................... **50-200**

Mother's Worry, 1963 .... **30-80**

Mr. Gasser, first kit released in Ed Roth series, 1963.. **50-150**

Outlaw with Robbin' Hood Fink, 1965.... **200-500**

Rat Fink, 1963.. **60-140**

Scuz-Fink, 1964.. **165-300**

Super Fink, 1964 .... **150-350**

Surfink, 1965... **55-165**

Revell - Plastic Kits, 1950s-present - Dr. Seuss Series, 1958-1960

Birthday Bird, 1960 .... **50-175**

Busby the Tasselated Afghan Yak, 1959.. **100-250**

Revell Cat in the Hat Kit

Cat in the Hat, 1959 (ILLUS.) **50-150**
Cat in the Hat with Thing 1 and Thing 2,
1960 .... **125-300**
Dr. Seuss Zoo Set, includes Gowdy, Tingo
& Norval, 1960, the set **250-600**

Gowdy the Dowdy Grackle Kit

Gowdy the Dowdy Grackle, plastic wrap
intact, 1958, 7 1/8 x 10 1/2" (ILLUS.) **100-300**
Grickily the Gractus, 1959 .... **100-250**
Horton the Elephant, 1960 .... **300-500**

Revell Norval the Bashful Blinket Kit

Norval the Bashful Blinket, 1959
(ILLUS.) **100-250**

Revell Roscoe the Many-footed Lion Kit

Roscoe the Many-footed Lion, 1959
(ILLUS.) **100-250**
Tingo the Noodle Stroodle, 1958 .... **100-250**

Revell - Plastic Kits,
1950s-present - General

Revell Astronaut in Space Kit

Astronaut in Space, 1968-present,
frequently reissued (ILLUS.) **5-10**

Revell Paul McCartney Kit

Beatles, John, Paul, George or Ringo,
1965, each (ILLUS. of Paul) **75-225**

Revell Challenger Space Shuttle Kit

Challenger Space Shuttle, 1/72 scale, 1982 (ILLUS.) **20-45**

Dracula, Monsters of the Movies series, Aurora reissue, 1999 .... **8-15**

Everything is "Go," Friendship 7 Mercury rocket, 1962 .... **25-75**

Revell Knight Rider Chopper Trike Kit

Evil Iron, Knight Rider Chopper Trike, 1976, 14" l. (ILLUS.) **15-40**

Flipper, based on dolphin TV series, 1965 .... **75-150**

Revell Frankenstein Kit

Frankenstein, Monsters of the Movies series, Aurora reissue, 1999 (ILLUS.) **8-15**

Revell Perri Squirrel Kit

Perri Squirrel, from Disney film, life-size w/sprinkle-on fur, 1958 (ILLUS.) **25-85**

Phantom and the Voodoo Witch Doctor, 1/8 scale, 1965 .... **125-350**

Quick Snap Dinos, tiny 1/100 versions of Aurora kits, 1994, each **4-8**

Titanic Kit

Titanic, 1/570 scale, 1976, 18 1/2" l. (ILLUS.) **400-475**

Revell - Plastic Kits, 1950s-present - General

Visible Woman, w/optional womb & fetus, 1950s-present, frequently reissued **8-20**

Revell/Monogram - Plastic Kits, 1990s

Dinosaurs, 1/13 scale, reissues from Aurora Prehistoric Scenes, 1992-93, each **12-30**

Revell/Monogram Elvira Figure & Certifcate of Authenticity

Elvira, Mistress of the Dark '58 Thunderbird with painted Elvira figure, limited edition of 10,000, together w/certificate of authenticity (ILLUS. Elvira figure shown by certificate) **25-45**

Jurassic Park, Lost World Tyrannosaurus
Rex, 1/25 scale, 1997 .... **10-15**

*Revell/Monogram Lost
World Velociraptors Kit*

JurassicPark, Lost World Velociraptors,
1/25 scale, snap-together, 1997
(ILLUS.) **10-15**

Jurassic Park, Lost World vehicle, Hunter's Humvee Snagger, snap-together,
1997 .... **7-10**

Jurassic Park, Lost World vehicle,
Mercedes-Benz, snap-together, 1997 .... **7-10**

Revell/Monogram Kothoga Monster Kit

Relic, Kothoga monster from the film,
limited edition of 5,000, vinyl, 1997
(ILLUS.) **20-35**

Screamin' Productions -
Large vinyl Kits, 1980s-90s

Cryptkeeper, w/book, real hair, 1/4 scale,
14" h. **50-85**

Screamin' Productions Elvira Kit

Elvira, 1/4 scale w/mini poster, 1988
(ILLUS.) **60-100**

Freddy Kreuger, 1/6 scale, reissue of
Kaiyodo mold **45-65**

Jason, from Friday the 13th, w/removable
mask, 1/4 scale, 1988, 18" h. **50-85**

Pinhead Cenobite, from Hellraiser,
1/4 scale, 1989 .... **75-100**

Screamin' Productions Pinhead Cenobite Kit

Pinhead Cenobite, from Hellraiser, w/altar
of souls, 1/4 scale, 1993 (ILLUS.) **75-100**

Tamiya - Plastic Kits
(Japanese), 1980s-90s

Brachiosaurus diorama, 1994 .... **70-90**

Chasmosaurus with baby diorama, 1994 ... **25-35**

Mesozoic Creatures, six different models,
1994, each **15-25**

Parasaurolophys and Nystosaur diorama, 1994 .... **25-35**

Triceratops with Velociraptor diorama, 1994 .... **35-45**

Tyrannosaurus Rex with figure diorama, 1994 .... **40-50**

Velociraptor pack, six different, 1 1/2 to 2", 1994 .... **15-25**

Tsukuda - Vinyl Kits (Japanese), 1980s-present

Alien, completed model sold boxed, Kenner mold, Hobby **90-130**

Tsukuda Frankenstein Kit

Frankenstein, 1/5 scale, painted by Joe Fex, 1986 (ILLUS.) **85-125**

Ghostbusters Terror Dog, 1/6 scale **75-100**

Gillman, Creature from the Black Lagoon, 1/5 scale, 1981 .... **150-200**

Godzilla 1964, 1/160 scale **125-150**

Jurassic Park, Tyrannosaurus Rex, 1/24 scale PVC kit **80-120**

Tsukuda King Kong Kit

King Kong, 1/5 scale, 1986 (ILLUS.) **85-125**

Mummy (The) No. 39, "Mummy Man," 1/5 scale, 1986 .... **80-120**

Rodan, 1/160 scale, 1994 .... **80-120**

Wolfman #40, 1/6 scale, 1986 .... **40-80**

X-Plus - Vinyl Kits (Japanese), 1980s-present

X-Plus Yeti Adult Kit

Yeti, half human adult w/optional bodies, 1/8 scale, factory paint, limited edition, 1988 (ILLUS.) **150-200**

X-Plus Yeti Child w/Rabbit Kit

Yeti, half human child w/rabbit, 1/8 scale, factory paint, limited edition, 1988 (ILLUS. front right w/adult figures) **75-100**

Miscellaneous

Dr. Phibes Bust

Dr. Phibes bust, painted by Joe Fex, maker
unknown, resin, small, 1990s (ILLUS.) **50-75**

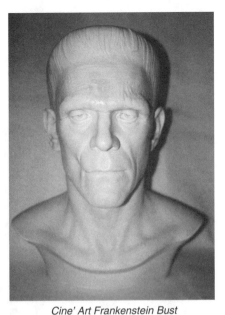

Cine' Art Frankenstein Bust

Frankenstein bust, Boris Karloff likeness,
by Miles Teves, life-size, resin, Cine'
Art, 1990s (ILLUS.)................................... **595-650**

Lil' Monsters Elvira Bust

Elvira bust, w/Bio-matched glass eyes, by
Lil' Monsters, life-size, 1990s
(ILLUS.) **150-175**

Vincent Price Bust

Vincent Price bust on pedestal, by Steve
West, resin, 1990s (ILLUS.)........................ **65-75**

Chapter 17
PLAYSETS BY MARX

Cape Kennedy Action Play Set

In 1919 Louis Marx set out to manufacture high quality toys for the mass market. His plan was to cut costs, but not quality, and make toys affordable for the general public.

A few years later he was joined by his brother, David. The firm's motto became "Give the customer more toy for less money and quality is not negotiable."

Over the years Marx signed exclusive toy deals with Walt Disney, Sears, Montgomery Ward and other large firms. In addition to toys and dolls, electric trains joined the Marx line-up.

After World War II the playset was born. Even though other companies moved into this business, when you mention "playset" to collectors today they think "Marx."

During the 1950s and '60s Marx sold playsets by the millions. They employed mass-production techniques to cut costs. At first the boxes were similar to their train boxes with just the company name but by the 1950s they had added graphics to the box designs.

Playsets provided countless hours of play for kids and mothers liked them because all the pieces went back into the box for storage. Each Marx playset contained one hundred pieces or more, so that was helpful.

Playsets based on popular television shows and movies were among leading sellers.

Some of the early favorites included Tom Corbett Space Academy, Gunsmoke, Wagon Train, Robin Hood, Roy Rogers, Rin Tin Tin at Fort Apache and Zorro.

Each set came with lithographed tin buildings, chairs, logs, flags, fireplaces, pots, bombs, guns, cannons and many other accessories.

Today playsets have become one of the hottest areas of toy collecting. Even though millions were made, it is difficult to find a set complete. Usually a collector has to hunt and put it together piece by piece.

Adventures of Robin Hood, based on British TV series, No. 4722, 1956 .... **$200-1,300**
American Airlines International Jet Port,
No. 4810, 1962 .... **125-400**

Army Training Center Headquarters

Army Training Center, No. 4102, 1955
(ILLUS. of one building) **150-450**
Bar-M Ranch, No. 3956 .... **75-250**

Battle of Iwo Jima, No. 4147, 1964 .... **100-500**
Battle of the Blue and Gray, Deluxe Civil
War Centennial Edition, No. 4744,
1963 .... **300-1,250**
Ben Hur, based on the movie, No. 4696,
1959 .... **200-750**
Big Top Circus, No. 4310, 1952 .... **100-600**
Boys Camp, No. 4103, 1956 .... **150-700**

Cape Kennedy Action Play Set

Cape Kennedy Action Play Set, w/metal
carry-all case, No. 4625, 1968
(ILLUS.) **50-150**
Cattle Drive, No. 3983, 1970 .... **75-300**
D.E.W. (Distant Early Warning) Line Set,
No. 4802, w/atomic bomb rack, 1958 ... **300-900**
Davy Crockett at the Alamo, based on
the Disney TV show, No. 3530, 1955 ... **125-450**
Desert Fox, No. 4177, 1966 .... **125-500**
Dollhouse, w/bomb shelter inside,
1958-59 (ILLUS.) **75-150**
Fort Apache, No. 6063, 1965 .... **125-575**
Fort Apache Stockade, No. 3610,
1951 .... **150-700**
Fort Pitt, No. 3741, 1959 .... **90-400**
Fort York, Canada, No. 3640,
1958-59, sold only in Canada **1,000-1,500**
Freight Terminal, No. 5220, 1955 .... **90-200**
I.G.Y. Satellite Base, No. 4800, 1959 ... **300-1,000**
Johnny Ringo Western Frontier Set,
No. 4784, 1959 .... **1,300-2,700**
Johnny Tremain Revolutionary War set,
based on TV series, No. 3402, 1957 .. **450-2,100**
Jungle Jim, based on TV series, No.
3706, 1957 .... **400-1,500**
Knights and Vikings, No. 4743, 1970 .... **75-250**
Lady and The Tramp, based on the
Disney movie, 1961 .... **125-400**

Lazy-Day Farm Set

Lazy-Day Farm, No. 3948, 1950s
(ILLUS.) **100-425**
Little Red School House, No. 3381,
1956 .... **100-450**
Navarone Mountain Battleground,
No. 3412, 1976 .... **30-150**
Operation Moon Base, No. 4654, 1962 ... **150-550**
Pet Shop, No. 4210, 1953 .... **50-300**
Project Mercury Cape Canaveral,
No. 4524, 1959 .... **100-500**
Rex Mars Planet Patrol, No. 7040,
1958 .... **125-450**
Rifleman (The) Ranch, based on TV
series, No. 3998, 1959 .... **150-750**
Rin Tin Tin, based on TV series, No.
3628, 1956 .... **200-900**
Roy Rogers Rodeo Ranch, No.
3979, 1952 .... **100-350**
Sears Store, No. 5490, 1961 .... **400-1,900**
Service Station, No. 3495 .... **30-100**
Sons of Liberty, based on TV series,
No. 4170, 1950s **50-350**
Strategic Air Command, No. 6013,
1960 .... **225-800**
Tales of Wells Fargo, No. 4260, 1950s .. **200-750**
Untouchables, based on TV series,
No. 4676, 1961 .... **300-700**
Wagon Train, based on TV series,
No. 4888, 1950s **300-1,700**
Ward's Service Station, No. 3488,
1959 .... **100-500**
Western Mining Town, No. 4265,
1950s **175-600**
Wyatt Earp Dodge City Western Town,
based on TV series, No. 4228, 1957 .... **200-800**

Zorro Playset in Box

Zorro, based on Disney TV series,
No. 3754, 1958 (ILLUS.) **300-1,450**

Chapter 18
PUZZLES

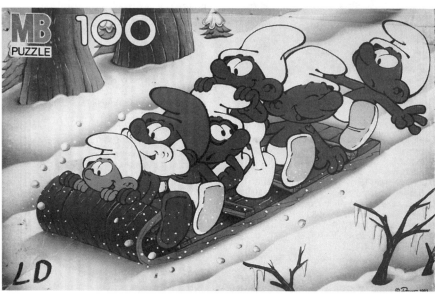

Smurf Puzzle

King Kong Jigsaw Puzzle

Jigsaw-type, Disney characters, "Disneyland Christmas," frame-tray type, Whitman, 1956 .... **11**

Jigsaw-type, Dracula, 200 pieces in canister, APC, 1974 .... **15-30**

Jigsaw-type, Dracula, 200 pieces, Western, 1991 .... **8-12**

Jigsaw-type, Dracula, frame tray-type, 11 pieces **8-10**

Jigsaw-type, Dracula, frame tray-type, Jaymar, 1963 .... **40-60**

E.T. Jigsaw Puzzle

Jigsaw-type, E.T., The Extra-Terrestrial, 15 pieces, frame tray-type, various designs, Craftmaster, 1982, each (ILLUS. of one) **10-18**

Farrah Fawcett Jigsaw Puzzle

Jigsaw-type, Farrah Fawcett photo, 200 pieces, Pro Arts, 1977 (ILLUS.) **12-30**

Fat Albert Round Jigsaw Puzzle

Jigsaw-type, Fat Albert round puzzle, baseball scene, 125 pieces, Whitman, 1974, 20" d. (ILLUS.) **15-25**

Jigsaw-type, "Fire in the Barnyard," Thomas Hart Benton, 304 pieces, 1949 .... **35-40**

Set of Flintstones Jigsaw Puzzles

Jigsaw-type, "Flintstones 4 Children's Puzzles," 10 pieces each, Warren, 1976, boxed set (ILLUS.) **10-18**

Jigsaw-type, Frankenstein, 200 pieces in canister, APC, 1974 .... **15-35**

Jigsaw-type, "Frankenstein Vs. Wolfman," Jaymar, 1963, 7 x 10" box **65-90**

Jigsaw-type, "Frankenstein Vs. Wolfman," Jaymar, 1963, 8 x 12" box **150-180**

Fred Flintstone Jigsaw Puzzle

Jigsaw-type, Fred Flintstone golfing, frame tray-type, Whitman,1969, 11 1/2 x 14 1/2" (ILLUS.) **10-18**

Gene Autry Jigsaw Puzzle

Jigsaw-type, Gene Autry color photo, frame tray-type, Gene nailing up wanted sign, Whitman No. 2628, 1950s (ILLUS.) **25-35**

Jigsaw-type, Godzilla, 150 pieces, HG Toys, 1975, 10 x 14" **25-45**

Jigsaw-type, "Godzilla - King of the Creatures," APC, 1978 .... **20-30**

Jigsaw-type, "Good Company," Donald Teague, 304 pieces, 1956........................... **20-30**

Jigsaw-type, Hopalong Cassidy frame tray-type, photo of Hoppy & Topper, Whitman, 1950 .... **20-35**

Jigsaw-type, Hopalong Cassidy, three different color scenes of Hoppy & Topper, Milton Bradley, Set No. 4025, 1950-52, assembled in original color illustrated box, the set **95**

Jigsaw-type, Jetsons, 70 pieces, Whitman, 1962.. **30-60**

Jigsaw-type, Jetsons w/Elroy at computer & George in tube, frame tray-type, Whitman, 1960s... **20-40**

Kiss Jigsaw Puzzle

Jigsaw-type, Kiss, Destroyer LP art on box, APC, 1977 (ILLUS.) **30-60**

Jigsaw-type, Lassie, 100 pieces, Whitman, 1971 .... **8-12**

Jigsaw-type, Lassie Jr., 63 pieces, Whitman, 1950s.. **10-12**

Lassie Jigsaw Puzzle

Jigsaw-type, Lassie & ranger w/mountain lion, 100 pieces, Whitman, 1966 (ILLUS.).. **10-12**

Jigsaw-type, Lassie, round form, 125 pieces, Whitman, 1972 .... **10-15**

Lassie with Puppies Jigsaw Puzzle

Jigsaw-type, Lassie w/puppies, frame tray-type, Whitman, 1980 (ILLUS.) **8-10**

Jigsaw-type, "Lazy River," Federic Mizen, 252 pieces, 1950 .... **5-15**

Jigsaw-type, Lone Ranger frame tray-type, Lone Ranger rides Silver across the desert, Whitman, 1950s, 11 x 15" **25-35**

Jigsaw-type, Lone Ranger frame tray-type, Lone Ranger & Silver & Tonto & Scout, Whitman, 1954 .... **25-35**

Jigsaw-type, Lone Ranger, photo with Siver in foreground w/the Lone Ranger & Tonto, 1978 .... **12-20**

Jigsaw-type, Lone Ranger set of three puzzles, Puzzle Craft, 1945, boxed, the set **100-150**

Jigsaw-type, "Main Street," M. DeV. Lee, 252 pieces, 1949 .... **35-40**

Jigsaw-type, "New England Winter Scene," George Durrie, 304 pieces, 1947 ...... **5-15**

Jigsaw-type, "New World," John Newton Howitt, 280 pieces, 1948 .... **20-30**

Jigsaw-type, "No Time to Waste," Harold Anderson, 204 pieces, 1951 ...... **20-30**

Outer Limits Jigsaw Puzzle

Jigsaw-type, Outer Limits, Milton Bradley, 1964, series of six different puzzles, each (ILLUS. of one) **150-200**

Jigsaw-type, Pebbles Flintstone, frame tray-type, Whitman, 1962 ...... **12-20**

Jigsaw-type, Pinocchio, Walt Disney, Jaymar, w/original box **25**

Jigsaw-type, Pup Named Scooby-Doo, 60 pieces, Milton Bradley, 1989 .... **3-8**

"Radiant as a Rose" Puzzle

Jigsaw-type, "Radiant as a Rose," Arthur Frahm, 204 pieces, 1954 (ILLUS.) **20-30**

Road Runner Picnic Jigsaw Puzzle

Jigsaw-type, Road Runner at picnic w/family, 100 pieces, Whitman, 1975, 14 x 18" (ILLUS.) **6-12**

Jigsaw-type, Road Runner - Big Little Book, 99 pieces, Whitman, 1974, 10 x 13" **5-10**

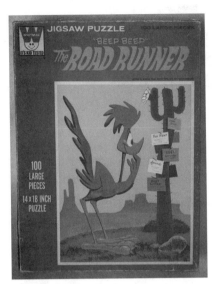

Road Runner & Signs Jigsaw Puzzle

Jigsaw-type, Road Runner looks at signs, 100 pieces, Whitman, 1968, 14 x 18" (ILLUS.) **8-15**

Bullwinkle & Rocky Jigsaw Puzzle

Jigsaw-type, Rocky and His Friends Jr. Jigsaw Puzzle, 63 pieces, Whitman, late 1950s - early 1960s (ILLUS.)...................... **25-50**

Jigsaw-type, Rocky & Bullwinkle in a car, 100 pieces, 1976, 14 x 18".......................... **15-25**

Jigsaw-type, Roy Rogers, frame tray-type, Roy on Trigger, w/cover photo to frame, 1950 .... **30-55**

Jigsaw-type, Roy Rogers, frame tray-type, Roy & Trigger stand together, Whitman, 1948 .... **30-50**

Jigsaw-type, "Seven New Playmates," Joseph F. Kernan, 280 pieces, 1948 .... **35-40**

Jigsaw-type, "Slaking Their Thirst Together," Belmore Browne, 529 pieces, 1951 .... **20-30**

Smurfs Jigsaw Puzzle

Jigsaw-type, Smurfs on sled, 100 pieces, Milton Bradley, 1983, 11 x 16" (ILLUS.)......... **4-8**

Jigsaw-type, Star Trek, frame tray-type, Spock & Kirk on bridge, Whitman, 1970s .. **15-35**

Jigsaw-type, Star Wars, 500 pieces, Kenner, 1970s, 15 x 18" **10-15**

Jigsaw-type, "Sunday Solo," Harold Anderson, 252 pieces, 1951................................. **20-30**

Superman Jigsaw Puzzle

Jigsaw-type, Superman smashing asteroid, 100 pieces, Golden, 1983 (ILLUS.)....... **4-10**

Jigsaw-type, "Surprise Attack," Anthony Cucchi, 280 pieces, 1951 .... **20-30**

Jigsaw-type, "Thatch-Roofed Cottage," Aston Knight, 252 pieces, 1949 .... **5-15**

Jigsaw-type, "The Critics," Charlie Dye, 437 pieces, 1952 .... **20-30**

Jigsaw-type, The Mummy, Jaymar, 1963, 7 x 10" box **75-130**

Jigsaw-type, The Mummy, Jaymar, 1963, 8 x 12" box **100-180**

Jigsaw-type, The Munsters Dragula, frame tray-type, Whitman, 1964 .... **35-60**

Jigsaw-type, The Munsters, frame tray-type, Whitman, 1964 .... **20-35**

The Munsters Jigsaw Puzzles

Jigsaw-type, The Munsters, series of four, 100 pieces, Whitman, 1964, 14 x 18", each (ILLUS. of two) **30-45**

Jigsaw-type, "Threesome," Frances Tipton Hunter, 378 pieces, 1950 .... **20-30**

Jigsaw-type, "Time to Look," Emmett Watson, 378 pieces, 1954................................. **20-30**

Jigsaw-type, Top Cat sips milk from straw, frame tray-type, Whitman, 1960................. **12-25**

"Twixt Love and Duty" Puzzle

Jigsaw-type, "Twixt Love and Duty," Jack Wittrup, 252 pieces, 1948 (ILLUS.)............. **20-30**

Jigsaw-type, "Two Friends," Adam Styka, 304 pieces, 1952 .... **20-30**

Underdog & Polly Jigsaw Puzzle

Jigsaw-type, Underdog flying w/Polly, 100 pieces, Whitman, 1975 (ILLUS.) **12-25**

Jigsaw-type, Underdog & phone booth, 100 pieces, Whitman, 1973, 14 x 18"........ **12-25**

Jigsaw-type, "Western Paradise," F. Grayson Sayre, 252 pieces, 1951 .... **5-15**

Jigsaw-type, "Westward Ho," Arthur Frahm, 252 pieces, 1950............................. **20-30**

Jigsaw-type, Wolfman, 200 pieces in canister, APC, 1974.. **15-30**

Jigsaw-type, Wolfman, 200 pieces, Western (Golden), 1991 .... **10-15**

Jigsaw-type, Wolfman, Jaymar, 1963, 7 x 10" box... **75-130**

Jigsaw-type, Wolfman, Jaymar, 1963, 8 x 12" box... **100-180**

Jigsaw-type, Woody Woodpecker, frame tray-type, Whitman, No. 4428-29, 1956 ...... **8-15**

Slide-type, Addams Family "2 Elementary Puzzles," featuring Fester & Lurch, Milton Bradley, 1965 .... **50-75**

Slide-type, Banana Splits, plastic, shows the group, Roalex **12-20**

Slide-type, Frankenstein, Roalex, 1960s....... **35-45**

Slide-type, Gremlins puzzleforms, 30 pieces, pictures Gizmo in bed, colorforms, foreign.. **20-30**

Slide-type, Marvin the Martian, 3-D type, DaMert Co., 1997, 4" sq. **5-8**

Mighty Mouse Slide Puzzle

Slide-type, Mightly Mouse & other character, plastic, Roalex, 1960s (ILLUS.)............ **20-35**

Slide-type, The Munsters, Roalex, 1964 .... **20-40**

Chapter 19
SCIENCE FICTION AND HORROR CHARACTERS

Addams Family Lunch Box

Uncle Fester Figure

Addams Family (The) action figure, any
character, based on cartoon series, Playmates, 1992, 4 1/2" h. (ILLUS. of Uncle
Fester) **$12-20**

The Thing Bank

Addams Family (The) bank, Thing in box,
Poynter Products, 1964, 4 1/4" h.
(ILLUS.) **45-95**

Addams Family (The) bop bag, Lurch or
Fester, blinking eyes & beeping nose,
1965, 42" h., each... 50-85

Addams Family (The) cartoon kit, Color-
forms, 1965.. 100-150

Addams Family (The) cereal box w/flash-
light, Ralston-Purina, 1991......................... 5-15

Addams Family (The) coloring book, Art-
craft, 1970s.. 15-25

Addams Family (The) coloring book,
Saalfield, 1960s 30-45

Addams Family (The) costume, Uncle
Fester, Rubies, 1990s................................. 15-25

Morticia Costume with Mask

Addams Family (The) costume w/mask,
Fester, Lurch or Morticia, Ben Cooper,
1965, each (ILLUS. of Morticia)............... 80-140

Addams Family (The) doll, Fester, plastic,
small body, big head, Remco,
1964, 5".. 200-600

Addams Family (The) doll, Lurch, plastic,
small body, big head, Remco, 1964,
5".. 100-400

Addams Family (The) doll, Morticia, plastic, small body, big head, Remco, 1964,
5".. 300-700

Addams Family (The) doll, Wednesday,
Aberiginals, 1965, 24"............................ 100-150

Addams Family (The) flashlight, any character, cereal premium, Ralston-Purina,
1991, each 5-15

Addams Family (The) flashlight, "Mon-
ster-Eyes" w/logo on side, Bantam-lite,
1965.. 50-75

Addams Family (The) flashlight, "Pin-On
Flashlight," pull tassel, nose lights, Ban-
tam-lite, 1965... 50-75

Addams Family (The) light bulb, "Uncle
Fester's Mystery Light Bulb," lights in
mouth, 1964... 45-95

Addams Family Lunch Box

Addams Family (The) lunch box, steel,
based on cartoon series, King Seeley
Thermos, 1974 (ILLUS.)............................... 65-95

Addams Family (The) model kit, "Addams
Family Haunted House," Aurora, 1965 . 200-600

Addams Family (The) model kit, reissue,
glow version of Addams Family Haunted
House, Polar Lights, 1995........................... 15-25

Gomez Puppet

Addams Family (The) puppet, any character, cloth body, soft vinyl head, boxed
version, Ideal, 1965, 10 1/2" h., each
(ILLUS. of Gomez) 75-250

Morticia Puppet

Addams Family (The) puppet, any character, cloth body, soft vinyl head, w/bag, Ideal, 1965, 10 1/2" h., each (ILLUS. of Morticia).. **75-150**

Addams Family (The) rings, flicker-type, series of six w/silver bands, Vari-View, 1965, each **20-30**

Addams Family (The) thermos, King Seeley Thermos, 1974... **20-35**

Addams Family (The) View-Master, three-reel set, Sawyer, 1965 .... **75-100**

Alf **costume,** Collegeville, 1986, w/8 1/2 x 11" box **12-20**

Alf lunch box, plastic, red w/decal, 1980s (no thermos) **20-30**

Alf phone, plastic w/plush Alf figure attached, boxed, 1980s.................................... **45-75**

Alf puppet w/record set, several styles, Burger King, 1987, each.................................. **5-8**

Alf Tales figures, Wendy's premiums, set of six, 1990, each **2-5**

Talking Alf Tape Deck & Tape

Alf talking tape deck w/tape, plush, Coleco, 1987, 24" (ILLUS.) **50-85**

Talking Alf Toy

Alf talking toy, plush, Coleco/Alien Productions, 1986, 18" (ILLUS.) **15-25**

Plush Alf Toy

Alf toy, plush, Coleco, 1986, 18" (ILLUS.)..... **12-20**

Alf toy, plush, suction window type, Coleco, 1988, 7 1/2" l. **4-8**

Alien action figure, Alien Queen, Kenner, 1993, 6" h.. **8-15**

Alien Action Figure

Alien action figure, articulated figure w/movable jaws, clear head dome, 1979, 18" h. (ILLUS.)... **250-500**

Alien action figure, Bull Alien, Kenner, 1994, 4" h.. **10-20**

Alien action figure, Flying Alien Queen, Kenner, 1993, 7" h... **8-15**

Alien action figure, fully posable, Real Action Series, Takara, Japan, 1996, 12" h.. **75-125**

Alien action figure, Gorilla Alien, soft vinyl head, squirts water, claws grasp, Kenner, 1992, 5 1/5" h....................................... **10-20**

Alien action figure, Killer Crab Alien w/dual launching chest busters, Kenner, 4" h. **4-8**

Alien action figure, King Alien, deluxe Alien leader, Kenner, 6 1/2" h....................... **9-20**

Alien action figure, Mantis Alien, Kenner, 1994, 5 1/2" h.. **5-10**

Alien action figure, Night Cougar Alien, Kenner, 1994.. **4-8**

Alien action figure, Panther Alien w/flying attack parasite, Kenner, 5 1/2" h.................... **4-8**

Alien action figure, Queen Face Hugger, Kenner, 2" h.. **5-10**

Rhino Alien Action Figure

Alien action figure, Rhino Alien, Kenner, 4" h. (ILLUS.).. **7-15**

Scorpion Alien Action Figure

Alien action figure, Scorpion Alien, Kenner, 1992, 5 1/2" h. (ILLUS.).......................... **7-15**

Snake Alien Bendee Figure

Alien action figure, Snake Alien, bendee, Kenner, 15 1/2" l. (ILLUS.) **5-10**

Alien action figure, Swarm Alien, electronic, laser eyes, Kenner, 6 1/2" h. **10-20**

Alien action figure, Warrior Alien from Aliens vs. Predator two-pack, Kenner, 1994, 5" h.. **10-25**

Alien action figure, Wild Boar Alien w/hidden power attack spikes, Kenner, 1994, 6" h. **4-8**

Alien collectors case, Operation Aliens, holds 12 figures, Kenner **12-20**

Alien costume, "Alien 3," ten-piece latex full body suit, Distortions **1,200-1,400**

Alien costume, black & white, Ben Cooper **50-100**

Alien model kit, "Alien Facehugger with Fetus," vinyl, Halcyon, 46" h. **50-115**

Alien model kit, "Alien Warrior," plastic aliens, base & egg, Halcyon, aliens 9" h. **30-90**

Alien model kit, "Facehugger," tan vinyl, Halcyon, 1992, life-size, 50" l. **200-250**

Alien model kit, plastic, MPC, 1979 .... **25-100**

Alien model kit, "Queen Chestburster," tan vinyl, Halcyon, 10 1/2" h. **125-175**

Alien movie viewer, hand-turned, w/"Alien Terror" film cartridge, Kenner **100-150**

Alien playset, w/Queen Alien, Kenner, hive is 11 1/2" h. **15-25**

Alien replica, "Facehugger," foam latex, life-size, Distortions **80-120**

Alien target set, "Blaster Target," tall outline target of alien, HG Toys, 1979, 33" h. **175-250**

Alien target set, "Chase Target," HG Toys, 1979, target 12 x 18 3/4" **125-200**

Buck Rogers action figure, Buck, Mego, 1979, 4" h. **30-70**

Buck Rogers figure, articulated plastic w/removable clothes, Mego, 1979, 12" h. ... **40-90**

Buck Rogers flying saucer, printed paper plates w/metal rim, S.P. Co., 6" d., each **400-600**

Buck Rogers playset, "Buck Rogers Spaceport," Mego, 1979 .... **125-200**

Captain Video alien figure, bird-like figure, plastic, blue, Post Raisin Bran premium, 1950s, 2 1/2" h. **60-100**

Captain Video alien figure, hard plastic, blue, hose on nose, Post Raisin Bran premium, 1950s, 2 1/2" h. **60-100**

Captain Video playset, "Interplanetary Space Men/Supersonic Space Ships," boxed, 1950s **150-200**

Captain Video ring, flying saucer, 1950s **200-300**

Creature from the Black Lagoon book, flip-type, "Monster Flip Movies," Topps Gum, 1963, 2 1/2", each **10-15**

Creature from the Black Lagoon book box, for "Monster Flip Movies," shows Creature, Topps Gum, 1963 .... **150-200**

Creature from the Black Lagoon button, black & white photo on colored background, 1960s, 7/8" d. **12-20**

Creature from the Black Lagoon Candy

Creature from the Black Lagoon candy & toy, Phoenix Candy Co., 1963, 3 1/2" h. box (ILLUS.) **30-40**

Creature from the Black Lagoon charm, bubble gum, 1960s **18-25**

Creature from the Black Lagoon figure, bendee, made in China, 1991, 4" l. **10-15**

Creature from the Black Lagoon figure, Figure No. 1, AHI, 1973, 8" h. **600-1,600**

Creature from the Black Lagoon figure, Figure No. 2, AHI, 1973, 8" h. **350-900**

Creature from the Black Lagoon figure, glow-in-the-dark, Marx reproduction of Uncle Milton, 1990, 6" h. **12-20**

Creature from the Black Lagoon figure, Hamilton, 1991, 14" h. **25-40**

Creature from the Black Lagoon Figures

Creature from the Black Lagoon figure, mini-monster, glow version, Remco, 1983, 3 3/4" h. (ILLUS. left) **20-40**

Creature from the Black Lagoon figure,
mini-monster, non-glow version, Remco,
1983, 3 3/4" h. ILLUS. right) **30-65**

Creature from the Black Lagoon figure,
nodder-type, Japan, 1960s **90-150**

Creature from the Black Lagoon figure,
nodder-type, plaster, unlicensed,
China **90-150**

Creature from the Black Lagoon figure,
nodder-type, soft plastic, Hong Kong,
China, 7" **75-130**

Creature from the Black Lagoon figure,
nodder-type, superdeformed, Uncle Gil-
bert **40-50**

Creature from the Black Lagoon figure,
plastic, unarticulated, Marx, 1963, 6" h. **15-20**

Creature from the Black Lagoon Figure

Creature from the Black Lagoon figure,
w/patch & ring, glow-in-the-dark, Remco,
1980, 8" h. (ILLUS.) **200-400**

Creature from the Black Lagoon Hallow-
een costume, Ben Cooper, 1973 .... **40-60**

Creature from the Black Lagoon Hallow-
een costume, Collegeville, 1993 .... **15-25**

Creature from the Black Lagoon Hallow-
een costume, Rubie's, 1980 .... **25-40**

Creature from the Black Lagoon mask,
children's size, 1970s, 11" **60-90**

Creature from the Black Lagoon mask,
Don Post, 1967 .... **200-300**

Creature from the Black Lagoon mask,
Don Post, 1980s **150-200**

Creature from the Black Lagoon mask,
Illusive Concepts, 1990, 18" **45-75**

Creature from the Black Lagoon
paint-by-number set, Hasbro, 1963 .... **165-300**

Creature from the Black Lagoon Pez
dispenser, green & red or black,
1970s, each **100-150**

Creature from the Black Lagoon Pez
dispenser, pearl green, 1965 .... **150-200**

Creature from the Black Lagoon
pinball machine, Bally, 1992 .... **1,700-2,000**

Creature from the Black Lagoon
pog, cardboard, "Slammer
Wammer #32," Universal Monsters ..... **.25¢-.50¢**

Creature from the Black Lagoon
puppet, Remco, 1980s **150-200**

Creature from the Black Lagoon ring,
flicker-type, round, 1960s **25-35**

Creature from the Black Lagoon ring,
flicker-type, silver base, 1960s **40-65**

Creature from the Black Lagoon squirt
gun, AHI, 1973 .... **75-100**

Creature from the Black Lagoon toy,
aquarium, moves & connects to
air pump, Penn-Plax, 1971, 5" h. **250-350**

Doctor Who action figure, Mego,
w/British box, 1976, 8" h. **75-175**

Doctor Who figure, Dalek, carded,
Dapol, British, 1986 .... **15-30**

Ice Warrior Figure

Doctor Who figure, Ice Warrior, carded,
Dapol, British, 1986, 4 1/4" h.
(ILLUS.) **20-40**

Doctor Who gift set, "Dalek Army
Fight Set," Denys Fisher, 1976 .... **60-100**

Dracula button, black & white photo on colored background, 1960s, 7/8" d. **12-20**

Dracula doll, Drac Bat in coffin box w/death
certificate, Travelers, 1985, 18" h. **40-75**

Dracula figure, 60th Anniversary, limited
edition, Placo, 10" h. **15-20**

Dracula figure, bendee, AHI, 1974 .... **30-40**

Dracula figure, bendee, Vic's, 1979 .... **5-10**

Dracula figure, Donatello, TMN Turtle-
Monster Turtles, Playmates, 1993 .... **5-10**

Dracula figure, Imperial, 1986, 6" h. **4-8**

Dracula figure, inflatable, Doritos/Pepsi
promotion, 1990s, 32" h. **20-35**

Dracula figure, mini-monster, glow version,
Remco, 1980s, 3 3/4" h. **15-30**

"The Dreadful Dracula" Figure

Remco Mini-monster Dracula Figure

Dracula figure, mini-monster, non-glow version, Remco, 1983, 3 3/4" h. (ILLUS.).. **20-45**

Dracula figure, MPC Plastics, 2 1/2" h. **10-15**

Dracula figure, No. 1, AHI, 1973, 8" h. **100-450**

Dracula figure, No. 2, AHI, 1973, 8" h. **100-250**

Dracula figure, No. 3, AHI, 1973, 8" h. **100-250**

Dracula figure, Palmer Plastics, 1963, 3" h. .. **15-25**

Dracula figure, plastic, unarticulated, Marx, 1960s, 6" h... **12-20**

Dracula figure, "The Dreadful Dracula," Mad Monster series, Mego, 1972, 8" h. (ILLUS.).. **75-250**

Remco Dracula Figure

Dracula figure, w/patch & ring, Remco, 1980, 8" h. (ILLUS.)................................. **100-200**

Dracula Halloween costume, Ben Cooper, 1963... **50-100**

Dracula mask, Don Post, 1967 .... **200-250**

Dracula model kit, "Bela the Vampire," res- in, Dimensional Designs, 1992, 7" h. **45-55**

Dracula model kit, Frightnin' Lightnin', Au- rora, 1969... **200-450**

Dracula model kit, Monogram, 1983 .... **20-30**

Dracula model kit, superdeformed, Mad Labs **20-30**

Lincoln International Dracula Figure

Dracula figure, removable clothes, Lincoln International, 1975, 8" h. (ILLUS.) **100-250**

Dracula motionette, Telco, 1992, 24" h. **30-40**

Dracula paint-by-number set, Hasbro, 1963 .... **165-300**

Dracula ring, flicker-type, blue base, 1960s .. **20-35**

Dracula ring, flicker-type, silver base, 1960s **35-50**

Dracula talking toy, plush w/coffin box, Commonwealth Toy, 14" h. **35-70**

Dracula toy, "Tricky Walker," Jaymar, 1960s **35-50**

Dracula wallet, Hasbro, 1963 .... **100-150**

E.T. Shrinky Dinks Activity Set

E.T. activity set, "Shrinky Dinks," by Color-forms, 1982 (ILLUS.)..................................... **15-25**

E.T. balloons, E.T. picture on front of pack-age, 1982 .... **4-8**

E.T. coloring set, three large pictures to color, together w/felt-tip pens, Fun Art, 1982 .... **8-12**

E.T. Costume

E.T. costume, vinyl w/light plastic string mask, Collegeville, 1982 (ILLUS.)............... **15-30**

E.T. Figure

E.T. figure, assortment A or B, any of 12 fig-ures total, LJN, 1982, 2 1/2" h., each (ILLUS. of one)... **6-12**

E.T. Pal Inflatable Figure

E.T. figure, inflatable, "E.T. Pal," Coleco, 1982, w/original box, life-size, 3' tall (ILLUS.)... **35-50**

E.T. figure, life-size replica, Sharper Image, 1990s..................................... **1,000-1,300**

E.T. figures, family gift set: E.T., Elliott, Gertie, Michael, Mom, Bad Guy, LJN, 1982, the set **40-60**

E.T. Lunch Box

E.T. lunch box w/thermos, Aladdin, 1982
(ILLUS.) **30-50**

Hasbro Talking E.T. Phone

E.T. phone, "E.T. Talking Phone," Hasbro
Preschool, 1982, boxed, 10" h. (ILLUS.) ... **40-60**

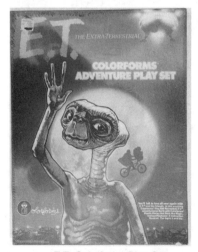

E.T. Colorforms Play Set

E.T. play set, Colorforms, E.T. illustration
on front, 1982, large box (ILLUS.) **20-35**

E.T. puppet, "E.T. Punching Puppet,"
brown face, polka-dot shirt, no mark,
1990s.. **10-15**

E.T. puppet, figural, vinyl w/red chest, blue
eyes, U.C.S., 6" h. **12-18**

Child's E.T. Riding Toy

E.T. riding toy, child's, E.T. head on front,
Coleco, 1982-83 (ILLUS.) **50-75**

Talking E.T. Figure

E.T. talking figure, dressed in robe, LJN,
1983, boxed, 7" h. (ILLUS.) **25-40**

E.T. talking figure, plastic w/pull string,
LJN, 1982, boxed, 7" h. **20-35**

E.T., the Extra-Terrestrial Action Figure

E.T., the Extra-Terrestrial action figure, several poses, LJN, 1982, 4" h., each (ILLUS.) **10-18**

E.T. toy, E.T. & Elliott Powered Bicycle, on card, LJN, 1982... **12-20**

E.T. & Spaceship Launcher

E.T. toy, "E.T. & Spaceship Launcher," on card, LJN, 1982, 3" h. (ILLUS.) **15-25**

Applause E.T. Plush Toy

E.T. toy, plush, arms folded across chest, pink, Applause, 1988, 10" h. (ILLUS.).......... **8-12**

E.T. toy, plush, brown w/blue eyes, Kamar, 1982, 16" h. **15-30**

E.T. toy, plush, brown w/blue eyes, red smile, Showtime, 1982, 8" h. **8-12**

E.T. toy, plush, brown w/blue eyes, Show-time, 1982, 12" h.. **10-16**

E.T. toy, plush, leatherette, Kamar, 1982 ...... **15-25**

Kamar E.T. Plush Toy

E.T. toy, plush, leatherette w/bean bag hands & feet, Kamar, 1982, 14" h. (ILLUS.).. **20-30**

E.T. toy, plush, pink w/hand raised, Applause, 1988.. **10-15**

E.T. toy, plush, pink w/vinyl head, green shirt, U.C.S., 1966, 7 1/2" h. **5-10**

E.T. toy, Pop-up Spaceship, on card, LJN, 1982.. **12-20**

E.T. toy, rubber finger, "Hong Kong," 8" l. (does not light up)... **8-12**

E.T. toy, window grabber, plush w/vinyl head & suction cup hands, "Phone Home" tee-shirt, 9" h. **8-16**

E.T. View-Master gift set, E.T. & Elliott photo on box... **15-25**

E.T. Wallet

E.T. wallet, vinyl, blue w/yellow moon & E.T. graphic in black, U.C.S., 1982 (ILLUS.).. **20-30**

Frankenstein book, flip-type, Monster Flip Movies, Topps Gum, 1963, 2 1/2", each.... **10-15**

Frankenstein bubble bath bottle, Soaky, 1960s......... **75-150**

Frankenstein bucket, for Halloween candy, figural Frankenstein head, Clinton, 1963...... **75-150**

Frankenstein candy & toy, Phoenix Candy Co., 1963, in 3 1/2" h. box...... **30-40**

Figural Frankenstein Charm

Frankenstein charm, figural, plastic, 1960s, 1" (ILLUS.)...... **10-15**

Frankenstein charm, plastic, Frankenstein head, 1960s, 1"...... **10-15**

Frankenstein figure, 60th Anniversary, limited edition, Placo, 10" h...... **12-20**

Frankenstein figure, bendee, AHI, 1974, 4" h...... **30-40**

Frankenstein figure, bendee, AHI No. 6050, 1970s, 6 1/2" h...... **30-40**

"Mighty Monster" Bendee Figure

Frankenstein figure, bendee, "Mighty Monster" by Ben Cooper, 1960s-70s, 8" h. (ILLUS.)...... **20-30**

Frankenstein figure, bendee, Vic's, 1979..... **10-15**

Frankenstein figure, glow-in-the-dark, Marx reproduction of Uncle Milton, 1990, 4 1/5" h...... **10-15**

Frankenstein figure, Imperial, 1986, 6" h........ **4-8**

Frankenstein figure, Imperial, 1986, 7 1/2" h...... **10-15**

Mad Monster Series Frankenstein Figure

Frankenstein figure, Mad Monster series, Mego, 1972, 8" h. (ILLUS.)...... **25-90**

Frankenstein figure, Mego, 1970s, in window box...... **25-300**

Frankenstein figure, mini-monster, glow version, Remco, 1980s, 3 3/4" h...... **15-25**

Frankenstein Mini-monster Figure

Frankenstein figure, mini-monster, non-glow version, Remco, 1983, 3 3/4" h. (ILLUS.)...... **15-40**

Monster-nik Frankenstein Figure

Frankenstein figure, monster-nik, plastic, removable clothes & shoes, 1960s, originally carded, 3 1/2" h. (ILLUS.) **65-125**

Frankenstein figure, No. 1, AHI, 1973, 8" h. **100-350**

Frankenstein figure, No. 2, AHI, 1973, 8" h. **75-200**

Frankenstein figure, No. 3, AHI, 1973, 8" h. **75-200**

Frankenstein figure, nodder-type, composition, name on base, 1950s-60s? **100-175**

Frankenstein figure, plastic, comic version, made in Spain, 4" h. **5-10**

Frankenstein figure, plastic, MPC, mid-1960s, 2 1/2" h. **15-25**

Frankenstein figure, plastic, Palmer Plastics, 1963, 3" h. **20-35**

Frankenstein figure, plastic, unarticulated, Marx, 1963, 6" h. **10-18**

Remco Glow Frankenstein Figure

Frankenstein figure, w/removable clothes, glows, Remco, 1978, 8" h. (ILLUS.) **40-100**

Lincoln International Frankenstein Figure

Frankenstein figure, w/removable clothes, Lincoln International, 1975 (ILLUS.) **100-250**

Universal Studios Frankenstein Figure

Frankenstein figure, waxy plastic, green, Universal Studios, 7" h. (ILLUS.) **20-35**

Frankenstein Halloween costume, Ben Cooper, 1963 .... **60-100**

Frankenstein mask, Don Post, 1967 .... **200-250**

Frankenstein model kit, 1/5 scale, Tsukuda, 1986 .... **85-125**

Frankenstein model kit, Luminators, Revell/Monogram, 1991 .... **12-20**

Frankenstein paint-by-number set, Hasbro, 1963.. **165-300**

Frankenstein pencil-topper, rubber, yellow Frankenstein head, 1960s, 1" **15-20**

Frankenstein Pez Dispenser

Frankenstein Pez dispenser, 1960s
(ILLUS.) **150-250**

Giant Frankenstein Poster

Frankenstein poster, mail-order offer
(w/small toys in tube), 1960s, 6' h.
(ILLUS.) **150-200**

Frankenstein puppet, plastic paper body
w/soft plastic head, Candy World, 6" h. **15-20**

Frankenstein ring, flicker-type, blue base,
1960s **35-50**

Frankenstein ring, flicker-type, silver base,
1960s **35-50**

Electronic Talking Frankenstein Figure

Frankenstein talking figure, electronic,
neon colors, Playskool, 1992, 16" h.
(ILLUS.) **20-35**

Frankenstein toy, glow putty, Larami, 1979 .. **10-15**

Frankenstein wallet, Hasbro, 1963 .... **100-150**

Godzilla action figure, 1964 style, Bandai,
1988, 18" h. **150-250**

Godzilla action figure, blue or brown vinyl,
small scale, Bullmark, 1975, each **50-100**

"Burning Godzilla" Action Figure

Godzilla action figure, "Burning Godzilla,"
black & orange plastic, Bandai, 1995,
9" h. (ILLUS.) **25-40**

"Disco" Godzilla Action Figure

Godzilla action figure, "Disco" Godzilla w/gold glitter, Godzilla Forever series, Bandai, 1996, 9" h. (ILLUS.).................. **150-250**

Godzilla action figure, Godzilla 1954, Bandai, 1995, 4" h. **25-50**

Godzilla action figure, Godzilla 1962, Bandai, 9" h. **200-275**

Godzilla action figure, Godzilla 1964, Bandai, 1983, 8 1/4" h. **100-150**

Godzilla action figure, Godzilla 1984, Bandai, 9" h. **125-200**

Godzilla action figure, Godzilla 1991, Bandai, 1991, 14" h. **125-175**

Godzilla action figure, Godzilla 1991, mouth closed, Bandai, 1991, 8" h. **100-145**

Godzilla action figure, Godzilla 1992, open mouth, arms out, 8" h........................ **35-50**

Godzilla action figure, holds red tower, Bullmark, 1970, large size, rare.......... **750-1,000**

Godzilla action figure, "Meltdown Godzilla," super big scale, numbered edition, 4000 made, 1995..................................... **600-750**

Godzilla action figure, plastic, arms move, black & silver, Bandai, 1992, 4 1/4" h........ **20-30**

Large Imperial Godzilla Figure

Godzilla action figure, rubber, painted green, Imperial, 1984, 15" h. (ILLUS.) **15-25**

Imperial Godzilla Figure

Godzilla action figure, rubber, painted green, w/tag, Imperial, 1984, 5" h. (ILLUS.).. **6-10**

Godzilla action figure, soft plastic, Big Godzilla boxed series, Bandai, 1994, 4 1/2" h.. **20-40**

"Theater Meltdown Godzilla" Figure

Godzilla action figure, "Theater Meltdown Godzilla," articulated translucent red & orange plastic, limited edition, originally sold only in Japanese theaters showing Godzilla vs. Destroyah, 1995, 9" h. (ILLUS.)... **200-350**

Godzilla action figure, vinyl, blue, Marusan, 1966.. **400-600**

Godzilla action figure, vinyl, Bullmark, made from Marusan mold, 1970s.. **300-400**

Godzilla action figure, vinyl, green, the very first Godzilla figure produced, Marusan, 1966... **500-750**

Godzilla bop bag, inflatable,
Imperial, 1985, 48" h. **20-30**

"Bubble Blowing Godzilla"

Godzilla bubble blower, "Bubble Blowing
Godzilla," Imperial, 1985, 6 3/4 x 9 1/4"
box (ILLUS.) **25-40**

Flix Godzilla Candy Dispenser

Godzilla candy dispenser, Godzilla head
on "collectible candy machine," bagged,
Flix, 1990s, 5 1/2" h. (ILLUS.)..................... **12-20**

Godzilla coloring book, "Godzilla - King of
the Monsters," Resource Publications
No. 630, 1977 .... **35-45**

Bendable Godzilla Figure

Godzilla figure, bendable, Trendmasters,
1994, 4" h. (ILLUS.)... **4-8**

Godzilla figure, bendee, Godzilla trading
card premium, Yamakatsu, 1983, rare.... **85-110**

Godzilla figure, bendee, Kaiju series,
1983... **125-175**

Godzilla figure, die-cast, brown version,
stomach holds weapons, Bullmark,
1970s, boxed, 4 1/2" h. **75-175**

Diecast Godzilla Figure

Godzilla figure, die-cast, green version,
stomach holds weapons, Bullmark,
1970s, boxed, 4 1/2" h. (ILLUS.)............. **50-150**

Godzilla figure, inflatable, Imperial,
1985, 12' h. **100-125**

Giant Inflatable Godzilla Figure

Godzilla figure, inflatable, Imperial, 1985,
6' h. (ILLUS.) **25-35**

Godzilla figure, inflatable, Imperial, 1985,
8' h. **60-80**

Godzilla figure, jump-up-type, Trendmas-
ters, 1994 .... **4-8**

"Shogun Warriors Godzilla"

Godzilla figure, "Shogun Warriors Godzilla," shoots hand, Toho Co., Mattel, 1977,
19" h. (ILLUS.)... **80-190**

Godzilla figures, White Castle
premium, complete set **35-50**

Godzilla play set, "Combat Joe
Godzilla," vinyl figures, 12" h., 1984 ... **600-1,000**

Godzilla play set, "Godzilla Attacks
New York," large boxed set w/great
figure, Trendmasters, 1994 .... **20-35**

Godzilla play set, "Godzilla's Gang,"
featuring Godzilla figure w/seven
ultra monster figures, Mattel, 1978 .... **250-400**

Godzilla play set, "King of the
Monsters" boxed set w/large Godzilla
figure & tank, Bandai, 1993, 16 x 19".... **200-300**

Godzilla Gymnast Puppet Figure

Godzilla puppet, push-type, plush gymnast
figure w/green or silver base, Toho Eiga,
1993, 5 1/4" (ILLUS.) **15-25**

Godzilla Squirt Gun

Godzilla squirt gun, plastic, blue w/Godzil-
la figure on top, Japan, 7" h. (ILLUS.)........ **15-22**

Popy Talking Godzilla Figure

Godzilla talking figure, plastic, pull string for roar, Popy, 17 1/2" h. (ILLUS.) .. **1,200-2,000**

Godzilla talking View-Master reels, "Godzilla - Godzilla's Rampage," GAF **20-30**

Godzilla toy, "Magic Rocks" w/paintable Godzilla figure, Crafthouse, 1995 .... **15-25**

Knickerbocker Plush Godzilla Toy

Godzilla toy, plush, Hanna-Barbera Godzilla Power Hour tie-in, Knickerbocker, 1979, 8 1/2" h. (ILLUS.) **75-100**

Godzilla toy, plush, hatching from styrofoam egg, w/potato chips, Concorde, 1994, 12 1/2" h... **30-50**

Hatching Monster Godzilla

Godzilla toy, plastic, hatching monster breaks out of egg, Trendmasters, 1994 (ILLUS.) **5-15**

Godzilla toy, plastic, mechanical hatching egg w/Godzilla figure inside, Takara, 1988, 3 1/2" h. **15-30**

Godzilla Sparker Friction Toy

Godzilla toy, sparker friction-type, plastic, green, poseable arms, no mark, Takara, 1 3/4" h. (ILLUS.) **10-20**

Godzilla toy, tin w/string remote control, from Marusan mold, Bullmark, early 1970s, 11" h................................. **600-1,000**

Godzilla View-Master reel set, "Godzilla - Godzilla's Rampage," GAF **20-30**

Small Gizmo Action Figure

Gremlins action figure, Gizmo, LJN Toys,
1984, 3 1/2" h. (ILLUS.) **15-35**

Large Gizmo Action Figure

Gremlins action figure, Gizmo, LJN Toys,
1984, 8" h. (ILLUS.) **20-50**

Large Stripe Action Figure

Gremlins action figure, Stripe, hard plas-
tic, real hair, LJN Toys, 1984, 14" h.
(ILLUS.) **40-95**
Gremlins costume, Stripe, vinyl suit
& plastic string mask, 1984 .... **20-35**
Gremlins figure, Gizmo, plastic,
LJN, 1984, 2" h. **5-8**

Stripe Bendee Figure

Gremlins figure, Stripe, bendee, LJN
Toys, 1984, 6" h. (ILLUS.) **15-30**
Gremlins figure, Stripe, plastic, LJN, 1984,
3 1/2" h. **5-8**
Gremlins gift pack, set of three plastic fig-
ures on card, LJN, 1984 .... **60-90**
Gremlins lunch box **20-30**
Gremlins mask, Gizmo, custom model,
latex & hair, by Don Post **400-600**
Gremlins mask, Gizmo, latex, by Don
Post **75-150**
Gremlins mask, Stripe, custom model,
latex & hair, by Don Post **350-500**
Gremlins mask, Stripe, latex, by Don
Post **75-150**
Gremlins model kit, Gizmo, Gremlins 2,
resin kit No. 980, Kaiyodo, Japan **50-75**
Gremlins model kit, Stripe, life-size,
Kalyodo **200-300**

Colorforms Deluxe Gremlins Play Set

Science Fiction and Horror Characters   228

Gremlins play set, "Gremlins Colorforms Adventure Set," deluxe set, 1984, 12 x 15 box (ILLUS.) **12-25**

Gremlins thermos, ... **5-10**

Gremlins toy, plush, black & white Gremlin from Gremlins 2, "Alberto CE Milano," 8" h. **25-40**

Gremlins toy, plush, Gizmo, Applause, 1984, 8" h. **20-30**

Gremlins toy, plush, Gizmo in Gremlins 2 crate-style cardboard box, JUN Planning Co., Japan.. **125-175**

Gremlins toy, plush, Gizmo, made in Spain, 8" h. **50-100**

Gremlins toy, plush, Gizmo, made in Spain, together w/box w/air holes, 14" h. **100-200**

Gremlins toy, plush, Gizmo, marked "CE, Cerato Marini," Europe, 8" h. **25-40**

Gremlins toy, plush, Gizmo, squeaks when shaken, Hasbro Softies, 1984, 10" h. **15-20**

Gremlins toy, plush Gizmo window-grabber, marked "CE," Germany, 7" h. **25-40**

Gremlins toy, plush, Stripe w/Gremlins 2 tag, Japan, 1996, large........................ **200-250**

Gremlins toy, "Water Hatchers," LJN, 1984, each... **8-20**

Gremlins View-Master reel set **15**

MPC King Kong Action Figure

King Kong action figure, based on 1960s animated series, MPC, 1967, 8" h. (ILLUS.)... **35-50**

King Kong action figure, carded, Imperial, 1992 .... **12-18**

King Kong action figure, w/tag, Imperial, 1985, 13 1/4" h... **20-30**

King Kong bank, on gray stone nameplate, Universal Studios, 1990, 6 1/2" h. **15-25**

King Kong bank, plastic, black, pounds chest, A.J. Renzi Corp., 15 1/2" h. **15-30**

King Kong bank, plastic, red, black & green, holding train, RKO, Relic art, 13" h... **45-65**

King Kong costume, DeLaurentis version, Ben Cooper, 1976 .... **45-65**

King Kong Bendee Figure

King Kong figure, bendee, based on cartoon series, mid-1960s, 5 1/2" h. (ILLUS.).. **20-35**

King Kong figure, chalkware, 1940s carnival prize, 14" h. **50-100**

King Kong figure, die-cast, Toho's Kong, boxed, Bullmark, 1970s **200-250**

King Kong figure, plastic, holding Fay over head, 1990, 4" h. **10-15**

King Kong figure, plastic, red, Palmer Plastics, 1963, 3" h..................................... **20-35**

King Kong lunch box, King Seeley Thermos, 1977 .... **60-85**

King Kong model kit, DeLaurentis Kong, Mego, 1976.. **25-40**

King Kong model kit, Luminators, Monogram, 1992... **15-20**

King Kong model kit, resin, GEOmetric **50-75**

King Kong model kit, Tsukuda Hobby Jumbo Figure Series No. 49 .... **85-120**

King Kong model kit, vinyl, brown, rocky base, RKO & Turner marks, Dark Horse, 16 1/2" h.. **75-100**

King Kong pogs, Holocaps set on blister pack, 1994 .... **4-8**

King Kong thermos, King Seeley Thermos, 1977 .... **10-15**

King Kong View-Master reel set **8-15**

Lost in Space costume, silver space suit w/show logo, Ben Cooper, 1965 .... **125-225**

Lost in Space Lunch Box & Thermos

Lost in Space lunch box & thermos, metal, dome-type, 1967-68, King Seeley Thermos (ILLUS.)........................ **450-650**

Official Lost in Space Robot

Lost in Space Robot Model Kit

Mego "The Horrible Mummy" Figure

Remco Mummy Figure

Mummy (The) figure, w/patch & ring, face & hands glow, Remco, 1980, 8" h. (ILLUS.) **40-100**

Mummy (The) figure, w/removable clothes, Lincoln International, 1975, 8" h. **100-250**

Mummy (The) Halloween costume, Ben Cooper, 1973.. **15-30**

Mummy (The) mask, Don Post, 1967 ...... **200-250**

Mummy (The) model kit, "Haunted Glow Head," MPC, 1975 .... **20-45**

Mummy (The) model kit, Luminators, Revell/Monogram, 1991...................................... **12-20**

Mummy (The) paint-by-number set, Crafthouse, 1975.. **15-30**

Mummy (The) ring, flicker-type, blue base, 1960s.. **35-50**

Mummy (The) ring, flicker-type, round, 1960s.. **20-30**

Mummy (The) ring, flicker-type, silver base, 1960s.. **35-50**

Mummy (The) wallet, Hasbro, 1963......... **100-150**

Munsters (The) coloring book, Whitman, 1964 .... **35-50**

Munsters (The) costume, Grandpa Munster, Ben Cooper, 1965........................... **150-225**

Munsters (The) costume, Herman Munster, Ben Cooper, 1964........................... **150-225**

Munsters (The) doll, Baby Grandpa lookalike, Mad Doctor series, Ideal, 1965, 9" h.. **75-150**

Munsters (The) doll, Baby Herman lookalike, Mad Doctor series, Ideal, 1965, 9" h.. **75-150**

Munsters (The) doll, Eddie look-alike, Mad Doctor series, Ideal, 1965, 9" h. **75-150**

Presents Eddie Doll

Munsters (The) doll, Eddie, w/velvet-like clothes, Presents, 1991, 8 1/2" h. (ILLUS.)... **15-25**

Munsters (The) doll, Grandpa, Presents, 1991, 11" h. **30-40**

Munsters (The) doll, Grandpa, Presents, 1991, 7" h... **15-25**

Munsters (The) doll, Herman, Presents, 1991, 13" h. **30-40**

Rare Herman Munster Doll

Munsters (The) doll, Herman, vinyl, Remco, 1964, mint in sealed box (ILLUS.)........ **1,980**

Presents Herman Doll

Munsters (The) doll, Herman w/clothes,
Presents, 1991, 8 1/2" h. (ILLUS.) **15-25**

Herman Munster Doll

Munsters (The) doll, Lily, Herman or
Grandpa, big soft head w/hair, hard
body, Temco, 1964, 5" h., each (ILLUS.
of Herman).. **250-550**
Munsters (The) doll, Lily look-alike, Mad
Doctor series, Ideal, 1965, 9" h. **75-150**
Munsters (The) doll, Lily, Presents, 1991,
10" h.. **25-35**
Munsters (The) doll, Woof-Woof, limited
edition of 100, from original, by Jim Mad-
den **1,000-2,000**
Munsters (The) figure, Herman, Lily,
Grandpa or Eddie, Presents, 1991,
3 1/4" h., each **6-10**
Munsters (The) flashlight, "Wrist Flash-
light," Bantam-lite, 1965 .... **50-75**
Munsters (The) kite, Herman Munster,
Pressman, 1964.. **20-35**
Munsters (The) lunch box, King Seely
Thermos, 1965...................................... **150-225**

Munsters (The) mask, Herman, Lily or
Grandpa, latex w/hair, Don Post,
1965, each.. **200-300**
Munsters (The) mask, Herman, Lily or
Grandpa, latex w/painted hair, Don
Post, 1965, each...................................... **100-150**
Munsters (The) model kit, "Munster
Koach," AMT, 1964 .... **50-175**
Munsters (The) model kit, Munster Koach
& Dragula, reissued in one package,
AMT/Ertl, 1991 .... **35-50**
Munsters (The) model kit, resin, Munster
family standing, Eddie holds bone **45-75**
**Munsters (The) paint-by-number oil paint
set,** Herman, Lily or Grandpa, Hasbro,
1964, each.. **100-150**
Munsters (The) paint-by-number set,
"Touch of Velvet," paint on black velvet,
Hasbro, 1964 .... **150-200**
Munsters (The) paper dolls, five charac-
ters w/clothes in cardboard folder, Whit-
man, 1965.. **75-125**
Munsters (The) pencil-by-number set,
twelve pictures & twelve colored pencils,
Hasbro, 1964... **65-100**
Munsters (The) play set, "Castex 5 Mold-
ing Set," includes plaster & paints, Eme-
nee, 1964 .... **150-225**
Munsters (The) play set, "Munsters Car-
toon Kit," Colorforms, 1964, 10 x 12"
box **100-150**
Munsters (The) play set, "Munsters Car-
toon Kit," deluxe set, Colorforms, 1964,
13 x 17" box **150-250**
Munsters (The) puppet, Lily, Herman or
Grandpa, cloth body, soft vinyl head, in
box, Ideal, 1964, each **75-250**
Munsters (The) puppet, Lily, Herman or
Grandpa, cloth body, soft vinyl head, in
plastic wrapper, Ideal, 1964, each.......... **75-150**
Munsters (The) squirt gun, hypodermic
needle shape, Hasbro, 1964, 8" l.......... **100-150**
Munsters (The) sticker fun book,
Whitman, 1964.. **25-40**

Herman Munster Talking Doll

Munsters (The) talking doll, Herman Munster, stuffed cloth, Mattel, 1964, 20" h. (ILLUS.) **200-400**

Munsters (The) talking puppet, hand-type, Herman, Mattel, 1964, 12" h. **150-300**

Munsters (The) thermos, King Seely Thermos, 1965 .... **25-40**

Munsters (The) toy, Munster Koach w/motor noise, AMT, 1964, 12"........................ **250-450**

Munsters (The) toy, Paint-A-Plaque, 3-D portrait of Grandpa, Standard Toykraft, 1964 .... **75-100**

Munsters (The) toy, Paint-A-Plaque, 3-D portrait of Herman, Standard Toykraft, 1964 .... **75-100**

Munsters (The) toy, Paint-A-Plaque, 3-D portrait of Lily, Standard Toykraft, 1964.. **75-100**

Munsters (The) View-Master reel set, Sawyer, 1964, set of 3 .... **35-50**

Nightmare Before Christmas action figure, Behemoth, Hasbro, 1993, 5 1/2" h. **30-65**

Oogie Boogie Action Figure

Nightmare Before Christmas action figure, Oogie Boogie w/bugs inside, Hasbro, 1993, 7" h. (ILLUS.) **100-300**

Nightmare Before Christmas action figure, Sally, Hasbro, 1993, 7" h. **40-100**

Nightmare Before Christmas action figure, Santa, Hasbro, 1993, 6" h. **100-300**

Nightmare Before Christmas action figure, Wolf, Hasbro, 1993, 5" h. **45-120**

Nightmare Before Christmas action figure, Zero, Applause, 1993, 3 1/2" h. **10-15**

Nightmare Before Christmas activity book, Golden, 1993, 5 x 7 3/4".................... **8-15**

Nightmare Before Christmas bank, Mayor, ceramic, Schmid, 1993, 8" h. **100-150**

Nightmare Before Christmas bubble bath bottle, Jack, figural, Centura Brand, Disney, 1993, 9 1/2" h. **20-40**

Nightmare Before Christmas doll, Oogie Boogie, boxed, Hasbro, 1993, 13" h. **50-140**

Dr. Finklestein Action Figure

Nightmare Before Christmas action figure, Dr. Finklestein, Hasbro, 1993, 5 1/2" h. (ILLUS.) **70-140**

Nightmare Before Christmas action figure, Jack as Santa, Hasbro, 1993, 9" h..... **30-65**

Nightmare Before Christmas action figure, Lock, Shock & Barrel in walking tub, Applause, 1993, 4 x 5"................................. **15-35**

Nightmare Before Christmas action figure, Mayor, Hasbro, 1993, 7 1/2" h. **70-140**

Hasbro Cloth Sally Doll

Nightmare Before Christmas doll, Sally,
cloth, removable limbs, boxed,
Hasbro, 1993, 14" h. (ILLUS.) **200-450**

Nightmare Before Christmas doll/puppet, Santa, plush, boxed, Hasbro, 1993,
12" h. **25-100**

Nightmare Before Christmas dolls, Lock,
Shock & Barrel, boxed, Hasbro,
1993, 4 1/2" h., set of 3 .... **100-250**

Nightmare Before Christmas figure, Dr.
Finklestein, plastic PVC, Applause,
1993, 4" h. **20-30**

Nightmare Before Christmas figure, Jack,
bend-em, Applause, 1993, 9 1/2" h. **12-35**

Nightmare Before Christmas figure, Jack
& Sally w/moon, plastic PVC, Applause,
video promotion figure, 6" h. **15-20**

Nightmare Before Christmas figure, Jack
& Zero, plastic PVC, Applause, 3 1/2" h. ... **12-20**

Nightmare Before Christmas figure,
Lock, Shock or Barrel, Applause, 1993,
2 1/2" h., sold separately, each **6-10**

Nightmare Before Christmas figure, Oogie Boogie, Applause, 1993, 3 1/2" h. **15-25**

Nightmare Before Christmas kite, pictures Jack on hill **15-20**

Nightmare Before Christmas puppet,
plush, Applause, 1993, 9" h. **25-60**

Talking Jack Doll with Zero

Nightmare Before Christmas talking doll,
Jack w/Zero, Hasbro, 1993, 15" h.
(ILLUS.) **100-250**

Phantom of the Opera candy & toy,
Phoenix Candy Co., 1963, 3 1/2" box **25-40**

Phantom of the Opera figure, glow-in-the-
dark, Marx reproductions, Uncle Milton,
1990, 6" h. **10-15**

Phantom of the Opera Mini-monster

Phantom of the Opera figure, mini-monster, glow version, Remco, 1980s,
3 3/4" h. (ILLUS.) **15-30**

Phantom of the Opera figure, mini-monster, non-glow version, Remco, 1983,
3 3/4" h. **20-40**

Phantom of the Opera Nodder Figure

Phantom of the Opera figure, nodder-
type, soft plastic, Hong Kong, 7" h.
(ILLUS.) **75-100**

Phantom of the Opera figure, plastic, unarticulated, Marx, 1960s, 6" h. **12-18**

Phantom of the Opera figure, w/patch &
ring, glows, Remco, 1980, 8" h. **150-400**

Phantom of the Opera Figure

Phantom of the Opera figure, w/removable clothes, Lincoln International, 1975, 8" h. (ILLUS.)... **100-250**

Phantom of the Opera Halloween costume, Ben Cooper, 1963.......................... **80-160**

Phantom of the Opera mask, Don Post, 1967... **200-250**

Phantom of the Opera ring, flicker-type, blue base, 1960s **35-50**

Phantom of the Opera ring, flicker-type, round, 1960s.. **20-30**

Phantom of the Opera squirt gun, AHI, 1973... **30-50**

Dr. Zaius Action Figure

Planet of the Apes action figure, Signature series, any character, Hasbro, 1998, 12" h. (ILLUS. of Dr. Zaius)......................... **10-25**

Zira Action Figure

Planet of the Apes action figure, Zira, Signature series, Hasbro, 1998, 12" h. (ILLUS.)... **10-25**

Planet of the Apes bank, plastic, figural Dr. Zaius, Play Pal, 1974, 11" h. **30-50**

Planet of the Apes figure, Cornelius, Zira, or Astronaut, Mego, 1973, 8" h., each **45-120**

Planet of the Apes figure, Soldier Ape, Mego, 1973, 8" h. **75-175**

Space Patrol "Space-O-Phone," w/original string attached, Ralston premium, 1950s... **85**

Star Trek coloring book, Saalfield, 1968, unused.. **46**

Star Trek costume, Mr. Spock, 1976................. **50**

Star Trek costume, Mr. Spock, Ben Copper, 1967... **100**

Star Trek Dolls

Star Trek doll, Capt. Kirk w/accessories, removable clothes, Mego, 1974, 8" h. (ILLUS. **30-75**

Star Trek doll, Captain Kirk, Mego, ca. 1979, never removed from box, 12 1/2" h. **45**

Star Trek doll, Mr. Spock w/accessories, removable clothes, Mego, 1974, 8" h. (ILLUS. right w/Capt.Kirk) **30-75**

Mr. Spock Mint in Box Doll

Star Trek doll, Mr. Spock, Mego, ca. 1979, never removed from box, 12 1/2" h. (ILLUS.) **50**

Star Trek dolls, "Barbie & Ken Star Trek Giftset" in window box, Mattel, 1996, the set **10-30**

Star Trek letter, signed by Gene Rodenberry on Desilu Productions stationery, 1966, very fine **163**

Star Trek Lunch Box

Star Trek lunch box, Aladdin, 1967 (ILLUS.) **350-500**

Star Trek magazine, "TV Showtime," January 6, 1967, Mr. Spock cover, near mint **30**

Mr. Spock Model Kit

Star Trek model kit, Mr. Spock, 1/12 scale, painted by Evan Stuart, AMT, 1968 (ILLUS.) **60-120**

Star Trek playset, Star Trek Mission To Gamma VI Playset, Mego, No. 51226, 1976, boxed, the set **650**

Star Trek playset, Star Trek Telescreen Console, Mego, No. 51232, 1976, boxed, the set **150**

Star Trek thermos, Aladdin, 1967 .... **75-125**

Star Trek toy, Ray Gun flashlight, Larami, No. 9238, 1968 .... **50**

Star Trek toy, St **100**

Star Trek wristwatch, U.S.S. Enterprise, round face, Bradley, 1980 .... **90**

Star Trek writing tablet, 1960s, unused **30**

Star Wars action figure, Luke Skywalker, 1st series card w/twelve figures shown on back, Kenner, 1978 .... **40-350**

Star Wars action figure, Luke Skywalker, Hoth Battle Gear (Empire Strikes Back), Kenner, 1981 .... **20-75**

Star Wars action figure, Luke Skywalker, X-Wing Pilot, Kenner, 1978-79 .... **30-150**

Star Wars "Chewbacca" Bank

Star Wars bank, Chewbacca, figural, ceramic, Sigma, ca. 1982, 10 1/2" h. (ILLUS.) **95**

Yoda Ceramic Bank

Star Wars bank, Yoda, ceramic, figural, painted green, white & brown Sigma (ILLUS.) 85.00

Star Wars bank, Darth Vader head, ceramic, Roman Ceramics, ca. 1977, 6 x 6" 95

Star Wars book ends, ceramic, figural Chewbacca & Darth Vader, Sigma, 1983, pr. 75

Star Wars clock radio, R2-D2 & C-3PO, Bradley Time, 1984 100

Star Wars cookie jar, ceramic, figural R2-D2, Roman Ceramics, 1977, 13" h. 150

Star Wars doll, Boba Fett, boxed, Kenner, 1980, 12" h. 125-400

Star Wars doll, Darth Vader, Star Wars Collector Series, No. 27726, Kenner, ca. 1996, 12" h. 20

Star Wars doll, Luke Skywalker, Star Wars Collector Series, No. 27724, Kenner, ca. 1996, never removed from box, 12" h. 20

Star Wars helmet, Darth Vader Collector Helmet, plastic, 1977........................ 200

Star Wars lunch box & thermos, metal box w/space battle scene on front & Tatoonie scene on back, w/Droids thermos, King Seeley Thermos, 1977 75

Star Wars mask, C-3PO, latex, Don Post Studios, 1977 100

Star Wars mask, Chewbacca, rubber, Don Post Studios, 1977 250

Star Wars mask, Chewbacca, rubber, Don Post Studios, 1978 reissue 100

Star Wars mask, Yoda, rubber, Don Post Studios, 1980s 60

Star Wars premium card set, Burger King, 1980, unused........................ 25

Star Wars teapot set, ceramic, figural Luke & Tauntaun, Sigma, 1983, the set 150

Star Wars toy, AT-AT walker, large plastic vehicle, boxed, Kenner, 1979-80 .... **100-200**

Star Wars Ewok Paploo

Star Wars toy, plush, Ewok, Paploo w/cowl, Kenner, 1983, 4" h. (ILLUS.) **25-50**

Star Wars Ewok Princess Kneesa

Star Wars toy, plush, Ewok, Princess Kneesa w/cowl, Kenner, 1983, 4" h. (ILLUS.)........................ **20-45**

Star Wars vehicle, Darth Vader TIE Fighter, Kenner, No. 39100, 1978, w/original Star Wars box 125

Star Wars vehicle, Darth Vader TIE Fighter, Kenner, No. 39100, 1978, w/original Star Wars box w/Battle Scene Setting 500

Star Wars vehicle, Millenium Falcon Spaceship, Kenner, No. 39110, 1979, in original Star Wars box 325

The Empire Strikes Back (Star Wars) lunch box & thermos, metal, Millennium Falcon on front, Luke, Yoda & R2-D2 on back, Yoda thermos, King Seeley Thermos, 1980........................ 60

Tom Corbett Atomic Pistol

Tom Corbett, Space Cadet Atomic Pistol, plastic, blue body w/red trigger & clear lens cap on flashlight tip, Marx, w/original box, 1950s, excellent condition (ILLUS.) 468

Tom Corbett, Space Cadet coloring book, Saalfield, 1950s........................ 25-50

Tom Corbett, Space Cadet lunch box w/thermos, metal, 1954, Aladdin 431

Tom Corbett, Space Cadet rifle, official Tom Corbett Sparkling Space Gun, plastic & metal, Marx, 1950s, 21" l................ 100-200

Tom Corbett, Space Cadet View-Master reel set, Sawyer, 1950s, set of 3 25-50

Twiki (Buck Rogers TV) action figure, Mego, 1979................................. 25-50

Twiki (Buck Rogers TV) doll, 25th Century Walking Twiki, Mego, ca. 1979, never removed from box, 7" h. 55

Wolfman bubble bath bottle, Soaky, figural, 1963........................ 85-140

Wolfman button, black & white photo on colored background, 1960s, 7/8" d. 12-20

Wolfman candy & toy, Phoenix Candy Co., 1963, 3 1/2" h. box 25-40

Wolfman charm, flicker-type, Wolfman/Phantom, silver frame, 1960s............ 10-20

Wolfman figure, 60th Anniversary limited edition, Placo, 10" h. 12-20

Wolfman figure, bendee, Just Toys, 1991...... 5-10

Wolfman figure, bendee, Vic's, 1979 10-15

Wolfman figure, glow-in-the-dark, Marx reproduction, Uncle Milton, 1990, 4 1/2" h.... 10-15

Wolfman figure, Hamilton, 13" h. **20-35**
Wolfman figure, Imperial, 1986, 6" h. **4-8**
Wolfman figure, mini-monster, glow version, Remco, 1980s, 3 3/4" h...................... **20-45**

Mini-monster Wolfman Figure

Wolfman figure, mini-monster, non-glow version, Remco, 1983, 3 3/4" h. (ILLUS.).. **40-75**
Wolfman figure, MPC Plastics, 2 1/2" h. **10-15**
Wolfman figure, No. 1, AHI, 1973, 8" h.... **100-300**
Wolfman figure, No. 2, AHI, 1973, 8" h.... **100-200**
Wolfman figure, No. 3, AHI, 1973, 8" h.... **100-200**
Wolfman figure, painted plastic, crouching position, 1991, 2 3/4" h. **4-8**
Wolfman figure, plastic, Palmer Plastics, 1963, 3" h.. **20-35**
Wolfman figure, plastic, unarticulated, Marx, 1960s, 6" h... **12-20**

"The Human Wolfman" Figure

Wolfman figure, "The Human Wolfman," Mad Monster series, Mego, 1972, 8" h. (ILLUS.) **75-300**

Remco Wolfman Figure

Wolfman figure, w/patch & ring, glows, Remco, 1980, 8" h. (ILLUS.).................. **100-200**
Wolfman mask, Don Post, 1967............... **225-300**
Wolfman mask, rubber, Don Post, 1976 .... **60-85**
Wolfman model kit, nodder-type, Uncle Gilbert.. **40-60**
Wolfman paint-by-number set, Hasbro, 1963.. **165-300**
Wolfman pencil topper, Wolfman head, no mark, 1960s... **10-20**
Wolfman Pez dispenser, 1960s **172-250**
Wolfman puppet, soft plastic head, plastic paper body, Candy World, 6" h. **10-25**
Wolfman ring, blue base, 1960s.................... **35-50**
Wolfman ring, round, 1960s.......................... **20-30**
Wolfman ring, silver base, 1960s.................. **35-50**
Wolfman View-Master reel set, GAF, 1978.. **10-15**
Wolfman wallet, Hasbro, 1963.................. **100-150**

X-files Action Figures

X-Files (The) action figure, Scully or Mulder, any variation, McFarlane Toys, 1998, each (ILLUS. of three) **12-20**
X-Files (The) dolls, Barbie & Ken, set No. 19630 w/long-haired Scully, Mattel, 1998, the set... **75-125**
X-Files (The) dolls, Barbie & Ken, w/normal-haired Scully, Mattel, 1996, the set..... **65-80**
X-Files (The) model kit, Flukeman, Dark Horse, 1990s.. **100-150**
X-Files (The) model kit, Mulder & Scully, by Men in Black, 1990s **175-225**
X-Files (The) model kit, "X-files: Paranormal Activities, 5th Sense," 1990s........... **125-175**

Chapter 20
TOY SOLDIERS

Reliable Fighting Commandos

Miniature or toy soldiers have been around for hundreds of years. The soldiers have taken many forms and have been constructed of wood, paper, metal, plastic, composition and other materials.Many figures have become scarce and valuable for several reasons. First, children played with them - shot things at them, dropped rocks on them, etc. Second, in the 1960s concerns were raised about the paint used on the metal soldiers and many were taken off the market because of the lead-based paint. Finally, some types deteriorated simply due to the fragile nature of the paper and composition they were made of. Especially during the Korean War era toy soldiers were made of composition material which does not hold up well. Soon collectors moved in and prices began to climb.

German-made soldiers from before or during World War II, such as those produced by Elastolin, Lineol and Heyde, have become scarce due to the ravages of the war. Also, after the war, surviving German toy manufacturers no longer produced anything related to the military or war. Elastolin, for example, produced cowboys and Indians.

The wonderful thing about collecting toy soldiers is that there is such a variety and various periods represented. There is something in everyone's price range. The dimestore soldiers that were sold at Woolworths and other chain stores in bins are still very affordable and even some fine Britains are within reason.

For the more upscale collector there are pieces from Minot of France where a single cavalry figure can cost $150 and a boxed set $700.

A few collectors only collect the boxes that held the sets. As with any good toy it is difficult to find a set complete in an original box.

Auburn, hard rubber, soldier w/bugle,
1930s **$5-10**

Auburn Trench Mortar Soldier

Auburn, hard rubber, trench mortar soldier,
1930s (ILLUS.) **20-45**

Auburn, soldiers, vehicle, truck & tank,
1950s, boxed sets, each **10-20**

Authenticast British Desert Troops Set

Authenticast of Ireland, metal, British Desert Troops of World War II, 1960s, boxed set (ILLUS.).. **15-25**

Authenticast of Ireland, original box for "History in Miniatures" set, red, white & blue (ILLUS. page 240).............................. **5-15**

Barclay Motorcycle with Gunner

Barclay, cast-metal, motorcycle w/driver & sidecar w/gunner, 1930s, 3" l. (ILLUS.)..... **25-45**

Barclay, cast-metal, soldier w/dog, 1930s..... **40-60**

Barclay, cast-metal, soldier w/range finder, early version w/helmet attached w/a pin, 1930s... **10-18**

Barclay Anti-aircraft Gunner

Barclay, cast-metal, anti-aircraft gunner, 1930s (ILLUS.).. **10-18**

Barclay, cast-metal, cannon, 1930s, 3" l. (ILLUS. right).. **10-15**

Barclay Motor Vehicle & Cannon

Barclay, cast-metal, Motor Unit Vehicle, 1930s, 3" l. (ILLUS. left).............................. **10-15**

Barclay Soldier with "Pod Feet"

Barclay, cast-metal, walking soldier w/"pod feet," 1950s, 2 1/2" h. (ILLUS.)..................... **8-12**

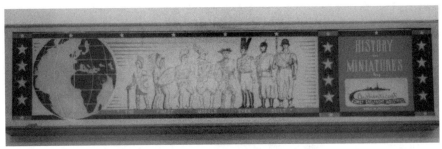

Authenticast Box

Beton (Bergen Toy and Novelty Company), plastic, five-and-dimestore soldier, machine gunner or ammo carrier, 1940s, 2 3/4" h., each **3-5**

Beton Five-and-Dime Plastic Soldier

Beton (Bergen Toy and Novelty Company), plastic, five-and-dimestore soldier, standing holding rifle, 1950s, 2 3/4" h. (ILLUS.) **3-5**

Britains, "Britain's Historical Series - Her Majesty's State Coach," No. 9401, cast metal, coach w/six-horse team, drivers & passengers, England, 1950s, never removed from box, box 8 x 18 1/4", the set **495**

Britains, cast lead, "Armies of the World - German Infantry," ca. 1940, set of 20 (ILLUS. of part below) **300**

British Soldiers by Britains

Britains, cast lead, British soldiers, various sets, ca. 1940, group of 20 (ILLUS. of part) **250**

Britains, cast lead, "Types of U.S.A. Forces," "Marines" & "West Point Cadets - Summer Dress," ca. 1940, group of16 .... **225**

Britains, cast metal, "Arabs of the Desert," five mounted & one marching soldier on slope, Model No. 164, original box, the set **144**

Britains, cast metal, Canadian Mounted Police, set of six w/one horse, mint in original box, ca. 1950-60, the set **99**

Britains, cast-metal, 25-pound howitzer cannon, 1950s.. **35-60**

Britains, cast-metal, Australian's Battle Dress World War II set, 1950s **130-150**

Britains German Infantry Soldiers

Britains Queen Elizabeth on Horse

Britains, cast-metal, Queen Elizabeth II on horseback, "British-Regiments" series, No. 7230, 1970s, boxed (ILLUS.) **40-75**

Britains, cast-metal, sound locator & operator, 1930s-40s **50-100**

Elastolin 1930s German Soldier

Elastolin, cast-metal, German soldier charging, 1930s, 2 3/4" h. (ILLUS.) **35-60**

Elastolin, cast-metal, German soldier kneeling firing rifle, 1930s, 2 3/4" h. **35-60**

Britains Stretcher Carriers Set

Britains, cast-metal, stretcher carriers, 1940, three-piece set (ILLUS.) **20-30**

Britains, original catalog of products, 1972 .... **20-50**

Built Rite, cardboard, soldiers, 1930s, each **10-20**

Comet of England, World War II soldier crawling **8-15**

Doepke (William) Mfg. Co., soldier, painted wood, tin soldier-style standing on spindle, painted face & uniform w/tall black hat, ... **22**

Elastolin, cast-metal, figure of Hitler, 1930s **150-300**

Early Elastolin Solider on Horse

Elastolin, soldier on horseback, figure wearing khaki uniform & helmet, naturally painted hands & face, on brown horse w/black harness, on narrow rectangular base, early, 5 1/2" h. (ILLUS.) **55**

German-made Flat Civil War Soldiers

Elastolin, soldiers, marching platoon, khaki uniforms, painted faces, ca. 1930s, each 3 3/4" h., set of 14 .... **138**

German-made, flat-style cast-metal, soldiers of the American Civil War, 1960s, boxed set of 10 (ILLUS. above) **10-20**

German-made, soldiers, cast lead, painted flat cast, some mounted, label on oval box says "No. 110 1/8, 10 stick pcs.," "Preussische Infanterie im Marsch" (Prussian Infantry Marching), the set **33**

Grey Iron, cast-metal, Foreign Legion soldier in blue uniform, 1930s **20-45**

Grey Iron, cast-metal, soldier w/radio & aerial, 1930s, the set **100-250**

Grey Iron, cast-metal, wounded sitting soldier, 1930s **40-65**

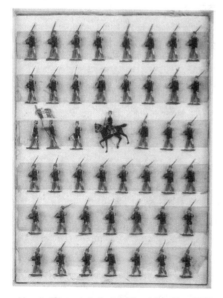

Heyde "French Infantry Marching No. 177"

Heycle Miniatures, cast-metal, "French Infantry Marching No. 177," comprising general, officer, standard bearer, drummer & 41 infantrymen, in maker's box, Heyde (box taped, lid incomplete); a partial set of the same comprising general, two officers, standard bearer, drummer & 18 infantrymen & 16 mounted French cavalry (possibly not Heyde), comprising general, two officers, bugler & 12 cavalrymen (ILLUS.)... **1,035**

Heyde Miniatures, soldiers, die-cast metal, "American Infantry Marching 12th Regt. No. 169," comprising mounted officer, marching officer, standard bearer, drummer & eighteen infantrymen, in original box, 20th c., the set (box taped)................... **431**

Japanese-made West Point Cadet

Japanese-made, cast-metal, West Point Cadet, copy of American piece, 1930s, 3" h. (ILLUS.)... **10-25**

Kellogg's Sugar Smacks premiums, plastic soldiers, 1951, 2 1/4" h., each............... **10-20**

Lineol Horse-Drawn Wagon & Driver

Lineol, cast-metal, horse-pulled wagon & driver, Germany, 1930s, overall 10" l., the set (ILLUS.)....................................... **100-250**

London Toys of Canada, cast-metal, soldier, two cannons & a Hurricane aircraft, 1939, boxed set **100-200**

Manoil, cast-metal, soldier throwing hand grenade, 1950s, 2 3/4" h. **13-18**

Manoil, cast-metal, soldier w/pistol, 1950s, 2 3/4" h. **13-18**

Manoil, soldier set, die-cast metal, including machine gunners, grenade thrower, pilot, doctor, nurse, stretcher bearers, casualty, soldiers in gas masks, two tents, ca. 1930s, 22 pcs. **546**

Marx, plastic, German soldier throwing grenade, 1963, 6" h.. **6-8**

Marx Roman Soldier

Marx, plastic, Roman soldier, from "Warriors of the World" series, 1960s, 2 3/8" h., each in box (ILLUS.) **8-15**

Marx Plastic Russian Soldier

Marx, plastic, Russian soldier, standing holding rifle, 1963, 6" h. (ILLUS.) **5-7**

Miller (J.H.) of Chicago, composition, General MacArthur, 1952, 5" h. **35-75**

Miller (J.H.) of Chicago, composition, machine gunner in prone position, 1952, 5" l. **15-25**

Minot of France Cavalry Figure

Minot of France, 1914 Dragoon Cavalry figure on horseback (ILLUS.) **100-150**

Minot of France, complete boxed sets **300-700**

Minot of France, World War I French Infantry set, in blue uniforms, 1970, the set **20-50**

Playwood Plastics, flag bearer, 1940s............. **6-8**

Playwood Plastics, soldier w/machine gun, 1940s **6-8**

Reliable Fighting Commandos

Reliable of Canada, plastic, "Canada's Fighting Commandos," World War II-style soldiers, boxed set (ILLUS.) **100-150**

Reliable of Canada Toy Soldier

Reliable of Canada, soldiers, 1950s, 2 3/4" h., each (ILLUS. of one) **3-5**

Silk Soldier Mortar Soldier

Silk of Lansing, Iowa, composition, Korean War mortar soldier, 1952, 5" h. (ILLUS.) **25-50**

Sonsco, Japan, soldiers marked "Made in Occupied Japan," 1947, each **25-100**

Tommy Toy, cast-metal, officer w/gas mask, 1930s **125-225**

Chapter 21
VEHICLES

"Atom Jet" Racer

Friction-Powered F-51 Airplane

1958 AMT Edsel Promo Car

Friction Action Lincoln Continental

Automobile, Lincoln Continental, friction-type, lithographed tin, red w/silver trim, metal wheels, Japan, 1950s, very good condition, 11" l. (ILLUS.) **193**

The Mattel Dream Car

Automobile, "The Mattel Dream Car," friction-type, plastic, blue & silver plastic body w/clear bubble top, Mattel, 1950s, w/original box (ILLUS.) **220**

Automobile, Volkswagon, pressed steel, Tonka Mfg., ca. 1950s, 9" **11**

Bandai Battery-Operated Volkswagon

Automobile, Volkswagon sedan, battery-operated, lithographed tin, grey w/silver metal trim & black & white tires w/metal hubcaps, Bandai (Japan), ca. 1960, very good condition, 10 1/2" l. (ILLUS.) **110**

Boat, battery-operated, plastic, "Lang Craft Powered Model Boat," cabin cruiser in brown, red & white, includes original box & outboard motor box, 1950s, mint toy, 13" l. **193**

The Marlin Cabin Cruiser Toy

Boat, plastic, "Fleet Line Speedboats - The Marlin," cabin cruiser in brown & white w/grey Star Flite Evinrude motor, w/original red & blue box, never played with, 1950s, 18 1/2" l. (ILLUS.) **825**

Bulldozer, pressed steel, Tonka Mfg., ca. 1950s, 12" l. **110**

Bus, friction-type, lithographed tin, sight-seeing style, cream w/black striped sections along body, multiple open windows, bullet-form silver roof projections at front & rear, red headlights, rubber tires, lithographed interior, marked "I.Y. Metal Toys - Made in Japan," ca. 1950s, 16 1/2" l. (denting, spotting, scratches & soiling, non-working mechanism) **149**

Camper, pressed steel, "Winnebago Indian," Tonka Mfg., 23" l. **44**

Combine, die-cast metal, John Deere Turbo Combine w/yellow cab, Ertl Toy Co. (Dyersville, Iowa), 15" l. **22**

Combine, pressed steel, John Deere model, green w/yellow trim, black rubber tires, Eska, ca. 1950s, w/original slightly damaged box, excellent condition **303**

Corgi vehicle, 1012 S.P.E.C.T.R.E. bob-sled, used by head of S.P.E.C.T.R.E. when fleeing from James Bond, good condition **140**

Corgi vehicle, 1102 Crane w/orange Frue-hauf bottom dumper & red Berliet cab, near mint toy & good box **65**

Corgi vehicle, 1106 Mack Container truck, yellow cab & trailer w/red containers marked "ACL," near mint toy & good box **65**

Corgi vehicle, 1130 Bedford Circus horse transporter w/horses, red cab & red/blue trailer, good toy & near mint box **200**

Corgi vehicle, 1154-A Mack Priestman crane truck w/red cab & yellow cabin, has "Hi-Lift" labels, good **75**

Corgi vehicle, 24-C1 Shazam Thunderbolt race car, yellow (from Capt. Marvel comics), near mint **35**

Corgi vehicle, 259 Penguinmobile, white body w/Penguin labels, near mint toy & good box **55**

Corgi vehicle, 260 Metropolis (Superman's city) Buick police car, blue & white body, mint toy & box **55**

Corgi vehicle, 267 Batmobile, black body/silver hubs/gold tow hook, Batman & Robin figures, mint toy & box **65**

Corgi vehicle, 303S Mercedes Benz 300 SL open roadster w/light blue body & white interior, good toy & box **95**

Corgi vehicle, 45 Blue Royal Canadian Mounted Police set, near mint toy & good box **110**

Corgi vehicle, 69 Massey-Ferguson 165 tractor, red body and unpainted shovel, near mint toy & box **95**

Corgi vehicle, 801-A Noddy's car w/three figures, yellow body & red fenders, near mint body & good box 310

Corgi vehicle, 96655 James Bond DB 5 Aston Martin, silver body & red interior, produced 1995, mint toy & box 35

Corgi vehicle, Co-op set, near mint 370

Corgi vehicle, GS-15-B1 Corgi Pony Club Land Rover & Horse Box, blue & white, good 80

Corgi vehicle, GS-24 Construction set, near mint toys & box 230

Corgi vehicle, GS-31 Buick Riviera (blue) w/boat on red trailer & water skier, near mint toy & box.................. 300

Dinky vehicle, 110, Aston Martin DB3S grey body & blue interior, racing decal, near mint body & fair box 80

Dinky vehicle, 147, Cadillac 72, blue body & red interior, near mint body & box 90

Dinky vehicle, 156, Rover 75 Saloon, maroon body & red hubcaps, near mint toy & box................. 140

Dinky vehicle, 162, Ford Zephyr, two-tone blue, near mint body......................... 95

Dinky vehicle, 165, Humber Hawk, green & black body, near mint toy 105

Dinky vehicle, 173, Pontiac Parisienne, red, near mint body & good box 55

Dinky vehicle, 194, Bentley Coupe, light grey body & maroon interior, near mint body & box.................. 95

Dinky vehicle, 257, Nash Rambler Fire Chief's car, good toy & box 110

Dinky vehicle, 294, Police Vehicles Gift Set (boxed), good toys & box 130

Dinky vehicle, 353, Shado 2 Mobile, olive green body & pale green base, near mint toy & box 60

Dinky vehicle, 370, Dragster set, good toy & box................. 55

Dinky vehicle, 678, Air Sea Rescue launch w/black hull & light grey deck, yellow superstructure, near mint toy & box................. 55

Dinky vehicle, 724, Sikorsky Sea King helicopter, white & blue w/red interior, near mint toy w/box 70

Dinky vehicle, 726, Messerschmitt B.F. 109E, tan & olive camouflage, near mint toy & box 60

Dinky vehicle, 732, Bell Police Helicopter, blue & orange, missing pilot, good toy & box 35

Dinky vehicle, 771, International Road Signs set, near mint toy & good box............. 210

Dinky vehicle, 784, Goods Train Set, near mint toy & box...................... 55

Dinky vehicle, 822, M-3 Half track, olive body & no machine gun, good body & box 150

Dinky vehicle, 945, A.E.C. Esso fuel tanker w/white body but no rear label, near mint toy & box.................. 85

Dinky vehicle, 948, McLean Tractor trailer w/red cab & grey trailer, near mint toy & box 475

Dinky vehicle, 957, Fire Service Gift Set, good body & box.................. 650

Earthmover, pressed steel, Structo Mfg. Co., ca. 1950s, 17" l. (repainted) 50

Fire aerial ladder truck, pressed steel, red cab & trailer w/adjustible silver ladder, black rubber wheels, "S.M.F.D." on side, Smith-Miller Toy Co. (Los Angeles, California), ca. 1950s, toy excellent, original box very good 825

Fire extension-ladder truck, lithographed tin, friction-type, automatic ladder mechanism, Cragston (Japan), 1960s, w/original box, 14 1/4" l. 81

Fire hook & ladder truck, pressed steel, Wyandotte Toys, ca. 1950, 25" l. 83

Fire ladder truck, pressed steel, Smith-Miller Toy Co., ca. 1950s, 36" l. 495

Fire ladder truck, pressed steel, William Doepke Mfg. Co., ca. 1950s, 33" l. 242

Fire snorkel truck, pressed steel, Tonka Mfg., ca. 1950s, 17" 66

Fire truck, pressed steel, Suburban Pumper #46, Tonka 180

Forklift, pressed steel, Tonka Mfg., ca. 1950s, 16" l. (repainted) 22

Gremlins automobile, die-cast, Gizmo in pink Corvette, small version, 1984 .... **125-275**

Gremlins automobile, plastic & metal, Gizmo in pink Corvette, Ertl, 1984, 5 1/2 x 12 1/2" **125-275**

Hay loader, pressed steel, "Barber-Greene" high capacity loader, William Doepke Mfg. Co., 22" l. (repainted) 187

James Bond automobile, lithographed tin, friction-type, multi-action 711 Aston Martin Secret Ejector Car, original receipt of purchase, good w/fair box, United, 11" l. 483

James Bond Moonbuggy, inspired by "Diamonds Are Forever," excellent w/good box, Corgi.................. 690

Jeep, "G.I. Joe Desert Patrol Attack Jeep," plastic, includes Jeep, machine gun & ring, portable radio, Hasbro Mfg., original box, ca. 1960s, 20" l. (missing antenna)....... 649

Machinery hauler, pressed steel, Structo Mfg. Co., ca. 1950, 13" l. 55

Matchbox set, "Sea Fury" play set w/carrying case & three figures, near mint toy & good box 105

Matchbox vehicle, Coronation Coach, small silver-plated, issued 1953 100

Matchbox vehicle, CY-104, Kenworth Superstar Transporter Sunoco Ultra Racing Team Set #94, without "Sterlin Marlin" on trailer, mint vehicle w/good box...................... 80

Matchbox vehicle, G-14, Grand Prix Set
w/near mint toys & good box **45**

Matchbox vehicle, G-6-B, Commercial
Truck set, pristine toy & box........................... **150**

Matchbox vehicle, K-11, DAF Car transporter w/blue cab & gold trailer, DAF la-
bels, mint vehicle w/poor box........................... **60**

Matchbox vehicle, Limited Edition #9729,
Yorkshire Steam Wagon w/Samuel
Smith logo & framed in case, near mint **60**

Matchbox vehicle, MB-16-3, Scammell
Mountaineer Snowplow w/grey wheels,
mint body & good box **100**

Matchbox vehicle, MB-41-3, Ford GT, rare
yellow body & black wheels, good car &
mint box.. **180**

Matchbox vehicle, MB-42-2, Studebaker
Lark Wagonaire w/rare dark blue roof,
good **75**

Matchbox vehicle, MB-46-1, Morris Minor
GPW in rare green color, good **135**

Matchbox vehicle, MB-66-2, Harley Davidson motorcycle & rider, good toy & fair
box **110**

Matchbox vehicle, MB-66-3, Greyhound
Bus w/silver body & rare clear windows,
both toy & box mint.. **85**

Matchbox vehicle, PS1000, Gift Set (road
construction vehicles) pristine toy & box....... **155**

Matchbox vehicle, SB-29-A SR-71, spy
plane w/USAF markings, preproduction
resin model, near mint w/fair box **120**

Matchbox vehicle, SB-34-A C-130, Hercules transport w/USCG markings, preproduction resin model, near mint toy &
fair box.. **170**

Matchbox vehicle, small covered wagon
w/barrels, issued 1955, good toy **195**

Matchbox vehicle, Y-5, 1929 Le Mans
Bentley w/green body, red seats & black
fenders, near mint toy & good box.................. **65**

Harley-Davidison Friction Motorcycle

Motorcycle, friction-type, lithographed tin,
black w/white trim & "Harley-Davidson"
on the side, working pistons, perfect
working order, Japan, ca. 1950s, 9" l.
(ILLUS.) **605**

Motorcycle & Rider

Motorcycle, w/rider, battery-operated, tin,
Modern Toys, 12" l. (ILLUS.) **770**

Moving van, painted metal, GMC semi,
"Mayflower," Nylint, boxed, modern,
22" l.. **44**

Tonka Allied Van Lines Truck

Moving van, pressed steel, orange cab &
trailer marked "Allied Van Lines" in black
& white, ca. 1950s - 60s, Tonka (ILLUS.)..... **303**

Super-Sonic Jet Pedal Toy

Pedal airplane, "Super-Sonic Jet," pressed
steel w/rubber-rimmed tires, white & red,
all-original, even overall wear,
Murray, ca. 1950s (ILLUS.)........................ **1,430**

English Austin J40 Pedal Car

Fire Chief's Pedal Car

Pedal car, pressed steel, "Austin J40" model, light blue, opening trunk & hood, electric headlights & horn, leatherette upholstery, nickel-plated grille, bumpers & hood ornament, surface rust to left front fender, England, 1950s, 61" l. (ILLUS.) **1,610**

Pedal car, pressed steel, fire chief's car, wood chassis, red w/yellow striping, Rickenbacker, American National (Toledo, Ohio), late 1920s, missing front bell, poor finish, surface rust, 42" l. (ILLUS. above) **1,840**

Pedal Fire Ladder Truck

Pedal vehicle, pressed steel, hook & ladder fire truck, painted red & white, bell on hood & battery-operated headlight, AMF, 1950s, ladders missing, overall excellent (ILLUS.) **858**

Early Eska John Deere Pedal Tractor

Pedal vehicle, tractor & wagon, pressed steel, John Deere model, green w/yellow wheels & trim, Eska, purchased in 1955, original receipt included, old repaint, 2 pcs. (ILLUS.) **1,128**

Nylint U-Haul Pick-up and Trailer

Pick-up truck & trailer, pressed steel, orange & white, original "U-Haul" stickers on each, Nylint, Model 4100, w/original box, very good condition, 2 pcs. (ILLUS.)..... **303**

Popeye vehicle, die-cast metal, Popeye's Paddle Wagon Jr., Corgi **100-200**

Popeye vehicle, die-cast metal, Popeye's Paddle Wagon, w/Swee Pea in lifeboat, Corgi, 5" l. **250-500**

"Atom Jet" Racer

Racing car, "Atom Jet" (ILLUS.)..................... **1,320**

Road grader, pressed steel, Tonka Mfg., ca. 1950s, 18" l. (repainted)................... **11**

Sand loader, pressed steel, Tonka Mfg., ca. 1950s, 11" **28**

Scooby-Doo vehicle, airplane, Scooby-Doo Bump & Go Airplane, Boley, 1998, boxed.. **15-20**

Scooby-Doo vehicle, friction-powered, Scooby-Doo on Ski Vacation, Boley, 1998, boxed.. **15-20**

Skidder, pressed steel, John Deere, #590, Ertl Toy Co., 16" l. **72**

Smurf automobile, die-cast metal, Smurf in car, "Smurf #2," Ertl, 1982........................... **10-20**

Smurf automobile, die-cast metal, Smurf in log car, "Smurf #3," Ertl, 1982, 1 1/2" l....... **10-20**

Smurfette in Car Toy

Smurf automobile, die-cast metal, Smurfette in car, "Smurf #1," Ertl, 1982,
1 1/2" l. (ILLUS.) **10-20**

Steam roller, pressed steel, Tonka
Mfg., ca. 1950s, 15" l. **17**

Early Tonka Steam Shovel

Steam shovel, pressed steel, red body &
platform w/black wheels, adjustable blue
digging arm, Model 50, Tonka, excellent
condition (ILLUS.) **248**

Tank, pressed steel, hand-crank rotating orange turret w/firing noise, sheet metal
body w/ten metal wheels, green body,
decals on both sides, Structo Mfg. Co.,
12" l. **407**

Tractor, cast metal, "John Deere 4WD 8960
Limited Edition-Sept. '88, 1/2000," Ertl
Toy Co., 16" l. **138**

Tractor, cast metal, John Deere 8010 die-
sel 4wd custom, Ertl Toy Co., 15" l. **215**

Massey-Harris Scale Model Tractor

Tractor, cast metal, Massey-Harris scale
model, red chassis w/silver driver, black
rubber tires w/yellow hubs, mint in origi-
nal box (ILLUS.) **303**

Tractor, pressed steel, International 6388
2+2, 15" l. **66**

Eska John Deere Tractor

Tractor, pressed steel, John Deere model,
green w/yellow trim & black rubber tires,
Eska, ca. 1950s, mint toy w/excellent
original box (ILLUS.) **787**

Train boxcar, Lionel Lines, New York Cen-
tral, No. 6464-125, 1954-56 .... **150**

Train caboose w/bay window, Lionel
Lines, Chessie System, No. 16518, 1990 ...... **45**

Johnny Lightning Car Hauler Car

Train car, car hauler, Lionel Lines, Johnny
Lightning, No. 16757, uncatalogued
1996 (ILLUS.) **100**

Lionel Double Roll Cable Car

Train car, double roll cable car on flat bed,
orange rolls tied down, grey body flat car,
Lionel Lines #6561, 1950s (ILLUS.) **100**

Train car, Lionel Lines, refrigeration car,
No. 214R, standard gauge, 1929-40 .... **800**

Lionel Work Crane Car

Train crane car, Lionel Lines, #6560, red w/smoke stack & control wheel on back, black crane arm w/large hook at end, 1950s-60s (ILLUS.) 100

Train engine, Lionel Lines 0-4-0 locomotive, No. 1061, 1963-64, 1969 40

Train engine, Lionel Lines 2-4-2 locomotive, No. 1688/1688E, "O" gauge, 1936-38, uncatalogued 1939-42 100

Train engine, Lionel Lines 2-6-2 locomotive, No. 2025, 1947-49, 1952 150

Train engine, Lionel Lines 2-6-2 locomotive, No. 224/224E, "O" gauge, 1938-42....... 250

Train engine, Lionel Lines 2-6-4 locomotive, No. 2037, 1953-64 125

Train engine, Lionel Lines 2-8-4 Berkshire locomotive, No. 736, 1955-66........................ 300

Train engine, Lionel Lines 4-6-4 locomotive, No. 2055, 1953-56 225

Train engine, Lionel Lines, Chesapeake & Ohio GP-7 locomotive, No. 2347, uncatalogued 1965... 3,000

Train engine, Lionel Lines, Joshua Lionel Cowen 4-6-4 Hudson locomotive, No. 8210, 1982... 375

Train engine, Lionel Lines, Lackawanna FM TrainMaster locomotive, No. 2321, 1954-56 550

Pennsylvania GG-1 Engine Car

Train engine, Lionel Lines, Pennsylvania GG-1 locomotive, No. 18313, 1996 (ILLUS.) 375

Train engine, Lionel Lines, Pennsylvania GG-1 locomotive, No. 2332, 1947-49............ 900

American Flyer Engine No. 3116

Train engine, lithographed tin, electric, American Flyer Model 3116, complete, very good condition (ILLUS.) 248

Train engines, Lionel Lines, Union Pacific GP-9 powered & dummy locomotives, No. 11956, 1997, the set 500

Lionel Lines Flatcar

Train flatcar, w/pipes, Lionel Lines No. 6511, 1953-56 (ILLUS.).................................... 35

"Lionel Visitor's Center" Gondola Car

Train gondola car, w/coil covers, Lionel Lines, marked "Lionel Visitor's Center," No. 19955, uncatalogued 1998 (ILLUS.) 35

Republican Party Observation Car

Train observation car, Lionel Lines, George Bush Whistle Stop, made for Republican Party campaign workers, uncatalogued 1992 (ILLUS.)................................. 3,500

Train operating bascule bridge, Lionel Lines, No. 313, 1946-49 550

Train operating gateman, Lionel Lines, No. 145, 1950-66.. 550

Borden's Milk Car

Train operating milk car, w/platform, Lionel Lines, Borden's, No. 9220, 1983-86 (ILLUS.).. 125

Train set, "American Flyer," Burlington Zephyr 9900, original box, the set 110

Canada Confederation Train Engine

Train set, Canada Confederation, Limited Edition HO set, engine white w/red stripes, marked "Canada—The Confederation Flyer" w/red Canadian maple leaf, 12 cars in set: engine, caboose & 10 cars representing each of the Canadian provinces, 1970s, rare (ILLUS. of engine only) **800**

Lionel Transformer Type ZW

Train transformer, Lionel Lines, type ZW, 275 watts, handles four trains & whistles, 1948 (ILLUS.) **350**

Trencher-backhoe, pressed steel, #2534, Tonka Mfg., boxed, ca. 1950s, 18" l. **14**

Truck, auto carrier, lithographed tin, Japan, ca. 1950s, 13" l. **22**

Mack Hollywood Film Ad Truck

Truck, B Mack Hollywood film ad, six-wheels, red, Smith Miller (ILLUS.) **1,843**

Dinky ABC-TV Truck

Truck, cast metal, van-style, pale blue over silver w/red band & logo, "ABC-TV" over front, Dinky Toy (Meccano, Liverpool, England), very good condition, 4 1/2" l. (ILLUS.) **193**

Truck, cement mixer, pressed steel, Tonka Mfg., ca. 1950s, 15" l. **127**

Marx Coal Delivery Truck

Truck, coal delivery-type, pressed steel, red, white & black paint w/the deep back marked "Glen Dale Coal Company," Marx, ca. 1950, 12" l. (ILLUS.) **248**

Truck, dump & plow, pressed steel, State Hi-Way Dept. truck, Tonka Mfg., ca. 1950s, 16" l. **352**

Smith-Miller Dump Truck

Truck, dump, pressed steel, reddish orange cab & dump box w/original decals, black rubber tires, Smith-Miller, ca. 1950s, all-original, very good condition (ILLUS.) **330**

Cragston Gasoline Tanker Truck

Truck, gasoline tanker, friction-type, pressed steel, yellow & red w/black rubber tires, "Shell" printed on the tanker, Cragston (Japan), ca. 1950s, w/original box, toy 6" l. (ILLUS.) **165**

Walgreen's Ice Cream Truck by Marx

Truck, ice cream delivery semi-truck & trailer, stamped steel, creamy white ground printed in blue on trailer "Walgreen's Ice Cream - Fresh Flavorful Delicious - It Tastes Better - Coast to Coast," the cab w/open windows & black grille printed w/"Walgreen Drug Co.," hard rubber wheels, rear door opens, Marx Toys, some rust spotting, scratches & soiling, 19 3/4" l. (ILLUS.) **330**

Truck, low-boy type, pressed steel, "Coast to Coast" on sides, Marx, ca. 1950, 25" l. **110**

Truck, machinery moving-type, pressed steel in black, red, yellow & silver, side labeled "Machinery Equipment Service" w/traversing crane, plastic motor & two wooden crates, w/original cardboard box marked "Machinery Moving Truck...," Marx, 1950s, 22" l. (truck w/rust & discoloration, box taped & water-stained)............... **173**

Truck, pressed steel, livestock van-type, No. 36, Tonka... **125**

Truck, pressed steel, semi w/trailer, "Kroehler Semi," Structo Mfg. Co., ca. 1950s, 23" l. **55**

Truck, pressed steel, Tonka Farms stock rack-type, No. 32 .... **146**

Winross vehicle, 1992 York Fair Doubles w/Wind-Up Music & Reithoffer's logo, Ford cab in orange w/orange & white trailer & tandem axles, issued 1992, mint toy & box **140**

Winross vehicle, A.D. Frey White 7000 cab in white w/red/white trailer, tandem axles, issued 1985, 120 made, near mint toy & box **425**

Winross vehicle, Branch Motor Express, White 9000 cab in green, grey trailer & tandem axle, issued 1982, near mint toy & box.. **240**

Winross vehicle, Cambell Express Inc. w/metal dolly, White 5000 cab in yellow, yellow & white trailer, issued 1975, near mint toy & box... **95**

Winross vehicle, Consolidated Freightways w/metal swing dolly, White 7000 cab in green/grey trailer, single axle, issued 1972, near mint toy & box..................... **130**

Winross vehicle, Goodwrench #3 Dale Earnhardt Dropped, International 8300 cab in black w/black trailer, tandem axles, two Special Edition Earnhardt Matchbox Chevy Luminas with special presentation box, issued 1992 & all mint toy and box **65**

Winross vehicle, Hanover Shoe Company 1st Edition, Mack cab in green, white trailer, tandem axles, issued 1991, near mint toy & box **80**

Winross vehicle, Helms Express, White 9000 cab in dark green/white trailer, tandem axles & issued 1980, near mint toy & box... **230**

Winross vehicle, New Penn 50 Years Of Service 1931-1981, White 9000 cab in green, white trailer, tandem axles, issued 1982, near mint toy & box **90**

Winross vehicle, Pilot TNT Freight, White 9000 cab in cream & orange, cream trailer, tandem axles, issued 1985, slight factory paint flaws on the cab, near mint toy otherwise & near mint box..................... **150**

Winross vehicle, Red Bubble Yum, White 5000 red cab w/red trailer, single axle, issued 1979, near mint toy & box **65**

Winross vehicle, Rutters Tanker, White 9000 cab in white, chrome tanker, tandem axles, issued 1986, near mint toy & box **105**

Winross vehicle, Schneider National Mack cab in dark orange w/orange trailer & tandem axles, one of 504 made, issued 1988, very good toy & box **410**

Winross vehicle, The Chief Freight Lines Co., White 7000 cab in red & white, white trailer, tandem axles, issued 1982, near mint toy & box **180**

Winross vehicle, Ward Trucking Corp., International 8300 cab in green, white trailer, tandem axles, issued 1991, near mint toy & box **60**

Winross vehicle, York Paper Box 100th Anniversary 1894-1994, Aeromax cab in metallic gold, pale yellow & cream trailer, tandem axles, issued 1994, only 600 made, mint toy & box **40**

Chapter 22
MISCELLANEOUS

Kiddies Play Pump

Texaco Service Station Boxed Set

Auto service station set, "Texaco Service Station - Steel with Plastic Accessories," color box cover w/red, white & blue house-form station w/vehicles & pumps, a young boy at one end, all on a greenish yellow ground, Tag No. 856, never out of box, minor box wear, the set (ILLUS.) **$385**

Auto service station set, "Uptown Service Center," lithographed metal w/plastic accessories, original box cover shows complete station w/young boy behind it, all on an orange ground w/blue wording, notes in one corner "New 'Clip Lock' Easy Assembly," unused in box, No. 860, ca. 1970s, the set (some wear & damage to box) **242**

Beetle, molded plastic, antenna moves up & down when rolled **17**

Bluey Blooper, Kosmic Kiddle, pink hair w/attached yellow plastic cap w/two antenna, yellow coat, black & white removable disc eyes, red plastic stand & spaceship **200**

Cannon, cast iron & pressed steel, "Big Bang Cannon," 1950s, 18" l. **58**

G.I. Joe Action Soldier

G.I. Joe Action Soldier, w/Army manual, in original box (ILLUS.) **88**

G.I. Joe doll, Collector's Edition "Home for the Holidays" Soldier, No. 35946, Hasbro Mfg. Co. (Pawtucket, Rhode Island), ca. 1996, never removed from box **30**

G.I. Joe doll, "G.I. Joe Action Soldier," black hair, blue eyes, green fatigues w/button accents, green plastic cap, brown boots, metal dog tag, Army Manual, Boot Instructions, Gear & Equipment Manual, two sticker insignia sheets, G.I. Joe Club folder (snap on shirt loose, box & papers discolored) **127**

G.I. Joe Space Capsule, w/Astronaut, the set **465**

"Hootin Hollow Haunted House"

House, "Hootin Hollow Haunted House," Marx (ILLUS.) **1,540**

Kaleidoscope, Steven, original box, ca. 1950s **14**

Kitchen stove, electric, chrome & cream enamel, oven & two burners, Lionel, 11 1/2 x 25", 33" h. **1,093**

Marionette, rabbit, rubber head, feet & hands, wearing skirt & long-sleeved blouse, ca. 1950 (skirt w/some holes) **17**

Matchbox toy, jigsaw puzzles featuring eight different vehicle toys issued in 1969, mint, set of eight **130**

Microscope set, includes accessories & handbooks, A.C. Gilbert Co., 1948, original carrying case............................... **39**

Military police outfit, plastic, model of a Trooper, pistol, billy club, whistle, belt & holster & arm band, Carnell Mfg. Co., ca. 1950, near mint in original box **165**

Monkey, lithographed tin, string climbing-type, marked "Made in USA," 5 1/2" l. **39**

Music box, model of a televison set, TV & clock music box plays as couple dance in TV screen, jewel musical alarm, Bradley Time of Germany, ca. 1950s, original box (back needs three small screws) **39**

Pop-up toy, cat, black w/white face, pull rings to make it stand up, Fisher-Price (East Aurora, New York), ca. 1950s **50**

Kiddies Play Pump

Pump, "Kiddies Play Pump," tin w/two small tin buckets, decorated w/children wearing fire hats, Ohio Art No. 262, 1950s, together w/original box (ILLUS.) **143**

Riding toy, horse, pressed metal, push down on stirrups & he walks, painted, Mobo, ca. 1950s **132**

Riding toy, pony, brown & white plush, standing on four-wheel platform, steering handle, ca. 1950s, 18" l., 20" h. **121**

Road construction set, cast iron, miniature vehicles & signs, Arcade Mfg. Co., ca. 1950s, near mint original box **605**

Sewing machine, "Kayanee" model, metal, made in U.S. Zone, Germany, 1950s **95**

Ship building set, "Kidstruction Ship Builder," plastic, builds 25 big ships, Lee Craft, ca. 1950s, original box **22**

Spurs, child's, ca. 1950s, Kilgore, mint in box, pr. **95**

APPENDIX
LIST OF WELL-KNOWN TOY MANUFACTURERS

A.C. Gilbert Co. (New Haven, CT)
A.C. Williams Co. (Ravenna, OH)
Acme Toy Works (Chicago, IL)
Airfix (England)
All Metal Products Co.
   (Wyandotte, MI— Wyandotte Toys)
All-NU Products, Inc. (New York, NY)
Alps Shojo Ltd. (Tokyo, Japan)
Althof, Bergmann & Co. (New York, NY)
American Flyer (Chicago, IL)
American National Co. (Toledo, OH)
American Soldier Co. (Brooklyn, NY)
AMT (Japan)
Andes Foundry Co. (Lancaster, PA)
Andre Citroen (Paris, France)
Arcade Mfg. Co. (Freeport, IL)
Arnold Co. (Nuremberg, Germany)
Art Metal Works
Auburn (Auburn, IN—
   Double Fabric Tire Corp.)
Automatic Toy Works (New York, NY)

Bandai (Japan)
Banner (Bronx, NY)
Barclay Mfg. Co. (Hoboken, NJ)
Barton & Smith (Philadelphia, PA)
Beckley Ralson (Chicago, IL)
Basset-Lowke (Northampton, England)
Beggs, Eugene (Paterson, NJ—1870-80)
Benjamin (Air Rifle)
Bestmaid (Japan)
Best Toy & Novelty (Manhattan, KS)
Bing Corp (New York, NY)
Bing, (Gebruder)
   (Nuremberg, Germany)
Bliss (R.) Mfg. Co. (Pawtucket, R.I.)
Blomer & Schuler
   (Nuremberg, Germany)
Borgfeldt (George) & Co. (New York, NY)
Bowen, James H. (Philadelphia, PA)
Bowman (Norwich, England)
Bradley, Milton & Co. (Springfield, MA)

Britains (William) Ltd. (London,
   England)
British Zone (Germany)
Brown (George W.) & Co.
   (Forestville, CT)
Bub, Karl (Nuremberg, Germany)
Buddy L (Moline Pressed Steel Co.,
   E. Moline, IL)
Buffalo Toy & Tool Works (Buffalo, NY)
Burnett Ltd. (London, England)
Butler Brothers (New York, NY)

C.B.G. Mignot Miniatures
   (Paris, France)
Cardini (Omegna, Italy)
Carette, Georges (Nuremberg, Germany)
Carpenter, Francis W. (Port Chester, NY)
Cass—see N.D. Cass
Chad Valley (Birmingham, England)
Champion Hardware Co. (Geneva, OH)
Charles M. Crandall (Covington, PA)
Charles Morrell (Courtenay (?), England)
Chein—see J. Chein
C.K. Co. (Japan)
Citroen—see Andre Citroen
Clark, D.P.—see D.P. Clark
Clark & Sowdon (New York, NY)
Clark, E.O.—see E.O. Clark
Comet Metal Products (Queens, NY)
Commonwealth Plastics Corp.
   (Leominster, MA)
Conestoga Co. (Bethlehem, PA)
Converse—see Morton E. Converse
Corcoran Mfg. Co. (Washington, IN)
Corgi Toys, Mettoy Playcraft Ltd.
   (Swansea, South Wales)
Courtenay Miniatures (Doran, England)
CR (France)
Cragston (Japan)
Crandall, Charles M.—
   see Charles M. Crandall
Crandall, Jesse—see Jesse Crandall
Crescent Toy Co., Ltd. (Great Britain)

D.P. Clark (New York, NY)
Daisy Manufacturing Co. (Rogers, AK)
Davis, A.A. (Nashua, NH)
Dayton Friction Toy Works (Dayton, OH)
Dayton Toy & Specialty Co.
   (Dayton, OH)
Deluxe Game Corp.
Dent Hardware Co. (Fullerton, PA)
Detroit Stove Works
Dinky Toys—see Meccano
Distler (Germany)
Doepke—see William Doepke
Doll Et Cie (& Co.)—
   (Nuremberg, Germany)
Dowst Bros. (Samuel)—(Tootsietoy)—
   (Chicago, IL)
Dunwell (Clifton, NJ)

E.O. Clark (New York, NY)
Ebert, Hans—see Hans Ebert
Edmund's Traditional Toy Soldiers—
   (Confederate)
Edward Katyll (Chicago, IL)
EFFanBEE (New York, NY)
Einfalt, Gebruder
   (Nuremberg, Germany)
Elastolin (Germany)
Elgo
Ellis, Britton & Eaton (Springfield, VT)
Enoch Rich Morrison
Enterprise Mfg. Co. (Philadelphia, PA)
Erie (Fairview, PA)
Ertl Toy Co. (Dyersville, IA)

Falk, J. (Nuremberg, Germany)
Fallows (James) & Sons
   (Philadelphia, PA)
Ferdinand Strauss Corp.
   (New York, NY)
Fisher Price (East Aurora, NY)
Fleischman (Germany)
Francis Carpenter (Port Chester, NY)
Francis Field & Francis
   (Philadelphia, PA)
Frog (England)

Gama (Germany)
Gebruder Bing—see Bing, Gebruder
Gendron
George Borgfeldt—see Borgfeldt
George W. Brown & Co. (Forestville, CT)
Georges Carette (Nuremberg, Germany)
Gibbs Mfg. Co. (Canton, OH)
Gilbert, A.C.—see A.C. Gilbert Co.
Girard Model Works, Inc. (Girard Mfg.
   Co., The Toy Works, Girard, PA)
Gong Bell Mfg. Co. (East Hampton, CT)
Gotham Press (New York)
Greppert & Kelch (Gundka, G.&K.)
Grey Iron Co. (Mount Joy, PA)
Gunthermann, S.G.
   (Nuremberg, Germany)
Gutmann (Paris, France)

H. & H. Novelty (Cleveland, OH)
Hafner Mfg. Co. (Chicago, IL)
Halsam Co. (Chicago, IL)
Hans Ebert (Nuremberg, Germany)
Hardware and Woodenware Mfg. Co.
   (New York, NY)
Harper (John) & Co., Ltd.
   (Willenhall, England)
Harris Toy Co. (Toledo, OH)
Hasbro Mfg. (Pawtucket, RI)
Hausser, O&M (Stuttgart—
   Ludwigsburg, Germany)
Hazelle (marionette)
Heinrichsen (Ernst) Miniatures
   (Nuremberg, Germany)
Henry Katz
Hess, J.L. (Nuremberg, Germany)
Heyde Miniatures (Dresden, Germany)
Hill, N.N.—see N.N. Hill
Hill Standard & Co. (Anderson, IN)
Hilpert, Johann Gottfried—
   see Johann Gottfried
Hoge Mfg. Co. (New York, NY)
Hornby-Dublo (England)
Hornby, Frank (Liverpool, England)
Hubley Mfg. Co. (Lancaster, PA)
Hull & Stafford (Clinton, CT)

Ideal (Brooklyn, NY)
Industria Nazionale Giocattoli
   Automatica (Padova, Padua, Italy)
Ives Corp. (Bridgeport, CT)

J. Chein & Co. (New York, N.Y.)
J.S. Wesby (Worcester, MA)
James H. Bowen—see Bowen
Jane Francis Toys (Pittsburgh, PA)
Jeanette Toy & Novelty Co.
   (Jeanette, PA)
JEP (Jouets en Paris)—(Paris, France)
Jesse Crandall (Brooklyn, NY)
Johan Distler (Nuremberg, Germany)
Johann Gottfried Hilpert
   (Nuremberg, Germany)
John C. Turner Co. (Wapakoneta, OH)
John Hill & Co. (Johillco)—
   (London, England)
Jones & Bixler Co. (Freemansburg, PA)
Jones (Metal Art Miniature Co.)—
   (Chicago, IL)
Judd Mfg. Co. (Wallingford, CT)
Judy Co. (Minneapolis, MN)
Jumeau (Paris &
   Montreil-sous-Bois, France)

Kansas Toy & Novelty Co. (Clifton, KS)
Katsumi (Japan)
Katz—see Henry Katz
KAYanEE (Germany)
Kellermann, George C.
   (Nuremberg, Germany)
Kelmet Corp. (New York, NY)
Kenner Products (Cincinnati, OH)
Kenton Hardware (Kenton, OH)
Keystone Mfg. Co. (Boston, MA)
Kienberger & Co.
   (Nuremberg, Germany)
Kilgore Mfg. Co. (Westerville, OH)
Kingsbury Mfg. Co. (Keene, NH)
Kingston Products Corp. (Kokomo, IN)
Kirchoff Patent Co. (Newark, NJ)
Knapp Electric Novelty Co.
   (New York, NY)
Kobe (Japan)
Kohnstam (Furth, Germany)

Kokomo Toys (Kingston Products Corp.,
   Kokomo, IN)
Kosuge (pre-war Japan)
Kyser & Rex (Philadelphia, PA)

Lancaster
Lefkowitz Toy Co. (Brooklyn, NY)
Lehmann (Ernest) Co.
   (Brandenberg, Germany)
Lenci (Turin, Italy)
Le Rapide (Paris, France)
Lesney (Matchbox)—(London, England)
Levy, Georg (Nuremberg, Germany)
Lindstrom Tool & Toy Co.
   (Bridgeport, CT)
Line Mar (Japan)
Lineol (Brandenberg/Havel, Germany)
Lines Brothers Ltd. (London, England)
Lionel Mfg. Corp. (New York, NY)
Louis Marx & Co. (New York, NY)
Lucotte Miniatures (Paris, France)

Maerklin (Gebruder)—
   (Goppingren, Germany)
Magnus Toy Co.
Manoil Mfg. Co. (Waverly, NY &
   New York City)
Markham Air Rifle Co.
Marklin (Germany)
Martin, Fernand (Paris, France)
Martin & Runyan (New York, NY)
Marusan (Japan)
Marx—see Louis Marx
Mason & Parker (Winchendon, MA)
Masutoku Toys (Tokyo, Japan)
Matchbox—see Lesney
Mattel Inc. (Hawthorne, CA)
McLoughlin Brothers (New York, NY)
McVitie & Price
Meccano (Dinky Toys)—
   (Liverpool, England)
Mechanical Novelty Works
   (New Britain, CT)
Merrythought (England)
Merrian Mfg. Co. (Durham, CT)
Metalcast (New York, NY)
Metalcraft Corp. (St. Louis, MO)

Metalgraf (Milan, Italy)

Mettoy Playcraft Ltd.—Corgi Toys
(Swansea, South Wales)

Microcraft (microscope)

Midwestern America

Mignot (C.B.G.) Miniatures
(Paris, France)

Miller (J.H.)—(Chicago, IL)

Milton Bradley & Co.
(E. Longmeadow & Springfield, MA)

Minot of France

Mokeiten (Japan)

Moline—see Buddy L

Morrison—see Enoch Rich Morrison

Morton E. Converse Co.
(Winchendon, MA)

Muller & Kadeder (MUK)—
(Nuremberg, Germany)

Murray Ohio Mfg. (Murray, OH)

N.D. Cass (Athol, MA)

N.N. Hill Brass Co. (New Jersey)

National Novelty Corp.
(N.N. Hill Brass)— (New Jersey)

Neff-Moon Toy Co. (Sandusky, OH)

Nifty

Noble & Cooley Co.

Nonpareil Toy & Novelty Co.
(Newark, NJ)

North & Judd (New Britain, CT)

Nylint (Rockford, IL)

O&M Hausser—see Hausser

Occupied Japan (Japan)

Ohio Art Co. (Bryan, OH)

Orkin (Cambridge, MA)

Par Beverage Co. (Cincinnati, OH)

Paris Mfg. Co. (South Paris, ME, USA)

Parker Brothers (Salem, MA)

Paya (Alicante, Spain)

Peco—Product Engineering Co.
(Tigard, OR)

Pente—see Will Pente

Penwood Toys (Philadelphia, PA)

Philadelphia Stove Works

Philadelphia Tin Toy Co.
(Philadelphia, PA)

Plank, Ernst (Nuremberg, Germany)

Playskool Mfg. Co. (Milwaukee, WI)

Playwood Plastics (Subsidiary of
Transogram, Brooklyn, N.Y.)

Portor Chemical Co. (The)—
(Hagerstown, MD)

Pratt & Letchworth (Buffalo, NY)

Ranlite (England)

Realistic Toys—Freeport Toys Mfg. Co.
(Freeport, IL)

Reed (W.S.) Toy Co. (Leominster, MA)

Reliable of Canada

Remco

Rempel Manufacturing (Akron, OH)

Rich & Co. (Clinton, IA)

Richter (Anchor Blocks)—
(Rudolstadt, Germany)

Richter's (U.S.A.)

Rico (Alicante, Spain)

Riemann, Seabrey Co., Inc.
(New York, NY)

Rissmann (William) Co. (RI-CO)—
(Nuremberg, Germany)

Rohrseitz, Karl (Zindorf, Germany)

Rossignol, Charles (Paris, France)

S.A. Smith Mfg. Co. (Brattleboro, VT)

S.A.E. (Swedish South African
Engineers)— (Capetown,
South Africa)

Samhongsa (Japan)

Samuel Dowst—see Dowst

Schieble Toy & Novelty Co.
(Dayton, OH)

Schlesinger (Leo) Co. (New York, NY)

Schoenhut (A) & Co. (Philadelphia, PA)

Schoenner (Germany)

Schuco Toy Co. (Nuremberg, Germany)

Secor (Jerome) Mfg. (Bridgeport, CT)

Selchow & Richter (Righter)—
(New York, NY)

Selwyn Miniatures (London, England)

Shepard (C.G.) & Co. (Buffalo, NY)

Shimer (William) & Son
(Freemansburg, PA)
Singer, J.H. (New York, NY)
Smith-Miller Toy Co. (Los Angeles, CA)
SON-NY—see Dayton Toy & Specialty
Stadden Miniatures (London, England)
Star Collectibles (Marlborough, Wales)
Steelcraft
Steiff, Margarete (Giengen, Germany)
Stevens, J.&E. (Cromwell, CT)
Stevens & Brown (New York, NY)
Stirn & Lyons (America)
Stock, Walter (Solingen, Germany)
Strauss—see Ferdinand Strauss
Structo Mfg. Co. (Freeport, IL)
Sturdy Corp (The)—(Sturditoys)—
Providence, RI)
Sun Rubber Company (Barberton, OH)
Swedish South African Engineers—
see S.A.E.

Taiyo (Japan)
Technofix (Nuremberg, Germany)
Thomas Toys (Newark, NJ)
Tipp & Co. (Nuremberg, Germany)
TN (Japan)
Tommy Toy (Union City, NJ)
Tonka
Tootsietoy—see Dowst
Tower (Guild)—(South Hingham, MA)
Toy Tinkers (Evanston, IL)
TPS (Japan)
Triang (England)
Trix, Mangold (Nuremberg, Germany)
Turner—see John C. Turner

Ultrahart
Union Hardware Co.
Union Manufacturing Co. (Clinton, CT)
Unique Art Mfg. Co., Inc.
(New York, NY & Newark, NJ)
U.S. Hardware Co. (New Haven, CT)
U.S. Metal Toy Mfg. Co.
U.S. Zone (Germany)

Warren Lines (New York City, NY)
Watrous Mfg. Co—branch of National
Novelty Co., New York—
(East Hampton, CT)
Weeden Mfg. Co. (New Bedford, MA)
Welker & Crosby (Brooklyn, NY)
Wells Brimtoy (Hollyhead, Wales &
Wells, London, England)
Wilesco
Wilkins Toy Co. (Keene, NH)
William Britains Ltd. (London, England)
William Doepke Mfg. Co.
(Rossmoyne, OH)
Williams, A.C.—see A.C. Williams Co.
Will Pente (Chicago, IL)
Winchester (Air Rifle)
Wolverine Co. (Pittsburgh, PA)
Wolverine Supply & Mfg. Co.
(Pittsburgh, PA)
Woodhaven (Woodhaven, NY)
Wyandotte Toys (All Metal Products
Corp.)— (Wyandotte, MI)

Yonezawa (Japan)
Yoshiya (Japan)

INDEX